DOYLE BRUNSON'S
SUPER
SYSTEM
2

D0043406

DOYLE BRUNSON'S SUPER SYSTEM 2

A COURSE IN POWER POKER

Contributions by:
Crandell Addington
Bobby Baldwin
Lyle Berman
Todd Brunson
Mike Caro
Johnny Chan
Jennifer Harman
Steve Lipscomb
Daniel Negreanu
Steve Zolotow

CARDOZA PUBLISHING

Play Poker Online!
Visit www.doylesroom.com

Cardoza Publishing is the world's foremost gaming and gambling publisher with a library of more than 100 up-to-date and easy-to-read books and strategies. These authoritative works are written by the top experts in their fields and, with more than 7,500,000 books in print, are the best-selling and most popular gaming books anywhere.

FIRST EDITION
Copyright ©2005 by Doyle Brunson
All Rights Reserved

All illustrations except page 7 by Russ Braun.
Page 7 illustration by Stan Hunt.

Library of Congress Catalog No: 2004101409
ISBN: 1-58042-136-9

Visit our new website (www.cardozapub.com)
or write us for a full list of books, advanced strategy guides,
and computer simulations.

CARDOZA PUBLISHING
PO Box 1500, Cooper Station, New York, NY 10276
Toll Free Phone (800) 577-WINS
email: cardozapub@aol.com
www.cardozapub.com

To Benny and Jack Binion and the World Poker Tour
for their contributions to poker.

———————————————————

*It is not the critic who counts, nor the man who points out how the strong
man stumbled, or where the doer of deeds could have done them better.
The credit belongs to the man who is actually in the arena; whose face is
marred by dust and sweat and blood; who strives valiantly, who errs and
comes short again and again; who knows the great enthusiasms, the great
devotions, and spends himself in a worthy cause, who at the best, knows
in the end the triumph of high acheivement; and who at the worst, at least
falls while daring greatly; so that his place shall never be with those cold
and timid souls who know neither victory nor defeat.*

—Theodore Roosevelt

Acknowledgements

Many people helped me in creating this book. I want to show my appreciation for their efforts by acknowledging them in alphabetical order:

Lenny Barshack
Jack Binion
Avery Cardoza
Doug Dalton
Richard Englesteen
Alixandra Gould
John Hill
Diane McHaffie
David Reese
Brian Saliba
Dana Smith

and

Russ Braun for his caricatures.

TABLE OF CONTENTS

8. OMAHA EIGHT-OR-BETTER   283
by Bobby Baldwin

9. SEVEN-CARD STUD HIGH-LOW EIGHT-OR-BETTER   361

by Todd Brunson

10. POT-LIMIT OMAHA HIGH   415
by Lyle Berman

FOREWORD
by Avery Cardoza

Super/System 2 gathers together the greatest poker players and theoreticians today. This book is not meant to replace the original *Super/System*, but to be an extension of that great work, with more games, new authors, and most importantly, more professional secrets from the best in the business. Doyle's expert collaborators have won millions upon millions of dollars in cash games—that's *each* one of them. You'll be learning expert strategies from a pool of talent that includes three world champions—Doyle Brunson, Bobby Baldwin, and Johnny Chan (Doyle and Johnny being two-time *consecutive* winners). Add to that an all-star team of contributors with so many World Series of Poker bracelets among them, you could fill a bucket with their gold. And, for good measure, throw in Mike Caro, a world-class player who is the leading poker researcher, theoretician and instructor. These are the superstars of the game.

With the completion of *Super/System 2*, Doyle has created two powerful works that every serious poker player simply must own. This makes the two-volume set of *Super/System* a full library of the best playing advice, strategies and professional concepts ever put into print. Own both these books, and you'll have the complete masterpiece of poker.

It is impossible to overstate the importance of Doyle's accomplishments and the tremendous impact he has had—and still has—on the game. He is the "Babe Ruth of Poker," a living legend who has been at this game for fifty years and still plays in the highest limit poker games in the world. Along the way he won back-to-back world championships in 1976 and 1977 and a total of nine WSOP gold bracelets, tied for the most ever at the time of this writing. I'd bet he's won more money playing poker than any man who has ever lived.

Along with Crandell Addington and a few other early players, Doyle introduced Texas hold'em to Nevada, an event that has had profound implications on the world of poker. In fact, the widespread popularity that televised no-limit hold'em enjoys today would never had occurred if not for these men. Crandell will tell you more about this event and its ramifications in his chapter on the evolution of hold'em. When the History Channel did a special on the history of poker, the producer, slightly embarrassed, told me that the program had turned into the Doyle Brunson hour—every player interviewed paid homage to the man that *is* poker, Doyle Brunson. The original *Super/System*, published in 1978, is the single most influential poker book ever written. Back then, the original price of $100 was a lot of money for a book, but this was no ordinary book; this was the bible of poker. *Super/System* was a steal at that price. The same holds true today. And why not? This book changed the way players looked at that game and, for the first time, gave away secrets that brought readers to a new level of expertise. The master of poker had spoken, and the game would never be the same.

I had always admired this book and through my friendship and association with Mike Caro, the "Mad Genius of Poker," Doyle and I got together. We made a deal to get *Super/System* out to the mainstream bookstores as a paperback for the very first time, and people who had never been exposed to this great work just went gaga over this bonanza of poker riches. Did they ever! *Super/System* hit #1 worldwide on Amazon, ahead of the Harry Potter books and best-selling authors like Steven King and John Grisham. Even as I write this, *Super/System* holds steady in the top 100 of all titles—usually in the top 40. Pretty heady stuff. In the bookstores themselves, *Super/System* sales eclipsed those of all other titles in the gaming category.

Doyle just keeps going. He's somewhat past the age where

the government kind of suggests you collect your paychecks and retire, but the competitive fire that has powered his entire career still burns fiercely. So what does the legend do? In late August 2004, at the Bicycle Club, Doyle plays against the largest field ever to play a World Poker Tour event to date—667 players. And he wins it all. Again. He takes home more than a million dollars cash. The legend grows. And the accolades and accomplishments keep coming—a World Poker Tour event named after him, a poker-playing website that bears his name, an autobiography due in spring 2005, a movie based on his life that may see the big screen one day soon. And on and on.

I've had the honor of getting to know Doyle away from the tables and have always enjoyed his company. He's gracious, wise, and has the big heart of a Texan. After spending time with him, you walk away feeling a little taller, because this ex-basketball player makes you a bigger person, and richer, because he's a man who's been a big winner in life—and you take a little bit of that away with you. I've seen the respect he gives and the respect he gets. All earned. Doyle is more than a great man in poker; he's a great man, and I say that with the utmost respect.

Well, it's time you move on and see the gems of knowledge this book has in store for you. My friend Doyle has taken good care of you in these pages. When you're done studying the wisdom within and have profited from that very powerful advice, you'll feel like Doyle's your good friend, too.

Enjoy this book, profit from it, and remember to give homage to one of the men who made this modern-day phenomenon possible, Mr. Doyle "Texas Dolly" Brunson, the greatest poker player who has ever lived. And remember to honor the game itself, something Doyle loves with every fiber of his being.

Avery Cardoza
Publisher

Johnny Chan

I first met Johnny Chan over 25 years ago when he was a novice player. I've watched him grow, step by step, into one of the greatest players in the world. Johnny is known in poker circles as "The Orient Express" because of his aggressive style of play.

In 1987 and 1988, Johnny won back-to-back world championships at the World Series of Poker and the prestigious Hall of Fame tournaments. At the 1989 WSOP, he finished second at the main event, completing the most phenomenal streak in tournament history.

Johnny is tied for the most bracelets won at the WSOP with nine victories. He was inducted into the Poker Hall of Fame in 2002 and plays regularly in the largest cash games in the world. Still a young man, Johnny will be a force to be reckoned with for many years to come.

PREFACE
by Johnny Chan

I learned poker the hard way, playing in games that were like street fights in the back alleys of Chinatown. Before anyone thought I was ready, I sat right down at some of the toughest tables in poker, staring down the best and meanest players I could find. And as you can see, I survived and prospered.

Some say I am one of the few players ever to conquer the poker world without any formal training. I'm proud of that accomplishment, but if I had it to do over again, I'd make it easier. Instead of learning the hard way, brawling my way up, risking my bankroll, and banging my head against those big bricks walls, I'd start by reading this book. How often are you going to get a chance to learn from the most feared poker player around, year after year: Doyle Brunson himself?

To be honest, at first I was upset that Doyle was writing this follow-up to his first *Super/System*, which all the players at my tables call "the bible of poker." Every time I heard that, hair stood up on the back of my neck. Who needs a bible of poker? I kept thinking that professional players like me would be better off without one. The secrets contained in these two books are so powerful that at first I would have paid considerable money to keep them out of print. Doyle "Texas Dolly" Brunson couldn't have been bought off, anyway.

I've changed my mind. I think about how poker has grown over the last few years and how many new players have joined the game. There must be millions of them. They're ready to treat the strategy of poker with respect, and I want them to treat it that way. Poker is a monster of a game that deserves respect.

When great players like Doyle and his expert collaborators are willing to share their secrets with you, poker creeps out from the rocks like a dragon that's been hiding for a hundred years. The dragon emerges, looks around, roars, and demands respect. Even though nobody noticed when that the dragon wasn't there, everyone hears it now. That's what happened to poker, and this book is part of that dragon's roar. If you're smart, you won't waste the opportunity to learn from it.

You see, poker isn't like other kinds of gambling. It fits better in the category of skill games, like chess and bridge. Would those games be as well respected or have such loyal followings if experts kept the secrets to themselves?

Before poker came of age, it was a hustler's game, hidden from the public and not entirely respectable. But that's not the case anymore, and probably won't be ever again. Tournaments are broadcast to hundreds of millions of television viewers, making people who have never played the game before take notice—and join in. So, now that the dark era of poker is over and the dragon has come out of hiding, I think it's important that this great book, which outlines the strategies and the plays that really win, take center stage.

You know, I'm not afraid to play in any game. But I was once asked which nine opponents I'd least like to play against at one table. Now, there's a tough question. But one player I could name without hesitation is Doyle "Texas Dolly" Brunson. Doyle isn't someone you want to play against, but he is someone you definitely want to learn from. And that goes for all the experts he has chosen to include in this book.

You're lucky that you don't have to learn poker the way I did. You won't need to brawl your way to profit. In the years ahead, if you stick with it, you'll play millions of hands and wager millions of dollars. I hope you'll play right and wager well, unless you're in my game, in which case I hope you'll play like a dummy and throw away all your money to me.

Doyle is ready to take you aside and let you in on poker's most powerful secrets, the ones that really win. If I were you, I'd pay attention. The other day, I started thinking about the big pie made up of all those billions of dollars that will be exchanged in poker hands this year. Well, it's already being carved up.

If you want a big slice, you hold the knife in your hands.

INTRODUCTION

INTRODUCTION
by Doyle Brunson

I'd been toying with the idea of revising my *Super/System* for years, but every time I discussed it with friends or fellow professional poker players, I always heard the same response: "Why? Almost all the advice in the book is as powerful today as it was twenty-seven years ago. It doesn't need a word changed." Not one to go against the advice of so many good folks, I put it off for a year, then another year, and time kept sliding away like chips slipping off a poker table.

It's mighty flattering to know that *Super/System* has stood the test of time. And I'm glad it has, because when I think back about how much time, money, and effort went into creating it, I shudder. I'd let myself get talked into writing and financing the book. I convinced the top five specialists in various poker games to collaborate with me.

None of us could have predicted how devoted to the project we would become. I think we all got a little bit nuts while we were writing the original version. Before long, we were running an informal contest to see who could contribute the most information to help people play better poker. And all of us swore that we'd never give up any of the key secrets that had helped us build our bankrolls, but eventually we found ourselves giving up everything that had taken us years to learn by the seat of our pants.

All those secrets ...

If you think that's crazy, listen to this: I not only let myself get talked into producing the book, I got suckered into forming a whole big company just to publish and promote it. It wasn't some mom-and-pop operation either—I went the whole nine yards. Rented an office building, bought the very latest computer typesetting equipment, hired a staff of graphic artists, editors, and receptionists, set up a marketing department, and even bought a commercial photo developer—all to publish one book! You might be thinking that nothing like that had ever happened in the history of publishing, and you may be right. Only a bunch of poker players could've dreamed up such a thing—sane people would've had better sense. And it only took me nigh on to twenty years to cover my investment. But you know what? It was worth it!

When I think about the people I chose as my expert collaborators way back in '77, the list reads like a "Who's Who of the Most Influential People in the World of Poker." They were all young men back then, in their late twenties to early thirties—I was the senior statesman at age forty-four. When you pick a group of people that young from among hundreds of outstanding prospects, you'd be lucky to see one or two of them go on to great success. But my team has flourished amazingly and has stood the test of time, just like the book they helped create. You'll find them all over the pages and often the covers of both poker and mainstream publications and even on TV. So, yes, I'm mighty proud that I trusted my instincts and had the foresight to select them.

Almost all of the poker principles in *Super/System* are still applicable today, and that's why you'll find them on these pages, along with analyses of more games and the unveiling of new secrets. When I decided to publish *Super/System 2*, the task seemed monumental to this seventy-year-old poker player who, after all these years, is still active in his chosen profession. But today's explosion in the popularity of poker has kept me inspired to push forward with *Super/System 2*, in which we have adapted our writings to account for the dramatic changes that have taken place in the world of poker over the past few decades. Today's younger players rising through the ranks, playing alongside old-timers who used decks of cards as baby rattlers when they were still in the crib, are playing a different brand of poker than we played in the old days. And we're playing new poker games that we didn't play back them, so I've drafted some new people to join my original team of writers.

ORIGINAL SUPER/SYSTEM TEAM

I'm very proud of my group of collaborators on the original *Super/System*—let's take a look at them before I introduce you to my new team members. You'll meet them as you read the chapters.

Mike Caro, who wrote the draw poker and statistics sections, was a draw poker champion when I first met him, but he has mastered all forms of poker since then. He's a legendary player and poker strategist known the world over as "The Mad Genius of Poker." In fact, Mike has become the strategic analyst of choice for many of today's top professional players. He reached an even wider audience a few years ago when he founded the Mike Caro University of Poker, devoted to educating aspiring players. His books, videos, and seminars clearly rank among the most sought after in the history of poker. Mike is an integral part of *Super/System 2*. Believe me, I would never have attempted to write this book without him.

If I had to choose someone to play for the survival of my family, it would be **Chip Reese**. "The best of the best!" are the words that Lyle Berman used to introduce Chip when he was inducted into the Poker Hall of Fame in 1991. At the age of 39, he was the youngest person ever awarded that honor. Chip was a very young poker player in 1977, right out of Dartmouth, when I asked him to write the seven-card stud chapter. In addition to his expertise at stud, a game at which I still believe he is the best ever, he has evolved into the world's premier all-around player. I would without hesitation bet on Chip against anyone who dares face him in mixed games.

Chip can consistently be found in the biggest games in the world. He has played in France, Germany, England, Australia, Greece, Ireland, and South Africa. Although he doesn't play many tournaments, Chip has won three World Series of Poker bracelets for seven-card stud, stud high-low split, and razz. Years ago he won a no-limit hold'em tournament and placed second in a deuce-to-seven tournament, while playing the two events simultaneously. Now that's what I call being versatile!

David Sklansky, who collaborated with me on seven-card stud high-low split, has generated a following of devoted poker enthusiasts, while proving himself among the most capable players. David has chosen to play a broad range of games, from middle to high limits and has been successful at all of them. Like Mike Caro, he has terrific insight into all poker games and has put his theories and plays into very readable strategy, producing some of the most highly regarded poker books in the world. He also has acted as a top advisor to casino owners and executives, and has tutored many of the world's foremost professional players. I recommend that every poker player read his books.

Bobby Baldwin hardly needs to be introduced, as just about everybody in gaming is familiar with his great success story. After winning the main event at the World Series of Poker in 1978, Bobby left professional poker and went into casino management. Within a short time, he had climbed to the top of the ladder and today is considered by his peers to be the premier gaming executive in the world. President of the multi-billion dollar Bellagio Hotel and Casino in Las Vegas, Bobby also acts as CEO of the Mirage Corporation. Somehow he still finds time to get together with us for some friendly high-stakes poker every now and then. In 2003 he was inducted into the Poker Hall of Fame.

With the exception of **Joey Hawthorne**, that completes the list of my original collaborators. Here's the sad part: Joey died from a drug overdose while he was still in his forties, and his brilliant career didn't have time to get off the ground. God, I hate drugs! If he were still with us today, Joey probably would be a part of this new edition.

Along with my old standbys, Mike and Bobby, I've chosen my newest group of collaborators carefully, and I hope that twenty-seven years from now, their success in poker and in life will be as outstanding as my original group.

MY STORY

MY STORY
by Doyle Brunson

A lot has changed since the publication of the original *Super/System* in 1978. I'll tell you about that shortly. But first I'd like you to know how I felt back then, at that halfway point in my poker career. It goes like this...

BEFORE 1978

At some time in our lives, I suppose we all reflect on the good and the bad that has happened to us and ask ourselves the question, "If I had it to do all over again, are there things I would change?" I'm no exception.

There's no one alive who could have had it much tougher than I had it in the early years, long before the publication of the first *Super/System*. I was in a photo-finish with death. That's as close as you can get to the ultimate bad beat.

And accompanying my early poker adventures, I experienced near tragedy due to the health problems of my wife Louise and my oldest daughter Doyla. We lost Doyla a few years after *Super/System* came out. It was the biggest heartbreak in my life.

I've been so broke early in my marriage that I couldn't afford bus fare from Las Vegas to my home in Fort Worth. And there were times I could barely scrape up a dime to call my wife and ask her to send me money for the ticket.

But there are two sides to the coin that's been flipping my life around. I finally got to the point where I got my bankroll up to one hundred thousand dollars, and I haven't looked back since. Years before *Super/System* was born, my wife and family lived in relative luxury, and now they'll never have a hungry day as long as they live.

I've made many millions playing poker, and at times early on, lost most of my bankroll betting on sports and golf. But I've always done my thing, and I'm a happy man because of it. The pleasures have definitely outweighed the pain.

Through it all, I've learned that in life, a man's not beaten even though he's all-in. You can't count him out until the fall of the last card. I've been tested time and again on many battlefields. I've lost a lot of little skirmishes, but I've won the big ones. That's what really counts.

The adversity I've faced has been a blessing in disguise. It's strengthened my character. I've had to draw on that strength many a time at the poker table, and I'll continue to draw on it for the rest of my years.

I need that strength, too. You see, I'm a gambler. I'll always be one. I couldn't be anything else. So my life will always be filled with wins—and losses. I wouldn't have it any other way. It's exciting. There's almost never a dull moment in my life, and I can't imagine anyone having a better life than the one I have right now. I've got just about everything I want.

That Elusive Something

Yes, the deck's been stacked against me at various times in my life, but I've overcome every cold deck I've faced. I'm enough of a dreamer to realize what got me through might have been that elusive something a gambler calls luck. But I'm also enough of a realist to know that, in general, we make our own luck—through knowledge, skill, and experience. And that goes for the game of poker as well as the game of life.

In the summer of 1933, I was born in the West Texas town of Longworth, a spot on the road consisting of a few houses and a general store. I don't suppose the population ever exceeded one hundred. We had only two industries in the area, farming and a

U.S. Gypsum plant. My dad worked for Planters Gin Company, and while he didn't make much money, there was always food on the table and a little extra for the kids once in a while. We lived in a four-room frame house at the time, with an outhouse at the back. I remember thinking when I was little that, if I ever got any money, I'd bring the plumbing indoors. It used to get mighty cold on those prairies during the winter.

There were five of us living at home when I was small: Dad, Mom, my sister Lavada, my older brother Lloyd, and myself. It was crowded but we didn't mind. There was a lot of warmth and a lot of love.

My mother was a religious, God-fearing woman who did her best to raise us with a sense of moral values. I suppose a good deal of that has remained with me. She used to tell us that you'll find good in every man if you look hard enough. I've always tried to remember that and act accordingly, although sometimes it's been mighty difficult considering some of the unsavory characters I've come in contact with.

My dad was perhaps the calmest, most even-tempered individual I've ever known. Nothing ruffled him. I can't remember ever seeing him get angry. When things went wrong he'd take it in stride, smile, and say that setbacks are only a temporary thing. Tomorrow would always be better. Of course we kids would get into a little trouble every once in a while, as all kids do, and there were times when he surely would have been justified in whaling the tar out of us. But he never even raised his voice. Not once. Nor did he ever hit us. He had an ability to make us know we'd been out of line without raising as much as one finger. He was a truly remarkable man. When the Good Lord made my dad, he destroyed the mold.

School Days

I attended grammar school in Longworth where several grades were held in one room. I recall that my third grade class consisted of only three kids, two boys and a girl. We got a lot of individual attention, that's for sure.

After grammar school and junior high, I entered Sweetwater High School with D. C. Andrews and Riley Cross, two of my closest friends from Longworth. We turned out for the basketball team. Before long, we were known as the Longworth Triple Threat, and the three of us took over the varsity team. Why not? We were in prime shape. We were always working out, running, and swimming. D. C., Riley, and I would run non-stop from Longworth to the swimming hole on the Barclay Ranch, which was about eight miles away. Sometimes we'd run from Sweetwater back to Longworth after school, but the coach didn't take too kindly to that. He gave us a station wagon so we'd be sure to make the practices on time. Sports were my whole life in those days. They were everything.

In addition to basketball, I also turned out for the baseball team and, at the suggestion of my coach, started running track. I was never much interested in track, but the basketball season was over and I needed something to do to keep in shape, so I took on the mile run. It seemed like a fair distance and with all the running I was doing, I felt I could do all right. I honestly didn't realize at the time how well I'd actually do.

In 1950, as a senior, I entered the Texas Interscholastic Track Meet as a mile runner and won it with a time of 4:38. Without really trying, I'd suddenly become the best high school miler in the state of Texas. In the meantime, I had also been chosen as one of the five best high school basketball players in the state, a rather heady experience for a boy of sixteen.

Riding High

After that, the scholarship offers started coming in. All told, there must have been a hundred or so from various colleges and universities throughout the country. I finally settled on Hardin-Simmons, a Baptist-affiliated college in Abilene that was known primarily for turning out teachers and coaches. At the time, I felt my life's work would be in one of these areas.

In my junior year at Hardin-Simmons, I was voted the most valuable player in the Border Conference, and the pro teams were beginning to show an interest. The Minneapolis Lakers, now the Los Angeles Lakers, were making overtures, and I began to set my sights on a career as a professional basketball player. *Dell Basketball* magazine picked me as one of the top ten college players in the country. I was riding high.

In addition to the basketball honors, I had run the mile in 4:18.6, which put me in contention for a spot on the national team. I often wonder what would have happened if I had trained as hard for track as I did for basketball. Thinking about it now, I'm sorry I didn't. I think I missed my true calling in sports. There's no doubt in my mind that a four-minute mile was possible.

The future looked bright indeed. In the summer, I got a job at the U.S. Gypsum plant. It wasn't any great shakes as jobs go, but I planned on saving enough to last me through my senior year. One day, I was unloading some sheetrock, and as I was hauling the sheets off and stacking them, suddenly, the pile began to shift. I tried to stop it with my body, jamming my knee into the lower half of the pile to keep it in place. What a dummy I was. I couldn't stop it. Two thousand pounds of sheetrock crashed on my right leg. It snapped in two places. I remember my first thought was, "My God, I'll never play basketball again." My leg was in a cast for two years due to complications. The fractures finally healed, but when the cast came off, my speed and coordination were gone. So were my hopes for the pros.

My First Poker Game

I'd been playing poker off and on since my high school days. In fact, I still remember my first game. It was five-card draw, and I ended up the big winner. I recall thinking at the time what easy money it was. After I entered Hardin-Simmons, I'd play in the usual Saturday night games. In general, I seemed to do pretty well. I got caught once or twice and was disciplined for gambling, but since I was one of the basketball stars nothing much came of it.

After breaking my leg, basketball was out of the question and I spent a lot more time playing poker. I began paying more attention to my studies also. Prior to my injury, I felt that basketball would carry me through school. But from here on in, I'd have to use my brain. My poker winnings paid for my expenses, and in 1954 I graduated with a bachelor's degree. I stayed on at Hardin-Simmons and earned my master's degree in Administrative Education the following year. With these credentials, I felt sure I'd be offered a job that would lead to a position as superintendent of schools or at least a principal. It didn't work out that way. In fact, the top job offered to me was that of a basketball coach at Dalhart (Texas) High School at a salary of $4,800 a year.

It didn't make sense; I was making more than that just playing poker. I used to travel around to the different colleges in Texas setting up games and making a fair living by my wits. At that time, however, the idea of becoming a professional gambler had not occurred to me even though it was apparent I played better than most.

After graduation, I went to work as a business machines salesman, a profession that ultimately could have made me some twenty-five or thirty thousand a year—or so I thought. But it wasn't in the cards. My first day on the job, I called on a few prospective accounts. I didn't get much further than the front door, and I wound up in a poker game before the day was out. It was a seven-stud game where I cleared a month's salary in less than three hours. "My God," I thought, "what am I doing trying to sell machines nobody wants to buy from me when I can sit down at a poker table and make ten times the money in one-sixth the time?" It didn't take me very long to figure out what to do. I quit the company and began my career as a full-time professional poker player. I've never regretted that decision.

Turning Pro

The first games I played that amounted to anything were down on Exchange Street in Fort Worth, Texas. I'd be surprised if you could find a tougher street in the whole world. There were shootings, muggings, robberies, and just about every kind of violence imaginable. The stuff we see on TV today is tame compared to what Exchange Street was like almost any hour of the day. But at the card table, amidst all that violence, everything was as gentlemanly as could be. They were two different worlds. My buddy Dwayne Hamilton and I frequented a card room run by a gangster named Tincy whose main claim to fame was having killed half a dozen people. He ran an honest game, though, and Dwayne and I did fairly well. No-limit hold'em was our main game. After we accumulated a good-sized stake we moved uptown to the three hundred and five hundred buy-in games where we played with doctors, lawyers, and other professional people.

For the next five or six years we made the Texas circuit, playing bigger and bigger games throughout the state. Occasionally we'd drop into the big games in Oklahoma and Louisiana. During this period, I met Amarillo Slim and Sailor Roberts, a couple of the finest poker hustlers I've ever met. We hit it off from the start and after Dwayne moved back to Fort Worth, Sailor, Slim, and I decided to go into business together. We must have hit every town in Texas, relieving the locals of their money. It was a sight to see, the three of us taking on all comers. And not just at poker. We got to the point where we were gambling on just about every game there was—golf, tennis, basketball, pool, sports betting. Just about everything. As long as we thought we had some sort of an edge, we'd bet. And we made money. Pretty soon we got to know most everybody in the games no matter where we played. We kept running into the same guys all the time—Jack Straus, Johnny Moss, Bob Hooks, and a lot of others.

Making a Name for Ourselves

As our reputations grew, we were invited to more and more games in private clubs and homes. For the most part, these games were for rich oil men and cattlemen who had a hankering to take on young professionals like us. It was safer playing in these games than playing in back rooms where you took a risk every time you won a fair amount. I've been hijacked a few times, and I can tell you it's not a pleasant experience to be looking down at the business end of a shotgun.

Sailor, Slim, and I stuck together for six years or so, and we had some mighty fine times. Once in a while we were down, but we managed to hold our own better than most. Our partnership finally broke up after our first big trip to Las Vegas. We lost our entire bankroll—close to six figures—and believe me, there's nothing more cantankerous than three broke gamblers. We went our separate ways after that but have remained close friends to this day.

In 1960, I met my wife, Louise. She was a pharmacist in San Angelo, Texas, and I courted her for about two years. She was something worth winning, you see, and I can tell you I had an uphill fight persuading my sweetheart that I was her one and only. She was convinced I was married, and it took a heap of testimonials to convince her that I was single and available. I worked harder for our first date than anything I've ever done in my life. After I asked her to marry me, she had to think twice about permanently hitching up with a professional gambler. She had a lot of doubts. It wasn't what most girls were doing at the time. I finally convinced her and we were married in August of 1962.

About four months after we were married, I woke up one

morning with a sore throat and thought I was coming down with a bad cold. There was a little knot on the side of my neck about the size of a pea. Louise insisted I go to a doctor, and so for about three weeks I was taking heavy doses of antibiotics every day. That didn't help, and the knot grew to the size of a hen's egg. By that time, I was plenty worried. My brother Lloyd had died of cancer a short while before, and I couldn't keep that off my mind. We consulted a cancer specialist in Fort Worth. He took one look at me and scheduled me for surgery the following Monday. He didn't think the tumor was malignant, but said it would have to come out.

Something Awfully Wrong

I went into the operating room at 6:30 a.m. When I woke up in the recovery room, it was dark. Even though I was very groggy, I could tell things weren't going too well for me. Not only were my head and back in bandages, but my entire chest was wrapped in gauze and completely covered with tape. I remember thinking, "Doyle, there's something awfully wrong." Louise was there at my side telling me everything was going to be all right, but I knew she was trying to hide something. I was in a lot of pain, and the drugs they kept feeding me kept me fairly stupified for the next few days.

I remained in the hospital for quite a while. My relatives and friends were always coming by to see how I was doing. That was a comfort.

Still, nobody had the courage to tell me what the real situation was. The only thing I knew was that I was going to be taken for further study to the Cancer Center at M. D. Anderson Hospital in Houston. What I had not been told was that when the doctors opened me up, they found massive cancer spread throughout my body. It had reached close to the base of my brain, and my chest and stomach area were riddled with it. Four surgeons had been called in and they all agreed that it was useless to proceed.

The cancer had attacked so much of my body that it was only a matter time before I died. I was a big dog to live longer than four months.

They Came to Say Goodbye

While I suspected the worst, it wasn't until I was taken home for one day, prior to flying to Houston, that I really knew I was going to die. Over two hundred people from all over the country came to our house that day. I was really surprised. I didn't think I had that many close friends. From the way everybody was acting it was obvious they'd come to say goodbye. My friend Dwayne Hamilton just broke down and cried.

Louise was pregnant at the time, and I thought to myself how sad it was that I'd probably never get to see my baby. By all rights, I'd be dead and gone before it arrived.

Louise was thinking the same thing and had made the arrangements for further surgery at M. D. Anderson. Though the doctors had told her there was no hope of my living, they said there might be a slight chance of prolonging my life a few more months through radical neck surgery. With that operation, there was a possibility that I'd be able to live long enough to see my baby before the cancer reached my brain.

We flew to Houston the next day. For the next two-and-a-half weeks, I rested in the hospital to build myself up for the surgery to come. I went into the operating room at 10:30 a.m. I spent eight hours under the knife and at 6:30 p.m., they gave Louise the news. I was going to make it. It had been touch and go.

The Impossible Had Happened

At one point during the operation, my blood pressure dropped to zero, but they pulled me through. What was truly incredible was that there was no longer any trace of cancer in my system. The doctors couldn't believe it. The impossible had happened.

The odds against merely surviving the operation itself were very high. A month earlier the black corruption of melanoma had been visible to the naked eye. That the cancer had disappeared was incomprehensible to the staff at the hospital. Five doctors had unanimously agreed that it was a medical impossibility for me to live longer than a few more months, with or without the operation.

For the next two weeks, Louise and Sailor took turns watching me twenty-four hours a day, since we couldn't afford a private nurse. I had to be observed closely. The tubes that led to my body had to be checked constantly, and my vital signs had to be monitored continuously. I don't know when Louise and Sailor got any sleep.

After leaving the hospital, I recuperated at my sister's. When my strength returned, I reported back to the hospital in Fort Worth for a checkup. The doctor who had first operated on me was at a complete loss for an explanation. The only thing he could say was that occasionally, spontaneous remissions occur, but in my case he could only believe a miracle had happened.

Later we found out that during the operation several friends had spoken to their church pastors about my case and entire congregations were praying for my recovery. Those prayers surely must have been answered.

A Higher Power

Louise had always been a religious woman, but this experience and two others in our lives reinforced her conviction that there's a higher power that watches over us.

Shortly after my recovery, Louise developed a uterine tumor. That normally requires extensive surgery and removal of the female organs. She was scheduled for surgery, but before the procedure, it was discovered that her tumor had disappeared. Another miracle.

In 1975, when my daughter Doyla was twelve years old

she was found to have idiopathic scoliosis, a debilitating spinal disorder. That affliction causes extensive curvature of the spine or permanent crippling. Specialists were consulted and radical procedures were recommended, including implantation of a steel rod in her spine or a full body brace. None of that was necessary.

Louise organized a marathon prayer session for Doyla that included radio broadcasts and correspondence with the late Katherine Kuhlman, the famous faith healer. Within three months, Doyla's spine had straightened completely. The doctors acknowledged that hers was one of only three known cases where the curvature was corrected without surgical assistance. The third miracle in our family.

Since that time, Louise has been extremely active in Christian ministry and heavily involved in work with foreign missions. She spends as much or more time as a servant of the Lord as she does in taking care of our family. She's said time and again: "It's so exciting to be a Christian. It's by far the most exciting part of living." And I know she believes that as strongly as any person on earth.

Fortunately, money was not a problem when the mountains of medical bills came pouring in for Louise and Doyla. I did very well at the poker table during all those years. When I left the hospital after my operation, I recuperated for a while and then I returned to the poker circuit with a zest and appreciation for life that I had never had before. Each day when I woke up the sky was bluer and the grass was greener. The world was as bright as could be. I was alive. From the first session I started playing again, I won fifty-four times in a row. I never booked a loser until the fifty-fifth session I played. Never before, or since, have I had such a streak. I won enough to completely clear my immense doctor and hospital bills and had plenty left over to keep my family comfortable for several years.

Everything Seemed to Click

Before the surgery, I would have classified myself as a slightly better than average player. However, after that ordeal, something happened. Everything seemed to click, and I was playing better than I had ever played in my life. My playing became almost instinctive. I was reading my competitors more accurately, and I felt a self-assurance I had never experienced. My brush with death had apparently triggered innate abilities that had never surfaced before.

The most important thing of all was that I discovered my true vocation. I had finally dispelled any doubts about what my profession in life was going to be. Because of pressure from my family and friends, I had thought about returning to "legitimate" work. But now I knew I never would. I was never going to be a working stiff, nor was I ever going to have a boss. I was going to make my way through life *my way*.

During the next few years, I shuttled between Fort Worth and Las Vegas, where more and more of the action was developing. I was still doing most of my playing in Texas, but it was getting difficult to find the really big games there. I was beating them so regularly that they were finally saying, "We can do without Doyle." The action, for me, was really beginning to dry-up.

Also, in 1970 Congress passed legislation making it even more difficult for a poker professional to make a living. The law that directly affected me made it a federal offense to run a large scale poker game from which five or more players derived an income, except, of course, in states where such gambling was legal. The handwriting was on the wall.

So in 1973, I moved my family—Louise; Doyla, 10; Pamela, 9; and my little boy Todd, who had his fourth birthday on the road—to Las Vegas where we established our home. It's a good place to live: good weather, good action, and good people.

Competitive by Nature

I'm known as a professional gambler rather than just a professional poker player, and I have to admit that I am. I've been known to bet on just about anything. And because of that, I've surely had my share of losers. If I had stuck to poker, I'd probably be a far wealthier man today. But old habits are hard to break, and I just like to gamble.

However, it's more than just liking to gamble. I'm very competitive by nature. As long as there's a contest—any kind of contest, even if it's a marble shooting contest—I want to be a part of it. If I can't be an active participant as I am at poker and golf—and therefore betting on myself—I have to bet on one side or the other, be it a football game, a prizefight, or whatever.

My competitive nature is one of the reasons I feel I've been so successful playing poker. You've got to play hard to be a consistent winner at poker, and I'm able to do that instinctively. I was a very fierce competitor as an athlete in high school and college. That competitive spirit remains with me. I'm sure it has a lot to do with my success at the poker table. I've never lost the feeling of exhilaration that comes when you're doing the best you can and gambling real high. There's no feeling quite like it.

Next to poker, golf is my favorite game, and I'm considered a pretty good player—probably a little better than the next guy. Unfortunately, quite a few of those next guys have played a shade better than me when we got to betting on the course. I remember going back east one year with my best friend Jack Binion and ending up playing golf with a millionaire. We kept raising the stakes until finally we had $180,000 riding on one hole. He putted out for a par to my bogey and all that money just flew away. And that's just one of several such stories I could tell you. Now, the title of the first *Super/System* was originally *How I Made over $1,000,000 Playing Poker*. The title of my next one is going to be *How I Lost over $1,000,000 Playing Golf*. There's definitely a moral in there somewhere.

A lot has been written about my winning the 1976 and 1977 World Series of Poker for a total of some $560,000. You may have read some of the many stories. They were tough games against tough competitors. The best players in the world sat at those tables and the pace was grueling. That kind of playing is not something I would care to do every day, but for a sheer gut-level contest, it can't be beat. There's a certain pride you take from knowing that you've taken on the best and come out on the top. But with this pride also comes the realization that you can never afford to become complacent. In both the 1976 and 1977 Series, I made a full house only when the final card was played. And perhaps there's a moral in that, too. As I noted, in poker as in life, you can't count a man out until the last card falls.

1978 AND BEYOND

Life is always changing, never constant. You really can't count on anything staying the same. Late in 1977, I added the finishing touches to the original *Super/System*, and its publication would change poker for me forever in ways I hadn't anticipated.

The people closest to me, both my friends and my poker opponents, continued to see me in pretty much the same light. But it was the people and the players I'd never met before who began treating me differently. For the most part, they treated me with more reverence, and that was flattering. Nobody ever sat in a poker game anymore who didn't know who I was. And so many strangers had read my book in the first months after its publication that I never knew when I was playing a student of my game plan, who was expecting me to play poker precisely as I had described and eager to take advantage.

Forging Ahead

Although I had to adjust my strategy a little to keep these players confused, I was able to pretty much stick to my game plan and play just as I had written. It worked, because the strategy was so powerful that you could almost tell your opponents what you're going to do—how you're going to bet, how often you're going to bluff—and there wouldn't be much they could do about it. I had devised a proven world-class game plan for winning. And when you have a world-class game plan for winning…well, you just win. Hardly anything else can happen, and I wasn't about to change my style of play dramatically, just because I'd shared my secrets with the world.

Strangers could take my secrets and beat almost everyone with them, but I was determined that they weren't going to use them to beat me. And they didn't.

But things changed some. Poker changed. More and more, a new type of player was coming on the scene—more literate, more refined. Old gamblers were true gamblers, ready to put all their money on the table anytime, anywhere. Most of them had no other option as a livelihood, either. Poker was a path out of poverty. Many old gamblers were uneducated. Today, players often have degrees and treat poker as a business rather than a pure form of gambling. Modern players are growing up in a world of the Internet, and many even play poker online, something that would have been beyond anyone's wildest imagination when the first copy of *Super/System* was purchased.

And poker has grown so vastly in recent years. So vastly. The old ways—those seedy games in the back of pool halls, in taverns, those private home games and the ones held by fraternal organizations like the Elks and the VFW—are quickly fading. It was so much more difficult to get good back then. You had to do it the hard way.

Today, you can take a shortcut to winning just by reading what the experts and proven players have contributed, rather than having to develop poker talents through trial and error.

Big Money

After 1977, I started accumulating big money. The regular games were good, and the side games at the World Series of Poker were excellent. But this golden age for poker profits didn't last.

Did you know that satellites ruined the cash games at the tournaments? The players who previously came to town eager to risk their bankrolls against the top pros in side games suddenly discovered they could get their adrenaline rush by playing in these one-table shootouts, trying to win entries into the tournaments just by beating everyone at a single table. It was addictive for them. And it worked perfectly to increase the number of entrants in the tournaments. But it didn't work well for those of us who had previously benefited when these inexperienced players bumped heads against us during those tournaments. Satellites had arrived, and that kind of easy profit was gone. A few adventurous players still sought us out, wanting the challenge. But mostly, the opportunities for super-soft side games at tournaments were gone.

Despite this, my poker bankroll continued to grow. It was almost all smooth sailing, almost all success. Everything went straight up.

It was a time when the Gamblers Invitational Golf Tournament, hosted by Jack Binion, brought all the gamblers together and boasted some of the biggest golf games in the history of the sport. Those who think that there's big money of the PGA tour have no idea what goes on when a bunch of golf-crazed gamblers get together. And it didn't matter how well or how poorly you played the game, if you had a bankroll and a set of clubs, we'd figure out a way to make it a fair gamble.

Dubious Reputations

I made a load of money golfing, partly because I had a reputation for giving action. You've got to give action to get action. I used sheer mental toughness and competitiveness, as well as a God-given gift for athletics, to come out on top. There were million dollar days.

Back then, not everyone we wagered with at golf belonged in the "reputable gambler" category. Take Jimmy Chagra, a convicted drug dealer who was later revealed to be one of the biggest suppliers in the United States. We're talking boatloads from Columbia. Well, that was the "successful" side of Chagra. On the less successful side, he had his golf game vastly overrated. He was so wrong about his ability that he demanded to play $100,000 Nassaus with automatic presses anytime someone got two holes down.

Nobody else could easily afford to play that high, so I decided take the challenge and also to stake the legendary poker player Puggy Pearson from Nashville and Jerry Irwin from Indianapolis, both participants in Jack's tournament. Now Puggy had a dubious reputation for taking advantages that were, well, let's just say they approached the gray area on a scale of golfing propriety. All three of us beat Chagra the first two holes and, on the third, the automatic press started.

Next hole. Puggy and I are on the green in two, while Chagra finds himself in a sand trap. There's a meaningless spot of sun-dried grass in front of Puggy's ball, a blemish on the green path to the hole, but not a hindrance to his putt in any way. For some reason I'll never live long enough to understand, Puggy moved his ball a few inches away from the sunspot, to no advantage. Maybe it's just Pug's nature.

Chagra had his bodyguard riding in the cart with him.

"Jimmy, Puggy moved his ball," the bodyguard announced.

Well, Chagra went ballistic, screaming, bellowing, threatening, "I'm gonna blow all you blankety-blanks away!"

I figure Puggy cost me $2 million in future earnings that day, maybe more, and I've never let him forget it. While I personally had success against Chagra after that, Puggy never got another chance. He was banished forever from our group.

My Saddest Hour

Life is like poker sometimes. Just when things are going so good that you think you're supposed to win every pot, you get a monster hand cracked, and it spells the beginning of a dizzying downward spiral. That's how it was when Doyla died at eighteen.

She'd been attending UNLV. We knew she had a valve problem with her heart, but it wasn't supposed to be serious. They say it was too much potassium that took her from us. It was so unexpected, like being kicked in the gut so hard you don't think you can ever stand up again, breathe again.

You know how each of us sometimes searches for the meaning of life? Losing Doyla started my search in earnest. Doyla was a devout Christian, as is her mother, Louise. To be sure, I had Christian beliefs, too. But I wasn't really practicing them. I guess I had strayed about as far away from God as you can and still be a believer. Thinking back, I was too caught up in myself and my quest for success, my desire to be rich and famous and such.

I sunk into a long depression. During this time I studied the Bible and other Christian literature. It awakened me. Gradually, so gradually over the next year, my strength returned, and with it my resolve and my spirit.

I came to realize that God allows us to have a free will and do as we please. And so, Doyla had used her free will when she took too much potassium, the event that put her system out of balance and stopped her heart. It must not have seemed like a big thing to her, such a small mistake. But sometimes choices we make have consequences beyond what we could ever imagine.

I remember Doyla every day, and the shock and the sadness of losing her will never end. But I'm at peace with God. Had I not come to accept that peace, I could never have returned successfully to poker.

I finally came to understand that Doyla's and Louise's Christian beliefs were right for me. And I was ready to revisit poker with a new vigor.

I moved to California and found very soft action at the poker tables. At the Bicycle Club, I won over a $1 million very quickly. I was back.

Essex, England

I've become more reflective about life as I've continued to mature. It's strange to realize that a man can get to be fifty, sixty, and now seventy and still find himself maturing. But that's what happens.

About twenty years ago, I took an interest in genealogy, wondering how I came to be. I learned that Roger Brunson, the first historically recorded Brunson in America, could be traced to Connecticut in 1625. And you can trace my lineage back to Essex, England in the 1500s.

Actually, the early surnames in my family weren't all Brunson. They were Brownson, meaning son of Braun, and Bronson. But these were all related, all from the same family tree. I discovered that, except for Native Americans, no families can trace their roots to this continent further back than the Brunsons.

Sometimes I wonder if any of the Brunsons who preceded me had gambling in their natures. Were they great risk takers? Did they overcome adversity or get buried by it? What anguish did they face that involved their families? What victories made them proudest? History doesn't provide me enough detail. Still, I wonder.

As for me, life's path has been peppered with pretty

panorama and disastrous detours. Maybe everyone's life is a little like that. Maybe things that happen to you just seem magnified and out of proportion when compared to events that happen to others.

Thinking Back

The events that I most remember play out in my mind like sound bites. Occasionally I can't recall details or events until one of these monumental moments in memory gets me started, and then that trigger leads me to the next remembrance and the next.

Like my children leaving the nest. Like when my closest friends and some of my family began to die off—Sailor, D.C., Mom, three aunts, and four uncles—all within two years. And this, once again, got me to wondering about the meaning of life. What's it all about? But this time, my newly discovered faith brought me through.

Then there were those bad investments—television stations, mining ventures, you name it. Despite my advanced education in business, I just couldn't seem to get it right. Maybe the Lord intended for me to be a poker player. Maybe poker *is* my path to greater awareness. Maybe whenever I stray from that poker path, the Lord decides to yank me around a little and remind me to stay on course, doing what I do best. It sure seems that way.

And I've noticed this in other great poker players as well. They yearn to take a shot at something beyond poker, and as likely as not, whenever they do it, they end up getting yanked around, too.

Enter the World Poker Tour, the tremendously successful televised series that's helped to popularize our game as much as anything else in poker history. When Lyle Berman, founder of the WPT offered me a chance to buy in, I was so gun-shy from failed investments that I turned it down.

Life's strange. Here I am, all my life, taking shots at shaky investments having nothing to do with poker. Many of those shots are doomed from the get-go, and here's one with the right people behind it, with the right vision, at the right time, involving the right game—my game—and I turn it down. Yeah, life's strange and so are the choices that people make in life. You never know what the next deal brings. Sometimes you play hands and wish you hadn't. And sometimes you throw away hands, only to see a perfect flop, and you wished you'd stuck around to enjoy it.

More Twists and Turns

My best friend over the past thirty years has been Jack Binion, who took over as principal owner of the Horseshoe after his legendary father, Benny Binion, died. Maybe you've heard about the family dispute that pitted Jack against his sister, Becky. It was highly publicized. Naturally, my friendship dictated that I side with Jack, and when he left the Horseshoe in his sister's charge and opened casinos down South, I deserted the World Series of Poker for four years.

It was a hard thing to do, because I was the leading money winner lifetime at the tournament, and I knew that with ever-growing tournaments and bigger prize money, other players would likely be passing me as I sat on the sidelines. Yet even today I remain in a tie with Johnny Chan and Phil Hellmuth for total first-place bracelets won. We've each won nine.

That family dispute has blown over, and maybe I'll be able to add more bracelets in the years ahead, although with the number of entrants per event often approaching 1,000 nowadays and surpassing 2,600 for the 2004 main event, that becomes a much tougher challenge.

Nightmare

I remember the last year I played in the WSOP before my boycott. I finished first, second, and third during the series of events. But on the negative side, I was robbed at gunpoint, beaten, and hit over the head. But the night it happened taught me just how saintly and brave Louise really was. I'd always known it in my heart, but this time she proved it in a way that will always haunt me.

You'd think I'd know better than to carry large amounts of money, and I do know better. Being held up and hijacked, rolled and robbed from my earliest poker days in Texas has taught me caution. But, apparently not enough caution. It wasn't cash I was carrying six years ago, just chips from the poker games at the WSOP. Big chips. Lots of them.

And I got home with them safely. Almost.

One of the worst nightmares, not only for a poker player, but for any citizen, is a home invasion. It was midnight. As I left my car, heading for my door, I was confronted by two men, one with a gun. They wanted the keys. I flung them far into the bushes, but not far enough. One of the men retrieved them. I decided I simply wasn't going inside the house. No way. So, I faked a heart attack. It was a convincing act, and they bought into it. But that didn't send them scurrying into the night. They simply unlocked the door and dragged me through it.

Naturally, we have all sorts of security features, as most high-stakes players do. One of those was a delayed alarm, which had been set by Louise, who was upstairs sleeping. When I didn't deactivate it, the alarm sounded, just as I'd hoped.

They demanded to know how to turn it off. I kept feigning semi-consciousness and giving them the wrong combinations, asking them to call the paramedics. Sympathy from them was not forthcoming, however. I was pistol-whipped and they broke my nose in the process. My face was badly cut up when Louise came downstairs to investigate the commotion.

The phone rang.

"That's the alarm company," one of the men growled. "Tell them everything's all right, or we'll kill you right now!"

It was, indeed, the security company, responding to a standard alert. In order to determine whether this was a false alarm, they asked for a password that would let them know everything was okay. Louise took the call and had the presence of mind to give the wrong password, just as I had given the wrong codes. But instead of picking up on the clue that something was terribly amiss at the Brunsons' residence, the woman on the other end admonished Louise, saying she had been given the wrong password.

"Yes, I know," Louise confirmed politely, hoping the intruders wouldn't divine the direction of the phone conversation. She again repeated the invalid code and hung up. Now, you'd think that was enough to send help on its way. But no. The phone rang again. And again it was the security company. This time one of the robbers answered and tried, pathetically, to sound like a woman. He was told that the code previously given is invalid. Belatedly, the agent got suspicious and figured it out. Finally, she hung up and called the police.

Slamming the phone down, the robber lost his cool, charged back into the room where the other bandit had a gun to my head.

"Don't kill him, kill me!" It was my dear Louise's voice. When the man had stepped back from me, she had jumped between me and the gun.

The robbers seemed flabbergasted. They threatened us again, then took chips and some money from my pockets. They didn't search the house, and they wouldn't have found any cash there, anyway. I don't keep cash at home, mostly because it could endanger my family. They sensed they were running out of time, and so they fled.

Even through the pain, one thought struck home. It was my astonishment at just how courageous Louise is. I'd always known she was like that, but that night set a new standard.

By the way, I'd learned that heart attack trick from another legendary gambler, Titanic Thompson. It was in his book. But he would take it a step further, coming out with a hidden pistol. They say he killed five guys that tried to rob him.

A Reunion

My life has been a long chain of adventures. And when I think back, I realize that the things you experience are your gifts to remember. Permanent gifts, like diamonds. They sparkle in your head, and they are yours forever.

And I journey back to my college years at Hardin-Simmons. It's as if I can remember it all, the games, the glory, the shots I made, the shots I missed. It all plays out again, like brand new, on a basketball court in my mind. Everyone's there. My friends. My teammates. The crowds.

It had been like that for many years, those vivid memories. And so, I invited my whole team to a reunion. Surprisingly, all but two were still alive—twenty-five of them. Would you believe that twenty-two showed up at my home, more than fifty years after we'd had our championship season in the Border Conference? Our conference included big time schools such as Arizona, Arizona State, New Mexico, Texas Tech, and UTEP, then known as Texas Western. Our Hardin-Simmons team was one of sixteen elite teams that comprised the NCAA basketball tournament at that time.

My old teammates had become educators and preachers and businessmen. None was a poker player. I was the black sheep of the university. Hardin-Simmons has strong religious roots, and I'm betting I was the only one who turned out to be a professional gambler in the history of the school.

No wonder I've been passed up for my college's Hall of Fame, despite my accomplishments in track and basketball there. But the reunion made up for it, and it turned out to be one of the fondest experiences of my life.

We all reminisced about that championship year, and time

stood still. And for a brief, whimsical, magical moment, I believed—maybe we all believed—we could still do it. We could do it again.

Heartbreak and Peace

And so my time on earth so far has been a journey. Along the way, I've faced heartbreak and found peace. I've struggled but ultimately conquered. And now, having completed my seventh decade on earth, I reflect.

That's one of the two things I do most nowadays. Reflect. And play poker.

I don't play in a lot of tournaments outside of Nevada these days, but because the WPT has grown so popular, there's a sudden interest in poker. I've been invited regularly to appear on TV shows, the interviews for major publications have become commonplace, and a movie script about my life has just been completed.

Poker is hot. And I'm proud of my part in it, honored by every award that ties me to our great game of poker—Poker Hall of Fame, Seniors Hall of Fame, Texas Hall of Fame, Tropicana Casino Legends Hall of Fame. As I sat writing this section, I had the honor of being interrupted by an invitation from the Commerce Casino near Los Angeles, the biggest poker palace in the world. I was one of three "players" to be inducted into their new Poker Walk of Fame, along with actor James Garner, who played Maverick on the most popular TV series in its day, and Gus Hanson, who won three major televised tournaments last year. That's an amazing feat, especially in light of the increased number of competitors per event. This surge in poker popularity means more players to beat, and you can go a long, long time before winning just one major tournament, no matter how skillful you are. Winning three in a season is remarkable.

And to show the importance of all this exposure, not many would have named Gus as a top contender until that. Today, if you play well and get on a streak, you'll be in the spotlight and can stay there for a long time. Gus will. People's impressions of those televised victories linger and are long remembered.

Gus's performance is the most extraordinary feat since Johnny Chan won two WSOP main events back-to-back in the same twelve months that he won the two prestigious Hall of Fame main events and then finished second at the WSOP the following year. With the dramatically increased number of entrants, a performance like that will surely never be repeated.

Changes

My life has evolved radically since the days that Slim and Sailor and I traveled Texas and the South in an old Fairlane Ford. Things have changed so much.

I still play poker regularly. But often I decide to escape, even though it means sacrificing some profit. Then I stay at my place on Flathead Lake in Montana, out of the Las Vegas heat, relaxing. At those times, life is passing me by, and I feel renewed. And there, as everywhere, I reflect. Reflecting on my life, and life in general, has become almost an obsession with me in recent years.

What good is life, you know, if you can only live it once? You own your experiences. They are yours to keep. You should think about that as you go through life. What you do now will become a permanent part of you. The good things and the bad things. I can't tell you that the cards you're dealt will be the ones you want, but whatever they turn out to be, play them wisely. That's the secret.

It all goes by so quickly, life. My son Todd and my daughters Pam and Cheryl were just kids yesterday. Now they're grown. And I've watched Todd quit college to follow in his father's footsteps in the poker arena. He's impressed me greatly, ever since he triumphed in one of his first tournaments at the Bicycle Club. Many world-class players have told me that Todd is one of the best young players today. So, don't just go by what I say. I could be biased. Todd has proven himself to the poker world, and that's why he's in this book.

I think back on why I liked poker in the first place. It was the freedom, I think. You're as free as a cloud floating in the sky. That's the most beautiful part of being a gambler.

Middle It at 120

As you probably know, I've been very heavy most of my adult life. People kept warning me of the health problems that go along with carrying around those extra pounds. But it didn't really hit home with me because I was able to move about swiftly, golf with a low handicap, and stay active.

But recently I sat down and chatted with myself. Things were not as they had been. I was over seventy. In recent years, like a classic car, my chassis wasn't in good shape. My legs weren't carrying me well and my shoulder ached. But my heart was healthy, like a great-working, tireless carburetor. Maybe that's because blood has flowed very fast through my veins during the pressure situations at poker. Maybe that cleansed me.

Two different doctors have told me that my body must be programmed to live 120 years, as badly as I've treated it. One said 130, one said 110, so I middled it at 120.

Then I decided that I may as well plan for a lot more hands of poker, and I had gastric bypass surgery to reduce my weight. I did that six months ago, and I feel a lot healthier now.

But what happens after those 120 years? I'll be gone and perhaps some aspiring players will read this book and new poker stars will be created. They'll keep poker's flame flickering, and if the Lord allows, I'll observe from above and share their adventures.

As for now, I'm looking forward to the next fifty years. And while that may not be exactly realistic and may not happen, in life and in poker, the best you can do is try. And I'll be trying.

THE HISTORY OF
NO-LIMIT TEXAS HOLD'EM

Crandell Addington

Some of my fondest memories of the old days include Crandell Addington. We met over forty years ago when we were both single and adventuresome. We played poker in backrooms, sawdust joints, and high stakes games throughout Texas, Alabama, Oklahoma, Louisiana, and other southern states. We survived numerous robberies, arrests and other situations that would rival the action scenes you see on the movie screens today.

Crandell, myself, and a half dozen other high stakes players from Texas introduced no-limit Texas hold 'em to Nevada in the late 1960's. Then later on in 1985, at the request of Benny Binion, Crandell and Jack Strauss went on a month-long tour of Great Britain to show their gamblers how to play the game.

Crandell was an original participant and the winner of the 1969 Texas Gamblers Convention held in Reno, the professional poker tournament that became the World Series of Poker in 1970. Crandell then played in the WSOP the next nine years at Binion's Horseshoe Casino in downtown Las Vegas. He compiled an outstanding record in the WSOP, including two second place finishes.

Now retired from poker, Crandell runs his oil exploration company, along with his precious metals and pharmaceutical companies. He remains one of the most colorful and greatest players in poker history.

THE HISTORY OF NO-LIMIT TEXAS HOLD'EM
by Crandell Addington

This is the story of how a small band of Texas gamblers unwittingly created the poker colossus that is currently enjoyed by more than fifty million professional and amateur players and is seen by millions of people worldwide on some of the most popular shows on television. Here's how it all started.

In the early 1960s, poker was an illegal activity throughout the United States, with the exception of Nevada and California. But that didn't stop Texans like Pinky Rhoden of Lubbock, "Duck" Mallard of Lockhart, Jesse Alto of Corpus Christi, Jack Straus of Houston, and Tom Moore of San Antonio from hosting high stakes games all over their state. Some game operators even disguised their organizations as fraternal organizations, such as the Redmen and Elks Clubs, hoping to prevent raids from the authorities. Sometimes this worked, sometimes it didn't.

These men and more—including the seven Texans who eventually brought no-limit Texas hold'em to Nevada—traveled from town to town across Texas and the deep South playing poker. They became known as "outside" or "road" gamblers, and they specialized in Kansas City lowball draw and Texas hold'em, then a new game that offered the best platform for developing multiple strategies and tactically implementing them.

Around this same time, Tom Moore, Slim Lambert, and Red Berry were running a weekend casino with table games in the heart of Texas. These "Boss Gamblers of Bexar County" operated their casino in the incorporated city of Castle Hills, which was entirely surrounded by San Antonio. In a rambling house attached to the casino on West Avenue, they ran a second illegal operation: a high stakes poker game six days a week—five days of no-limit, one day of limit.

In 1963, at the age of twenty-five, I began to play in this game. This was one of the softest high stakes no-limit games in the state due to the number of producers it drew, such as John Monfrey, the Falstaff beer distributor for South Texas; Austin Hemphill, a Ford dealer; and other oilmen, bankers, ranchers, restaurateurs, contractors, and car dealers. Because of this, Moore was protective of his game, and the only outside gamblers welcome to play were those of us who were his personal friends.

However, as soft as this game was, sometimes the fish ate the pelicans. One night on West Avenue, I witnessed one of the biggest laydowns and three of the highest hands that can be dealt in Texas hold'em. The fish was a San Antonio contractor who was a regular at the game, and fortunately for the two pelicans—Gilbert Hess of Dallas, who would later marry Felton McCorkindale's widow, and Doyle Brunson—it occurred on the one night of the week when the limit game was in session. Otherwise the pelicans would have had a smooth spot to shuffle on where all their chips had been.

The limit was $80/$160, cheap by today's standards, but high enough back then. There was a round of raises before the flop, then the flop fell A-4-2. The maximum bets and subsequent raises were made and called by all three players. At this point, Doyle was holding trip aces, Gilbert Hess was holding trip deuces, and the fish was holding trip fours.

The turn came a deuce. Doyle led with aces full, but when the double raise came back to him, he laid down the hand. Since I have already told you that on this particular night the fish ate the pelicans, you already know that the river card was the fourth four. So the contractor won the hand against odds that only some top poker mathematician and theorist, such as Mike Caro, might be interested in calculating.

Anyway, four years later, Tom invited me to participate in the acquisition of the Holiday Hotel in Reno, and thanks to my success at his table, I was able to accept. In 1967, I moved to Nevada with him and his family. Unfortunately, we ran into trouble securing a gaming license, so the Holiday Hotel never quite panned out, for me at least.

The original licensees of the Holiday Hotel in Reno became Tom, John Monfrey, and Austin Hemphill, who would later partner with Red McCombs, owner of the Minnesota Vikings and former owner of the San Antonio Spurs and Denver Nuggets.

But, hotel or not, I was playing enough poker to keep me occupied. I had decided against becoming an inside gambler and instead continued traveling all over the country and Mexico playing high stakes games. What I didn't know—what no one could have known—was how our introduction of Texas hold'em would end up changing the landscape of poker forever.

At the time, Nevada had only one legal poker room, which was located in the Golden Nugget and operated by Bill Boyd, a master five-card stud player. It was truly a "sawdust joint," with red-flocked wallpaper on the walls and oiled sawdust covering the floors. Nevada and California players came there to play five-card stud, razz, and California lowball draw. This would change when a small group of Texans, led by Felton McCorkindale and including Doyle Brunson, Bryan "Sailor" Roberts, Johnny Moss, Amarillo Slim, Jack Straus and me, introduced high-stakes no-limit Texas hold'em to Nevada.

Texas hold'em proved popular among the players, but for years there was no casino other than the Golden Nugget in which to spread a game. The Golden Nugget didn't exactly attract the same number of high roller casino patrons that the Strip casinos reeled in by the thousands. This meant there was very little opportunity to catch a drop-in player or producer at the poker room. But in 1969, Sid Wyman, the boss of the Dunes

Hotel and Casino, today the site of the Bellagio, invited us to spread a high-stakes no-limit game just outside the entrance to his main showroom, where we were able to catch lots of drop-ins, including the late Major Riddle, the majority owner of the Dunes.

Remember, Nevadans and Californians were primarily five-card stud players. And although he was originally from Lockhart, Texas, Riddle was by now a transplanted Nevadan. As such, he had no experience playing a game that required such sublime strategy, and it is fair to say that he and others new to the game were faced with a steep learning curve. Their inexperience helped fill the lockboxes of the outside gamblers from Texas who brought the game west.

One such incident took place at the legendary poker table in the Dunes. On one hand, all but Texan Johnny Moss and Major Riddle folded, leaving a huge heads-up pot. Johnny was in the lead and never checked his hand; Riddle never hesitated to call Johnny's bets from before the flop or after the river. When all the cards were out, the board was K-K-9-9-J. Moss moved in on Riddle, and Riddle called him. Moss rolled a pair of nines out of the hole for four of a kind. Major Riddle rolled a pair of deuces out of the hole. See what I mean about the five-card stud players and their learning curve? Riddle had a wired pair, and he was not about to lay them down, not realizing that he had the worst hand possible in this situation and could not even beat the five cards on the board.

One player, Joe Rubino, who was from Alabama and a good Kansas City lowball player (but not much of a Texas hold'em player), went so far as to register an objection to Johnny winning the pot. Rubino claimed that since Riddle could not beat the board with his two deuces, he should be able to take his last call back. It didn't take Johnny but a second to tell him that sometimes the board is the best possible hand in Texas hold'em and that his comment showed how little he knew about the game. He also told him a couple of other things about minding his own business when he was not involved in a pot.

As the game began to catch on in Las Vegas during the late sixties and early seventies, high stakes no-limit Texas hold'em games ranged from $10,000 to $100,000 change-in (that's about $60,000 - $600,000 in terms of today's dollar).

In 1968, Tom and Lafayne Moore decided to hold a table games tournament in order to promote the Holiday Hotel in Reno. They designed elaborate invitations to The First Annual Gaming Fraternity Convention and sent them to a select group of approximately fifty high rollers. The event met with limited success, so in 1969 Tom decided to change the format to a high-stakes poker game and invite all the top players and some of the biggest bookies in the U.S.

Moore, a good poker player himself, knew that the bookmakers would be the producers of The Second Annual Gaming Fraternity Convention. This was the first ever major poker tournament, and it drew twenty or thirty poker players, bookmakers, and pool hustlers, including myself, Johnny Moss, Doyle Brunson, James "Longgoodie" Roy, Aubrey Day, Benny Binion, Amarillo Slim, Puggy Pearson, Jimmy Casella, Minnesota Fats, Bill Boyd, Jack Straus, Felton "Corky" McCorkindale, George Barnes, "Sailor" Roberts, Johnny Joseph, and the notorious father of actor Woody Harrelson, Charles, now serving life for the 1979 assassination of John H. Wood, a U.S. District Court justice in San Antonio.

The event, which lasted one week, featured Texas hold'em, Kansas City lowball draw, razz, stud, and ace-to-five lowball draw. All the games were "live" games, that is, players could rebuy chips if they went broke. This meant that the winner had to be the best player, not just the luckiest.

At this tournament, I won the "Mr. Outside" trophy, designating me as the best outside or road gambler at the tournament. Oddly enough, both Tom Moore and Bill Boyd, who ran their own games and therefore were thought of as inside gamblers, were under consideration for the award as well.

Benny and Jack Binion were impressed with the success of the tournament and acquired the rights to it when Tom Moore sold the Holiday in 1970. They renamed it the World Series of Poker. For the inaugural tournament, which was held at Binion's Horseshoe Casino, he retained the multi-game format of Moore's Gaming Fraternity Convention, but with the exception of a few bookmakers, there were no producers. Even though the producers had not yet found their way to the World Series of Poker, this tournament was as successful as its predecessor. But unlike Tom Moore's tournament, the first World Series of Poker was attended by various representatives of the print media.

The following year, *Los Angeles Times* journalist Ted Thackrey suggested to Binion a new format: a single no-limit Texas hold'em tournament. Thackrey promised that he and Jimmy "The Greek" Snyder could get nationwide publicity if the event were billed as a winner-take-all world championship. That was all Benny Binion needed to hear.

The PR campaign worked and players from far and wide flocked to the World Series of Poker. Interestingly enough, the principal attraction of the tournament was not the tournament itself, but rather the opportunity to win large sums from the producers in the live games or side games, as they were sometimes called. In live poker games, players can buy more chips—as opposed to tournament games, in which players are eliminated when they lose their original buy-in. Live games need producers; that's a cardinal rule of high stakes no-limit poker. Although a group of superior players might spread a game amongst themselves, as we often did, it is the producers (bookmakers, oilmen, businessmen, and so on) that make a no-limit game thrive. Thanks to the excitement generated by Binion's PR campaign, there was no shortage of producers at the 1971 World Series of Poker. In Las Vegas, this was the beginning of the halcyon days of no-limit poker.

At one such live game in the seventies, Doyle Brunson and I took on a producer named Rex Cauble, a Texan who owned two exclusive western wear and tack shops in Dallas and Houston, which he named "Cutter Bill's" after a famous cutting horse. As it later turned out, Rex was also importing certain agricultural products from Mexico that the DEA objected to. Anyway, Rex liked to play high change in no-limit Texas hold'em, and he would show up at the Horseshoe during the World Series of Poker with a sizeable bankroll.

Now, Doyle and I have been friends for over forty years, and we've played in countless games together—but none have ever been as strange as this one. On this particular evening, Rex wanted to play a $50,000 change-in game. Four or five of us took him up on the challenge. But first, Doyle was gracious enough to give Rex a thirty-minute crash course on the finer points of hold'em. Only after Rex was certain he had enough of the basics to play credibly, did we all sit down.

Less than thirty minutes into the game, an unraised pot came up between Rex and poker world champion Bobby Baldwin, who beat me in 1978 for the title and who is now President of the Bellagio and CEO of the Mirage properties. There came a flop of K-J-2, three suits. Bobby checked in front, and Rex checked. The turn card was a 6, and both players again checked. The river showed a 4, with no flush possible. Bobby checked, Rex bet $1,500, and Bobby raised $30,000.

Rex, with $60,000 in front of him, pondered and pondered, seeming to consider folding in order to preserve half his stack. Finally, clearly intimidated, he reluctantly called.

Bobby triumphantly rolled 3-5 out of the hole for the nuts. His straight couldn't possibly be beat. What do you think Rex rolled out of the hole? Since Rex was last to act and had $30,000 in chips still in front of him, you would never guess his holecards to be 3-5, the same as Bobby's, but they were. Rex had just smooth called with the nuts.

At this point, Doyle uttered his favorite phrase of astonishment: "I'll be a sunburned son of a bitch." I had to suppress a laugh. But back in the early days of the World Series of Poker, this kind of thing happened. The tournament attracted many producers like Rex, and some played with us for even higher stakes.

The popularity of the World Series was not lost on Sid Wyman, an affable man and the public relations director for the Dunes and the Aladdin. In 1973, Wyman brought the game of no-limit Texas hold'em across Las Vegas Boulevard to the Aladdin, which was operated by Sam Diamond. Hosted by Johnny Moss, this high-stakes no-limit Texas hold'em game attracted not only the Texas and Nevada gamblers, but also more and more drop-ins. It was so well attended that games often ran for days at a time, and fortunes changed hands. Major Riddle was a frequent player at the Aladdin table, and his poor play led to his losing majority control of the Dunes to parties represented by Sid Wyman.

Moss eventually moved his game to the oldest casino on the strip, the Flamingo, which again found itself the subject of debate and criticism. More than thirty years earlier, in 1946, the Flamingo proved the critics of the 1940s wrong about the possibility of successful expansion of casinos from downtown to a dusty, remote location that eventually became known as the Strip. In 1976, at the same hotel, Johnny Moss would prove the critics of the 1970s wrong by successfully operating a poker room in a Strip casino.

At the time, other notable poker players were beginning to see the advantage of hosting high stakes games, including Chip Reese at the Dunes and Eric Drache and Doyle Brunson, who partnered up to operate the game at the Silver Bird, the casino that Major Riddle had acquired after losing control of the Dunes. The excitement generated by new poker rooms on the Strip and the World Series of Poker fueled Texas hold'em's meteoric rise in nationwide popularity.

These prosperous days lasted until about the middle eighties. By that time, satellites had become so popular that they were running twenty-four hours a day and were occupying more and more of the limited floor space in the Horseshoe. While at first, this was seen as a positive change for the tournament, it had the ironic effect of crowding out the live games—the very reason we had started the WSOP in the first place!

Today, the game of no-limit Texas hold'em that we introduced to Nevada so many years ago has been transformed, thanks to its entertainment value, to television audiences. Ever increasing participation in major freeze-out tournaments (more than 2,500 players in the 2004 World Series of Poker) have forced tournament hosts to impose rapidly increasing ante and blind structures in order to keep the tournament times manageable. And this has produced an aberration of the pure form of the game. With certain notable exceptions, the game of no-limit Texas hold'em is a game designed to be played *after* the flop. That's when the real play is supposed to begin. However, many hands seen at televised events today are played before the flop, when the players have received only their holecards. This style of play, sometimes referred to as "catch an ace and take a race," re-introduces a substantial amount of luck into a game that had always favored the best player over the best card catcher.

But it appears that nothing can stop an idea whose time has come. And for the hundreds of thousands, if not millions, of players now active on the online poker sites around the world, surely the time has come. In the future, you can expect to see time management problems develop for the tournament hosts as more and more of the Internet players gain entries into the major tournaments.

Looking into the future, it's not hard to imagine the creation of a professional poker league, with several teams selected by some sort of draft. In fact, just such a league is in an early investigative stage today.

The creation of new opportunities to exploit the poker phenomenon is limited only by the imagination of men like Benny Binion.

So now you know the history of no-limit Texas hold'em—the story of a small band of Texas gamblers who changed the game of poker forever and of how the modern poker tournaments are descendants of an illegal high stakes game in San Antonio that gypsied to Reno, then blossomed into the World Series of Poker, the progenitor of every poker tournament played and televised today.

ONLINE POKER

ONLINE POKER
by Doyle Brunson

Technology surrounds us. Things change. And the swiftness of change today is unparalleled in history. Nothing makes poker players more aware of this change than the advent of online poker.

Computers changed everything—from productivity, to research, to games. Poker, too. You see, along came the Internet and suddenly you could find almost any answer in seconds, be anywhere in the world, instantly—not physically, of course, but we learned we didn't need to be physically present to be there. And so we could play poker without being physically present. We could be at the table. Instantly.

I remember the first time I played poker online was in 1999. I think it was a tiny $3 limit game, and I was used to playing $2,000 limit and higher games where you could win or lose upwards of $1 million without leaving your seat. I'd gotten curious, because Mike Caro had endorsed an online poker site, and I thought this was strange, considering he had previously written a column warning of the pitfalls of online play. If he'd changed his mind, then the least I could do was investigate for myself. Remarkably, it was as exciting as any poker I'd ever played. There I was, participating in poker on the screen with opponents seated inches away, but knowing they weren't actually inches away. They were in England and Germany and Hong Kong. Everywhere. I was playing poker in a game that could never have been possible before.

A TORNADO

And so, unexpected and out of nowhere, online poker blew onto the scene. It was like a tornado sweeping down the Texas Panhandle. And I realized—grudgingly at first—that it was here to stay. You could now put poker into two main categories: online poker and real-world poker. Notice that I'm saying "real-world" poker, not "real" poker. That's because online poker *is* real poker. It is certainly real for the hundreds of thousands of new players around the world who are playing for real money! In fact, what is there about online poker that makes it unreal? Not much, and that's why I think most of us have started differentiating poker by just these two terms: online poker and real-world poker.

And real-world poker, the kind you sit down and play with physical cards at a real table against opponents you can reach across the table and shake hands with, can itself be divided into subcategories. For instance, we could talk about home poker and casino poker. Each offers a slightly different flavor. That's the same with basketball, you know. There is basketball played outdoors on concrete slabs, high school basketball, college basketball, NBA basketball, and international basketball that you see in the Olympics. But it's all basketball.

And I'm here to tell you today, that online or real world, poker is poker. It's all poker. There's hardly any advice on these pages that won't help you become a much better online player, simply because it will help you to become a much better poker player, period.

DOYLE'S ROOM
www.doylesroom.com

Before I give you some specific tips and insights about playing poker online, I want to tell you something that may surprise you. The truth is, it surprises me, because not too many years ago, I couldn't imagine myself being involved in online poker at all. Briefly, I got myself talked into endorsing a friend's start-up website, but I extricated myself from that fiasco as soon as I realized that nowadays only the big boys can afford to play in this business. Chalk it up as another of my bad ventures when trying to help others out.

Well, then I got smart. If you want to know how smart, check out www.doylesroom.com for actual play in practice games—and beyond! And for other things about learning poker, try its sister site, www.poker1.com. I'm happy to be the Doyle's Room consultant and that they're putting my name on the site— because they're paying me a handsome endorsement fee, and because it's a site I'm proud to be part of.

Using doylesroom.com as an example, I'll walk you through online poker. Remember, by the time you read this, doylesroom.com and other competing sites may be even more advanced. I envision being able to bet just by speaking and being able to scrutinize live, moving images of opponents, bringing to the online world the most sorely missed element of traditional poker: tells.

The one thing that will shock you most is the number of poker players currently online. Just before this book went to press, I was honored to be inducted into the Poker Walk of Fame at the Commerce Casino, near Los Angeles. Have you ever visited that casino? It's the biggest physical cardroom in the world. There are hundreds of poker tables!

Now, in my whole life as a poker player, I never envisioned that there would ever be fifty games going under one roof, let alone hundreds. And Commerce isn't the only major poker room to host a huge number of poker tables. Also, near Los Angeles, you have the Bicycle Casino, Hollywood Park Casino, Hawaiian Gardens, and the Hustler. And there are now huge poker rooms in Las Vegas casinos, including the Bellagio, the Golden Nugget, the Mirage, and others.

Jack Binion launched large-scale poker rooms in the Midwest, and there are now big rooms on the East Coast, too, including those in Foxwoods in Connecticut and others inside several casinos in Atlantic City. Poker is booming everywhere.

But put those all together, and you have maybe 1,000 tables. This is something I never imagined when I started my career, steering around the frequent tumble weeds that walked across the highways of Texas, going from one single-table private game to another.

When you play real-world poker games, you have to travel from one casino to another to find the right games. When you play poker online, however, you're instantly within reach of any table. A few clicks of your mouse and you're at another table, maybe at the same online casino, maybe at another.

Just how many tables are we talking about? You'll often find over 7,000 real-money online tables going on at the same time—some tournament tables, some regular ring games. Most days there will be over 50,000 real-money players that you can choose to play against in minutes, without leaving your home. And then there are the free, practice games, and I'd hesitate to count how many players and tables there are of those.

Between the sudden surge of televised poker and online poker, more new players have been exposed to our game than ever before in history. And it helps everyone. The real-world casinos are flooded with new players. Did you ever think poker would get this hot? I didn't. It's a fantasy come true.

I believe many potential players, who otherwise would feel too embarrassed to walk through the front doors of a public casino to play poker against more-experienced opponents, will find that courage now that they can play their first hands on the Internet.

So, let's see how poker is played online.

TWO REASONS WHY ONLINE POKER IS WORSE

Here are two ways that online poker is worse than real-world poker. I readily acknowledge that there are other minor grievances that could be added, but to me, these are the only two that stand out as important.

Reason #1: Where Did the Tells Go?

I think every serious player prefers real-world poker at times. There's no substitute for being able to stare an opponent down and make decisions based on your observations. And there's no greater feeling in poker than that of intimidating opponents into making costly mistakes. Those elements are missing—and missed—when you play online.

The first thing you need to know is that, at the time of this book's publication, you can throw your skills at reading opponents' body language out the window. But if you're reading *Super/System 2* just a couple years down the road, you may well be able to see real opponents on your screen. Poker will be like a video conference, and you'll be able to focus on the players across the table from you and read them. I predict, through live video of each player replacing the icons in the seats, tells will be everywhere, and then full-scale psychological warfare will come to the online poker battlefield—and nothing will be missing.

But for now, online poker sites—including doylesroom.com—depict players as icons. Sometimes those are cartoon characters, but Doyle's Room uses your choice of symbols, including flags, scenery, and artistic words, like TILT.

Here are some of the icons you can choose to differentiate yourself from other players at the tables:

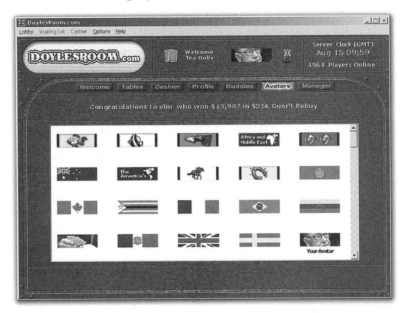

Think of it as selecting one of those weird pieces to represent yourself at Monopoly as you roll the dice and prance around the board. Players think it's kind of fun choosing their icon, but you're not going to gain any tells staring at them. Well, maybe that's not quite true. For instance, my guess is that players who choose an icon featuring the word TILT are actually fairly tight players, trying to deceive you.

Are there other tells online? Indeed there are! Almost all of them center around the use of early action buttons. Those are one of the inventions that make online poker the fast-paced game it is.

What are early action buttons? They are ingenious innovations that take advantage of the fact that you can secretly tell the software what your next action will be—before it's your turn to act! Since your opponents are sitting in their own homes, possibly on the other side of the earth, they have no idea which button you've decided to push.

Later, I'll discuss specific tells associated with early action buttons. But, overall, you're going to find yourself at a disadvantage online if you earn a lot of your real-world profit by reading your opponents.

Reason #2: Can't Spend the Money Immediately

Part of the thrill of the poker I grew up with is that you can send your opponents home with their tails tucked between their legs, whimpering and whining, while you're spending some of your freshly won money. Sadly, that thrill is gone from online poker. You can't send opponents home whimpering, because they're *already* home whimpering. And you can't spend their money yet, because you can't physically touch it. It's there in your account, but if you want to spend it, you'll have to request a cash-out and it will be several days before it arrives.

Now, I'll wager you're thinking that that might be a good thing. I'm sure there are thousands of poker players who unwisely wasted big chunks of their bankrolls after a big win and wish they'd had to wait a few days to receive their winnings. It's hard for most players to acquire the discipline needed to hang on to a bankroll, and I think that playing online helps promote that necessary habit. But I'm listing this fact as a negative simply because I believe a grown-up poker player should be able to enjoy his winnings by stuffing them immediately into his pockets. Call me old fashioned, but anything else doesn't set quite right with me.

But except for that and the fact that you can't reach across the table and shake an opponents' hand or read him the way you can in a real game, online poker is just as good as the traditional kind we're accustomed to—and in some ways better.

22 REASONS WHY ONLINE POKER IS BETTER

There are a great number of ways in which online poker actually excels. Each player has his own favorite reasons why he thinks online poker is in some way superior to real-world poker. These are mine...

Reason #1: Always a Game

Online poker makes a mockery out of how I went about finding good games when I traveled the poker circuit throughout Texas and the South in the 1960s and early 1970s. I mean, sometimes you'd drive all day only to find that the lucrative oil well you were hoping to drill had just dried up an hour before you got there. Then you had to swallow the disappointment and plan your next move in accordance with how much it would cost to travel. Was the game you'd heard about, far down the road, worth the hassle and the expense?

Then came casino poker. That helped, because there was often a choice of games in town. But many nights there was only one game of interest, and some nights there weren't any. So, imagine how I feel—having expended most of my effort finding the right games, rather than enjoying them—being able to sit down at my computer on a sleepless night and find the best game in the world after a few mouse clicks.

What's even greater is that online poker never sleeps. It's always prime time for poker somewhere in the world, and you can join those games, even if nobody else is awake in your neighborhood.

Reason #2: Play Against Opponents You'd Seldom or Never Meet in Person

The Internet has made the world so much smaller. It might not look like it now, with all the political flare-ups and regional wars in the news, but I believe that encountering people from far away places and striking up instant friendships is bound to make the world more civil eventually. You read about Internet romances that lead to marriage. Business associations are formed that would have been physically improbable.

It's a good thing. And one of the best effects of the Internet is what's happening to poker. Bit by bit, poker is becoming the world's common language of gaming. In a real sense, online poker is doing its part to make the world better—as well as helping to showcase the game.

A main virtue of online poker is that it makes games possible among eager players who live so far apart that they'd seldom have a chance to sit down together at a real-world table.

Reason #3: Take a Quick Five-Minute Break to Play

Often you only have a half-hour or less to spare, sometimes as little as five minutes. If you had the urge to play poker prior to online play, there wasn't anything you could do about it. There certainly wouldn't be time to sit down and be dealt in. Now, that's all changed. Sometimes, I'll log into a game when I have just a few minutes to spare. I might only play half a dozen hands at $100/$200 limit, but so what? Usually, I wouldn't play that small, because—for me—it's not worth the effort. But those are hefty limits by online standards, where the majority of people play $15/$30 limits and often much smaller.

So, I play those few hands, and I can do the same thing again on my next break. Those hands all add up, and so does the profit.

Reason #4: Great Practice for Those New To Poker

I'm betting one of the reasons that players didn't flock to the poker rooms in years past is that they just didn't know what to expect when they got there. That can be intimidating, stepping into a real world game for the first time, not knowing how you'll be accepted by the other players. And for beginners, the anonymity of online play gives timid people the courage to dive into the poker pond, whereas, if it were a face-to-face game, they'd just never go near the water.

I believe many players will learn to excel at poker who might otherwise never have played the game. It's all because of the online poker opportunity.

Reason #5: No Need to Dress Up or Groom

I got to thinking—there are times when you like to dress up and times when you don't. I try to look my best when I go to church or go to a decent restaurant with my family. It makes me feel better about myself.

But there are times when I'd rather be flat-out comfortable and I don't care if I'm dressed to impress. One of those times is when I'm playing poker. Unless I'm being filmed, I'm less choosey about what I wear to a poker game. Of course, I dress reasonably well, even then, because I think some of the attire seen at the poker tables is a downright disgrace and reflects poorly on our game. But, basically, I don't overdo it.

The truth is, though, if it weren't for how others might view me, I'd rather not bother about how I look when I play poker. And online play gives me the opportunity to dress however I like. As many have noted, you can play poker online in your pajamas and no one will care. Now, that's definitely a bonus you get *only* when playing poker by computer.

Reason #6: Heads-Up Challenges

If you like to play heads-up, online cardrooms are beginning to provide previously unavailable opportunities. Have you ever wondered why there are so few heads-up matches in real-world casinos? Surely, heads-up can't be that unpopular, because just the thought of a high-intensity one-on-one game can make pulses race. And aren't the final heads-up hands in a tournament the most exciting to watch on television? Let me tell you, having enjoyed a lot of experience in this situation, those final heads-up hands are not just the most exciting to watch—they're also the most exciting to play!

So, why no heads-up? It's because those games are not economical for casinos. Each game takes up valuable real estate—a full table. Worse, each game requires a dealer—who is hired to provide service to up to ten players at a table—just to accommodate two customers.

But online, this all changes. It costs nothing to set up a new table for two players, and online casinos don't worry about you using up their tables, because they can provide as many as they want at no cost. No tables to purchase. No cardroom floor space limitations. But bigger than that is the fact that online casinos don't worry about paying dealers. The cards are all shuffled and distributed by computer. There's no cost involved in dealing more cards or adding more. That's one reason why I believe you're going to see a surge in heads-up play online.

There's another, darker reason why some players might choose heads-up online. They fear collusion, because they've heard that opponents might be on the phone sharing information about each other's hands in order to gang up on honest players. Now, while collusion is always something to be alert to—whether you're playing poker online or in the real-world—the fact is that online poker has an advantage in that there's a database of every hand ever played. Each hand you play is worth money, when you're playing the way I advise in this book, and twice the hands can mean up to twice the profit.

Real-world surveillance and game protection has also increased dramatically in recent years, and I'm certain that, on average, poker is more honest today than it's been at any time in history. If you doubt this, just look at the players who are regularly winning the major tournaments. Often, these are unknown players—some rank amateurs. That, in itself, is a testament to the integrity of real-world poker today.

Still, for those who are so concerned that they don't trust anyone and don't want to risk playing against multiple opponents they can't physically scrutinize, heads-up just might be the answer. One opponent can't collude. To me, that isn't an issue. Online games can be monitored in ways so sophisticated that they'd shock those who aren't technically savvy. While I enjoy shorthanded games and even heads-up games, I'm very comfortable against multiple opponents and sometimes prefer to play against a table full of opponents online.

Heads-up is often a war of egos. And only online can you sit in London and play a hotly contested match against someone at home in bed with a laptop computer in Australia.

Reason #7: More Hands Per Hour

When online poker first debuted in the late nineties, poker rooms actually built in a delay to simulate the time it took to deal cards in the real world. Boy, was that a mistake! It quickly became apparent that players didn't want the delays. The faster their cards arrived, the happier they were. That's why doylesroom.com and most other online rooms have taken all the air out of dealing and shuffling. There is no delay.

You can play many more hands per hour online, about twice as many as you'd play in the real world. That means you can make more money faster. Each hand you play is worth money when you're playing the way I advise in this book, twice the hands can mean up to twice the profit.

Reason #8: Play Two or More Games at Once

You see some pretty weird things at poker. I've seen players hold seats at adjoining tables and scurry back and forth, trying to play both games for short periods of times. This usually happens when the player has free hands remaining before the blind at one game and has been called to a seat from the waiting list for another game. Needless to say, playing two games at once in the real world doesn't work well. It's physically impractical, and you're almost certain to rudely delay the play of a hand at one table, while completing action at another.

But online, it's much simpler. You just click to enter a second, third, or even more games. When it's your turn to act, the software notifies you, and you simply click on your decision to fold, call, check, or raise. Since you don't have to get out of your seat and physically move to the other table, multiple game play becomes practical online.

Does this mean more profit for you? It can—if you're good enough. Try to remember, though, that you won't be able to focus as closely as you would on a single game. You'll miss some of the nuances and won't be able to track your opponents' tendencies as readily. That means your average earnings per game are sure to suffer when you play more than one. But when you add those slightly diminished profits from multiple games together, you'll probably find that you'll earn more total profit. Whether you do depends on your skills.

I recommend that you stick to just one game at first, because it can be quite hectic concentrating on two or more at once. But as you get accustomed to playing multiple games, you might find it exciting and rewarding. Certainly, there's no equivalent in real-world poker.

Reason #9: Pre-Select Buttons

One of the great inventions of online poker are the early action or pre-select buttons. Since you aren't being watched by other players, you can decide what to do in advance of the action reaching you. In real-world poker, pre-selecting wouldn't be appropriate, because that would let opponents who act before you know how you planned to respond.

The early action choices help speed up the play, and they're especially useful if you're playing other games simultaneously. For instance, when you know you're going to fold, no matter what, you can just click the fold button before the action gets to you and concentrate on a different table, where you hold a more promising hand.

The pre-select choices change according to the action. Here's an example from Doyle's Room:

Here I'm holding the seven and three of clubs on the left side of the table. It's a straight limit game, and I'm waiting for Dr. Blueberry, at the bottom of the screen, to act. But, if you're in a situation like this, you don't have to wait until it's your turn to make a decision. Look at the bottom of the screen. You can click right now Fold, Call 5, Call any, Raise 5, or Raise any.

There is something I find useful about these pre-select buttons: they can provide tells. Watch the speed with which someone acts. If a decision is pre-selected, then it usually will occur instantly when the action reaches that player. I say "usually," because occasional lapses in Internet communication can cause a delay. Most of the time this delay won't happen, and you can get some information because of opponents' use of these special buttons.

The main thing I keep in my head is that when an action happens instantly, it's probably a result of a pre-selected action. Why would an opponent pre-select? There's only one reason I can think of. That opponent knows that he's going to take that action, no matter what anyone else does in front of him. That puts an added emphasis to that opponent's decision, in my mind.

Although the screen shot you just looked at was for a situation where someone had already bet, sometimes no one has bet. Then one of the pre-select buttons will be to check. What if an opponent checks instantly? Chances are, that player has determined in advance that he is going to check. At Doyle's Room, he may have selected either the Check/Fold button, which is a very frequent choice, or the less likely Check/Call any button. If Check/Fold is the choice, then I can assume that the instant check means the player probably would have automatically folded if there had been a bet. In that case, I give the player less credit for having a strong hand.

Similarly, if an opponent raises instantly, I'm pretty sure he intended to raise no matter what, and that usually indicates a very strong hand.

There are other tells you can divine from these pre-select buttons, when you take the time to think about what an instant action means. If an opponent seems to frequently use the pre-select buttons, but occasionally hesitates, you can figure him for a type of hand where the decision is not obvious. So, always consider what an instant action—or the lack of one—might mean.

You can, of course, wait until the action reaches your seat. Here's a no-limit example of what your choices would look like then:

Reason #10: The Shuffle

Some players doubt whether the shuffle in online poker is as random as in real-world games. In fact, online shuffles are instant and more random than real-world shuffles. That's because any competent online cardroom knows the right formulas to put into the software. They tell me that the science of simulating random events, including card distribution, is very mature. I guess that means that a lot of research has gone into it, and it's impossible for a human dealer to even come close in dealing cards with the same efficiency or unpredictability.

Another impressive thing about computerized shuffling and dealing is that you won't have any misdeals. And you'll never encounter one of the common irritations of real-world poker, because no cards will be inadvertently flashed.

Reason #11: Rakes Are Actually Less

At the higher limits I play, pots are seldom raked. Instead there's an hourly seat rental. But most everyday limits, $10/$20 and often higher, are raked. If you're looking for a bargain, you'll find that those rakes are a little less online.

Reason #12: No Tipping

It's customary to tip the dealer when you win a pot. It's not mandatory, but most players do it. In a $5/$10 game, you might throw a dollar the dealers way whenever you win a pot with any size to it. The dealer's make most of their income from these tips, because they're paid very low base wages. These dollars you tip add up, and you could buy some nice Christmas presents at the end of the year if you didn't have to pay them. Well, online, you don't. In fact, you can't, because there is no real dealer to appreciate or accept your gesture.

But I had a strange thought. Players being as superstitious as they are, I'm wondering if Doyle's Room should add an optional Tip button. I believe so many players would choose to tip the non-existing dealer that I might waive my endorsement fee and get rich off those tips.

Reason #13: Poker Clock

In poker, an opponent can't stall forever, whether it's an everyday game or a tournament.

Although it's rare, you'll sometimes see a player take a long time before acting on a hand. Now, in no-limit play, this is occasionally acceptable. Decisions can have extreme importance, and a player needs time to think about the situation and study his opponent.

But even in no-limit, most players act more quickly than you'd expect. It's rare for them take a lot of time to ponder. And in limit games, it's downright rude to waste time over and over again when the action gets to you. I believe, if you know you're going to fold, then you should usually just fold. Don't make a show of it.

Sometimes players take so long that if you allowed them to stall forever, the game would come to a halt. That's why in real-world poker, you can always ask to put the clock on an opponent. That gives him a set amount of time to complete the decision. Failure to act constitutes a fold.

The problem with that system is you don't want to be needlessly rude to opponents. Maybe they really do need the time. Maybe they're losing and confused. Maybe they're daring you to ask for the clock, so they can be hostile in return. Who knows?

The good thing about online poker is that it takes away the awkwardness of asking for the clock. If a player doesn't click on a decision button, after 10 seconds or so he'll be prompted to do so. Some sites provide a countdown clock. Doyle's Room uses gentle chimes to warn that you have 10 seconds left to act. What happens if you don't act online differs from cardroom to cardroom and situation to situation. If you haven't put any money in the pot, your hand will be folded. If you have, you'll usually be treated as if you're all-in, even though you still have chips in front of you. That means competing for a partial pot.

Yes, unscrupulous players sometimes try to use the all-in feature unfairly to their advantage. They'll pretend to be having Internet communications problems, not realizing that most sites can tell if they're actually still connected. Sometimes they'll succeed in getting a free shot at part of a pot, when they would otherwise have folded. That's why most sites only allow one or two artificial all-ins to be used per session, beyond which hands are folded, no matter what. That's also why players who abuse the treat-as-all-in privilege are suspended or barred.

Despite this timed-out issue, which is hard to deal with and unique to online poker, the presence of an automatic clock keeps the games moving swiftly. It's part of the reason why there are so many more hands dealt to you each hour online.

Reason #14: With More Hands, Your Results Will Even Out More Quickly

In most games of skill, the right decisions are quickly rewarded. In poker, the right decisions can cause misery in the short term. If you're not prepared for the frustrations that go with quick changes in fate, you don't have the right temperament to be a professional poker player.

Although superior players win in the long run, and you hardly ever hear about any full-time pros having a losing year, it's not hard to spend weeks or even a month suffering a net loss. But the longer you play, the more quickly that familiar law of probability takes hold, and the closer your results get to what really should happen.

But even though we talk about chance taking time to even out, it really doesn't take a lot of time—it takes a lot of hands. What if you could get all those hands played in a short time? Well, suddenly, when you're playing online, instead of in a physical casino, you're playing a lot more hands. The deals are amazingly brisk. The action is swift. Expect to get twice as many hands played each hour. And that's if you only play at a single table. Many winning players regularly play two or three games at once. That's up to six times as many hands per hour.

What does this mean in terms of a bad streak? It means that a streak that would have droned on for six days will stop showering misery on you after only one day. For certain, things will even out faster online. So, if you're a superior poker player, you can expect to win more consistently on a week-to-week basis when you play online.

Reason #15: Tournaments on Demand

This is among online poker's greatest advantages. You can play tournaments day and night. You might see events scheduled for three in the morning—so, if you happen to be awake, dive right in. Why so early in the morning? Remember that poker is now a worldwide sport, and when it's early in the morning for you, it's afternoon somewhere else.

But if tournaments scheduled around the clock aren't enough for you, try the unscheduled ones! There's a fast-and-furious form of tournament poker—the single-table shootout. You play down to one winner, with second and third place finishers also receiving money. It's the same as those popular one-table satellites that annoyed me by drying up the side action years ago at the major tournaments. The difference online is that you're playing for cash, not for a seat into a larger tournament.

What you need to know about these tournaments is that there's no scheduled starting time. That's why the popular name for them today is Sit-and-Goes. You take a seat at the table (or put your name on the list), and as soon as there's a full table, the cards automatically get dealt. You can put your name on other SNG lists and then play several of these tournaments at a time. Usually, they take less than an hour—and a typical player will last about 20 minutes, on average, sometimes being eliminated almost immediately, sometimes surviving long enough to win. You can play them all day if this is your favorite poker form. Just take a seat or click to get on the list. In other words, sit. As soon as there's a full table, it's time for the tournament to begin. A table often fills in a matter of a minute or two. In other words, go.

Sit-and-goes can get to be a habit in a hurry—and a very profitable one for accomplished players. The trick is to play a solid game, trying to survive and share in one of the three payouts for first, second, and third. As much as my temperament tells me to always go for first place, this really isn't the best strategy in these one-table shootouts, where nobody keeps track of your "championships" anyway. It's better to play a more conservative game than you would in a regular ring game. You should play a little more selectively, trying to survive until there are just two players left, and then open up.

The same is true of all online tournaments where you play down to a few players who share the prize money. You won't have the same opportunities to psychologically conquer opponents as you would in real-world games, so the proven best choice is to play more solidly.

Reason #16: More Comfortable Than at a Crowded Table

I hate sitting elbow to elbow. I'm a big man—at least I was until my recent gastric bypass surgery—and you can imagine how important it has been throughout my poker career to have enough room to feel comfortable. In the real world, I usually play shorthanded, but when I have to crowd into a nine- or 10-hand game, as I do for tournaments, I'm always wishing for more space. Online, I don't worry about that. I can play from a recliner with a keyboard in my lap, if I want to, and still be at a full table.

Reason #17: Small-Limit Games That Are Un-Economical in the Real World

In my mind, this is online poker's greatest contribution to our game. Most professionals don't think of $2 and $4 games as meaningful limits. But when you're just starting out and on a small bankroll, even the difference between a $50 win and a $50 loss can be important. Those small limits can be uncomfortable for players just learning the game.

I'll bet it's occurred to everyone who plays poker seriously that it would be a great idea to have formal games for beginners where you could bet just 10 cents. Those would be the training ground for those neophytes who are too timid to risk meaningful money at poker. You'd let new players get comfortable with the game, players who would otherwise never experience the thrill of poker in a casino.

As I pointed out earlier, real-world casinos can't afford to do this, because of the costs involved in providing physical tables and paying human dealers. But online poker rooms can and do make this great contribution to our game.

Reason #18: Free Games for Practice

But why not take this advantage of being able to spread games economically online a step further? Why not offer just-for-fun games for those who aren't ready to play poker for keeps?

Most online poker rooms do exactly that. They let players learn the mechanics of the game by playing for imaginary money. And they charge nothing for this promotional service to the poker community. Real-world casinos can't afford to do that.

Look closely at the game below. Notice that this Doyle's Room game says, "Play Money Table," down toward the bottom of the cloth.

I wouldn't be surprised if many successful real-world players, and even future World Poker Tour and other champions, will launch their careers on free online tables just like this one.

Reason #19: High Percentage of Real-World Tournament Players Who Qualified Online

Yes, I was skeptical of the value of online poker a few years ago. So were many of the people who managed real-world cardrooms. They were afraid that online poker would siphon off their business more than it would help bring in new players to their physical cardrooms.

That argument has been resolved. Today, it's hard to find anyone in the industry who doesn't realize that online games have helped in the resurgence of real-world poker. I meet players everyday at the Bellagio, Commerce, and elsewhere who began by playing poker online.

And the one thing that proves the point most convincingly is the number of players at the major tournaments who qualified online. For some, these real-world tournaments constitute their first exposure to casino poker. They like the adventure of playing against live opponents they actually can shake hands with and speak to at the tables. And they enjoy trying to read them and spot tells—something that isn't possible online.

Count the new players pouring into casino poker tournaments through online channels, and you'll be as convinced as I am that online poker has helped greatly to bring our game into the public spotlight, giving it the respect it always deserved, but never had.

Reason #20: Optional Four-Color Decks

I've got to confess, I've never been a fan of four-color decks. With the traditional deck of cards I grew up with, hearts and diamonds are both red, and spades and clubs are both black. They tell me that four-color decks, with each suit having its own color, were tried over a hundred years ago. Apparently, it wasn't as economical to print them that way, and two colors became the custom.

I prefer two-color decks, because that's what I'm used to.

But, there's obviously a strong argument for a four-color deck. It makes it much easier to spot flushes and flush possibilities at a glance. When Mike Caro publicly started making a big deal about changing to four-colors ten years ago, I thought he was goofy. He tried unsuccessfully to introduce four-color decks to real-world casinos, even going so far as promoting a "C-Day" for Color Deck Day where this novelty was introduced to sixty-five casinos simultaneously.

The effort fell flat, because poker players don't like change and because the differences in colors that he chose were too subtle to be easily distinguished across the table. Old timers like me balked, while many beginners liked the decks. It would have been nice if everyone could play with the deck they preferred, but that was obviously impossible. You had to choose one or the other, and the traditional two-color deck continued to rule in real-world casinos.

Online, it's different. You can play with the deck of your choice. That's because the deck you choose is only displayed on your own computer screen. Your opponent can be looking at a different deck, and it won't make any difference to you. That's why four-color decks have gained a new lease on life online—and only online, so far.

Reason #21: Software Lets You Know When It's Your Turn

You've had this happen before. A player sits patiently, because he doesn't realize it's his turn. You sit patiently, too, because you don't want to be rude while, you assume, he's making a decision. Yes, we've all seen this impasse time and again.

Online, this awkward moment never happens. The software prods players for a decision, letting them know precisely when it's time to act.

Reason #22: No Social Stigma About Leaving a Game Early with Your Winnings

I believe that a player should never need to provide a reason for leaving a game. The common notion that you're being unfair if you sit down for a short time and leave with a big profit is nonsense. In poker, you put your money at risk. If you win, it's your money, and you can get up and leave anytime you feel like it.

Still, this is sometimes hard to do in the real world. If you hit and run too often, you're apt to get a reputation as the type of player some don't like to play against. It never bothers me when players win and leave quickly, but it does bother others. Personally, I usually prefer to play longer sessions, but I don't frown on those who'd rather play short ones.

Online, you won't encounter any resistance when you take the money and run. Opponents realize that you might only have ten minutes to play right then, and you can just click Leave Table and be out of the game without fanfare or making excuses. In fact, players need to pay attention to even notice who comes and goes in a game, because it happens so quickly online. If you're one of those players who likes to play short sessions and leave with your winnings intact, online play is your kind of poker. For the most part, nobody cares or even notices.

WHAT ADJUSTMENTS WILL YOU NEED TO MAKE ONLINE?

Finally, I'll give you some basic advice about how to win online. Almost everything in this book applies. Online poker is real poker.

Keep in mind how I advise playing against bad players, because you can just assume most of the players you'll confront online are bad. Or at the very least, you'll find yourself up against more unsophisticated and too-loose players than you will in real-world casinos.

The trick to beating games against that type of player is to seldom do anything fancy. You don't need to. Most of your profit will come from choosing to do the obviously correct thing. Raise when your logical first choice is raising. Fold when your hands are weak. Bluff sparingly in limit games. Against the type of player you meet online, you should try a lot less tricks than you would in the real world.

Mike Caro and I are in the process of making instructional videos about real-world poker and online poker. Some of these videos will be given away at doylesroom.com exclusively. Many others will be available to the public. We expect this project to do for poker videos what *Super/System* did for poker literature.

Use all the professional techniques you've learned in this book, but keep it simple whenever possible. That's the purest path to online poker profit.

43 EXCLUSIVE
SUPER/SYSTEM 2
TIPS FROM
MIKE CARO UNIVERSITY

Mike Caro

From his earliest days as "Crazy Mike" to his current stature as the legendary "Mad Genius of Poker" and "America's Mad Genius," Mike Caro has pioneered some of the most important concepts used by the top players today. In public, he can be off-the-wall and entertaining, but when he offers advice and research, world-class poker competitors take his word as gospel. And even those players who haven't had personal contact with Mike have no doubt been greatly influenced by his pioneering theories in ways they don't even realize.

When I met him in 1977, Mike was thirty-two and already the best draw poker player in the world. Since then he has evolved into the premier authority on poker strategy, psychology, and statistics. Now at sixty, he has helped generations of players reach levels of achievement they never dreamed possible through his books, columns, seminars, and videos.

A few years ago, he founded Mike Caro University of Poker, Gaming, and Life Strategy with an online campus located at www.poker1.com, yet another innovation that electrified the poker community. Recognized as "the man" in poker circles, his unquestioned integrity, unprecedented ingenuity, and tireless devotion to our game have left their mark throughout the world of poker.

In the following pages you'll get a taste of what Mike teaches at his standing-room-only seminars. These powerful tips and concepts will likely be as valuable as any advice you'll ever receive.

43 EXCLUSIVE SUPER/SYSTEM 2 TIPS FROM MIKE CARO UNIVERSITY

By Mike Caro

Each tip in this chapter works in conjunction with everything Doyle Brunson and his collaborators teach in the following chapters. I know this because poker is powerful science. I know this because, in many ways, poker is exact science. I know this because any true world-class player—particularly one selected by Doyle—must honor all established laws of poker science. I also know this because I've already seen the chapters.

The following tips are selected from over 1,000 candidates in the library of articles, lectures, courses, and seminar transcripts found at Poker1.com. That's the online home of Mike Caro University of Poker. MCU serves as the exclusive educational wing for doylesroom.com, where you can play internet poker against real opponents worldwide. You'll find Doyle's teachings online, along with my own, at Poker1. But this is the way I still prefer to teach—offline, in traditional print.

For many years, I didn't want my poker concepts to appear in print at all. I never wanted to share poker secrets. I was perfectly content to be a professional poker player for the rest of my life. But in 1977, Doyle persuaded me to create the draw poker and statistics sections for the original *Super/System*, and in doing so, he opened my eyes to the prospect of propelling poker beyond its dark and dingy history. He dreamed of bringing our great game into the light of day, writing openly about tactics, and helping the public see poker as a worthy strategy game, just like chess, backgammon, and bridge.

As soon as *Super/System* was published in 1978, I realized the scope of Doyle's dream. Poker players, who had been hungry for real analysis—not homespun hit-and-miss wisdom found in previous books—expressed their gratitude openly, not just to Doyle, but to me and all the experts on the first *Super/System* team.

Yes, the early research I contributed back then was ahead of its time, but it doesn't compare with the truths we've learned since. Today, we're unraveling some of poker's great tactical mysteries, as you'll discover when you move beyond this chapter.

DRAW IS DEAD

"Draw poker is dead," Doyle said, and he suggested that, rather than revising and modernizing both the five-card draw high and lowball sections for *Super/System 2*, I create an introductory "seminar," based on the ones I present to casinos, but with deeper explanations worthy of *Super/System*. The tips would appear on "screens," just as they do at my live performances. Fine. I don't agree that draw poker is dead, but let's do that seminar, anyway.

I've divided the presentation into four sessions:

(1) Insights and Attitude;

(2) Strategy and Tactics;

(3) Psychology and Tells; and,

(4) Two Final Bonus Tips.

If you're ready, I am, too, so let the exclusive MCU *Super/System 2* seminar begin!

INSIGHT AND ATTITUDE

I know what you're thinking. That's a strange way to begin a chapter targeted to readers who seek to play poker seriously. I read your mind, right? Get used to it.

You're looking at my most famous quote, so let me explain why it is an important starting point.

The main skill that successful people possess is the ability to closely estimate their chances in life. The main skill that winning poker players possess is the ability to closely estimate their chances of winning a hand or making a profit in a game.

How do you closely estimate your chances? It's a matter of observing what goes on around you and determining how likely events are to affect you. Easier said than done, right? Right! And you'll never get anywhere near perfect when it comes to estimating your chances. But the closer you come, the more likely you are to conquer opponents at life and at poker.

But, here's what you need to understand: If you don't know how to estimate chances or you don't have any information at all about a situation, then that event appears to be an even money situation.

Experience tells us that some things are not even money. If you leap from a twenty-story building, you probably won't land safely. But, wait! You *might* land safely. You might have your fall broken by a giant pile of feather pillows. Of course, you and I know it's not an even-money proposition that this will happen. We know that leap probably isn't going to end pretty.

Okay, so how would you know it wouldn't end pretty if you didn't understand gravity or falling or collisions with concrete or anything else? You wouldn't. You'd just jump and take your chances. To you, the act would seem no more or less dangerous than sleeping. Landing safely would seem like an even-money bet to you.

But as you gain experience and gather information, you're able to better assess your chances. In fact, your goal in poker and in life is to defeat the notion that a situation is even money and replace it with truer odds—which sometimes might actually turn out to be even money after all. You don't necessarily do this by keeping actual odds or numbers in your head, just by using good judgment based on the information available. In the long run, the person who does that best succeeds most.

We want you to succeed at poker. The information in this book will help you monumentally when it comes to assessing your chances, making the right decisions, choosing the right games, and deciding which gambles are good for you.

MCU Tip #2

MONEY YOU DON'T LOSE...

buys just as many things as money you win.

The Super/System 2 collection

Again, you're probably bewildered, because the tip seems too simple. I'm betting you're thinking something like, "Obviously money you don't lose is just as good as money won, because you saved it. And saved money can be spent." Fine, but then how come most players, even most professionals, often play poorly when they're losing? If you sometimes find yourself doing that, then you need to pay close attention now.

Here's the way I explain the concept at live seminars. If you're losing $9,225 in a $50/$100 limit game, it probably won't feel much different to you if you lose $9,925 instead. Even though logically you know that the difference is $700, emotionally it doesn't seem like $700 you can spend. When you lose $9,225, you're thinking in terms of that money no longer being available. Same goes for losing $9,925. You're not thinking that you can spend anything, in either case. But you can!

If you lost just $9,225, you'd still have $700 to spend that you wouldn't have if you had lost $9,925. Obvious, I know. But the difference doesn't feel like much in the heat of poker combat. When you began playing for the day, though, you would have felt that you were ahead if you'd won $700—obviously. That's because it would be very clear to you that you have $700 extra to buy things with. Well, the same is true if you play as well as you can when you're running bad and cut the loss by $700 through superior play. You have $700 to spend, even though, in our example, you lost over $9,000.

If you're unable to see it that way, maybe this will help. Suppose you were having a really rotten year and had lost $240,000. Now a genie pops out of a bottle. Don't snicker—this actually happens to me regularly. The genie says, "Wanda," assuming your name is Wanda, which it might not be, "I can rewrite history and make you even for the year."

You say, "That's great, genie! Thank you so very much!"

"There's just one thing I need to know."

"I knew there was a catch," you complain.

"Just tell me," the genie continues, ignoring your unappreciative remark, "whether you want me to rewrite history by adding a little to each of your wins, so that they total $240,000 more, or take a little from each of your losses, so that they total $240,000 less."

Immediately you blurt, "I don't care, genie. It doesn't matter. Just do it."

And then you recognize the meaning of your own words. It really doesn't matter, because saving a little from each loss—even a big loss—is just as important as adding to a win. It's not almost the same money or theoretically the same money, but *exactly* the same money. And once you realize the truth of this, you will always play poker with the same amount of care, whether you're winning or losing. It always matters equally.

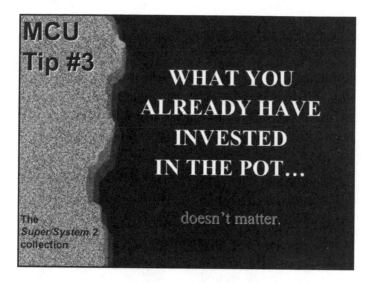

MCU Tip #3

WHAT YOU ALREADY HAVE INVESTED IN THE POT...

doesn't matter.

The *Super/System 2* collection

In order to be successful at poker, you must understand this. Always make your decision about whether to call, fold, check, or raise in accordance with how much money is in the pot, weighed against what it will cost you to wager. That decision should be the same whether the pot is provided as a promotion by the casino or you somehow put the entire sum in yourself. Once you put money in the pot, it's up for grabs and is no longer yours, any more than it is anyone else's. For that reason, you should *never* consider how much you personally have invested in a pot in evaluating a poker decision.

The same concept governs your everyday life. Let's suppose you fancy yourself a world-renowned collector of antique radiator caps, as many of us dreamed of being when we were kids. Two years ago you were able to acquire a radiator cap signed by Edward Jones Miscellania, a respected local automobile mechanic, for $300,000. Two years later, an appraisal places the true value at a disappointing $75,000.

Then a fellow collector offers you $150,000. Okay, now you have a choice. You can say, "Don't be ridiculous! I already have $300,000 invested in this radiator cap." Or you can correctly reason: *What I personally have invested doesn't matter. The only thing I should consider is whether the $150,000 is a good price for my radiator cap.* If you opt for the second choice and pocket the $150,000, you've learned a key secret in life and poker: *What you personally have invested never matters.*

MCU
Tip #4

YOU DON'T
GET PAID
TO WIN POTS.

You get paid to make
the right decisions.

The
Super/System 2
collection

Years ago a reporter asked me, "What's the main objective in poker—except, of course, winning pots." Well, I had to explain to him that winning pots isn't an objective in poker, at all.

You shouldn't even care whether you win a pot. You should only care about making the correct decisions. Making quality decisions is the only thing you get paid for in poker. In fact, it's easy to become the grand champion of winning pots. All you need to do is call and raise your way toward the showdown every chance you get. If you don't pick up the pot early, every hand that could possibly have gotten lucky enough to win, will win that final showdown. Many of these will be hands with long-shot, unprofitable chances that you stubbornly continued to play against the odds. If you'd thrown all of them away, you would have saved a lot of money, but you wouldn't have won any extra pots. If you don't throw any hands away, you're probably going to win more pots than anyone else—right up until you go broke.

So, obviously, the object in poker isn't to win pots. You need to take that attitude to the poker table. Whenever you make the correct decision to fold a hand, you've *made* money. Notice that I didn't say that you saved money. That's because—as you learned from the previous tip—money made and money not wasted can be spent equally well. So, there's profit in throwing hands away.

Of course, making the right decisions can sometimes help you win a pot, especially when you bluff at a profitable moment. But it's that decision you get paid for, not winning the pot. Striving to make the right decisions—not to winning pots—is so important that I do something you're going to consider weird: I root for my opponents to win pots. This keeps me good-natured in a poker game and makes my opponents believe I genuinely care about them—because it's true. By rooting for an opponent to win the pot, only two things can happen:

(1) If the opponent wins, I'm happy.

(2) If the opponent loses, I get the pot as a consolation prize.

I'm always aware that the more times my opponents go against the odds and win, the poorer they're playing, and the more money I'll earn eventually—especially in limit games, where average players enter too many pots. This attitude and this success come from realizing that winning the pot is not the object of poker.

MCU Tip #5

TABLES WITH LAUGHTER ARE THE MOST PROFITABLE.

Avoid silence!

The *Super/System 2* collection

You want to be in the most profitable games, right? Well, when you hear laughter, it's often an indication that players are there to enjoy poker, not to take it seriously. On average, friendly games, especially those with laughter, are the most easily beatable. Conversely, silence is usually an indication that opponents are playing way too seriously, and your prospects for making a profit are diminished. When you have a choice, choose a table where players are laughing.

MCU Tip #6

DON'T TREAT YOUR BANKROLL LIKE A TOURNAMENT BUY-IN.

If you do, you'll eventually go broke.

The Super/System 2 collection

Typical poker tournaments continue until one player has all the chips, and everyone else goes broke. But if the stakes just stayed the same, a tournament might last many years. It would be very hard to eliminate players. So, in tournaments, the stakes keep getting larger and larger periodically, until all but one player is gone.

But, you know what? If you only have a small bankroll, you can make your own tournament any day. Buy into a small game and keep moving to a bigger limit every hour until you either go broke or win at the $5,000/$10,000 limit or larger. You see what I'm getting at, right? You're almost certain to go broke, but you might get extremely lucky and increase your bankroll hundreds of times. Most likely, you're going to end up miserable.

You'd be surprised how many otherwise skillful players fail at poker, simply because they treat their bankrolls like tournament buy-ins. Sure, they don't do it all in one day, as in the exaggerated example I provided. But they keep promoting themselves to higher and higher levels that the size of their bankrolls can't justify. Almost all of them go broke, despite their skills. Please don't do that.

MCU Tip #7

IF ONE PRO PLAYS TWICE AS MANY HANDS AS ANOTHER...

both might earn the same profit!

The Super/System 2 collection

"What percentage of hands should I enter pots with?" It's a common question.

"It depends on your image and what you're trying to accomplish." That's my answer. As strange as it may seem to you, one professional can play twice as many hands as another and both can earn the same amount of profit in the long run.

How come? It's because so many hands are marginal, meaning they will break about even, that you could play almost all of them or almost none of them and still earn the same. Most of your poker profit comes from relatively few quality hands.

Still, you need to consider the good and the bad about playing a lot of marginal hands. When you do, you're seen as an action player, and you're likely to make more money when you hold your best hands, because opponents feel comfortable playing against you. That's good. But, because opponents don't perceive you as conservative, it will be harder for you to bluff profitably. That's bad. Also, when you play most of your marginal hands, the size of your bankroll becomes more volatile, and that means you need more money to afford the same size games.

When I've established a friendly, carefree image, which is

what I usually strive for, I generally play most marginal hands. In addition to fitting my image, this strategy gives me opportunities to extract profit from small edges later in hands when opponents make mistakes. These small-profit opportunities add up, and they wouldn't be available to me if I didn't play those hands. In general, Doyle and almost all world-class players agree and play a lot of marginal hands.

But, you need to keep in mind that marginal hands are marginal for a reason—they about break even. And since there are so many hands in this category compared with so few high-quality hands, it's easy to see how one professional player can contend for twice as many pots as another and both can eventually end up with about the same profit.

MCU Tip #8

IF YOU
AVERAGE
A BIG PROFIT
BY CALLING...

you're not calling enough!

The Super/System 2 collection

Don't be too proud of your success calling bets in limit poker games. Remember, the pot is always larger than the size of the bet, because there will always be some money in the pot when the bet is made. In limit games, the pot is usually many times the size of the bet. Let's say you're heads-up and your opponent bets $400 into a $2,400 pot on the last betting round. Clearly your call only needs to be successful once in a while, not every time. Specifically, there's $2,800 out there to win (the $400 just bet, plus the $2,400 that was already there), and it will cost you $400 to find out if your hand is best. You're getting 7 to 1 odds ($2,800 to $400).

That means if you win once in eight times when you call in this circumstance, you'll break even (seven $400 losses, totaling $2,800, versus one $2,800 win). So, this is a call you should make, even if you estimate that you're going to lose 5 out of 6 times. That would cost $2,000 for the five unsuccessful $400 calls and provide $2,800 for the one successful call—a net gain of $800 for six calls. That's about $133 profit per call, on average. So, if you don't make that call—because you know you're usually going to lose—you're costing yourself a lot of money.

Now, sometimes you call because you've read your opponent and are acting in response to a powerful tell. If you're good at reading opponents—and I'll help you out with that in a few minutes—you will increase the profit you make by calling. Otherwise, most of your calls will be made on the basis of evaluating the cards in relation to the size of the pot. You see, in those cases, you're usually not supposed to win when you call. Burn this into your brain once and for all: "I'm probably going to lose when I call, but it's a good thing!" You could, of course, only call with your most-likely winning hands. Then you'd average a lot of profit per call. But that would be very bad, because in order to average a lot of money calling, you must sacrifice by not making calls that are individually less profitable, but hugely profitable combined. The truth is that you don't want to average a lot of profit per call, and you shouldn't be proud of the fact, if you do.

MCU
Tip #9

**NEVER STAY
IN A POKER GAME,
HOPING TO
GET EVEN.**

You already
are even!

The
Super/System 2
collection

It makes no sense to stay in a poker game, struggling to get even, unless you would normally continue to play that game if you were ahead. If you're a professional player, then the more hours you spend in games, under good working conditions, the more profit you'll earn. You get paid by the hour—pure and simple. Sometimes it might not seem that way, because the fluctuations in poker are so great that it's hard to imagine yourself working for an hourly wage. But that's what's happening.

Eventually, the more hours you play under profitable conditions, the more your bankroll will grow. But, you only have so many hours to invest in poker, and you need to invest them wisely. Find the best games. Make sure you're playing when you're in condition to do the best job. You need to weigh everything. For instance, it's not good to play poker when you're tired. But if the game is very good, you might occasionally choose to continue playing, even if you're tired. Conversely, sometimes you might choose to go home early and rest, even though the game is profitable, because you think another game will be more profitable tomorrow.

So you need to make choices about which hours will be the most profitable. Okay, but what you do *not* need to do is choose to play for hours on end in an attempt to get even for the session. Whether you win or lose today has nothing whatsoever to do with your overall success. It doesn't matter when you quit or when you play—as long as your decision is based on how profitable the next hour will be.

Think about this: You start every pot even. Your bankroll is always only as big as when the pot begins. You're never winning or losing when the cards are dealt. You're always even. So it makes no sense to try to *get* even. You already are.

MCU
Tip #10

The Super/System 2 collection

DON'T MANUFACTURE A WINNING STREAK.

A long, contrived winning streak can be expensive!

"I've won twenty-three days in a row!"

Peter was proud as he told me this. But he shouldn't have been. Earlier during this win streak, he'd bragged about having been buried one day for $1,100 in the $10/$20 hold'em game he played as an aspiring professional. "I stuck it out like a world-class pro," he'd bragged. "At a quarter to five in the morning, I counted down my stack and I was $8 ahead. I didn't even bother to play out my free hands until the next blind. I just cashed out immediately. That gives me seventeen wins in a row!"

Now, you see the problem here? Peter was manufacturing his win streak. It's a pretty easy thing to do. You just refuse to take a loss until it gets so big that there's hardly any hope of recovery. If you get lucky and recover, you cash out immediately with a small win. If you start off winning, you're quickly satisfied, and you also settle for a small win. The hallmark of a player who manufactures winning streaks is that his average wins are much smaller than his average losses.

Yes, you tend to have a lot of long winning streaks, but at what cost? By trying to recover from a deep loss, you're likely to find yourself playing in the worst conditions—when games yield smaller profits, on average. Although there are exceptions, always keep in mind that games where you're losing are likely to be made up of stronger opponents. These games will therefore be less profitable than games where you're winning, which tend to consist of weaker opponents. Also, when you're losing, many opponents are aware of this and don't see you as much of a threat. Often they're motivated by your bad run and play better. For these reasons, you'll probably be in a less profitable situation if you stick around, struggling to get even. Remember, you're getting paid by the hour, and here you are, putting in lots of extra hours under poor working conditions, with poor pay.

It's also bad to quit when you're winning, just to keep your streak alive. You'll very likely be deserting a good game. When you're winning, games are more profitable on average than when you're losing. And players you're beating are more easily intimidated, because they've seen you winning, fear you more, and are less likely to play their best game against you. So, when you leave a game to enhance a winning streak, you're usually taking off work under the best conditions, where the hourly wages were highest.

Put it all together and you can see why a manufactured win streak isn't a good thing. It's certainly nothing you should be bragging about.

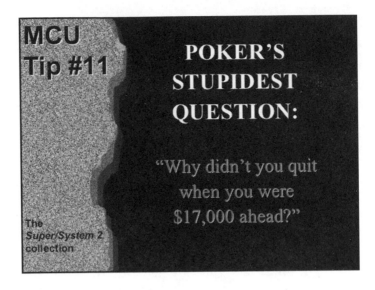

MCU Tip #11

POKER'S STUPIDEST QUESTION:

"Why didn't you quit when you were $17,000 ahead?"

The Super/System 2 collection

This brings us to poker's stupidest question: "Why didn't you quit when you were ahead?" Specifically, people will ask this question after you've lost a lot of your winnings or unfortunately turned a win into a loss. Often they know approximately how much you were winning and will phrase the question similarly to what you see above: "Why didn't you quit when you were $17,000 ahead?"

I'll tell you why I didn't quit when I was $17,000 ahead! I didn't quit, because I wanted to make more money. I didn't quit, because when I'm winning, game conditions tend to be best, and since I get paid by the hour, I wanted to get in more hours under those conditions. I didn't quit, because neither you nor I had any way of knowing at the time whether the cards would be good or bad from that point on.

Here's the main reason that "Why didn't you quit when you were $17,000 ahead?" is the stupidest question in poker: When you win $50,000, nobody ever asks it.

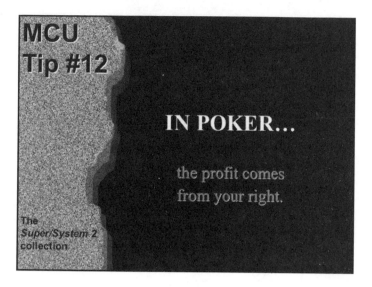

MCU
Tip #12

IN POKER...

the profit comes
from your right.

The
Super/System 2
collection

Most serious players understand this tip, but few understand its full value. Since the action moves clockwise around the table in poker, players to your right usually act before you. I say usually, not always, because if the player on your right is in the dealer position, he'll act last throughout the hand. Or if he's in one of the blinds and you're not, he'll act after you on the first betting round. Also, in a stud game, the face-up cards—not table position—dictate who goes first, but you still have an overall positional advantage against stud players to your right.

For the most part, you will act after players to your right, and this means you'll usually get to see what they do before making your decision. That's called positional advantage.

In fact, positional advantage is so huge in full-handed games that most of the money you make in your poker-playing career comes from the players one or two seats to your right, and most of the money you lose goes to players one or two seats to your left.

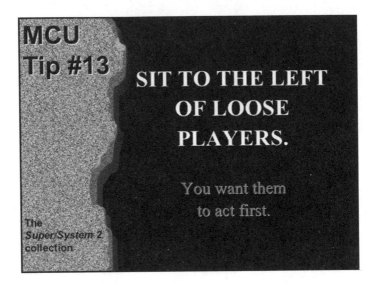

Because most of your lifetime profit comes from players who act before you do, it's important to choose a seat, whenever possible, that places the correct types of players to your right. In other words, you sit to the left of them.

When you have a choice, sit to the left of players who either pose the biggest threat or who supply the most money. In the biggest threat category are players who are sophisticated, aggressive, and unpredictable. You can greatly diminish their effectiveness by forcing them to act first, giving you positional advantage over them. If they were seated to your left, they could use that advantage to pummel you.

But even more important to your long-range profit is sitting to the left of loose opponents, particularly non-aggressive ones. Loose but non-aggressive players supply most of the money you win, because they enter too many pots and don't always take full advantage of profitable opportunities by betting or raising when they have you beat. They're likely to lose, and you'll have a better shot at their money if they act first. When you hold your most profitable hands, you'll frequently see them calling a bet with weak hands before you raise. Then, when you do raise, they're trapped for more money. If the situation were reversed and you acted before them with an opportunity to raise another opponent, your raise would likely scare away those weak players to your left (along with their weak hands).

The two types of players you want to sit to the left of are almost opposite in nature. One type is loose and timid; the other is selective and aggressive. You'll often have to choose between having your biggest money supplier or your biggest threat on your right. But try to make sure one or the other is there—and sometimes you'll be fortunate enough to accomplish both when your loosest opponent and, also, your most threatening one sit in the two seats to your right.

Now let's talk about the seat on the other side of you. What type of player can you sit to the right of, thereby surrendering your positional advantage? Here's the secret: Ideally you should have very conservative but unimaginative players acting after you. These players don't enter enough pots to interfere with your strategy very often and don't play aggressively enough to exploit their superior position, even when they do get involved.

Given all these considerations, my first priority is usually to sit to the left of my loosest opponents. I want to act after them, because they're the most likely to build my bankroll.

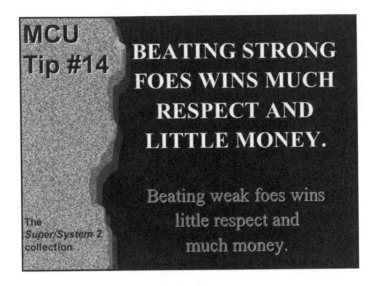

I'll admit I spent a lot of my energy in my younger days playing against the toughest opponents. This was valuable as a way to hone my skills, but I overdid it. Although, I played professionally for fourteen years, I think I would have made even more money had I concentrated more on finding weaker games, rather than gaining respect by beating world-class opponents.

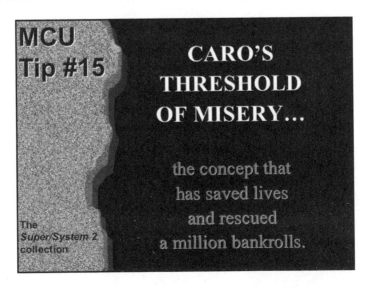

The full name of MCU is Mike Caro University of Poker, Gaming, and Life Strategy. I take the life strategy part of that seriously, and in my teachings there are many overlapping themes between poker and everyday endeavors.

Few concepts have resonated with students more than Caro's Threshold of Misery. I continually receive letters, e-mails, and face to face thanks from both poker players and people in the "real world," telling me how much this simple truth has meant to them.

Here's how it goes: Suppose you're a small- to medium-limit player, and you can envision yourself comfortably losing a maximum of $1,500 today. I'm not suggesting that you'll be happy about losing that much, just that you can comfortably handle it and that anything more will begin to feel uncomfortable.

Okay, now you find yourself down $500, then $1,100, then— before it registers—you've zoomed past $1,500 and are losing $1,800. You've entered dangerous territory. And it gets worse. And worse. Hours later, you find yourself losing $4,530. Now, your mind is numb. I believe that most people at this point can't mentally comprehend added losses. It all feels the same. You've crossed Caro's Threshold of Misery, which is the point at which mental and emotional pain is maximized and anything further won't register.

You must be aware when you cross the threshold, because beyond it decisions don't seem to matter. This is true in real life, too. When romances unravel or businesses fail, you might cross the Threshold of Misery and stop caring about making critical decisions regarding other things. That's because the pain is already maximized and anything else that goes wrong can't add to the agony. Listen closely. At these times, in poker and in life, the secret is to keep performing as if you care. Remember that, although you can't emotionally feel the importance of making quality decisions at the moment, there will come a time when you will feel that importance and be grateful for the good decisions that you make now. Yes, you've crossed the threshold and decisions don't seem to matter. They *do* still matter, and anything that suggests otherwise at this moment is an illusion.

STRATEGY AND TACTICS

MCU
Tip #16

WHEN DECEPTIVE
PLAYERS CHECK
TO YOU...

bet less often.

The
Super/System 2
collection

Even some professional players make the mistake of betting aggressively after deceptive players check. They'd earn much more money if they didn't have this bad habit. Throughout your poker playing years, always think about the player you're about to bet into before firing away with a medium-strong hand. If it's a tricky player, you should be much less motivated to bet, because he won't just fall in line and call meekly. He will surprise you occasionally by raising as a bluff, sometimes getting you to throw away the best hand. And he will also tend to get maximum value out of his strong hands by raising daringly, costing you an extra bet whenever you call and lose the showdown. You should tend to bet much more often when the check comes from meek and non-deceptive foes. So, you should not bet as frequently or as willingly after a deceptive opponent checks. Make that a part of your permanent game plan.

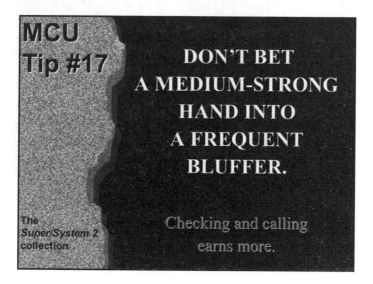

MCU Tip #17

The *Super/System 2* collection

DON'T BET A MEDIUM-STRONG HAND INTO A FREQUENT BLUFFER.

Checking and calling earns more.

This is another MCU maxim that some professionals too often ignore, costing them extra profit for their whole careers. When a frequent bluffer waits to act after you, there can be considerable value in letting him make his primary mistake— bluffing too often. Against this type of player, a medium-strong hand will often earn more in the long run as a bluff catcher than a hand you would bet aggressively for extra value.

MCU
Tip #18

The
Super/System 2
collection

WHEN A
FREQUENT
BLUFFER CHECKS
TO YOU...

don't bluff.

One of the reasons bluffs are successful is that they often beat other equally weak hands. Had you checked, you would have won some showdowns between garbage hands. And you would have lost some. By betting, you ensure a win under those circumstances, and that adds substantially to the value of the bluff.

But when a frequent bluffer checks, it's much less likely that you can win by chasing away an almost equally weak hand that might have squeaked through in a showdown. So that factor won't work in your favor. Additionally, frequent bluffers check a disproportionate number of hands that they intend to call with. That makes a bluff even riskier.

I won't tell you to *never* bluff when a frequent bluffer checks, but you wouldn't cost yourself much by adopting that policy. You need to be very certain you're on solid ground. Otherwise, don't bluff.

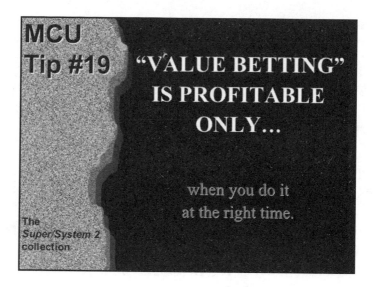

MCU
Tip #19 "VALUE BETTING"
IS PROFITABLE
ONLY...

when you do it
at the right time.

The
Super/System 2
collection

A value bet is simply an aggressive wager that targets every last dollar of potential profit. Whenever you value bet, the decision is close enough that you could easily have checked, instead, without sophisticated opponents thinking you did anything strange.

The problem with value betting is that many players do it as a matter of policy, without realizing that there are times you should and times you shouldn't. By value betting without applying the correct guidelines, these players turn a tactic that should add greatly to their profit into one that may do little more than break even.

I don't want that to happen to you. So here are two lists telling you whether to value bet or to check:

Four Conditions That Favor a Value Bet:

1. You've Established a Dominant and Unpredictable Image
This intimidates your opponents, making them more likely to call with weaker hands out of confusion.

2. You're Winning

This also intimidates your opponents, making them less likely to raise aggressively, which will cost you extra money when their hands are somewhat better than yours.

3. Your Opponent Is Timid

Opponents who are, by nature, timid, are unlikely to press a superior hand for maximum value or steal the pot with an unexpected bluff-raise.

4. Your Opponent Tends to Call More Often Than the Average Player

That's exactly what you're seeking from your value bets— lots of calls with weaker hands.

Four Conditions That Favor a Check:

1. You've Failed to Establish a Dominant and Unpredictable Image

This usually means your opponent is not intimidated and less likely to call out of confusion.

2. You're Losing

Your opponents, aware that you're losing, often gain the courage to get maximum value by raising with hands that may be slightly better than yours, costing you extra bets.

3. Your Opponents Have a Tendency to Raise Liberally

This means that due to their nature, they get maximum value from hands that are slightly better than yours.

4. Your Opponent Plays Tight

Tight players are unlikely to call liberally with weaker hands than yours, taking the value out of your bet.

These lists don't cover every conceivable thing you might consider. But they do include the things I consider first when deciding whether or not to value bet. If you do that, too, you'll make a lot of extra money. Value betting just for its own sake doesn't make much money. Value betting for the right reason does.

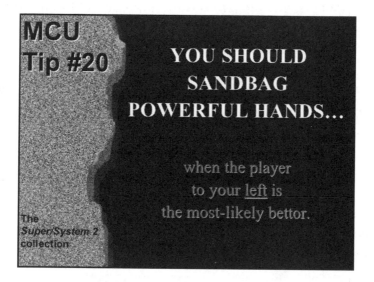

MCU Tip #20

YOU SHOULD SANDBAG POWERFUL HANDS...

when the player to your <u>left</u> is the most-likely bettor.

The Super/System 2 collection

Whenever you hold an unbeatable hand—or one close to it—you might consider checking and then raising if an opponent bets, also known as sandbagging. But when two or more opponents are involved in the pot with you, there's an important factor you'll need to consider before deciding whether to bet or to sandbag.

Here it is: You should sandbag your strongest hands when the player immediately to your left is the one most likely to make the first bet, and usually not otherwise. Why is that? Because by sandbagging with a powerful hand, you're trying to win more money. You're declining to bet, risking direct money through calls, in the hopes that someone else will do your betting for you, and then you can raise and win extra.

Well, suppose there are three players in the pot. If you check, the player to your left checks, and the other opponent checks, you win nothing. You gambled that someone else would bet, and you lost that gamble. If you check, the player to your left checks, and the other opponent bets, that's not so good, either. You get to raise, but your seating position relative to your opponent's greatly reduces the effectiveness. Your raise will make it very difficult for the player to your left to justify calling with anything but a nearly unbeatable hand. You'll almost certainly chase that player away. You might get the bettor to your right to call your raise, but you might not.

What you'd really like to see happen after you check is a bet from the player to your left. Then, if all goes well, the other opponent will call, and *then* you can raise and hope they both call the raise. This call and overcall often happens in a limit game, because the pot is so large, relative to the cost of the call.

That great outcome, where you win four bets—two from each opponent—is only likely to happen if the opponent to your left is the most likely bettor. So, because sandbagging a huge hand is often only marginally superior to betting, usually you should try it only when the player to your left is the one you think will bet.

This happens a lot in hold'em when the player to your left got the last raise in before the flop and many players are still contesting the pot. Now, if the flop hits you perfectly and might be satisfactory to the player to your left, you often should check. If that first-round aggressor again bets, you might see a lot of other callers before the action returns for your raise. You should also consider the playing styles of the players you're checking into. In particular, you should be more willing to sandbag your strongest hands when the player to your left is a liberal bettor.

When you're first to act, have a big hand, and are considering a sandbag against two or more opponents, ask yourself who's most likely to bet. Left is right. Right is wrong.

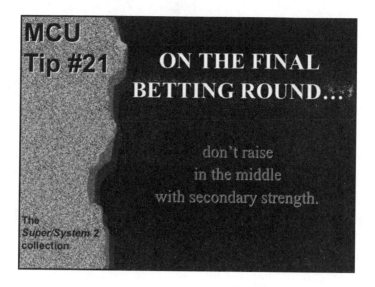

MCU Tip #21

ON THE FINAL BETTING ROUND...

don't raise
in the middle
with secondary strength.

The Super/System 2 collection

Lots of money is lost in pots with at least three players when one of them raises from a middle seat on the last round of betting. Lower level professionals quite often make the mistake of raising with fairly strong, but not invincible, hands.

You seldom want to raise with this secondary strength. By "secondary," I mean that the hand is very powerful, but falls short of primary strength, which consists of hands that cannot be beat or, at least, are very nearly invincible. Aggressive players that are accustomed to dominating the game by getting maximum value through betting, typically raise much too liberally in this situation. The mistake costs them dearly, but they probably don't even realize it.

The problem with this middle raise is that hands with secondary strength usually make more money if you give a third player the chance to overcall. A raise will likely chase away that money and, if the first player is bluffing or has a hand too weak to call, that raise gains you nothing. By not raising, you also protect yourself against losing more money with a second-best hand when you collide with the perfect hand. The solution: Seldom raise in the middle position on the last betting round.

You can make an exception and raise if:

(1) You have a weak hand and you think you're being bluffed; or

(2) Your hand is extremely strong.

In the first case, you raise to eliminate the player waiting to act behind you, so you can beat the possible bluff. In the second case, you raise strictly because your hand is strong enough to withstand a reraise from anyone and you'll beat the player behind you, if he calls a raise. Even in the second case, you might choose to just call.

So seldom raise.

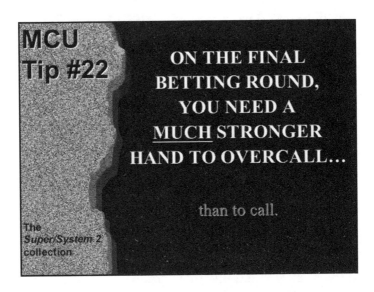

MCU Tip #22

ON THE FINAL BETTING ROUND, YOU NEED A MUCH STRONGER HAND TO OVERCALL...

than to call.

The Super/System 2 collection

While most top professionals understand this, some don't. And the majority of second-tier professionals, along with most serious amateurs, don't seem to understand it at all, based on the way they play in this situation. I'll try to explain it as simply as I can, but you'll need to work with me a little.

The mistake happens mostly in limit games. Imagine this:

You're playing $200/$400 hold'em. Three of you have survived to see the river card and here comes the final round of betting. You'll be last to act, and you're holding A♥ J♥ with a board of J♣ 4♥ K♥ 9♠ Q♠. The pot is $3,100 and the first player bets, making it grow to $3,500. You examine the situation and estimate that you have roughly 1 chance in 6 of beating this bettor in a showdown. As you know, 1 chance in 6 means that the odds are 5 to 1 against you. That means, in order to break even on the call, the pot would need to be at least five times as large as your $400 call.

Well, the pot in this case is already $3,500—much larger than the $2,000 needed to justify a call—so obviously you're supposed to call. In fact, if you made six calls and won once, you'd lose $400 five times, for a total of $2,000, and win $3,500 once—an overall gain of $1,500, or $250 per call.

But, wait! There's another player involved in this pot. Her name is Beth and you've played poker with her many times before. She gets to act before you do. Beth calls the bettor, and you estimate her chances of having a better hand than his to be just about the same as yours. Now what? Now you need to consider what your chances are of beating both the bettor and Beth. The mistake players make here is that they tend to overcall with the same hands—or only slightly stronger ones—than they would have called with had Beth folded. That's wrong! You need a significantly stronger hand to overcall than you need to call.

Here's why: Remember, you feel that you have an equally good chance of beating the bettor as Beth does. Mentally, here's where most players—even very experienced ones—go off course with their logic. They think, "If she can call, then so can I, because I have just as good a chance as she does and now the pot is even bigger." And they're partially right: The pot is even bigger now; it was $3,500, and now, with Beth's $400 call, it's $3,900.

So, should you overcall? No! If your estimates are correct,

and we're assuming they are, then you still have 1 chance in 6 of beating the original bettor in a showdown. But, if you succeed there, you still must beat Beth, and you've estimated that you have an even money shot of doing that. So, if a very similar hand were played over and over through eternity, for every two times you beat the bettor (and that would only happen 1 out of 6, or 2 out of 12 attempts), you'd also need to beat Beth (and that would only happen half the time). So, Beth's presence takes away half your chances of winning the pot, making your real chances only 1 in 12, instead of 2 in 12.

How does that translate in terms of money chances? How big would the pot need to be to call? If you followed the earlier logic, analyzing the odds before Beth's call, you know that at 1 chance in 6 , you needed a pot five times as large as the call to break even. Now, at 1 chance in 12, the odds are 11 to 1 against you, and you need a pot eleven times the size of the $400 call to break even. So, in order to justify this overcall, the pot needs to be at least $4,400 large. It isn't. It's only $3,900. Using the same formula as before, we see that we're going to lose $4,400 on those eleven failed calls, and win $3,900 once. That leaves us $500 short of breaking even over twelve tries, so the average cost is just less than $42.

Do you see what happened here? It was worth $250, on average, every time you called just the bettor, but costs you $42 every time you overcall after Beth. I know this was a tough lesson, but it's something you need to know.

Thanks for indulging me. Let's move on…

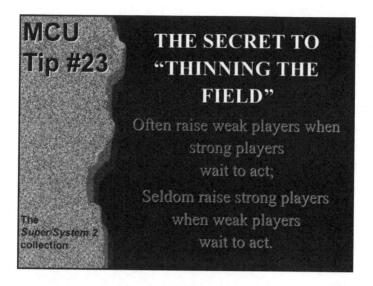

MCU Tip #23

THE SECRET TO "THINNING THE FIELD"

Often raise weak players when strong players wait to act; Seldom raise strong players when weak players wait to act.

The Super/System 2 collection

You've heard a lot about thinning the field. The term refers to eliminating some of the players that are in competition for the pot. Thinning the field is sometimes an important weapon. Indeed, there are hands that can be played more profitably against one or two opponents than against a whole herd of them.

I'm on record as not being a fan of thin-the-field strategy, because I believe that players usually attempt it at times when they would make more money by allowing extra opponents in. The really big issue I have with this strategy is that, if you succeed in thinning the field, you very likely have chased away the weakest hands, which might have provided profit to you had they stayed in the pot. Instead, you've left yourself stranded against only the stronger hands that you wanted to chase from the pot, but didn't.

Okay, now that I've shared my innermost thoughts about thinning the field, here's when to try it and when not to try it. The most advantageous time to thin the field is when weak players are already committed to the pot and strong players are waiting to act behind you. If you raise, you're likely to chase strong players out and play against weak opponents and weak hands. The worst time to use this strategy is when strong players are committed to the pot and weak players remain to act behind you. If you raise, you're likely to chase weak players out and play against just the strong players with strong hands.

Next time you attempt to thin the field, don't just think about the number of opponents you'd like to thin, think about which players you're going to thin.

TELLS AND PSYCHOLOGY

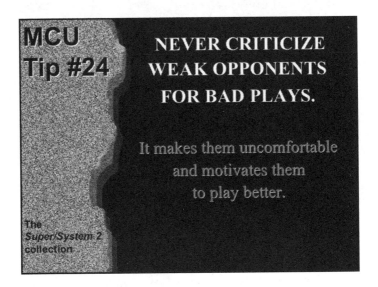

MCU
Tip #24

NEVER CRITICIZE
WEAK OPPONENTS
FOR BAD PLAYS.

It makes them uncomfortable
and motivates them
to play better.

The
Super/System 2
collection

You want weak players in your game. Usually, they're playing recreationally, not seriously. They're apt to play hands for the sheer fun of it. They may even enjoy going up against the odds. When you insult them for their "bad" plays, you're making them uncomfortable and motivating them to play better in the future. Don't do that.

Concluding his seven-card stud high-low chapter, Todd Brunson gives further insight about the disastrous mistake some professionals make by rudely criticizing weak opponents. I feel so strongly about this that I often give encouragement to players who go up against heavy odds to win a pot from me. I'll say, "Wow! Most people don't even play 4-3 offsuit, and usually I don't, either. But I won with it three times yesterday. Maybe you and I are on to something!"

Do you understand why I say that? I'm making the weak player feel good about getting lucky. I'm practically making him into a hero. At the same time, I'm telling him that I "usually" don't play that hand, making me sound sincere and believable. (At a poker table, it's perfectly permissible to lie about your hands and about the way you play them. In fact, it's part of the psychology of winning. And once in a while, you should throw in the truth, just to keep opponents off balance.) But, I'm saying more. I'm claiming that I played the same hand successfully, even though I suggest that I know better. This gives him "permission" to play badly again in the future. If I do it, so can he. It will be fun for him to try to succeed again and be rewarded with more praise. When players make him feel badly about weak plays, they're prodding him to play better. That's exactly the opposite of what they should want. And it isn't fair to other competitors to make their money suppliers uncomfortable about supplying money.

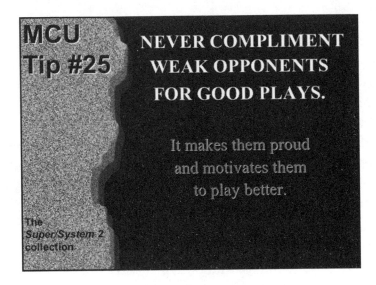

MCU
Tip #25

NEVER COMPLIMENT
WEAK OPPONENTS
FOR GOOD PLAYS.

It makes them proud
and motivates them
to play better.

The
Super/System 2
collection

While I often praise weak opponents for bad plays, I *never* praise them for good plays. That would make them proud of "pleasing me." They might decide to take the game seriously— and wouldn't that be a disaster?

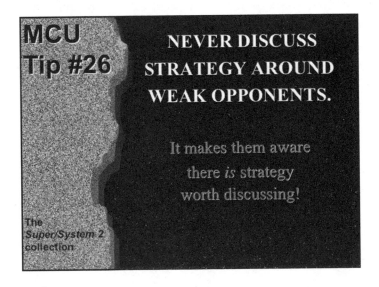

MCU
Tip #26

NEVER DISCUSS
STRATEGY AROUND
WEAK OPPONENTS.

It makes them aware
there *is* strategy
worth discussing!

The
Super/System 2
collection

I've seen even some of the best players in the world violate the advice shown above. Never forget that recreational players supply most of your profit. They came for the fun of poker, not to analyze it to death or to take it seriously. When you sit at the table discussing the finer points of poker strategy, you're alerting the players who supply your profit that they might be competing above their league. You're making them uncomfortable, and it's quite possible that they'll either decide to sit in your games less often or to play better. You don't want either of those things to happen.

I often hear sophisticated players debating the technical merits of how a hand was just played in the presence of weak opponents. Serious discussions of strategy can alert these recreational players to the notion that there *is* strategy. You don't want to do that. And, even more peculiar to me, the debates are usually over something as inconsequential as whether a call or a raise in a borderline situation was the better choice. These way-too-technical arguments can never really be resolved (except, possibly, by me), because there are too many side factors involved, such as how opponents were likely to respond emotionally at the moment and what the bettor's image was.

The truth is, the discussion is often about which choice is 37¢ better, when just by talking about it in front of a recreational player, the debaters potentially are costing themselves thousands of dollars. Let me put in gently, without insulting some of my poker-playing friends who've made this mistake: The economic advisability of discussing advanced strategy at a poker table populated with weak opponents is hereby brought into question.

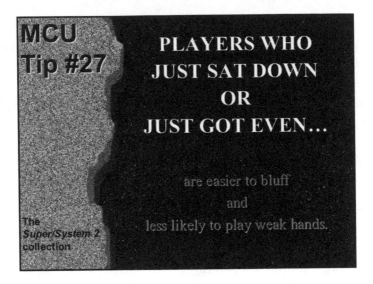

MCU Tip #27

The Super/System 2 collection

PLAYERS WHO JUST SAT DOWN OR JUST GOT EVEN...

are easier to bluff and less likely to play weak hands.

Now I'm going to tell you a story. I've told it many times, but I think it illustrates this point so well that I've chosen to immortalize it by including it in *Super/System 2*.

I'm not sure what year it was—1985, I think. Well, actually, it was both 1985 and 1986, because this happened on New Year's Eve and shortly thereafter. Okay, I'm playing poker at the Bicycle Casino near Los Angeles, not because I'm a poker junkie, but because my wife Phyllis Caro is in charge of the dealers and is working that night.

Anyway, as the hour approaches midnight, games start to break as players head home to their families. Pretty soon there are sadly no games with much size to them. Don't you hate it when players get their priorities confused? So I settle for killing some time playing a tiny no-limit game with $1 and $2 blinds. As you're probably aware, no-limit isn't about the size of a poker game; no-limit is a method of betting in a poker game. Since the forced-blind bets are the initial targets, all wagering should be in proportion to the size of those blinds. Theoretically, no-limit games with $100 and $200 blinds should result in pots that are, on average, 100 times as large as the pots in the game where I now sit, with paltry $1 and $2 blinds. Actually, I could have sat in that game for that hour before midnight, seen about twenty deals, folded every hand, and it would have only cost me $6 in blinds. That's how small the game should have been.

Notice that I said, "should have been." You see, something strange was happening. I'm sure the average pot was over $700, and many pots were thousands of dollars large. I was suddenly winning a great deal of money in a game I hadn't even considered to be a profit-making opportunity. I mean, here was the loosest, wildest game of poker I'd ever seen in my life!

Midnight approaches. The Bicycle Casino staff passes out those annoying noise makers and goofy hats. They also give away streamers you're supposed to throw in the air to show how thrilled you are that time moved forward smoothly to the next year, just as most scientists predicted it would. I know I sound grumpy, but lucrative poker games should not be interrupted for this sort of silliness.

It gets to be a couple minutes to the hour. That hour. A second-by-second countdown begins. Everyone has left the table, getting ready to kiss their girlfriends, boyfriends, or spouses. Me too. I figure, "Why not?" Nobody's sitting at the stupid table anyway. So everyone smooches and hugs and produces strange, loud bellows that sometimes sound more anguished than joyful. I kiss Phyllis, but make no loud noises whatsoever. Streamers snake through the air and sully the carpet. More obnoxious sounds are coming from everywhere, courtesy of the Bicycle Casino's free noise makers.

It goes on for a couple of minutes and everyone returns to the poker table. Let me tell you, this is now the tightest poker game in the history of our planet. Nobody's gambling! You know why, right? New Year's resolutions. Everyone has decided to play good this year, and—knowing poker players as I do—this resolve might last for twenty minutes. So, I cash out my winnings and hurry home.

What's the point of this story? The point is that your opponents resolve to play well from time to time, not just on New Year's Eve. And you need to be prepared for it. Typically, players will resolve to play better when they just sit down for the night. They're probably thinking: "This is the day I'm finally going to stay disciplined and play good." And like I said, their resolve can last up to twenty minutes, but never any longer. During this brief window of opportunity, you can bluff successfully against them. And they won't be playing weak hands. The same holds true for players who were buried in a game and played recklessly with the faint hope of getting even. If they miraculously do get even, expect their style of play to tighten. Again, you can bluff them, and they won't be playing frivolous hands.

So, adjust your strategy accordingly.

MCU Tip #28

PLAYERS COMPLAINING ABOUT THEIR BAD LUCK SELDOM BLUFF.

The Super/System 2 collection

So, seldom call.

When players complain about bad luck, they're seeking sympathy. They're feeding off their own misery, and they want to show you the hands they lose with to prove their point. It's rare that players who are complaining in this way will try to bluff. More often they'll simply show you that they missed and, perhaps, say, "See what I mean."

So, when they bet, it's very unlikely that they're bluffing, and it's usually safe to fold medium hands you might otherwise call with.

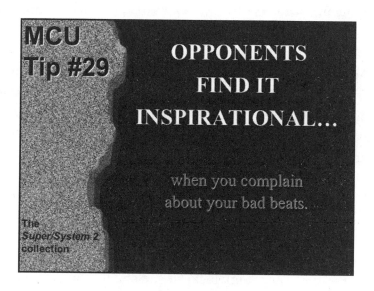

MCU
Tip #29

OPPONENTS
FIND IT
INSPIRATIONAL...

when you complain
about your bad beats.

The
Super/System 2
collection

What happens when you complain about bad beats? Do your opponents grow sympathetic and teary eyed? No. They might feign sympathy, but actually they're thinking, "Hey! There's someone more unlucky than I am! There's somebody I can beat!" And they become inspired and play better against you.

There probably aren't any poker players who haven't sometimes felt as if they were setting the world record for bad beats. That's because it's lonely at the table, and when your luck turns terrible, you're the only one that's paying full attention to it. The most you get from anyone else is vague awareness and an occasional half-hearted, "Wow! Bad beat!" And that's it.

It gets so bad sometimes that you wish you could show a video of what happened to you, so everyone could ooh and ahh about what you went through. "Want proof? Y'all meet me over at my house, we'll have a barbeque, and then we'll all sit around and watch televised evidence of how badly I've been suffering at poker." Forget about it! Except for being inspired by your sadness, nobody cares. Keep your bad luck to yourself.

Now, the last thing I want is for superstitious opponents to get inspired because I'm running poorly. So, I don't broadcast my bad beats. I deny them.

And I make a deal with my students. I explain, "When you tell me a bad beat story, I don't really listen. I nod sadly and pretend to care, but actually I'm using the time to think about more important things. That way, you feel the sympathy you're seeking, and I put my time to good use. It works for both of us."

I even deny that I'm having a bad run, if someone mentions it at the table. I'll often say something like, "That was a pretty strange beat, but actually I've been very lucky lately." While I'm not superstitious and don't allow my students to be, many opponents are. They think luck runs in streaks. But, as I've been pointing out for twenty-five years, a streak is just something you see in the rearview mirror. It might continue and it might not, but you're gauging the length of a streak on the basis of what's already happened, what's behind you in the mirror.

You see, the latest lab research suggests that cards lack the physical strength to reposition themselves. So, even if they were determined in their tiny brains to make your life miserable, their muscles are too weak to follow through.

MCU Tip #30

YOUR OPPONENTS HAVE A "CALLING REFLEX"

... and they'll call anything that moves!

The Super/System 2 collection

Your opponents didn't come to the card room hoping to throw hands away. They have a bias toward calling. And most of them are looking for reasons to call, even if they have to invent those reasons.

That's why you're more likely to be called if you're slightly animated. Opponents might unconsciously be aware that you twitched or sipped your coffee. They're instinctively thinking, "That's strange; maybe that means he's bluffing." They're a little bit like snakes, predisposed to strike at the slightest move. Except they're poker opponents, predisposed to call for the slightest reason. I've given this universal poker condition a name: The Calling Reflex. And it's easy to take advantage of it.

In fact, here's one huge tip: When you hold a strong hand and you know your opponent is about to fold, do anything! It's a freeroll, because you're already about to lose the call, and if you can change an opponent's mind at the last moment, you'll win a whole bet you would have lost by just sitting there. It's pure profit.

So, always keep in mind that your opponents have calling reflexes. As they begin to fold—assuming you want to be called—jitter, shift your weight in your chair, knock over some chips, just do something new. Once in a while, you'll get your opponent's attention, he'll get suspicious, reconsider, and call. You won't usually be able to trigger that calling reflex at the last moment, but you will sometimes. It's like making a snake strike. And it doesn't cost anything to try!

MCU
Tip #31

PLAYERS STARING AWAY...

are almost always more dangerous than players staring at you!

The
Super/System 2
collection

I've written a whole book about the body language of poker—about your opponents' mannerisms that suggest whether they're holding strong or weak hands and whether they're bluffing or not. These mannerisms are called "tells" in poker, because they often tell you something about your opponents' secret cards. The main thrust of the book is that opponents are either acting or they aren't. If they're acting, you should usually determine what they're trying to convince you to do and disappoint them. If they're exhibiting what I term "involuntary tells," they're not acting, and if the tell is strong enough, you should react directly in accordance with what it implies. Be aware that the most experienced players in the biggest games exhibit tells less frequently. And when they do, the tell is likely to be a more subtle variation of the one you'll see when confronting weak and average opponents.

One of the core principles governing acted tells is that a player looking away is always more dangerous than a player staring at you. A player staring away from the approaching action, as you see here, is pretending to be uninterested in the pot. Actually, he has a strong hand and is preparing to get involved. He'll probably raise if you're silly enough to bet a vulnerable hand into him.

If you see a player staring away like this when it's your turn to act, beware!

MCU Tip #32

A SUDDENLY SHAKING HAND...

almost never indicates a bluff!

The Super/System 2 collection

Here's one of the most misunderstood and most profitable tells in poker. It's not acted. It's a natural reaction that your opponents can't control. You'll occasionally see this even among a few top players in the biggest limits—and when you do, you can save a lot of money by folding.

I'm talking about a suddenly shaking hand. Please pay attention to what I just said—a "suddenly" shaking hand. If your opponent's hands tend to be unsteady most of the time, this tell won't help you much. But, fortunately, few players exhibit constant trembling. So, what happens when—all of a sudden—the opponent bets and his hand begins to tremble.

I'll tell you what happens in a lot of opposing players' minds. They think, "Look at that hand shake. That guy's nervous. I'll bet he's bluffing, so I'm going to call" Now, there's a thought that's guaranteed to cost you money! Typically, players who bluff bolster themselves and often become rigid. They don't allow themselves to shake, because they're afraid the shaking would make you suspicious and prompt you to call.

When you see an opponent shaking, it's a release of tension that comes automatically when the suspense ends. That opponent has made a big hand—often a truly monumental one—and expects to win. If this seems counter-intuitive to you, start watching. A suddenly shaking hand signals the happy ending to a drama. It indicates that the player has gotten lucky and is mentally already stacking those chips. The trembling means a strong hand, and you should almost always fold— unless your own hand is also very powerful.

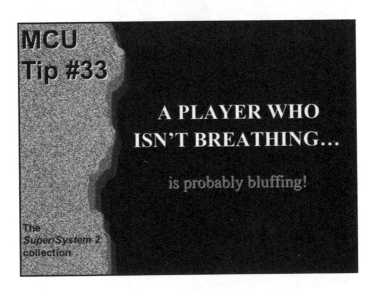

MCU Tip #33

A PLAYER WHO ISN'T BREATHING...

is probably bluffing!

The Super/System 2 collection

We talked about the calling reflex, and oddly, most opponents are instinctively aware of it. They're not aware to the extent that they're able to harness their own calling reflex, but subconsciously they're aware that the other players have one—although they've probably never put it in words.

Because of this vague awareness, your opponents are afraid of triggering your calling reflex after they bet weak hands. So, they instinctively make themselves less noticeable. Sometimes they freeze and sometimes they even stop breathing! When opponents appear not to be breathing after they bet, there's a much higher-than-normal chance that they're bluffing.

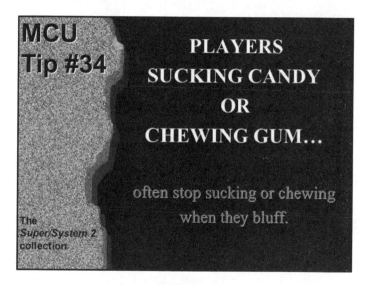

MCU Tip #34

PLAYERS SUCKING CANDY OR CHEWING GUM...

often stop sucking or chewing when they bluff.

The Super/System 2 collection

Here's just another member of the same powerful family of tells. Closely observe opponents who are sucking on candy or chewing gum. If they continue to do so naturally after betting, they're probably relaxed and hoping for your call. If they stop sucking or chewing, it's likely that they're bluffing.

You can sometimes force this tell when you're holding a marginal calling hand by reaching slightly toward your chips. Often a player who is bluffing will grow concerned and all sucking or chewing will suddenly cease. That's when you should call. If you don't get that reaction, fold.

MCU Tip #35

SHRUGS, SIGHS, AND SAD SOUNDS...

indicate strong hands.

The *Super/System 2* collection

Your opponents are always conscious that you might be observing them. It makes them uncomfortable, and that's why they become actors, especially in the low- and medium-limit games. They try to fool you by almost invariably acting weak when they hold strong hands and strong when they hold weak hands.

This means that when you see an opponent shrug or hear a sigh, that's an act intended to convey sadness. Don't be fooled. You're probably facing a powerful hand. Why would players go out of their way to convey sadness and make you suspicious if they didn't want you to call? They wouldn't. Confronted with conspicuous sadness, you should usually fold all medium-strong hands.

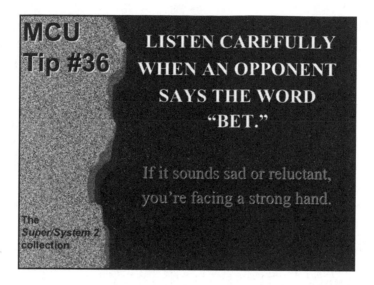

MCU Tip #36

LISTEN CAREFULLY WHEN AN OPPONENT SAYS THE WORD "BET."

If it sounds sad or reluctant, you're facing a strong hand.

The Super/System 2 collection

Another common way that opponents try to convey sadness is through the tone of their voices when they say "bet." Listen closely for it. Whenever you hear, "I bet" spoken in a singsong, drawn-out manner that suggests, "Gosh, I wish I didn't have to do this," that's almost certainly an indication of a powerful hand. Seldom call unless you have one, too.

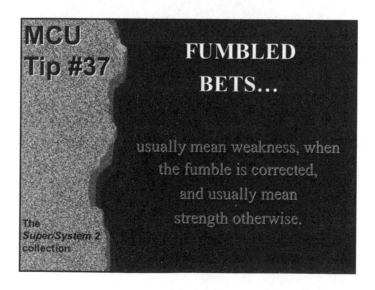

MCU Tip #37

FUMBLED BETS...

usually mean weakness, when the fumble is corrected, and usually mean strength otherwise.

The Super/System 2 collection

Here's an occasional tell that you'll see, sometimes even in the biggest-limit games. Suppose an opponent tries to bet a stack of chips, but some spill off the top as he positions them in the pot.

What does that imply? Usually nothing.

It's what happens next that matters. If the player is holding a weak hand or is bluffing, he's probably worried that the mistake will make you suspicious and invite you to call (remember the calling reflex?). So if you're facing a weak hand, you're likely to see the opponent try to neaten up the chips—to erase the error. If that happens, you should be much more willing to call.

But, if there is no attempt to correct the fumbled bet, you're likely to be against an opponent who isn't worried, and you should be reluctant to call.

MCU
Tip #38

DON'T WATCH
THE FLOP...

watch your opponents
watch the flop.

The
Super/System 2
collection

One of the strongest tips for hold'em or Omaha players is to avoid watching the flop. It will still be there later. As the dealer turns over those first three board cards, observe your opponents. This is a goldmine for tells.

Most players are unaware that you're watching them at the

moment the flop hits, so they're unlikely to be acting right then. What you're looking for is primarily this:

(1) Players who instinctively glance immediately toward their chips liked the flop and are considering betting.

(2) Players who stare at the flop a little longer probably didn't get any help. This falls somewhere in the gray area between acted tells and involuntary tells. Staring for a short time is involuntary, indicating the player didn't get help and has no reason to either look at his chips or look away as if uninterested, in an effort to make your bet seem safe. Continued staring for a longer time usually indicates weakness—the player is feigning interest, but probably won't call a bet.

The flop affords you the opportunity to read both acted and non-acted tells. The first instinct of some players who help their hands is to glance toward chips, preparing to put them to use. That's non-acted. The player, having helped his hand, will often closely follow this involuntary glance by looking away from the approaching action as if uninterested. That last part is an act, portraying weakness, which actually indicates strength.

Players who continue to stare at either the flop or their chips long enough that they think you're watching are trying to convey an interest in the pot that their cards don't merit. They're usually not a threat. And many players, who see a flop that helps them, *don't* instinctively glance toward their chips at all before looking away. They'll jump right to the looking away part—an act that also tells you they're holding strong hands.

Paying attention when the flop hits can earn you a lot of money. But, this can only happen if you're paying attention to the players. If you're paying attention to the cards instead, like almost everyone else is, you'll miss this opportunity.

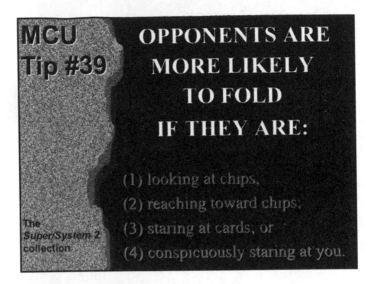

MCU Tip #39

OPPONENTS ARE MORE LIKELY TO FOLD IF THEY ARE:

(1) looking at chips,
(2) reaching toward chips,
(3) staring at cards, or
(4) conspicuously staring at you.

The Super/System 2 collection

Before you act on your hand, examine the players who will act after you. The four points above are strong indications that opponents aren't interested in calling any bets.

This is particularly important on the first round of betting. I'm able to convince even professional opponents that I'm in the game to gamble, playing hands that are too weak for my position—without actually doing it!

How? It's simple. I just look behind me and when I see one or more opponents providing these strong indicators that they're going to fold, I relax my hand requirements, substituting what I would need if I were that many seats later in position. It means I can profit from hands I wouldn't have been able to play if I weren't observant, and, at the same time, it does wonders for establishing my carefree image.

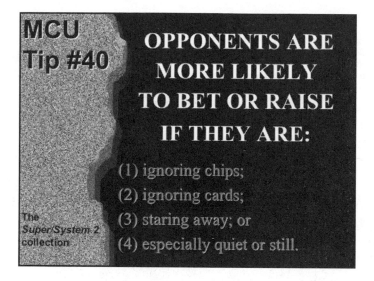

MCU
Tip #40

OPPONENTS ARE
MORE LIKELY
TO BET OR RAISE
IF THEY ARE:

(1) ignoring chips;
(2) ignoring cards;
(3) staring away; or
(4) especially quiet or still.

The
Super/System 2
collection

But, if I see these indicators when I examine players who will act after I do, then I'm in trouble with a weak or medium hand. I need real strength to justify a bet. And I'll be more willing to sandbag a super-strong hand on later betting rounds, because it looks like someone will do my betting for me, if I check.

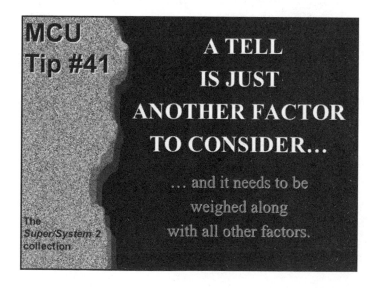

MCU
Tip #41

A TELL
IS JUST
ANOTHER FACTOR
TO CONSIDER...

... and it needs to be
weighed along
with all other factors.

The
Super/System 2
collection

Now that we've discussed some key tells, I need you to understand something. Very few tells are 100% accurate. You need to use them like you would any other bit of information.

For instance, if you're playing seven-card stud and you raise with a queen showing on the first betting round, a reraise from an opponent with a king showing very likely indicates a pair of kings. But it might not—the clue isn't perfect. You need to adjust your tactics so that you give more consideration to a pair of kings than you would have, while keeping open the possibility that you're facing a pair of buried aces, a smaller buried pair, three suited cards, or an outright bluff. The raise is an indicator that makes you reevaluate the likely hands your opponent has. A pair of kings becomes more likely, other hands less likely, but still possible.

It's the same with a tell. It's just another factor, just an indicator. The stronger it is, the more it should influence your decision. But you should seldom let a tell be the *only* factor that goes into your decision.

One other word of caution: Because players have a bias toward calling, many will use tells incorrectly. They'll go out of their way to spot imaginary tells that prompt them to call and almost completely ignore actual tells that prompt them to fold. If you do that, you'll probably lose money with tells and would be better off not using them at all.

My advice is that you get as good as you can at using tells and applying poker psychology. If you're a serious winning player, you might easily double your income by mastering these skills.

TWO FINAL BONUS TIPS

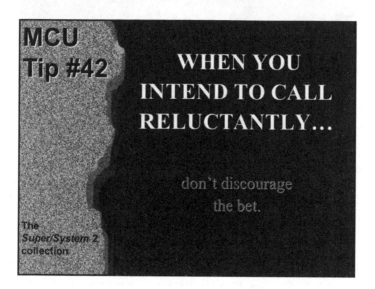

MCU
Tip #42

WHEN YOU
INTEND TO CALL
RELUCTANTLY...

don't discourage
the bet.

The
Super/System 2
collection

I see this mistake quite often, and it drives me crazy. (I have to blame my condition on something, right?) Let's say your hand is fairly weak for the situation, but the pot is so big that you're going to call a bet no matter what.

Faced with this circumstance, players instinctively try to prevent a bet, perhaps by reaching for their chips menacingly. Listen, if you know you're going to call, you should encourage your opponent to bet, even if you're hoping he doesn't!

That's because the only times you're likely to succeed in discouraging a bet are when your opponent holds weak hands or would have bluffed. Those are precisely the hands you would have beaten with your call. By not discouraging a bet, you're inviting an opponent to bet all the hands that will beat you—which he would do anyway! Plus, you're making him feel comfortable about betting all those extra hands you can beat when you call. Discouraging a bet you intend to call only stops opponents from betting hands you'll beat, not from betting hands you won't beat. So don't do it.

MCU Tip #43

The Super/System 2 collection

HOW TO MAKE ANY POKER BULLY BEG FOR MERCY:

(1) call more often;
(2) raise less often;
(3) seldom value bet.

For most players, it's very uncomfortable facing a poker bully—one that tries to dominate the game through super-aggressive plays, mixed with bewildering bluffs.

But it's easy to defeat poker bullies and send them home crying for their mommies. You're looking at the three-step formula now. If you follow it—rather than be lured into an escalating battle to determine who can be more forceful and creative—bullies can't damage you. There is no counter-strategy available to them, and ultimately they have no choice other than to give you their money or behave.

I've enjoyed spending this time with you. And now I'll return the stage to Doyle Brunson and the rest of his world-class experts.

Todd catches a record 18-pound trout on an Alaskan fishing trip about 1996.

In Montana, the deer love to eat my apples.

Rare photo of participants in first World Series of Poker in 1971.

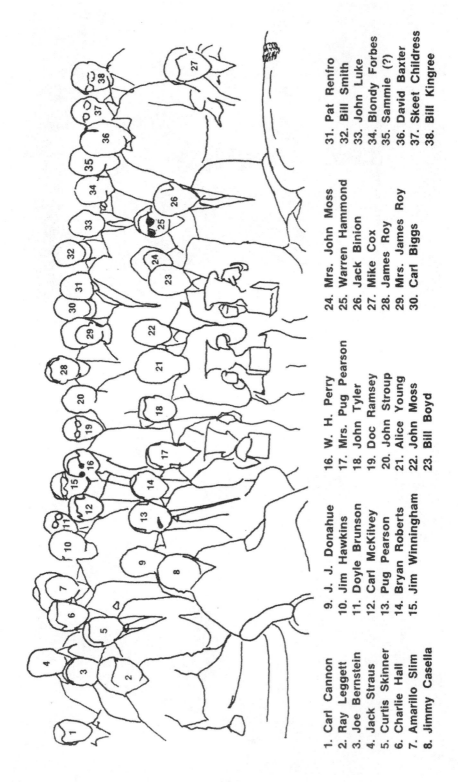

1. Carl Cannon
2. Ray Leggett
3. Joe Bernstein
4. Jack Straus
5. Curtis Skinner
6. Charlie Hall
7. Amarillo Slim
8. Jimmy Casella
9. J. J. Donahue
10. Jim Hawkins
11. Doyle Brunson
12. Carl McKilvey
13. Pug Pearson
14. Bryan Roberts
15. Jim Winningham
16. W. H. Perry
17. Mrs. Pug Pearson
18. John Tyler
19. Doc Ramsey
20. John Stroup
21. Alice Young
22. John Moss
23. Bill Boyd
24. Mrs. John Moss
25. Warren Hammond
26. Jack Binion
27. Mike Cox
28. James Roy
29. Mrs. James Roy
30. Carl Biggs
31. Pat Renfro
32. Bill Smith
33. John Luke
34. Blondy Forbes
35. Sammie (?)
36. David Baxter
37. Skeet Childress
38. Bill Kingree

181

Rare photo of participants in second World Series of Poker in 1971.

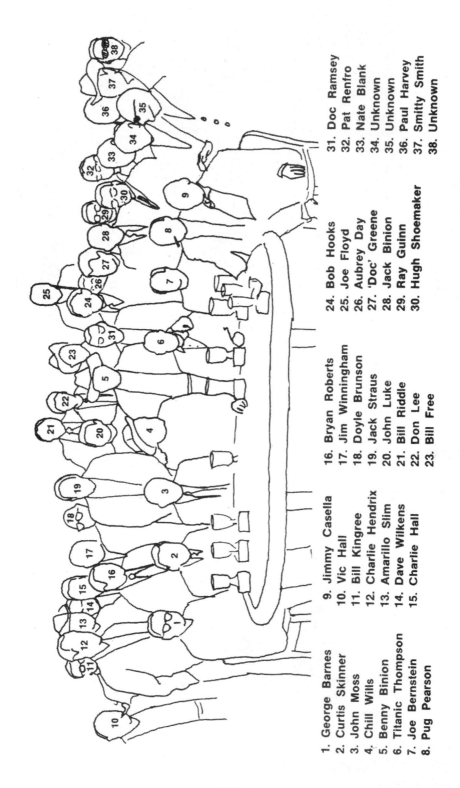

1. George Barnes
2. Curtis Skinner
3. John Moss
4. Chill Wills
5. Benny Binion
6. Titanic Thompson
7. Joe Bernstein
8. Pug Pearson

9. Jimmy Casella
10. Vic Hall
11. Bill Kingree
12. Charlie Hendrix
13. Amarillo Slim
14. Dave Wilkens
15. Charlie Hall

16. Bryan Roberts
17. Jim Winningham
18. Doyle Brunson
19. Jack Straus
20. John Luke
21. Bill Riddle
22. Don Lee
23. Bill Free

24. Bob Hooks
25. Joe Floyd
26. Aubrey Day
27. 'Doc' Greene
28. Jack Binion
29. Ray Guinn
30. Hugh Shoemaker

31. Doc Ramsey
32. Pat Renfro
33. Nate Blank
34. Unknown
35. Unknown
36. Paul Harvey
37. Smitty Smith
38. Unknown

Bobby moves all-in on Chip Reese in the 1979 World Series of Poker.

Mike Caro

This is the Brunson Invitational Golf Tournament that I hosted for seven years, held at the old Dunes golf course. The pros call it the "Dolly."

My daughter Cheryl, her son Jeff and his daughters Christian and Loren.

Family in harbor: Wife Louise in the front; back row shows my son Todd, his wife Angela, and my daughters Pam and Cheryl.

Two black bears protect the entrance to my Montana retreat.

This is my second house on Flathead Lake in Montana. It's where I'll retire if I ever get to where I can't win at poker anymore.

Fifty-year reunion of my college basketball team that went to the NCAA tournament.

Warming up for the mile run the year after I won the Texas High School State Championship. I'm on the right.

Louise and I in Greece around 1994.

This is how my kids looked twenty years ago: Todd, Pam, and Cheryl.

Todd's first championship at age twenty-one. He netted over $200,000 at the Bicycle Casino in Los Angeles.

My pride and joy, Casper and Cutie.

Pam and Barry at sunset.

My daughter Pam with her husband
Barry on a poker cruise in 2004.

Then and now…still smiling 43 years later.

Crandell finishes second in the 1978 World Series of Poker and congratulates new champion, Bobby Baldwin.

Crandell Addington in the 1970s.

This photo from 1977 shows me surrounded by original *Super/System* collaborators. Left to right: Bobby Baldwin, Mike Caro, Joey Hawthorne, David Sklansky, and Chip Reese.

"The Godfather"

I was honored to grace the cover of this short-lived magazine.

SPECIALIZE OR
LEARN THEM ALL?

Steve Zolotow

Steve Zolotow doesn't remember a time in his life when he wasn't playing games. Beyond approaching games as opportunities to make money gambling, he considers them intellectual challenges.

When I first met him, he was the head of one of the first and most successful sports betting groups. His team was one of the first to use computer modeling and high-powered statistical techniques to handicap sports. He has also won championships in backgammon and bridge.

As a teenager he dropped out of college to study acting. When that proved too unstable a profession, he turned to gambling to make a living. That turned out to be a good choice, and he has been a successful gambler for over forty years. Along the way, he earned a BS in Statistics, an MBA in Finance, and an MA in English from NYU.

In poker, he has concentrated more on live-money games than on tournaments. Still, he has managed to finish in the money twenty-five times at the WSOP, including two bracelets. One of these came at 6:00 a.m. after a marathon struggle against me in Chinese Poker. Shortly after Steve won this event in both the WSOP and the Hall of Fame tournaments, it was removed as a WSOP event. He has recent tournament wins that stretch from Tunica, Mississippi, to Melbourne, Australia, and his conquests cover the broad spectrum of poker forms.

Nobody understands the importance of being able to build a bankroll by diversifying your play more than Steve Zolotow, and nobody is more qualified to write about it.

SPECIALIZE OR LEARN THEM ALL?
by Steve Zolotow

THE FOX AND THE HEDGEHOG

Seven-hundred years before the birth of Christ, the Greek poet Archilochus distinguished between the fox and the hedgehog, saying "The fox devises many strategies; the hedgehog knows only one, but he uses it very effectively." As a gambler which should you strive to be? Should you try to learn a lot of games or just one?

Many poker players adopt the hedgehog's strategy. When presented with an encyclopedic book such as this one, they immediately turn to the chapter that covers their favorite game and study that chapter exclusively. They either give a cursory glance to sections dealing with other games, or they opt not to look at them at all. The advantage to being a hedgehog is very simple. You can become very good, perhaps even great, at your specialty. What could be wrong with that? If you become an expert at one game, you won't be afraid of any opponent, and you'll win consistently.

So why would you even consider the fox's strategy? Why learn a variety of games, especially if it is virtually impossible to play multiple games as well as you can learn to play just one? Here are five reasons why:

1. Times Change

Your chosen game might not stay popular forever. Some games that were once very popular have faded almost completely away. Imagine how much the five-card-stud or draw-high experts make now. When I first played in New York City, many home games played high-low declare. I never see declare games being played these days.

2. Adaptability Means Higher Profits

You never want to pass up the opportunity to make money at another game. Say you have a choice between a tough stud game and an unbelievably weak Omaha eight-or-better game. A great seven-stud hedgehog might barely cover the rake, while a fox who is barely competent in Omaha will opt for the weak game and clean up.

3. Knowing More Never Hurts

While learning one game, you might pick up something that helps you master another. Before I started playing pot-limit Omaha, I didn't understand the importance of making big laydowns on the river in that game. And you need to be versatile in learning the difference between cash games and tournaments, too. You never know where the profit will be. In cash games, how you play with or against a short stack isn't very important. In tournament play it is a crucial skill you can develop.

4. Flexibility

If you are a fox, you will be able to play mixed games or dealer's choice games. Many home games and most of the biggest games are mixed games, in which the game changes after a set number of hands is played or a certain amount of time elapses. The most popular multi-game mix in casinos is H.O.R.S.E., an acronym for the combination of hold'em, Omaha eight-or-better, razz, stud-high, and eight-or-better stud. Some common two-game mixes are stud and hold'em; no-limit hold'em and pot-limit Omaha; and high-low stud and high-low Omaha. With so many games to play, a hedgehog would have a lot of trouble competing at these tables.

5. Versatility

A fox is much better prepared for any new games that develop than a hedgehog. The more versatile you become, the easier it will be for you to pick up a new variation when you are faced with it.

WHAT TO LEARN

What poker variations should you learn first? To some extent that depends on where you are and what game you normally play. No-limit hold'em is a good game to master first. Not only is it the most popular game, but it's also growing faster than any other. If you intend to play a lot of tournaments, you should definitely learn no-limit hold'em, but don't forget to study the limit and pot-limit variations.

On the East Coast, stud is popular and should be your second choice. In Europe and the South, pot-limit Omaha should be your second choice. In Vegas and California, Omaha high-low split is a reasonable second game to learn, but make sure you learn how to play both tournaments and live games. Eventually you should practice enough to feel comfortable playing limit, pot-limit, and no-limit games. You should also strive to learn all the most popular games, including hold'em, seven-stud, Omaha high, Omaha high-low, seven-stud high-low, deuce-to-seven triple-draw, razz, and lowball draw—both ace-to-five, usually played limit, and deuce-to-seven, usually played no-limit. The top players know and play all of them. Why shouldn't you?

I would even recommend the study of certain academic disciplines, especially mathematics and psychology. Psychology will help you better understand your opponents and what they are doing. It may also enable you to find, understand, and eliminate some of your own mistakes. Probability and statistics are extremely useful as well. Poker players have been known to use game theory to determine the percentage of bets that should be bluffs. Assuming you are extremely intelligent—and you must be if you are reading this book—and hard working, you should be able to master all of these games and academic disciplines in approximately five lifetimes. That's why, in order to make the most money, you should master one or two games, while achieving high competence in the others.

LIMIT HOLD'EM

Jennifer Harman

Though Jennifer Harman is proficient in all poker games, I chose her to write the limit hold'em chapter because I've seen her win consistently at this game, often beating the best players in the world. Having played high-stakes poker with Jennifer the past few years, I'm convinced that she's not only the best all-around female player alive, but also ranks among the elite poker players of the world.

Her aggressive play, a style that fits right into the power poker I have always recommended, has impressed me for years. Jennifer is one of the few women who have won open events at the World Series of Poker, and she is the only woman who has done it twice. In 2000 she won the deuce-to-seven title—a game that was new to her at the time—and in 2002 she won the limit hold'em championship.

To further illustrate her versatility, Jennifer also has appeared at the final table at the WSOP in seven-card stud, pot-limit hold'em, and twice in limit hold'em events. She won the no-limit hold'em championship at the Commerce Casino in 1998, the same year that she won the limit hold'em event at the Orleans Open. In 2002 Jennifer made her final table debut at the prestigious World Poker Tour in Aruba. We'll be hearing more roars from this 100-pound poker lioness in the future.

LIMIT HOLD'EM
by Jennifer Harman

INTRODUCTION

There are significant differences between limit and no-limit hold'em. One obvious difference is that in no-limit, if you play your cards right, you can trap your opponents for all their chips. That's just not the case in limit hold'em. While no-limit is a game of traps, limit hold'em is all about value betting, which means you want to get maximum value for your hand, often through aggressive betting. You'll find that in limit hold'em it's best to play in a straightforward manner, that is, bet and raise when you actually have a decent hand. But don't be predictable, and don't forget that bluffing is one of the most powerful weapons you can use in limit hold'em. Let's get to it!

BLINDS AND ANTES

I would like to start with a discussion of blind structures. After all, posting the blinds is the first step in any hold'em game. In this chapter we are going to cover the different approaches that should be considered based on the blind structure .

A full-limit hold'em game has either nine or ten players seated at the table. These games are often referred to as **ring games**. Typical lower limit games are played ten-handed, but as the limits go up, eight- and nine-handed games are more common. Games with three to six players are called **shorthanded games**, and those played with just two players are called **heads-up** games.

Hold'em is a positional game. A little puck or **button** moves clockwise around the table representing the dealer. In home games, the deal simply moves to the left each hand, but casino games use a professional dealer. The position of the button on the table determines the order of action. After the first round of betting, the button always acts last, which is a great advantage. As the last player to act, the button is able to watch his opponents act on their hands, revealing possible strengths and weaknesses, before he makes his own decision.

Two players, the blinds, are forced to put money into the pot before the hand is dealt. The **small blind** sits directly to the left of the button, and the **big blind** sits directly to the left of the small blind. There are two basic types of blind structures: a **two-and-three chip** and a **two-and-four chip**. In a two-and-three chip blind structure, the small blind puts in two chips, while the big blind puts in three chips. For example in a $15/$30 limit hold'em game, the small blind must bet $10 while the big blind must bet $15.

In a two-and-four chip blind structure (a one-and-two chip structure is identical), the big blind posts double the amount of the small blind. So in a $20/$40 limit hold'em game, the small blind would be $10 and the big blind would be $20.

Optimal limit hold'em strategy differs depending on which blind structure you are playing. A two-and-three chip blind structure will cost you more money proportionately per round than the two-and-four chip structure. As a result, two-and-three chip games are looser than two-and-four chip games, and you will need to compensate for this by playing more hands.

The difference between the two structures seems pretty insignificant, so why the need to adjust your play?

Two-and-Three Chip Structure

In the two-and-three chip structure, the small blind already has 2/3 of a bet in the pot. If there is no raise before the flop, it's highly likely that the small blind will complete the bet and see the flop. There are few, if any, situations in which the player in the small blind should fold a hand rather than kick in one more chip. For example, let's say you are in the small blind in a $30/$60 hold'em game. A player from middle position calls $30, as does the button. As the player in the small blind, you already have $20 invested, and including the big blind's $30, the pot already stands at $110. Since calling will only cost you $10, you are getting 11 to 1 odds on your investment. And since there are very few hands that would be worse than an 11 to 1 underdog to win, it's basically an automatic call no matter what you are holding.

If only you and the big blind remain, remember that there is already $50 in the pot and you have to throw in just one more chip to call. In this case, you are getting 5 to 1 on your money, and you only have to beat one player. Even if you limp in with a marginal hand and the big blind raises you, it's not the end of the world; you've still made the right play.

In a two-and-four chip blind structure, the game should be played a bit more conservatively. As the small blind, you'll have to put in one-half more bet to see the flop, as opposed to the 1/3 bet in the two-and-three chip structure.

Let's apply the scenario above to a two-and-four chip structure. Once again, you are in the small blind, this time with a $10 bet invested. A middle position player limps in for $20, as does the button. There is $70 in the pot, and you have to call $10 more to see the flop. In this scenario, you are getting 7 to 1 on your money, which isn't bad. You should still play a majority of your hands, but not as many as you would have in the two-and-four chip structure. If only you and the big blind remain, you'll have to call $10 into a $30 pot—not that high a price against just one player, but it's still much less enticing than in the two-and-three chip blind structure. As the small blind in this type of game, you should play more conservatively, as it costs you less money per round.

When deciding what limit to play, consider what type of blind structure suits your style. If you are an aggressive player before the flop and like to play a lot of hands, the two-and-three chip blind structure is probably the best choice. Conversely, if you are the type of player who likes to sit back and wait for big hands, then the two-and-four chip structure is definitely better suited to your style.

PRE-FLOP STRATEGY

When people who are new to poker ask me for pointers, I usually tell them to play fewer hands. If you are a beginner, you should stick to strict guidelines with your pre-flop hand selection. This will benefit you in two key ways:

(1) You'll learn the importance of patience and discipline.

(2) Your daily swings won't be as large.

When you are just starting out, your goal should be to get accustomed to the game. As you improve, you'll be able to expand your starting requirements and play even more hands for a profit. As with strategies for any poker variation, there are basic principals and guidelines you should keep in mind, but remember that nothing is set in stone. As your poker abilities improve, you'll want to add some creativity to your pre-flop play so your opponents will have a tougher time getting a read on you.

Your pre-flop strategy will differ greatly depending on the number of players at the table. Later in the chapter, we'll discuss different strategies for games of all sizes, but for now let's look at optimal pre-flop strategy for ring games, those played nine- or ten-handed.

Position is an important factor in helping you decide how to play any given hand. In a typical ten-handed game, there are three positions other than the blinds (we'll get to blind play later in the chapter) you can bet from: early, middle, and late. The later you act, the better your position, and the more hands you can play for a profit. Conversely, if you are in a bad position (early position), you need a premium starting hand to enter the pot. For the sake of this discussion, we'll call positions three through five to the left of the button the **early positions**, positions six through eight the **middle positions**, and positions nine and ten (the button) the **late positions**. In a nine-handed game, players one and two are in the blinds, players three and four in early position, five through seven in middle position, and eight and nine in late position. The last player of each position falls in the middle of the two positions.

Early Position

When in early position, it is important to remember that the rest of the players act behind you, so your hand has to be strong enough to stand a raise. So as a general rule, you should only play the following hands in early position: A-A, K-K, Q-Q, J-J, 10-10, A-K, and A-Q—plus A-J suited and K-Q suited. These may sound like strict guidelines, but keep in mind that the texture of the game will dictate whether or not you can expand on them. If you find yourself in an aggressive game with a lot of pre-flop raising, you're better off sticking to these guidelines. On the other hand, if you are in a passive game with little aggression or pre-flop raising, you can broaden your hand selection to include A-10 suited, 9-9, and 8-8.

If you are dealt a premium hand in early position, you should raise. If you always raise with a premium hand, you'll actually be giving away *less* information about the strength of your hand than if you only raise with aces and kings. If you adopt this strategy of always raising with a premium hand, your opponents won't know if you are raising with A-A, A-K, K-Q, and so on down the list. However, if you always limp in with hands other than aces and kings, your opponents will soon be onto you and learn to never call when you raise.

Your pre-flop raise with these hands serves two purposes:

(1) It enlarges the pot. When you are holding premium cards, you want as much money as possible in the pot.

(2) It narrows the field. The value of your big pairs decreases in multiway pots. By narrowing the field with a raise, you increase the chances that your premium hand will stand up.

As you become more comfortable with the game, you might consider occasionally limping in with a premium hand in order to throw off your opponents. By limping in, you might cause many players to rule out the possibility that you're holding aces or another premium hand. Your pre-flop deception might win you more bets in later rounds. You could even consider limping in with A-K suited in early position. If it is raised behind you, you could go ahead and reraise when it gets back to you. By doing this, you could actually represent aces or kings. So even if you miss the flop, you can bet out and try to take it on the flop.

Limping in from Early Position

Some expert players like to limp in with kings in early position. I'm not a big fan of this play. If someone is going to beat me with an ace-rag hand, I want to make sure I make him pay for it before the flop. If more than three people see the flop and an ace flops, you can quietly deposit your kings in the muck.

If the pot was three-handed or heads-up and an ace flops,

you might want to test the waters and bet out. If you get raised, you'll have to rely on your judgment when it comes to deciding whether to call or fold. Your decision should be based on your read of your opponent. Would he raise me here with a draw? Might he even raise me with middle pair? Does this guy ever bluff? Would this guy play ace-rag? By answering all of these questions, you should have a sufficient number of clues to help you make the right choice.

This is why it's so important to pay attention to the hand you're involved in, as well as hands you've already folded. By watching the game, you should be able to figure out who likes to limp with A-x and who prefers playing suited connectors.

You may consider limping with K-Q suited as well. Unlike high pairs like A-A or K-K and other premium hands, this hand plays well in multiway pots. Deception and mixing up your play should be an important part of your game, but unfortunately there is only so much you can do from early position. For the most part, you just want to play fundamentally sound poker. When you find yourself under the gun, don't try too hard to be creative, because it may cause you to be faced with more difficult decisions later in the hand, and you can end up outwitting yourself!

Middle Position

In middle position, you should definitely play the premium hands we mentioned above, but now, with fewer players acting after you, you can play a few more. Although middle position allows you to broaden your hand selection, remember that, unlike early position, you now have to take into account what has happened in front of you.

Playing Premium Hands from Middle Position (A-A, K-K, Q-Q, A-K)

For the most part, you should play your premium hands from middle position the same way you would from early position. If you are the first one in with A-A, K-K or A-K, you should raise. If somebody has raised in front of you, you should be aggressive and reraise. As you read on through this chapter, you'll find a recurring theme: aggression!

Sometimes, you might want to practice a little bit of deception by calling a raise with a hand like A-K suited, the best drawing hand of them all. Even if you flop a flush draw with no pair, you still have fifteen outs against a hand like Q-Q, which, by the way, would make you the favorite to win the pot. If you are up against another unpaired hand, you'd have the best hand, as well as the best draw.

There are other reasons why you might just want to call a raise with A-K suited. Say you are holding A♠ K♠ in a loose game with lots of action. By smooth calling, you might persuade others to stay in the pot. Being heads-up with the initial raiser wouldn't be horrible, but it might be even more profitable to let others in. So let's say you call, as do three others, and the flop comes bad for your hand—7-8-9 with two hearts, for example. No problem—just check-muck it, thus saving one bet.

Playing Middle Pairs from Middle Position (J-J, 10-10, 9-9)

If you are the first to enter the pot, you should raise coming in. Remember: aggression, aggression, aggression! If someone has raised in front of you, you should reraise to narrow the field and give yourself the best chance to win the pot. Unlike a hand such as A-K suited, these middle pairs don't play very well in multiway pots. By reraising, you'll get a little bit more information about the initial raiser's hand.

If the initial raiser makes it four bets, he probably has a bigger pair or at least A-K. Defining your hand as a strong one is a good idea, and by reraising you can represent a premium hand. Why is this good? Take this example: Say you reraise with 10-10 against a player who has raised from early position. You get it heads-up and the flop comes down 7-3-2. The initial raiser checks, and you bet your 10-10. If your opponent has A-Q, he would be correct in calling one more bet on the flop. However, since you've represented a stronger hand than you actually have, the initial raiser may fold thinking that you might already have A-A.

Playing A-Q from Middle Position

As when playing middle pairs from the middle position, if you have A-Q and are the first to enter the pot, you should raise coming in. On the other hand, if you are facing an early position player who has already raised, playing A-Q from the middle can create some potentially sticky situations. What you should do against an early position raiser will depend heavily on your read of that player. If the Rock of Gibraltar raises from first position, you're A-Q isn't worth two cents! However, if you know the raiser to be a loosey-goosey type player, you should probably try to isolate him by reraising.

There are a few situations where simply calling an early position raise is acceptable, but if you think the hand is worth calling with, you should go ahead and reraise. Otherwise, dump it. You'll then want to keep the lead on the flop whether you flop a pair or not. What you do after the flop will depend on the texture of the flop, your opponents, tendencies, and the number of players in the pot. But as a general rule, you should never call a raise and a reraise with a hand as weak as A-Q.

Playing Marginal Hands from Middle Position (A-x suited, K-Q, K-J, Q-J, J-10, 10-9 suited, 7-8 suited, and Small Pairs)

This is where your starting requirements get a little tricky because there is an added variable: what has happened in front of you. For example, let's look at a hand like J-10. If no one has entered the pot, you should consider raising it up, hoping to pick up the blinds. But if someone has already raised in front of you from an early position, chances are they can beat jack high.

Since it's no longer possible to pick up the blinds, your best play here is usually to fold.

I say usually, because there are very few absolutes in poker. Each situation is unique and varying your plays will help confuse your opponents. How often you use these variances depends on many factors, including table composition, table image, and more.

Here are a few general guidelines to think about when playing marginal hands in middle position:

(1) In an aggressive game with pre-flop raises coming from all positions, you should avoid getting involved if you are holding only small suited connectors. While these hands play well in multiway pots, they do much worse in heads-up situations, especially when played from early or middle position.

(2) In a passive game you can open up a little bit with a marginal hand. If no one has entered with a raise, you might want to raise with all of your big card and small pair hands (K-J, Q-J, J-T, 10-9 suited, 7-7, 6-6, etc.). You should also raise with any suited ace if you are the first one to enter the pot. In a passive game, playing aggressively with a marginal hand is the way to go, as it gives you the opportunity to pick up the pot when no one calls pre-flop. Even when your raise is called, you could still win the pot with a bet on the flop. That is, if an opponent doesn't catch a piece of the flop, which will happen more often than not.

(3) In a loose game with many pre-flop limpers, you should still play the majority of your marginal hands—but unlike in a passive game, you should not play them aggressively. In this situation, your objective is to get full value on your hand, and a raise will only deter others from calling. In these more liberal games, your motto should be "The more the merrier!" For instance, if you are holding 7-8 suited and one player raises while two others call, you should call the raise. Chances are there is a big pot developing, and you've got the right kind of hand to take it down.

Late Position

Now it's time to have some fun! Late position is definitely my favorite place to be and once you've finished reading this limit hold'em section, you'll know why. Playing late position is fun for several reasons. For one, you get to play a lot more hands than you do in early and middle position. Secondly, as a late position player, you have access to a lot more information than the other players, such as who called, who raised, how many have called, etc. Furthermore, late position is the position from which you'll want to do the majority of your stealing—but only when no one has entered the pot ahead of you. If you are in the button, the last seat, you have the opportunity to knock off other late position steal attempts by isolating them and making it three bets. Confused yet? Don't worry, I'll explain.

Stealing from Late Position

When I say **stealing**, I'm referring to a late position player's attempt to grab the blinds with a less than premium hand. A stealer comes in with a raise, hoping to represent a premium hand, which will cause all of the stealer's remaining opponents to fold. Remember, it's hard to hit flops, and your opponents know it. So by staying aggressive, you can pick up a lot of loose change when your opponents miss and give up on the pot.

Sometimes, though, steals don't go quite this smoothly. If your opponents disappoint your steal attempt and call your raise, you'll have to try to pick up the pot on the flop whether you have anything or not. A player might even call behind you or try to isolate you by making it three bets. If you do happen to get reraised, you are now at the mercy of the deck.

If you don't catch a piece of the flop, your best play is usually just to give it up, but depending on what type of hand you have, you can also take one off and try to pick up something on the turn. If your opponent doesn't reraise but smooth calls your late position raise with position, you are presented with a new set of dilemmas. The first thing you need to consider is what hands might this particular opponent play this way. Typically, strong players will three-bet you in these situations, while some weaker players who see lots of flops might call you with just about anything. So, unless the flop looks extremely bad for your hand, you should continue leading and bet the flop.

Let's say that you are holding 6-7 suited in the nine position of a ten-handed game. Everyone has folded to you, and you raise before the flop. The button, seated right next to you in the ten position, calls the raise and both blinds fold. Now it's heads-up, and the flop comes A-9-2 **rainbow**—three unsuited cards. What is your play here? I would advise you to bet just as you normally would when you're the initial raiser and find yourself heads-up. Since the button almost certainly has the better hand, you're hoping that he will throw it away based upon the strength you showed by raising. If he doesn't have an ace he'll probably just dump his hand, and if he does have an ace…oh well. It's only going to cost you this one bet to find out. However, if he calls or raises you, you should shut down and fold your hand.

This ace flop is a good one to bluff. It is unlikely that your opponent has an ace. Unless he is a passive player, chances are your opponent would have reraised with a big ace, such as A-K, A-Q, A-J, or A-10.

The flops you should worry about are those that connect to hands like 8-9, 9-10, 10-J, J-Q, Q-K. More often than not, your opponent's holdings will fall into this range, so, you may want to save a bet if the flop comes down 8-J-Q or K-J-9. If your opponent bets one of these flops, you are done with this hand. If he checks one of these flops behind you, it can mean only one of two things:

    (1) He flopped a monster and is trapping you; or

    (2) He missed the flop as well.

Isolating from Late Position

You'll hear me use the term "isolation" several times throughout the chapter. To put it plainly, if you are going to succeed playing higher limit hold'em, you are going to have to learn the nuances of isolation plays.

So what is an isolation play? Quite simply, **isolation** is a play you make in order to create a one-on-one situation with your opponent and take the flop heads-up, usually with position. For example, say an aggressive player raises from middle to late position and you find 8-8 on the button. With no one else in the pot other than the raiser, you would reraise him and hope to knock both blinds out, thus isolating him and allowing you to play the hand against just one opponent, with the added advantage of having position on every street.

This example puts you in a marginal situation, but it is a situation from which you should profit due to your favorable position. Ideally, your opponent will have a non-paired hand like A-K, A-10, Q-J, or even 7-8 suited. Your pair of eights is a mathematical favorite over any of these hands. Couple that with the fact that you may be able to get your opponent to fold on the flop and it makes this play a profitable one.

In addition, you may even be able to bluff your opponent off of the best hand! How? Well, let's say your opponent has 9-9.

The flop comes down A-J-10. It looks like a horrible flop for you, but if your opponent checks and you bet, how can he call you? He doesn't know that you hate this flop just as much as he does! But because you took the initiative and made it three bets to go, your opponent is in no man's land—virtually forced to fold the best hand. There are many similar examples, all based on a combination of pre-flop aggression and position. The more you play limit hold'em, the more you'll understand how deadly this combination can be.

What do you do when the flop comes a little more difficult—something like J-9-2 rainbow? What happens if your opponent checks, you bet, and your opponent calls? He could have a number of different hands, so what you do on the turn should be determined by the card that comes off and your read of your opponent. In these situations, as well as virtually all hold'em hands, the most difficult street to play is the turn. Hey, no one said this was going to be easy!

If your opponent check-raises you on the flop, that's a different story all together. In this case, your opponent most likely has better than you, but there are still a few hands you can beat. Depending on the opponent, you might be up against nothing more than a pair of deuces! Again, your decision on what to do here and on the turn depends on your read of your opponent and the situation.

As a general rule, you should rarely try to isolate somebody who has raised or called from early position. Here's why: unless you're facing an extremely weak or wild player, you can assume that anyone entering a pot from such a dangerous position probably holds an extremely strong hand—and why would you want to isolate a hand like that? Against an early position raiser, the chances are just too good that your opponent has a big pair, making the odds of outdrawing him more than 4 to 1 against you. Even if it's not a big pair, your opponent might still be holding A-K or A-Q, hands that he might be willing to go to the river with. This means that you are less likely to win the pot right on the flop when they miss. It's also less likely that they are raising with suited connectors and such, hands you could move them off of on the flop.

General Hand Selection Advice for Late Position

Your starting requirements in late position should be wide, to say the least! Play all of the premium hands, of course, all the hands I mentioned for middle position, and—in the right situations—some offsuited connectors.

Here are some more guidelines and basic principals to consider when you are in late position:

(1) If no one has entered the pot in front of you, you should raise, as there is a decent enough chance that no one will call the raise.

(2) If there are several limpers in front of you and you are holding a weaker hand, you can go ahead and limp in. In fact, with hands like 10-9 or 9-8 suited, you might even want to raise from time to time—not because you think you have the best hand, but because it adds a little deception to your play and at little cost. With these types of drawing hands, playing larger pots with multiway action is going to be a profitable decision, not to mention the fact that your pre-flop raise might earn you a free card on the flop. This might give you an opportunity to pick up a draw on the turn if you didn't already flop one. If you did flop a draw, you might be able to pick up a free card on the turn! Huh? Well let's say you do flop a draw and bet it from last position. If you miss the draw on the turn and no one has bet

in front of you, you'll get a free shot to make your hand on the river.

(3) Avoid being overly aggressive in multiway pots with hands that play better shorthanded. If six people have already limped in before you, raising with hands like A-Q offsuit or A-J offsuit is counterproductive. With so many players in the pot, the chances of running the hand through to the river without improvement aren't good. You will need to flop at least a pair, and even that doesn't guarantee you will win the pot. The more players in the pot, the more likely it is that someone will make two pair, trips, a straight, a flush, or better. Furthermore, by raising pre-flop with A-Q offsuit or the like in multiway pots, you also induce your opponents to take long-shot draws against you. Of course, this doesn't mean you should fold these hands in multiway pots, but you should certainly proceed with caution. Limp in cheap, and hope to flop something solid. If the flop comes 10-6-7 to your A-Q, for example, you would be foolish to call any bets on the flop.

These three rules are simply guidelines. Each poker hand contains a completely different set of variables, so there will always be scenarios where you might want to bend the rules just a little.

THREE IMPORTANT LIMIT HOLD'EM CONCEPTS

Learning the fundamentals, improving your hand reading skills, and fighting the psychological wars at the table are three essential ingredients in becoming a fierce, winning player. You might be able to get by in the lower stakes games by simply playing fundamentally sound, but once you are up against some tough competition, relying on fundamentals alone will get you crushed. Hand reading skills and psychological warfare are certainly valuable tools, but again, without any fundamental understanding of the numbers you won't be able to succeed at the highest levels.

1. Fundamentals

In order to play fundamentally sound limit hold'em, you need to do your homework. Once you've studied the odds of, say, making a flush with two cards to come or hitting a straight with one card to come, making fundamentally sound decisions is much easier. So if you find yourself on a drawing hand, simply compare the odds of hitting your hand with the price you are being laid.

Comparing the Odds

To illustrate this point, let's look at a typical hold'em hand: Playing $20/$40 and holding 6-7 of clubs, you've called a raise from the big blind. It's a five-way action pot, so that's $210 (5 players x $40 + the $10 small blind). Now the flop comes Q♣ 8♥ 4♠, giving you an inside straight draw and a backdoor flush draw. You check, one player bets, and three call. That's an extra $80 added to the pot for a new total of $290.

The price you are being laid to make your straight on the next card is 290 to 20, or 14.5 to 1. You know that the odds of hitting the straight on the next card are 43 to 4 or 10.75 to 1. So on the flop, you are getting 14.5 to 1 in a situation where the true odds are 10.75 to 1. You'll take those odds any day, so you call.

The turn brings the 2♠, which is no help. The first player bets again, and all fold back to you. Should you call or fold? Let's take a look inside the numbers. There is now $350 in the pot ($210 pre-flop, $100 more on the flop, and now $40 bet at you on the turn). It will cost you $40 more to see if the river card is a 5, which would give you the nut straight. In deciding how to proceed, you should go through the same mental process as above. Since you know there are forty-six unseen cards remaining and only four helpful cards, there must be 42 unhelpful ones. Divide 42 by 4 and you know you're a 10.5 to 1 underdog.

Are we being laid enough pot odds to call? No. Our $40 investment will only earn us $350, not including bets we may make up on the river. But 350/40 equals only 8.75 to 1. Even if you know your straight cannot be tied, unless you're certain you'll be able to check-raise the river and get called, folding is still the correct decision, even though it's very close now.

Casinos make a fortune by taking the best of it on propositions similar to these. If you are mindful of the pot odds you are being laid, and have a good understanding of the situation, you too could make a fortune by making fundamentally correct decisions. As you get more playing experience, these exercises become second nature. A second or two is all you'll need to figure out the correct play.

2. Hand Reading Skills

In order to make fundamentally correct plays, it's important to have some idea about what you are up against. So how do you put your opponent on a hand? Simple: pay attention! I can't stress this enough. Whether you are in the current hand or not, you need to pay attention to the action at all times in order to learn what your opponents' tendencies are. By simply watching the action, you'll likely be able to find the answers to the following questions:

On the Pre-Flop

    (1) What hands will opponents raise with?

    (2) What hands will they call with?

    (3) Do they play conservatively or loosely from early position?

    (4) How often do they defend their blind to a raise?

    (5) Do they raise a lot of hands, or are they on the careful side?

On the Post-Flop

    (1) What type of hands will they check raise with?

    (2) Do they play draws aggressively or passively?

    (3) Do they slow-play made hands?

    (4) Do they ever bluff?

    (5) Do they fold often on the flop, or will they call all the way to the river?

These are ten questions that you'll learn the answers to simply by paying attention and making mental notes. If you spent the last forty-five minutes watching the ball game, how can you possibly be ready to answer these questions when the time comes? These questions are just the tip of the iceberg, but think about how much better you'd do against an opponent if you knew the answer to all ten! And the more you play, the better you'll get at it.

If you make the most of your time at the table, your skills will improve that much quicker. When you are out of a hand, make a game of it. Before the flop, put an opponent on a range of hands based on his pre-flop action. Then, try to narrow his holding down further after the flop, again on the turn, and finally on the river. Don't get discouraged if you are way off at first. I promise you that the more you try this exercise the better you'll get at it.

3. Psychology

What distinguishes a good poker player from a great poker player is simply the ability to read the thoughts of his opponents. When I first get into a game, I sit back for about ten minutes and watch how the others are playing. It's important to know how the game is playing in order to make better decisions. Does the game seem more aggressive than normal? Does it seem looser or tighter? Are there any players who are upset and playing badly or on tilt? Or conversely, who is winning and really playing their A-game?

The texture of the game can change in an instant, and a player can go from being on his A-game to being on tilt with just one bad beat. You need to keep tabs on all of your opponents and their ever-changing states of mind. When it comes to improving your ability to focus and your people reading skills, nothing is more valuable than experience at the table. This book should help prepare you for the tables, but the rest is up to you. The more intense and focused you are at the tables, the better your results will be. That, I can guarantee.

Understand also, that while you are focusing on your opponent's emotional and mental states, they will be doing the same to you! Whatever your table image is at any given time, it will inevitably have an affect on how your opponents choose to play against you, so it's important for you to be aware of your image and make the necessary adjustments to your play. If you have just raised, lost your fourth hand in a row, and turned beet red, chances are your opponents will assume that you are steaming. If you decide to raise a fifth consecutive hand, chances are your opponents won't give you credit for aces! In fact, if they are perceptive, they will likely play back at you with marginal hands assuming that their hands probably stack up pretty well against the trash you are raising with!

If your table image is shot, it's time to throw your opponents a curve ball and tighten up a little bit. Stealing blinds is only possible if your opponents have some respect for your raises. If they think you are steaming, they won't let you get away with anything! Of course, the opposite is true as well. If you have been winning every chip in sight, your opponents may fear you. They may decide to simply get out of your way. If they do that—pound 'em!

THE FLOP

This is the street where you have to be aggressive. If you play too passively on the flop, you risk being run over and giving away pots you should win. I don't advocate betting with reckless abandon, but when you have the lead and flop something, think about protecting your hand more than worrying about whether or not your opponents have the nuts. If you miss the flop entirely, there may be situations where it would be correct to take one off, hoping to pick up a draw or make a pair. Otherwise, it might be a good time to muck your hand.

This is why aggression is so important. If you had the pre-flop lead, meaning you were the raiser, you can usually keep the lead on the flop. So if both you and your opponent miss the flop, which often happens, your aggression might just win you the pot. If you use good judgment and play your hands aggressively, you'll be one step ahead of the game. You'll find that the best way to go in limit hold'em is playing in a straightforward manner, that is, betting and raising when you actually have some kind of a hand.

Fancy Play

When I say that you should play straightforward, that isn't to be confused with predictable. You still need to think about playing deceptively, but you want to avoid what Mike Caro terms **Fancy Play Syndrome** (FPS). FPS leads to missed bets, giving away free cards, or even playing a hand in such an unorthodox fashion that it actually costs you a pot! More often than not, fancy plays will minimize your profit on a hand. Sure, when these plays work you feel like a genius, but you're better off playing a more fundamentally sound game.

Before we go any further, I want to help you with a common scenario that arises when you are playing fundamentally well. Let's look at an example and go from there.

You are holding A♠ K♦ in early position. You are the initial pre-flop raiser and get two callers behind you, as well as the big blind. Now the perfect flop comes down: A♦ 4♥ 9♣. So here you are with top pair and top kicker. The big blind checks, so it's your turn. Since you were the pre-flop raiser, it's natural for you to bet here. The fancy play, the check, might work, but it won't necessarily win you any more money than a bet would. You have a strong hand, and a check-raise would only give away information. The right move here is to simply bet.

Of course, a check might do more harm than giving away information — it could cost you the pot! The right free card might give your opponent a big draw on the turn. You're better off taking what's in the middle and getting rid of hands like 10♣ J♣. If your opponent was lucky enough to get a free card with that hand, he could pick up as many as fifteen outs against you going in to the river. An 8♣ on the turn, for example, would pose a serious threat to your hand.

What else could happen? You could miss a valuable bet. Many of your opponents might call once more on the flop with a hand like 10-10 or even 8-9. Say it gets checked around on the flop and a king hits the turn. With a bet now, you will probably lose both the 10-10 and the 8-9, costing you two bets on the flop, not to mention the fact that you allowed both of your opponents to draw out on you for free.

So in this situation, the fancy play, the check, could do one of three things:

(1) Give away the strength of your hand.

(2) Cost you the entire pot.

(3) Miss bets on the flop.

On the flip side, what could you gain? You may be able to get a check-raise in and look cool—whoopee. Stick to straightforward play, and leave the fancy plays to the hotshots. When you are the pre-flop raiser, you should usually bet the flop whether you like it or not. Of course, there are several exceptions to this rule. Remember, in poker there are very few rules that are set in stone; always betting the flop when you raised pre-flop isn't one of them.

Two A-K Scenarios

If you have A♣ K♣ in a multiway pot and the flop comes 7-8-9 of diamonds, save your money and just give up. You can't run this hand through often enough to make a bet profitable.

Let's look at a less obvious and more difficult example: With your A♠ K♦ again, you raise after two people limped in, and get one player behind you to call So it's four-handed to see a flop of 6♦ 7♦ 8♥. Even if the first two limpers check to you, I would still advise you to check more often than not. This flop just connects with too many hands that players would limp in with, such as 9-10, 6-6, 9-9, A-7, and about a million others. If there is a bet on the flop, you should probably give up. Sure, you may be folding the best hand every now and then, but folding here is the safe, straightforward play.

Now let's look at a situation where you might decide to continue after the flop. What if, in the same scenario, everyone checks to the player in last position, who bets and sees both limpers fold. You have a decision to make. The last player may only be on a straight steal here, just taking advantage of his position. But then again, maybe he's got a hand. Here is where you'll need all of your poker skills to answer some important questions: If he held a high pair before the flop, would he have reraised you? Would this player call your raise with a marginal hand that hits this flop? Would he bet here with a hand like A-J or A-10? Is he a habitual bluffer, who always bets when checked to regardless of his hand? Or is this player a careful bettor, who only bets with strong hands?

Once you've answered the important questions, you'll have a much better idea about whether or not you should take one off, hoping to catch an ace or a king, or even whether or not you should call your opponent down all the way to the river. In general, if you've answered your questions about your opponent and still haven't found very strong reasons to proceed, you should fold.

So now that we are all warmed up, let's look more closely at the play of specific hands on the flop.

Playing Big Pairs

As I mentioned previously, you should play big pairs aggressively before the flop in order to narrow down the field. Big pairs do extremely well against one or two players, but the more opponents you have, the more likely it is that your big pair will get cracked. If the flop doesn't go your way, it's important to avoid getting too attached to your hand and fold in the face of too much action. Imagine you have two black aces in a multiway pot and the flop comes 6-7-8 of diamonds. I don't know about you, but I really don't like this flop for two black aces. Now, you shouldn't necessarily fold on the flop, but if the action gets hot and heavy, you can probably assume that you are dead or that your opponents at the very least have several outs against you.

Again, even if you're A-A is good at the moment, a 4, 5, 9, 10, any diamond, or an 8 could seal your fate. Another scary flop for aces is one that contains high straight cards like J-10-8. While aces are good here a high percentage of the time, there are several cards that could potentially kill you on the turn: 7, 9, 10, jack, queen, king. You shouldn't muck those aces just yet, but you should consider taking your pedal off the gas until you see the turn card. If the turn card is safe—2, 3, 4, etc.—you might want to get aggressive and try to eliminate players. However, if a scare card comes on the turn—a 9 or a queen would be the scariest—and the action gets heavy, you should consider folding.

While Q-Q is still considered a big pair, there are even more trouble flops to that hand than to A-A. In addition to all the scary flops A-A faces, any ace or king on the flop might do you in, as well. Let's say you raise with the Q-Q and are reraised pre-flop. Now the flop comes J-10-4, giving you an overpair. Only problem is, what can you beat? Well sure you have A-K or A-Q beat, but if your opponent has A-A, K-K, J-J, or 10-10, you are in pretty bad shape. Again you shouldn't automatically fold in these situations, but it's probably best to play a small pot and simply call your opponent down. If he does have a big ace, then you are simply letting your opponent bluff his chips off to you. True, you may be missing some bets along the way, but that's better than getting in a whole lot of bets when you are dead to two outs.

Flopping Top Pair

When flopping top pair, your main objective should be to narrow down the field, while punishing those opponents that are drawing to beat you. Aggression, which is the theme of this entire chapter, is key in this situation. Of course, there are certain types of flops that you should play carefully and other, safer flops that can be played full speed ahead. Let's first take a look at some of the more friendly flops.

Safe Flops. A scenario mentioned earlier is a good example of a safe flop. Say you have A-K and hit an A-9-4 rainbow flop. There is no legitimate straight draw out there, and no flush draw either. At this point, only two pair or trips would have you beat. This is a great flop for your hand, and ideally you'd be up against a player holding a hand like A-Q, A-J, or even A-10. You are a huge favorite against any of these hands, as they can only beat you if they hit one of three remaining kickers on the turn or the river. Of course, if either one of those cards is a king, they simply can't win unless they happen to make a backdoor flush. This is a dream situation for you, not only because it's unlikely that you'll lose, but you also stand to win several bets from your opponent. How you go about doing this depends on several variables, including your table image, your opponent's tendencies, your position, and so on. You might even choose to make a fancy play on a flop, but remember that I recommend straightforward, brute aggression. If you play the hand aggressively you should be able to win the maximum amount of bets, or close to it.

Let's look at a more detailed example of how you'd go about playing this hand in a specific situation. Say you are in the big blind with an A-K. A player in first position raises and gets two callers. Calling here will help disguise your hand more than raising will, and since you can't really narrow down the field any more, calling is probably the best way to play it.

Okay, so your hand is A♠ K♦, and the flop comes A♦ 4♥ 9♠. You're first to act. This is a good opportunity for you to get a check-raise in. Since there was an early position raiser, it's likely he'll bet this flop whether or not he has the ace. By check raising, you'll be able to trap anyone who called on the flop. Of course, this is not the only way to play this hand, but it is certainly the best or the second-best way to go. Your other option would be to lead right into the pre-flop raiser, hoping that he raises you with a weaker ace, thus giving you the opportunity to make it three bets. What method you choose will once again depend on those variables we've discussed: table image, your opponents' tendencies, history, and so on.

Let's move you to late position with this same hand and same flop, but this time, only you and an early position raiser remain. Holding A♠ K♦, you decide to smooth call here, because you know your opponent is a tight player who only raises with premium hands. The flop comes A♦ 4♥ 9♠, and your opponent bets into you. There is a chance he also has A-K or even A-A, but it's more likely that he holds a hand like A-Q, A-J, or maybe K-K, Q-Q, or J-J. Since this is such a safe flop, smooth calling on the flop might just work. If your opponent bets the turn, you can go ahead and raise him now that the bet has doubled.

What if he checks the turn? Well, there goes the raise-the-turn plan. This is another good illustration of the importance of aggressive play on the flops. Against most opponents, the raise the turn play will only work when your opponent actually flop an ace as well. If he doesn't, he may be leery of your call on the flop and decide to shut down on the turn. So the raise-the-turn play has some merit, but I recommend using it simply as a variation play against an opponent that may be getting a line on your play. Otherwise, you should play these flops in a straightforward manner.

Dangerous Flops. A dangerous flop for top pair is one that puts your hand in jeopardy due to the presence of a straight or flush draw. Depending how high your top pair is, you have to consider the added risk of an overcard hitting the turn. Obviously, more flops are dangerous to a hand like 8-8 than to a hand like A-A. For this reason, if you are holding 8-8 or the like, it's extremely important to narrow the field on the flop by playing aggressively, hoping your opponents won't draw out to overcards. You should be aggressive with the A-A hand as well, but for different reasons. With A-A, your goal is to get more money in the pot.

Let's look at an example. You are on the button with the 8-10 of hearts. You limp in, as do two other players. The small blind also calls, making it a five-way action pot. The flop comes 8♦ 4♣ 3♠, and all check to you. You should always bet here. Now, I know I've told you that there are only a few absolutes in poker—this is one of them. You simply cannot give free cards to hands like Q-J, A-5, K-10, etc. So you bet and get two callers. At this point, you should feel good about having the best hand. No one check-raised, so it's unlikely that anyone holds an overpair or even an 8 with a better kicker.

The real threat to your hand is an overcard on the turn or an opponent slow-playing a set, looking to check-raise you on the turn. You should always have an idea about what your opponents are going to call you with on the flop, so that you'll have a better idea of what to do on the turn.

Let's say you are on the button with the same hand (8♥ 10♥) in the exact same situation (the flop comes 8♦ 4♣ 3♠), only this time somebody leads into you on the flop. Based on what we've discussed earlier, you should know that a raise is your best option. Your goal here is to drive out the overcards and play the hand heads-up.

Raising will also give you a better idea about what the lead bettor's hand is. If he reraises you, chances are he has your pair of eights beat. Of course, if you pick up no help on the turn, it is time to make a difficult decision, one based on the read you've acquired on your opponent. If he is a conservative ABC-type player, he probably does have an overpair, a set, or an 8 with a better kicker. If he is a fast, loose, and aggressive type of player, he may have a hand like 8-9, A-4, or even a draw like 5-6. So in closing, aggression on the flop here helps narrow the field and defines your opponent's hand a little more clearly. You'll find that this will be the case in most situations when playing limit hold'em.

Flopping Middle Pair

When flopping middle pair, your choice of strategy heavily depends on the number of active players. The more players in the pot, the less likely it is that your hand is good enough to hold up. In a heads-up pot, you are simply going to have to take this hand to the river more often than not. The only time you should fold is if the board came extremely bad on the turn and river, or if you have a good read on your opponent and know that he wouldn't bet with a hand you could beat. Your kicker should also be a key consideration as well. Generally, the higher the kicker the better, but it might be even better if your kicker presented you with added outs—for example, if you held 7-8 and the flop came 6-7-10. In this case, a 9 would make you a straight, while an 8 would make you a dangerous two pair—or your kicker might even give you a flush draw.

Furthermore, say you held Q-J with the jack of hearts, and the flop came K-Q-4, all hearts. In this case, you might have the best hand with the pair of queens, but if not, the jack of hearts gives you a backup plan.

It's also important to consider what may happen if you do hit your kicker. Could it complete the hand of one of your opponents? Let's say you held K♣ 10♣ and the flop came Q♥ 10♦ 8♥. With a flush and straight draw present, you could hit your kicker but still need help. The K♥ of hearts would be considered a good card for your hand, but it could also be the worst card in the deck for you! It would fill any flush, as well as make the A-J straight—not to mention the possibility of kings and queens, or the fact that you could be up against a made straight or a set already.

In a situation like this, you'd want to proceed with caution, that is, if you continue with the hand at all. Despite this, added outs are always good, even if some of them aren't live outs. That's especially true in heads-up pots.

Playing Middle Pair from the Blinds—Heads-up Pots

This just might be one of the trickiest scenarios in limit hold'em. You are usually out of position with a marginal hand. The great players thrive in these situations, while average players are often overwhelmed by them. There are several different ways to approach playing middle pair from the blinds. Again, the number of players is the key, as are the raiser's tendencies, the position the raise came from, and so on. Answer these questions each time you are faced with this scenario and you'll be one step ahead of the game. Once you've gathered this information, you'll have to decide whether to lead-bet, check-raise, check-fold, or check-call.

Let's look at an example: You have 10-8 in the big blind, and a player on the button raises it, so the two of you see a flop of K-8-4 rainbow. Folding in this situation is far too weak a play. So, that leaves you with three legitimate options: check-call, check-raise, or bet right out.

This is a good opportunity to go for a check-raise. As the pre-flop raiser, your opponent should bet regardless of his holecards, and by check-raising, you'd also be representing a king. If your opponent has A-J in this spot, he would be correct in calling another bet on the flop. However, since you are representing a king, he might fold, thinking he can only win if he catches an ace.

When you check-raise, you are risking two small bets on the flop and are committed to one more when you lead out at the turn, so if you go for the check-raise when you are up against a better hand, it's usually a more expensive loss than it would have been had you just led out. If your opponent has a hand like A-K, you are going to get punished. But, that's not going to happen often enough for you to worry too much about it.

If you are really averse to taking risks, you can minimize your losses (as well as your profits) by leading out at the flop. If you lead out and your opponent has nothing, you'll likely be losing a bet—the one your opponent probably would have made—on the flop. If he raises you, he probably has at least a pair, but not necessarily one that beats eights.

Some believe that you gain more information about your opponents by leading out rather than check-raising, but I disagree. Your bet on the flop, known as the **weak lead**, doesn't do much to define your hand at all, which might make your opponent may play 7-8 aggressively, thinking it's the best hand. After all, he may be thinking, "If the big blind has a king, why wouldn't he have check-raised?"

Against a tough player, the weak lead does little to define his hand, though leading here with middle pair might be the right move. It all depends on your opponent's impression of your play. What has he seen you do thus far? When you led out in the past, did you always turn over a draw? If so, a lead here might fool your opponent into thinking that you are on a semi-bluff, and he might call you down the whole way with ace-high.

Deciding whether to lead or check-raise adds deception to your game. Situations like these are great opportunities to keep your opponents off balance. You want to use the information players gather about your playing style against them. If they think you will bet with nothing, bet with something. If they think you will only check-raise with something, check-raise with nothing! Just stay aware of your table image and avoid being too predictable. Think of it like a game of paper-rock-scissors. "Well, he went rock two hands in a row, I think he'll go paper this time." Or even, "I went scissors three times in a row, now my opponent will think I'll go for it four times in a row!"

If the raise comes from early position, the situation changes dramatically. If you have that same 8-10 on the K-8-4 flop, you might decide that you'll get more information if you lead right out. If you are raised, you should probably give your opponent credit for a king or maybe even a pocket pair like J-J. If you don't improve on the turn, you should probably let it go. Of course, if you make two pair or trips, it would be the perfect opportunity to go for the check-raise, but since it's so much more likely now that your opponent actually has something, it might be safer to lead out.

Playing Middle Pair with Multiway Pots

Things get even more troublesome with your middle pairs when more players are in the pot. If you are in the blinds, you'll have to play the hand from the worst position possible on the flop, turn, and river. If there is any real action on the flop, you should take the safe route and dump your hands. Again, even if you have the best hand on the flop, there is a very good chance that it won't be by the time the river card hits. In a multiway pot, you should usually check the flop to see what develops.

If it's bet and raised in front of you, the decision to fold has been made for you. However, if it looks like there is a good chance no one has top pair, you should commit to your read and get aggressive. If the flop isn't too scary and it's checked around, you should fire at the turn. If a player in a favorable position bets, check-raise to isolate him.

Let's look at another situation. You find yourself in the big blind with Q-6 off. Two early position players limp in, as do the button and small blind. The flop comes J♥ 6♠ 2♥. The small blind checks, as do you. In fact, all check to the button who bets.

Let's assume the button is an aggressive player who will bet all types of hands. What is your play? Raise. Yes, I realize there are still several players to act behind you, but since they all checked the flop, they probably don't have much. Otherwise they would have bet themselves. True, they could be check-raising, but in order to become a top limit hold'em player, you are going to have to take some calculated risks. Consider how many good things can happen if you raise. What if the first limper actually had 7-7? That hand has you beat, but is he willing to call two bets, hoping that you don't have jacks? Chances are, you'll get him to lay down the best hand. Even if you are wrong and the original bettor does have the jacks, you could still hit a queen or a 6 on the turn.

Now if the bet were to come from early position, raising after you checked would be dangerous. For example, if the first limper bets and all call, it might be a good idea to just call the bet and hope to make two pair or trips.

Playing Middle Pair from Early Position

If you are entering the pot from early position, chances are you've raised coming in. If you happen to flop middle pair, you should continue with the lead since you were the aggressor before the flop. Let's say you've raised coming in with A-Q and the flop comes K-Q-2. Go ahead and bet if no one else has bet in front of you, regardless of the number of players in the pot. By betting, you'll get a better idea of whether or not you have the best hand at the moment. If you get raised on the flop, it's time to reevaluate the situation. Again, you'll have to ask yourself some questions. Would my opponent raise with a draw? Would my opponent raise with a queen and a worse kicker?

If the answer to both questions is no, you have to give your opponent credit for at least a pair of kings. You should still call one bet on the flop, though, and if you don't improve on the turn, you should probably fold.

Let's say you decide to check-raise rather than lead out. Now the questions you'll have to ask yourself are more difficult to answer. If one of your opponents bet after you showed weakness by checking, he could have a number of hands. He may decide to bet with anything from K-Q, 9-9, Q-10, A-J, or J-10. Figuring out which hand is being bet is a difficult task. Had you just bet out on the flop as I recommended, you'd have a lot more information to go on, which in turn would help you make correct decision.

Let's look at a slightly different situation. Again, you are in early position with the A-Q on a K-Q-2 flop. This time, the big blind bets into you. What now? Unless you have information that indicates immense strength from the big blind, you should go ahead and raise him! If you know that this player always has at least top pair when he bets, folding would be correct. However, most players don't play that way. A typical opponent might have a Q-2, J-10, A-J, or the like, and is trying to pick up the pot on the flop. There is an excellent way to find out: raise. Your raise accomplishes two things:

(1) Narrows down the field;

(2) Helps define the bettor's hand.

If the lead bettor just calls your raise, there is a very good chance your pair of queens with an ace kicker is the best hand. If this is not the case, and your opponent has something like K-5, you still have five outs to improve with an ace or a queen.

Playing Middle Pair from Late Position

Whether or not you are in a heads-up pot or a multiway pot, you should usually bet middle pair when you opponents check to you on the flop. For example, say you have A-6, and the flop comes K-6-2 rainbow. Since everyone has checked to you, it looks like your pair of sixes is the best hand here.

Of course, if you get check-raised, you'll be faced with a difficult dilemma. Since you are betting in last position, a player check-raising you doesn't necessarily have to have you beat. He may be testing the waters, hoping that you are on a steal. If the small blind had 6-7, he may raise to isolate your likely bluff. As discussed in the section on playing middle pair from the blinds, a good player will often make this play against you when you've bet from steal position. Your goal then, is to figure out what type of player you are up against and play accordingly. If you are check-raised by a tight player who limped from first position, chances are he has the king. You should still call one more bet, hoping to hit an ace or a 6, but if you miss, be prepared to dump your hand.

So what do you do if you flop middle pair, and it's already bet in front of you? Again, as is true with most poker situations, it depends on a number of factors. Let's look at a couple of examples.

Example One: In a four-way pot you hold 6-6 on the button. The flop comes K♥ 4♣ K♣, and the player to your immediate right bets. In this spot, you'll want to raise for four reasons:

(1) To narrow the field;

(2) To find out if any of the other players have a king;

(3) Your 6-6 is likely the best hand;

(4) You may knock a higher pair than yours out of the pot.

Unless you are up against an extremely careful player, raising here is your best option. The lead bettor may have a 4, a flush draw, or even a hand like A-10—or nothing at all. He certainly doesn't need a king to make a bet here.

Example Two: In a five-way pot made up of two limpers, two blinds, and yourself on the button with J-8 of hearts, the flop comes 10♣ 8♣ 6♣. Everyone checks to the player on your immediate right who bets. So you raise, right? Wrong. I think this board is a little too scary. I'd suggest avoiding this dangerous flop and moving onto the next hand. If your opponent happens to have the flush or straight already, you'd need two perfect cards to win.

Flopping a Set

Your approach to playing sets should depend on the texture of the flop. Make your decision as to whether or not you can set a trap or whether you'll be forced to play it fast based upon how dangerous the board looks. The scarier the board, the more aggressive you should be. Don't worry too much about aggressive play costing you action. Strangely enough, many of your opponents will mistake your aggression for weakness! Here is an example: Let's say you limp in from middle position with 6-6. The flop comes K♠ 6♠ 7♣, and the pot is raised behind you. With five of you in the pot, the first two players check to you.

A busy flop like this is the perfect opportunity for you to ram and jam the flop with your set of sixes, maximizing your profit. Try betting right out into the raiser and see what happens. If the pre-flop raiser has a hand like A-A, A-K, or even Q-Q, he may decide to protect his hand and raise your bet. This will give you the opportunity to raise it once more on the flop, building a sizeable pot. By playing the hand straightforward—raising with what's likely the best hand—you may get even more action than if you had slow-played it. After all, the pre-flop raiser may put you on a hand like K-x or even a flush draw or straight draw, thinking that you would have checked a set. Again, play your sets according to the flop texture, your position, and your opponents' tendencies.

So what about setting a trap? Let's take a look at another example. From middle position with 6-6, you raise and are reraised by the button. All others fold, and you and the button take a flop of 10-6-2 rainbow heads-up. You have numerous options in this situation. You could bet, hoping to reraise; bet and just call a raise now, and then check-raise on the turn; check-raise; or check-call, and then check-raise the turn.

This is where playing hold'em gets fun. You've got your opponent right where you want him and will be using one of these plays to make him pay the maximum. So how do you figure out which one works the best? All of these options are good, so you have to base your decision on your opponent's tendencies, as well as his impression of you. The hands you've played against him should be considered when deciding on a course of action.

Let's say you know your opponent to be an extremely aggressive player who won't give away any free cards. In this case you know that a check-call followed by a check-raise on the turn will work.

What if your opponent likes to keep the lead on the flop? In this case, you might choose to bet right out and look to get extra bets in on the flop. Or you might check-raise the flop and try to win even more bets if you think your opponent is aggressive enough to reraise after you check-raise. Whatever you decide to do, make sure you don't get stuck playing a made hand the same way every time.

Using all of the tools available will help you in various other situations as well. How? Well, let's say you used the check-call, check-raise on the turn play. Once your opponents see this, they will now be worried that when you check twice, it doesn't necessarily mean you have a weak hand. That way, when you actually are on a draw, you may win yourself a free card. Flopping a set in position gives you even more leeway than if you had players behind you. In position, you never have to worry about missing a bet and giving away a free card. Being in position also allows you to safely set traps as well. For example, say you limp on the button with 3-3 in a four-way action pot, and the flop comes K-8-3 rainbow. This would be a very safe flop to smooth call and hope to raise the turn.

Flopping Flush Draws

There are several variables that will affect how you proceed with flush draws on the flop: your position, the number of players, the texture of the game (passive or aggressive), whether or not you have the nut draw, where the pre-flop raise came from, and so on. Depending on the variables, the correct strategy might be to play the hand very aggressively, very cautiously, or somewhere in between.

Monster Flush Draws

If you were to flop an open-ended straight flush draw, you'd most likely want to get as many bets in on the flop as possible since your hand would be favored over most of the hands you'd be up against. You would certainly be a money favorite regardless of the number of players in the pot. For instance, if you held 7-8 of hearts and the flop came 5♥ 6♥ J♠, you should try to get as much money in the pot as you can. However, simply raising and reraising may not necessarily be the best way to do that. You want more money in the pot, sure, but you also want as many players to stay in the pot as possible. If it's checked to you, you should always bet the hand. However, if the bet comes in front of you and there are still three players to act behind you, you have a dilemma. Raise or call?

If you raise you might knock out players you want in the pot. In this situation, you should probably just call and invite others to do the same. If they raise…great! That's not going to hurt your hand one bit. In fact, if a player raises behind you and all call, you may even consider jamming the pot! Of course, the problem is that the more players that are in the pot, the better the chances are that one of them has a bigger flush draw than yours. No matter, you can still hit the straight or the two key hearts to fill your straight flush.

Playing monster draws aggressively adds deception to your game at absolutely no cost. Often times that draw of yours will actually be a favorite over your opponent's hand anyway. Let's say you held A♥ K♥ on a flop of 2♥ 7♥ 10♠, and your opponent held Q♦ Q♠. Despite the fact that the Q-Q appears to be leading at this point, your two overcards and a flush draw is actually the favorite to win the pot! Or let's say you put your opponent on a pair of aces while you hold the 9♦ 10♦ to a flop of 8♦ 10♠ J♦. Again, all you have is a pair of tens, but with all those outs you should be happy to put in as many bets as the aces would like. In this situation there are twenty cards that help you, and you have two chances to hit one. That's what I call a good spot.

What about another monster draw, like A♠ K♠ on a flop of A♦ 6♠ 10♠? Here again, you should jam the pot—cap it if you can. True, you might be beat at this point, but even so, a spade that doesn't pair the board makes you the nuts. You should lead out if it's up to you, or raise and reraise if you get the opportunity. In some cases, it might be better for you to set a trap with this hand, but as a general rule, you don't want to slow-play it.

Marginal Flush Draws

So what happens when you don't flop such a monster draw? All of the above examples are dream hands. Any monkey can play hands like those. What separates the really good players from the rest is how they play marginal flush draws in marginal situations. Whenever you don't have the nut flush draw, you are vulnerable to losing a lot of bets. To avoid losing the maximum with less than stellar flush draws, you should be a lot more cautious than you would with a monster draw.

If all you have is a **naked** flush draw—meaning you have no other added outs—you don't want to get involved in a raising war. You should try to make a hand like this as cheaply as possible, and then if you do, you are left hoping that no one else has a bigger flush draw than yours. Remember now, the more players and more action you see on the flop, the more likely it is that someone else is also drawing to the flush. In multiway pots, you really have to pay attention to the action. It's important to get a good read on your opponents when you are holding a small flush draw.

Based on the flop action, you need to decide whether or not one of your opponents has a better draw than you and go with it. To do this, it helps to watch their body language and to know their tendencies with drawing hands in these situations.

You should also be cautious when three of a suit flops, say three hearts, for example. In this situation, you shouldn't proceed past the flop in a multiway pot without the nut draw. Even with the nut draw, I'm not all that crazy about this hand. After all, if a fourth heart hits the board, the flush would be obvious, so it would be difficult to extract any more bets from my opponents.

Obviously, you shouldn't fold an ace-high flush draw, but you don't want to put in too much action unless you also flopped a pair or think your ace-high might be the best hand. Any other flush draw should be thrown away on the flop in a multiway pot. For example, if the flop came K♥ 6♥ 4♥, you probably shouldn't put in another chip with a hand like 10♥ J♣. Sure you have a 10-high flush draw, but even if you make it, keep in mind that any ace, queen, or jack of hearts beats you.

If you are lucky enough to flop a flush, you want to make your opponents pay to outdraw you, but you may be better off doing so on the turn. How so? Well, let's say you have the 5♥ 6♥ on a 10♥ J♥ 2♥ flop. Anyone with the ace of hearts is going nowhere. A set or two pair are also going nowhere. If you are in a looser lower limit game, you may not even be able get a hand like 9♥ 9♦ out! Not to mention the fact that anyone who's flopped a bigger flush than you is certainly not going to fold if you play your hand aggressively. Well since a heart on the turn completely destroys your hand, why put in extra bets on the flop? Why not wait to see what develops on the turn and then get aggressive? Playing this way, you'll lose the minimum if a heart does hit the turn, and you may be able to better protect your hand with a timely raise on the turn.

If you happen to get reraised on the turn, you are going to have to use your reading skills to figure out whether or not your opponent is bluffing. If you know the player has to have the nuts to make a raise like this, it's time to dump your hand to the third bet. However, if you are up against a maniac, you can forget about folding. In fact, you might even want to make it four bets! I wouldn't recommend that play too often though; the situation has to be perfect. Normally, just calling down the maniac is acceptable.

Playing Flush Draws Out of Position

Playing marginal flush draws is even more difficult when you are out of position. Let's get straight to an example: You are in the big blind with 8-9 of hearts in a raised multiway pot. The flop comes 2♥ 3♥ 10♠. In this situation you should probably just check to the original raiser, especially if he raised from early position. If you were to bet out, there is a very good chance that the initial raiser will raise you to knock out the players behind him. Don't help him. Help yourself by keeping them in! The worst-case scenario for you is that your bet, coupled with your opponent's raise, takes you to the turn heads-up. Not good. So now that you've checked, the initial raiser bets, and all others call. It's time to check-raise, right? Wrong. If you check-raise, you run the risk of the initial raiser three-betting you in an attempt to thin the field. You want a big field, so check-raising here is a no-no.

Playing Flush Draws in Position

Drawing hands are much more profitable when played from late position. In late position, you have more control over what's happening on any given street. Since you get a chance to see what everyone in front of you does, you will be better equipped to maximize your profits or minimize your losses. If you flop the nut flush draw, you can jam the pot on the flop. Since you played so aggressively on the flop, chances are that your opponents will check to you on the turn. Obviously, if you make your hand you should bet, but if you miss, you can take the free card.

Just to make sure we are on the same page, let's look at an example: An early position player raises, there are two calls in between, and you call with A-10 of diamonds on the button. The flop comes 2♦ 9♦ Q♥. The initial raiser bets, and both players in front of you call. In this case, you should raise, even though you run the risk of the initial raiser three-betting it and knocking out the other two players. That wouldn't be good, but it doesn't happen often enough to negate the value of the raise. If the initial raiser reraises, it's not a complete disaster. If he doesn't, you've succeeded in getting more money in the pot, and you may just pick up a free card for yourself on the turn if you miss.

Playing Flush Draws Heads-Up

A lot of the rules that would apply to playing flush draws in multiway pots go right out the window when you are heads-up. Heads-up poker is like a power struggle, each player trying to get last action and force the other player to back down. More often than not in heads-up poker, both players will flop nothing. The player that wins the majority of those pots usually comes out ahead. Although it has no real value at the time, flopping a flush draw gives you the opportunity to take the initiative on a hand with the hope of either semi-bluffing your way to a flush or forcing your opponent to fold.

In heads-up situations, you can check-raise with a flush draw out of position. In fact, it's often a very good play. Of course, you can always bet right out as well. If you have position, raising your opponent on the flop or the turn might help you win the pot, whether you make the flush or not. How you decide to play a flush draw heads-up on the flop depends on a few key factors: your position, the pre-flop action, your opponent's tendencies, your table image, and your personal history with your opponent.

Flopping Straight Draws

There are three types of straight draws that we will cover in this section: open-ended draws, double belly-buster straight draws, and gutshots. An **open-ended straight draw** would look something like this: You have 9-10 and the flop reads 7-8-2. In this case, you have eight cards that would make your straight (four sixes plus four jacks).

Then there is the **double belly-buster**: Say you have 7-8 and the flop comes 4-6-10. Both a 5 and a 9 would make you a straight, which gives you the same amount of outs as the open-ended draw (eight). This draw would be exactly the same as an open-ended straight draw, except these belly-buster draws can be slightly more profitable since the hand is less obvious.

Finally, we have the **gutshot straight**: You have 9-10 and the flop reads Q-8-2. In this case, you can only make your straight with a jack. The open-ended draws give you eight outs, while this gutshot gives you just four.

Playing Open-Ended and Double Belly-Buster Straight Draws

These draws can be played much like a flush draw on the flop, even though the flush draw gives you nine outs, while these draws only give you eight. There are other drawbacks that affect the straight draw which don't affect the flush draw. If there is also a flush draw on the flop, you might make your straight with the same card that fills your opponent's flush. For example, you hold 9-10 and your opponent holds A-3 of hearts. The flop comes A♣ 7♥ 8♥. In this case, you'd have eight cards to fill your straight, but notice that if you fill it with the 6♥ or the J♥, you'd lose anyway, leaving you with only six pure outs. Even if you hit your nut straight on the turn, your hand is still vulnerable to any of nine remaining hearts on the river.

There are some hidden advantages to open-ended straight draws. When a third flush card hits on the board, it sets off alarm bells in your opponents' heads, knowing that any two hearts make a flush. If they hold top pair, two pair, or even a set, a third flush card might cause them to put on the breaks.

Straight draws aren't quite as obvious. When you hit one, you will likely gets lots of action from anyone holding an overpair, two pair, or a set. If you flop 10-9-6 to a hand like 7-8, an opponent holding a hand like 10-10 will go to war with you. You would need to have precisely 7-8 to have him beat, which wouldn't be the case with a flush board. If the board is 10-7-2 of hearts, that same player with a set of tens may be a little more cautious, realizing that any hand with two hearts has him beat.

Semi-Bluffing with Straight Draws

Again, if you bet when two hearts flop, your opponent might decide to put you on a flush draw. However, when you bet a straight draw on the flop, it's not quite as obvious. This actually gives you more semi-bluffing opportunities than you would have when betting flush draws.

Let's look at an example of a situation where you may decide to run a semi-bluff with a straight draw. You find 6-7 in the big blind. An early position player raises, and you call. The game is six-handed, and you know that your opponent would raise with any two cards 10 or higher, most ace-high hands, and any pair. (Later, in the shorthanded section, you'll learn why this is not a bad strategy.) The flop comes 4-5-9 rainbow, giving you an open-ended straight draw. This flop gives you an excellent opportunity to win this pot, whether you make a hand or not. You can play it several ways: bet out, check-raise, or check-call. Let's look at each option:

Betting Out. This play is acceptable but not exceptional. By leading out, you should be able to gather some information about your opponent's hand. If he folds, great! If he decides to call, it's unlikely—but not impossible—that he has a pair of nines or better. More often than not, he'll be trying to make a pair on the turn with a hand like K-J. If he calls, you should usually bet the turn no matter what card hits. If he raises you on the turn when you miss, it's time to make a straight on the river! If he raises you on the flop, you have to give him credit for having you beat; after all, you have 7-high! True he might be looking for a free card with A-K, but as long as an ace or a king doesn't hit the turn, you will most likely be the one getting the free card.

Check-Raising. This might be an even stronger play. Since your opponent came in raising, he'll usually keep the lead and bet the flop. By check-raising him, you are letting him know that you have a good hand and that you are going to fight for this pot. If he has a hand like A-J he'll probably take one off, but if he misses on the turn, you might be able to win it right there with a bet. In fact, depending on your opponent and his impression of you, you might even be able to force him off a hand like 7-7! Now that would be an excellent result.

Checking and Calling. If you choose this option, you give up any chance of winning the pot without improvement. You completely give up control of the hand. You may end up letting your opponent win the whole pot by default with J-10 high. Of course, if for some reason you think there is absolutely no chance you can win the pot by outplaying your opponent, checking and calling might be your best bet.

Gutshot Straight Draws

A gutshot straight draw is a real long shot. With one card to come, you are an 10.5 to 1 underdog to hit your straight. If you decide to call with a gutshot, be sure that the pot size is big enough and that all of your straight cards will win. If there are two hearts and two spades on the board in a five-way action pot, you may only have two outs to win the pot, as the other two straight cards may complete someone else's flush. That would make you a 22 to 1 underdog!

With one card to come on the turn, it's rarely correct to call with a pure gutshot, unless you have added outs, such as a pair or overcards. Since the bet size doesn't double until the turn, it will often be correct to call on the flop.

Let's look at a typical example: Playing $10/$20, you are in the big blind with 9-10 of clubs. The small blind folds, and you call a raise in a four-way action pot. The flop comes Q♠ 3♦ 8♥. You check, the first player bets, and one other calls. There is $105 in the pot, and it's $10 to call. It's 10.75 to 1 against you making the straight on the turn. Should you call? Based on the exact price you are getting at this point, the answer would be no. So we fold then, right? Wrong. There are three more variables you need to think about: implied odds, the potential to see two cards for the price of one, and extra outs—you may have more than you think.

Your implied odds in this situation are more than enough to call. You are already getting 10.5 to 1 as an 10.75 to 1 underdog. If you get just one more bet out of your opponents on the turn or river, you would be getting the right price. Also, the pre-flop raiser bet the flop, but who's to say you won't get a free card on the turn? There is also an outside chance that if you hit a pair of nines or tens you'd win. It's possible that the first raiser could have A-K and the caller A-8. Think about what might happen if your opponent flops a set and you hit that straight on the turn. Chances are, you'll win at least four more big bets on the turn and river, provided the board doesn't pair on the river. Any time you hit a pure gutshot it's going to be hidden. It's going to be difficult for your opponent to put you on a draw like that, so they'll often lose more bets than they should.

Let's say you are in a multiway pot and hold 6-4 of hearts in the big blind. The flop comes K♥ 7♠ 3♣, and the pot justifies a call. Now, off rolls the 5. Bingo! If one of your opponents have A-A, A-K, two pair, or a set, you should be able to win a lot of bets here. Remember, you pick up value with the implied odds.

Flopping a Made Hand

A **made hand** is a five-card hand, such as a straight, flush, full house, or better. There are times when you'll want to slow-play a made hand, and others where it might be correct to jam the pot. In this section, I hope to help you make better decisions when you flop a made hand.

Flopping a Full House

When you flop a full house your goal simply is to get as much money in the pot as possible. How you do that will depend on many factors.

Let's look at an example: You have pocket kings and the flop comes K-8-8. How nice! So you must decide whether to play it fast or let long shot draws in cheaply. Your decision should be based on what you think your opponents have. If you think one of your opponents flopped three eights, you should play it fast. Hopefully, your opponent will think you have A-A or A-K and continue to raise you.

So how will you be able to figure out if one of your opponents has an 8? Well, that will depend on several bits of information you've gathered pre-flop and on the flop. Let's say you bet and are raised on this flop, knowing no flush draw is possible. Then the big blind decides to call two bets cold. Chances are, he's flopped three eights. What else could he have? Unless it's a very bad player, he at least has the case king, but more likely three eights. It's also possible that he's flopped quads, but that would be a rare occurrence.

If there is a flush draw on the flop, then slow-playing would be silly. Your opponent with the flush draw isn't going to fold anyway, so you might as well make him pay to draw dead! After all, if he misses his flush, you aren't going to get any more bets on the river. Put those bets in on the flop; your opponent won't put you on a full house. If you know the player on a flush draw to be extremely conservative and won't draw to the flush with a pair on the board, you may not want to go too crazy on the flop. He is drawing dead, and you always want to encourage that!

Flopping a Full House, Heads-Up. In a heads-up pot, it's more than likely that your opponent has flopped nothing to the K-8-8 flop. Unless he has an 8, A-A, A-K, or a flush draw, it will be difficult to get much action. The best course of action here may be to slow-play your hand a little bit. Let's say you have position on your opponent, and he decides to bet out. This is a tricky situation because you don't want to lose him. If you raise here, he might throw away his hand. If you call, he might just check and fold on the turn. All you need to be concerned with is keeping your opponent interested in this pot. Hopefully he's flopped trips, a flush draw, or has the A-A or A-K hand. If not, hopefully he makes a smaller full house on the turn. Maybe he has 9-9. How sweet a 9 would be on the turn!

Again, you need to pay attention to the information you received pre-flop. Did your opponent raise coming in? Was he in early position? If so, the chances that he's flopped three eights is remote, though A-K, A-A, or another pair is very possible. Against one of these hands, it's usually a good idea to jam the flop as you are sure to get action. If your opponent calls from late position or from the blinds, you'll be hoping now that he's flopped three eights or maybe a flush draw. More often than not, your opponent is going to miss this flop. It's unlikely he has the case king and also unlikely that he has an 8. In this situation, it might also be correct to slow-play your hand and hope that your opponent picks up a draw on the turn. You can do that only if you feel that your check on the flop won't give away your hand. The tougher your opponent, the less often the check on the flop is going to trap him. To trap a tough player here, play straightforward and bet the flop.

Flopping a Flush

We touched on this subject a little when we discussed playing flush draws on the flop. In that section, we talked about playing a baby flush carefully on the flop and getting aggressive on the turn. Interestingly enough, we probably want to play our nut flushes similarly, waiting until the turn before getting busy.

Of course, this all depends on the texture of the flop. If you hold A♥ 8♥ on a K♥ 7♥ 2♥ flop, the only real draw out there would be the nut flush draw—but you already have that covered. Chances are you will get more action if the flop comes 10♥ J♥ 7♥. More of your opponents are going to hit this flop with a pair, two pair, a straight, or even a straight draw. If your opponent has a hand like K♥ J♣, he may decide to play it really fast on the flop. With that first flop you want anyone interested in the pot to stay in, so make it cheap on them. On that second flop however, you will get away with jamming it because the chances of your opponents continuing anyway are much greater.

Flopping a Straight

When flopping a straight you need to consider the risks involved. For example, say you've flopped a straight, but there are two flush cards on the board, or you've flopped the bottom end of the straight, and so on. When you flop a lower-end straight, it's important to try and knock out higher straight draws or at least have them pay the maximum if they choose to call. Or, if you put your opponent on a flush draw, you should play any straight fast on the flop. You aren't playing your hand fast only to try to knock a flush draw out of the pot, but rather to get more money into the pot as the favorite.

For this reason, I rarely slow-play a straight on the flop. There are too many cards on the turn that could hurt your hand. A board pair, a flush card, or even a higher straight card can turn your nut hand into a loser. Of course, in heads-up situations, I may choose to slow-play a straight on the flop, hoping to get two bets in on the turn. Say you hit a flop of 6-7-8 to go with your 9-10 in the hole. It's a great situation, but a 9 or a 10 puts your hand in jeopardy. The 9 fills the J-10 straight and the 10 fills the J-9 straight. Be aggressive on the flop, but if a dangerous card comes off on the turn, don't put in unnecessary action. I'm not saying that you should fold, but if you get raised on a 6-7-8-9 board, you shouldn't always reraise. Chances are, your opponent also has a 10-high straight, but it could be worse than that for you. He may have the J-10, or even a 10 with a flush draw giving him a freeroll. Or, if he has Q-10 and a jack hits the river, he'll have a freeroll against you.

Here's a final example of when you should play a straight fast on the flop: You have Q-J, and the flop comes 8-9-10. This is a flop that will hit a lot of people. Of course, none of your opponents can hit it better than you have, but that won't stop them from putting in lots of bets. You might win a monster pot if all goes well on the turn and river. If you are up against any of the following hands you should win tons of bets by keeping your foot on the gas and firing away: 6-7, 10-10, 9-9, 8-8, J-J, Q-Q, K-K, A-A, 10-J, 10-Q, K-Q, K-J, A-J, 9-10, 9-8, 10-8, and similar holdings. Of the sixteen hands I mentioned, most of them would be played only by average players—and I didn't even get to the hands where an opponent flops a flush draw! When you flop a monster on what I call an action flop, it will often pay big dividends. Of course you will sometimes be outdrawn on these hands, but you'll do yourself a great service in the long run by putting in as many bets as possible on the flop.

PLAYING THE TURN

The turn is probably the most difficult street to play. This is where you will need all of your poker skills to make the right decisions. As Daniel Negreanu wrote in one of his *Card Player* columns, "By the turn, you should have enough information about your opponents' hands to narrow down their holdings some. After factoring in their pre-flop action, their play on the flop, and the texture of the board, the turn is the street where you'll need to make the key decision as to what your opponents are holding." A big reason for this is that the bets now double.

When To Call

In many cases, calling on the turn is your best course of action. Let's look at four situations.

1. Against a Bluffer

Normally when you feel like there is a good chance you have the best hand on the turn, you should put in as many bets as possible. However, against a habitual bluffer, your raise may scare him off, costing you a bet on the river. Let's say you raise with A-10, and only Mr. Bluffer in the big blind calls. The flop comes A♠ 9♦ 4♠, Mr. Bluffer bets, and you decide to call. The turn brings the 7♥ and Mr. Bluffer again bets out. Chances are that your pair of aces with a 10 kicker is the best hand. However, it is possible that Mr. Bluffer woke up with a hand and has you beat. Regardless, you are convinced you have the best hand, but you know that Mr. Bluffer will fold if you raise. Since there isn't much of a draw present, why not just call the turn and hope that Mr. Bluffer wastes one more bet with a desperation attempt at the river? This helps you in two ways:

(1) You'll lose the minimum when he has you beat.

(2) You'll gain an extra bet when he tries to pick it up on the river.

In this case you run the risk of possibly giving your opponent a free shot to beat you on the end, but since it's a remote possibility with this board, calling will get the most out of him.

2. When Out of Position with Marginal Hands

In this example, you raise with 9-9 from late position. The button reraises you, so it's heads-up to see the flop. The flop comes down Q♥ 7♣ 2♥. You check, and your opponent bets the flop. Check-raising is an option here, but for this example let's assume you checked and called. Now the turn brings a 5♣. This presents you with a dilemma.

Since you raised in late position, and it was the button that reraised you, he might hold one of a wide range of hands that have you beat, as well as one of many others that don't. Let's assume that the button is the type of player who will raise you with any pair, any suited ace, any two picture cards, and any A-8 and above. Also throw in the occasional variation raise with hands like 8-9 suited or even 5-6 suited. If you know your opponent will three-bet you with these types of hands, your hand is just too good to fold. At the same time, you don't really want to lose any unnecessary extra bets.

In this situation, you are better off playing the hand to the river as cheaply as possible. You don't want to go crazy and put in a lot of action. Remember, you are out of position and could get moved off the best hand here. What if your opponent had A-K of hearts and decided to reraise you as a semi-bluff? Well, you can't really justify putting in three bets on the turn and then another one on the river when you are likely drawing dead to two outs! Play the hand carefully. Win the small pots while avoiding the big ones. Sacrifice some potential value and lean toward caution; that way you won't get outplayed.

3. To Avoid Costly Fancy Plays

Throughout this chapter you'll notice that I preach straightforward play. Why use a fancy play that might work when a straightforward play will do just as well? To be specific, raising on the turn with drawing hands in an attempt to force your opponent to lay down the best hand is a play that should be used infrequently. It works best on timid, careful players, but even they won't fold if they have top pair or better. Instead, they'll call you down on the turn and again on the river. After all, by raising the turn you've made the pot so big that your opponent is almost forced to call. Maybe years ago you could use this play more often, but these days many players are aware of it. So if there is a draw present, they'll likely call, hoping you are making a move. Don't bluff—value bet. That's what limit hold'em is all about.

4. When Drawing To Hands in Multiway Pots

The last thing you want to do when on a draw is narrow down the field. The more players in the pot the better. Attempting a long shot raise in hopes of bluffing everybody out is just a bad play. It's not going to work nearly often enough to make it profitable.

When To Raise

Raising the turn in marginal situations can be an expensive play, but it's one you'll need to make more often if you are playing in higher limit games. Before you go raising up a storm, consider the following four situations where this play is most effective.

1. To Maximize Your Profit

You should only make this play when you feel you have the best hand. Your goal isn't to drive your opponent out of the pot, although that wouldn't always be a bad thing; rather, you are simply trying to get maximum value for your hand. Let's look at an example.

In the middle position with K-K, you raise, and only the big blind calls. On a J♠ 7♣ 3♦ flop, the big blind check-raises you. Reraising on the flop wouldn't be a bad play, but what about just calling? By simply calling on the flop, you will entice your opponent to bet the turn unless a scare card hits. When he does bet the turn, you can go ahead and raise him.

This would be considered a variation play. You should only use it on a relatively safe flop. If there is a flush draw or straight draw present, there are too many potential scare cards out there that would cause your opponent to check the turn, thus costing you a bet. For example, on a flop like 9♥ 10♥ 5♠, any heart or any overcard may scare your opponent into checking. So on a dangerous flop, you're better off playing the K-K fast.

2. Semi-Bluffing on a Scare Card

Earlier, I advised you to avoid fancy plays when the straightforward play will work. That still holds true, but there are certain situations where a well-timed fancy play will win you the whole pot with little risk. Consider the following situation. You have J♥ 10♥ from early position. Although you'd often just call, this time you mix up your play and raise, and only the big blind calls you.

YOU   **FLOP**

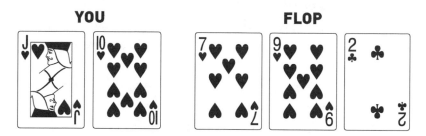

The flop comes 7♥ 9♥ 2♣. The big blind check-raises you on the flop, and you decide to just call. Now the turn card comes the K♠, and your opponent bets. If you don't think your opponent can beat a pair of kings, this wouldn't be a bad spot to try to take the pot from him. Since you raised from early position, you could easily be representing A-K. You are playing the J♥ 10♥ exactly as you would the A-K, and if your opponent believes you've got A-K, he may decide to fold a pair of nines. If not, oh well. You were going to call the turn anyway, so it only cost you one extra bet. If he does in fact have a pair of nines, you may have as many as twenty-one outs, including an 8 or queen for the straight, any heart, or possibly a jack or a 10!

There is one important thing to consider when making a play like this: What do you do on the river if he called your turn raise, and you have missed your hand? Betting here is not automatic. Unless you have reason to believe that your opponent was on a draw as well, I would recommend giving up at this point. If he called you on the turn with a pair, he's going to call you on the river as well. It's that simple. Of course, there is still a chance that you might win the pot with jack high in a showdown! Think about it: if your opponent was on a draw, maybe he has 8-10, 6-8, or even two baby hearts. If he has one of these hands you'll win the pot because of your turn raise.

3. Isolating Against a Possible Bluffer

This advanced play is exclusive to multiway pots, and I recommend you use it only if you have a solid feel for the game. In order for this play to work, you've got to have a good read on the turn bettor. You've got to know that he is a very aggressive player, and you also have to believe he is either bluffing or simply betting a draw. Let's use an example so that we can paint a clearer picture. You raise from middle position with the A-7 of spades, and the button calls as does the big blind.

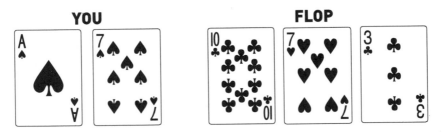

YOU   **FLOP**

The flop comes down 10♣ 7♥ 3♣. The big blind checks, you bet, and the button raises. Then the big blind calls, as do you. At this point you put the button on a pair of tens and the big blind on some kind of a draw.

The turn brings the Q♥. Out of nowhere, the big blind bets out. You still put him on a draw, maybe now a straight draw and flush draw. However, you know the player behind you has you beat. How about a raise? If you raise here, the button would be hard pressed to call two bets. So your raise would accomplish the following:

(1) Knock out the best hand.

(2) Get maximum value for your hand.

Again, this is an advanced play and depends heavily on your reading ability. Use it carefully.

4. When You Are Going To Call Anyway

On the turn, you are often going to find yourself in marginal situations where you think you have the best hand and decide to just call your opponent down. Well, rather than simply calling your opponent on the turn and river, many times it might be profitable to put both of those bets in on the turn. Here's an illustration. You raise in late position with A-7 of clubs, and only the big blind calls you.

The flop comes K♣ 7♥ 3♥, your opponent check-raises you, and you decide to call. Now the turn brings the 9♦. With 8½ small bets already in the pot, you feel that you are being laid a good enough price to call—especially considering that you may still have outs and that your pair might be the best hand. So now you decide that you are going to call the turn and then be forced to call on the river whether or not you improve.

Here's an idea: raise! So many good things can come as a result. For one, you might force your opponent to fold the best hand. What would your opponent do, for example, if he's holding a hand like 8-8 or even K-2? Depending on your opponent, he might even lay down top pair here.

What I like most about this play is that it usually costs you no extra bets, but you can win an extra bet if you improve. Let's say your opponent calls your raise. Unless you catch an ace or a 7 you'll just check it down and hope it's good. When you improve, you get the opportunity to value bet the river.

There is a downside to this play, however, and that comes

when your opponent reraises you on the turn. If your opponent makes it three bets, he probably has a very strong hand. You can safely assume that your pair is no good and should fold your hand. You lose the opportunity to outdraw him.

When To Fold

Sometimes the turn card comes so bad for your hand that you'll have to fold. Other times you'll have picked up enough information before the turn that you can safely put your opponent on a better hand than yours.

1. Draws

This is a question of pot odds. When the pot isn't laying you the correct price to call, you'll have to fold. Here's an example. With 6-7 in the big blind, you find yourself in a three-way, unraised pot.

YOU   **FLOP**

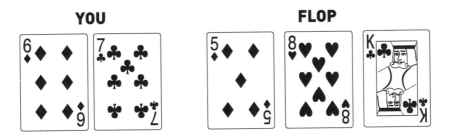

The flop comes 5-8-K, and it gets checked around. Now the turn brings a queen. Again you check, but this time the first player bets, and the second player raises. What do you do? The answer here is the result of a simple calculation. There are thirty-eight bad cards for you and only eight good ones, so the odds of you catching the straight are 4.75 to 1.

All you need to figure out now is whether or not the pot is giving you approximately 5 to 1 odds. In a $10/$20 game, there already would be $90 in the pot, and it will cost you $40 to call. The first player will probably call too, so let's make it $110 to $40.

Let's assume that you'll somehow win an additional three bets on the river, bringing the pot total to $170. Even after that, you are still only getting 4.25 to 1. In other words, this one is a fold.

2. When Potentially Drawing Dead

Situations like these are easier to identify in multiway pots. The more players in a pot, the more likely it is that the turn card helped someone. For example, if you flopped top pair in a multiway pot but the turn brought a third flush card, you should seriously consider folding. Folding will depend on your read of the player as well as the situation. If you are up against a wild player, don't be too quick in giving him credit for a made hand. Conversely, against a conservative ABC-type player in most situations, it should be an easy laydown to make.

There are other situations where you might even flop a flush draw, but then release it on the turn. Let's say you have the 5-6 of hearts and find yourself in a multiway pot with multiple bets in it. The flop comes K♥ J♥ 4♠, followed by the 9♦ on the turn. If there are four players in this pot, there is a very good chance someone has a bigger flush draw than yours, leaving you drawing dead. So, even if the pot is laying you the right price to draw to the flush, you'd still want to muck this hand if there is a reasonable chance that you are drawing dead.

3. When You Know You Are Beat

If after the flop you feel confident that you are beat, you should fold—unless of course you are getting the right pot odds to outdraw your opponent. Let's say with 7-7 you raise pre-flop and get two callers. The flop comes K-Q-4, so you bet and are raised. You call, hoping to see whether or not you can spike a 7 or that your opponent checks behind you with a draw. If the turn comes with a 9 and your opponent bets, you can safely fold the 7-7 . After all, what can you beat? Even if he was raising with a draw like 9-10, 9-J, or J-10, he now has you beat. Realistically you can only beat hands like A-4, A-J, and A-10. The odds here are stacked against you, so unless you have reason to believe your opponent is on a total bluff, this would be a good time to give up on the hand.

Aggression on the Turn

As you move up in limits, you'll notice that the better players are the ones who play ferociously on the turn, fearing nothing. In $10/$20, $15/$30, and $20/$40 games, many players tend to play passively on the turn, always fearing the worst—checking Q-Q when a king hits, checking when a straight card hits, and so on. In order to reach the elite levels of limit hold'em, you have to be a little fearless and keep the pressure on.

Let's look at a situation where you are faced with a choice: either give away a free card or risk being check-raised. You raise on the button with 7-8 of spades, and only big blind calls. The flop comes J♥ 8♣ 4♥. You bet the flop, and your opponent calls.

The turn brings the Q♦, and again your opponent checks. That Q♦ looks like a terrible card for your hand, and it very well could be. However, your opponent did check and call on the flop, and he has now checked the turn. Could he be setting a trap for you? Possibly. If in fact he is setting a trap, checking would certainly be the best play, as you would, in effect, be taking a free shot at a 7 or an 8.

But what if he's not setting a trap? If you check here you might be giving your opponent the free card he needs. If he's a typical player, he might have any of the following hands: A-K; A-10; ace anything, for that matter; K-10; a pair of fours with a random kicker; or even a gutshot straight draw, like 6-7 or 10-7. With your hand, it's important to bet here and knock one of these hands out—and you'll knockout the possibility of causing your opponent to fold if he's holding an 8 with a better kicker!

As a general rule in this situation, I would advise keeping the lead and staying aggressive. If you happen to get check-raised, so be it. It's not the end of the world. You'll simply have to make an educated decision as to what your opponent has and proceed accordingly. Don't be afraid to force yourself to make these types of plays. Making decisions like these will help you become a better player.

Semi-Bluffing the Turn

In situations where you've decided to check and call the turn anyway, you might be better off betting. Remember, taking the lead and being aggressive are probably the most important factors in limit hold'em.

For example, say a fairly tight early position player raises your blind and you decide to defend with the A-7 of spades. The flop comes 6♣ 7♦ 8♠. Rather than go for a check-raise, you decide to bet and see where you are. Unfortunately, this tight player decides to raise you, which means you can safely assume that you are beat. Of course, with a backdoor flush draw, trip draw, and two-pair draw, you are going to call one more bet.

Now the turn brings the 4♠. How about betting again? After all, you now picked up a flush draw and are going to call anyway, so why not represent the straight and possibly force your opponent off the best hand? It's highly unlikely that your opponent will raise you here, as he would need to have at least a 5, or maybe even 9-10. Since you know him to be a tight player, chances are he has an overpair or possibly a set. If he does call, oh well. You still have lots of outs and would have called a bet anyway. If you miss on the river, you should probably abort the bluff. If he decides to call you on the turn, he is going to make one last desperation call on the river if he has you beat. Save your money and check it down.

THE RIVER

Not a lot needs to be written about the river. At this point, the pot is usually large enough that making decisions is easy. If you have a legitimate chance to win the pot, you should call. Generally speaking, when in doubt, check or call. There are other elements related to the river that are worth mentioning: when to call or raise, when to fold, when to value bet, and when to bluff. Let's take a look at the choices.

Calling

In the world of poker, you hear a lot of talk about what separates the great players from the good ones. Some will say the difference lies in the great players' ability to lay down strong hands in difficult situations. While that may be true to some extent, trying too hard to play carefully on the river often leads to getting bluffed off of pots that were rightfully yours.

Often times, one bad decision can negate as many as ten great laydowns. Let's think about that for a minute. If there is $200 in a pot, and it will cost you $20 to see if you have the best hand, you better be almost 90 percent sure that folding is correct. Even if you were right to fold in eight out of ten situations, you've still lost money! Now I don't know about you, but to me that's a lot of pressure. I would advise you to avoid disastrous errors in favor of minor, less harmful ones.

Folding

Although I recommend calling if you have any chance to win the pot, there are times when you are so obviously beat that it would be silly to call. The majority of these situations arise in multiway pots. Here is an extreme example: Say you have bottom pair and a bet and three calls are on the table. Sure, the first player might be bluffing, but one of the three callers certainly has you beat. It doesn't matter how big the pot is here, you can safely assume that you are beat. Even when it is simply bet and raised to you, the safe move would be to fold any hand that could only beat a bluff. After all, even if the raiser is bluffing, the first player probably isn't.

Another key factor to consider is the price you'd have to pay to find out. Since you're faced with calling two bets instead of one, it cuts your pot odds in half. I could list several situations where you could make more sophisticated laydowns, but the one key factor is your ability to read your opponents. If you don't have an excellent understanding of your opponents' capabilities and tendencies, making monster laydowns is foolish. The more time you spend playing against any given player, the easier it will be to define his hand. If you get really good at it, you'll no longer have to make automatic calls on the river. As your skills improve you'll be able to pass up 10-1 pot odds because you'll trust yourself to be right 97 times out of 100. Until that time however, the best advice I can give you is: pay and see.

Value Betting

As we've said throughout the chapter, sheer aggression is key in limit hold'em. It is a mathematical game, one in which you want to maximize your wins while minimizing your losses. In order to maximize your wins, you'll need to be sure that you get full value for even the most marginal of hands. To value bet in the correct spots, it's important to think about what your opponent could have.

If you put your opponent on nothing but a draw, he simply won't call you on the river unless he makes it. Even then he probably won't just call you, he'll raise you! For example, say you hold A♣ J♣, and you take the lead the whole way. The turn comes J♥ 9♠ 6♥ 2♣. At this point, you are quite sure you have the best hand and think your opponent is on a flush or straight draw, or possibly a pair of nines or even jacks.

So now the river comes with the 9♦, and it's up to you. If

your opponent was on a draw, there is little value in betting here; he's obviously missed and will fold. If he also has a pair of jacks, there is a good chance he will bet when you check anyway. More importantly, if your opponent does have the three nines, he'll raise you, and that will usually cost you an extra bet. These are situations where you might want to avoid value betting.

Notice that in this example you are out of position. When you are in position, you will have at least twice as many opportunities to value bet than when out of position. If a player has checked the river to you, you should usually bet if you feel you have the best hand. Unless your opponent is setting a trap for you, his check on the river will mean it didn't help him. If you had the lead going into the river, chances are you still have it.

Basically, you should value bet any time you feel that your opponent will call with the worst hand more than half the time on the river. If you have bottom pair but feel your opponent would call you with ace-high, you should bet. Furthermore, if you feel your opponent is calling you down with ace-high, you might even bet with as little as A-K high! That situation is rare, but not unheard of. In closing, don't be overly worried about a check-raise. It's not like no-limit, where a check-raise could cost you your whole bankroll. In limit poker, it's only going to cost you another bet. You should be able to make up for a lost bet or two by picking up your fair share of value bets on the river.

Bluffing

Bluffing on the river is less effective than bluffing on the turn. Usually when your opponents get to the river, they are going to throw in that last bet if they have any chance of winning. As you've learned in this chapter, that's not exactly a bad strategy.

However, the pay-off for a bluff on the river that does work is tremendous, but in order for one to work, it has to be set up before the river. Simply calling all the way to the river and betting when an innocuous 2♣ hits won't get the money. River bluffs will work only if you had the lead going into the river, or a significant scare card hits that you can represent.

For example, say you are holding J-9, the board reads Q♥ 10♥ 2♣ 3♠, so you are drawing at an open-ended straight. You check-call on the turn and put your opponent on at least a pair. Now the river comes the A♥. That is the scare card of all scare cards. If your opponent held Q-J, he now couldn't beat any flush, any ace, or K-J. Since you played the hand like a draw, your opponent might think he can't beat anything, and fold his hand. Now remember, this play doesn't have to be successful too often in order to be profitable. If there is $200 in the pot, your $20 bet has to win the pot only one out of eleven times to break even. When it doesn't work, oh well, chalk it up to your advertising budget.

Don't Bluff with A-K High

I often see players make last ditch efforts to win pots on the river, thinking, "I can't win if I check. This is the only way I can win." The problem with this logic is that this player can't win by betting either! A-K high is going to beat any busted draws. If that's what your opponent has, there is no reason to bet. If your opponent does in fact have a pair, he's simply not going to fold—not very often, anyway.

Here is an example of a big but common mistake. Player A has been betting at a board of 3♣ 2♣ 6♦ 3♠, and finally the Q♠ comes on the river. Player A decides to check, and Player B foolishly throws in a desperation bet with A-K high. Player A quickly calls, and player B is left cursing his bad luck as Player A shows him his pair. This bet is flat out silly. Most likely, Player A checked the river fearing the queen. He didn't want to get raised, but that doesn't mean he isn't calling with even a pair of deuces. Player B's best bet with the A-K would have been to check it down and hope that Player A gives up on his bluff.

Of course, there is an argument for value betting A-K high if you put your opponent on A-x high, but that is a rather advanced play. In order to value bet A-K on the river, you'd have to have tons of data on your opponent backing up your decision. It's important to clarify that if you made this play you would be value betting, not bluffing.

Setting Up Bluffs

Earlier I talked about how successful bluffs start before the river. In order for a bluff to work, it's important to play in accordance with the hand you are trying to represent. If you are going to bluff when a flush card hits the river, you better have played the hand like you would have if you'd the flush draw. You'll also want to pick the right target—not the guy with the unbluffable sign on his forehead. You should pick the one who prides himself on making masterful laydowns on the river.

If that's your opponent's strength, it can be turned into a weakness, and bluffing is the way to exploit it. If you haven't set up your opponent for a bluff along the way, it would be foolish to attempt it on the river. Even the laydown artist, lets call him "Mr. Genius," will call you if it looks too suspicious. So how is it done?

Let's look at an example. You hold the 5-6 of diamonds. Mr. Genius limped in early position, as do two other players from middle position, so you welcome the pot odds. Four of you take the flop of J♥ 3♥ 4♣, giving you an open-ended straight draw. Mr. Genius bets the flop, and you raise looking for a free card, while all the others fold. Now the turn brings the 8♦ for no help and Mr. Genius checks, as do you. At this point Mr. Genius feels a little silly. He now "knows" you have a flush draw and has given you a free card. The river brings the K♥. Mr. Genius decides to check. Here is your chance.

You've played the hand as you would have if you'd actually had the flush, and the river brought an overcard as well. Take a chance and bet it. Hopefully you'll hear Mr. Genius go on about how he was so unlucky this hand. "I had you beat until that card came, but I know you have the flush. Take it." Music to your ears! Whatever you do, don't show Mr. Genius your hand. Let him continue to think he is the master of poker. In fact, you can even take it one step further, saying, "Good laydown." No need to tell him the truth, that you are robbing him blind!

SHORTHANDED PLAY

A game played five-handed or less is generally considered shorthanded. When playing shorthanded, remember the two keys to success: aggression and isolation. Shorthanded poker is an aggressive battle for the antes. Since the price per hand is higher, you need to get in there and fight as well. If you sit back and wait, you will be giving up too much and get blinded to death. Raise and reraise with a playable hand, taking the lead and pushing small edges. In the blinds, understand that you are getting excellent pot odds, and there is no reason to worry about being dominated.

Shorthanded, your goal is to isolate a lone opponent and fight for what's in the middle. Since winning the pot uncontested or getting the hand heads-up with position are both favorable situations, it makes sense that you want to raise with any hand you are going to play.

As Bobby Baldwin wrote in the original *Super/System*, when it comes to limit hold'em, "All hands worth playing are now worth raising." Limit hold'em, especially shorthanded, is all about taking the lead and being the aggressor. By doing this, you will force your opponent to hit flops. When your opponent misses, your aggressive pre-flop play will often win you the pot regardless of what your holecards are.

Let's look at an example of how this works. Say a player

opens for a raise and you find J♣ 10♣ on the button. Rather than simply call the raise, why not reraise? That will help you get the hand heads-up with position and will also give you the lead—both good things, by the way. Now the flop comes 6♦ 7♣ Q♥. Your opponent checks to you, and you bet. Unless your opponent started with a premium hand or hit the flop, he often will throw his hand away right there.

One important thing to understand when playing shorthanded, is that you are paying more in blinds per hand dealt. For example, in a ten-handed $20/$40 game you are paying $30 to see ten hands, or $3 a hand. Compare that to a five-handed game where you are paying that same $30 to see five hands, or $6 a hand. Knowing this, you can see why you simply can't wait for premium hands all the time. If you do, you'll get eaten up by the blinds. With fewer players at the table, high pairs, ace-anything, big cards, and small pairs all go up in value. At the same time, small suited connectors lose some value since you won't be getting multiway action, and these hands hold up rather poorly in aggressive shorthanded games.

Small Pairs

While small pairs often do well in multiway pots, they also do quite well shorthanded, especially with position. For example, if you are facing a late position raise with 5-5 on the button, reraising would likely have positive value. Unless your opponent is already paired, you have a slight edge with the best hand, position, and the lead. As long as your opponent misses the flop, chances are you will win it either on the flop or with another bet on the turn. This play doesn't even need to work 50 percent of the time for it to be profitable since there often will be added dead money in the pot, like the blinds.

Kickers

In hold'em, you'll often find yourself with kicker trouble when holding hands like A-7, K-8, Q-10, and so on. In a typical ring game, an early position raiser dominates these hands. That's not necessarily the case shorthanded. For example, if you hold Q-J on a flop of Q-7-2 against an early position raiser in a ring game, there is a very real chance that you are up against A-A, K-K, Q-Q, A-Q, or even K-Q. That's simply not as realistic a threat shorthanded since your opponents will be raising with a much wider variety of hands. If they aren't, they simply aren't playing correctly and are playing far too tight.

When you flop a pair shorthanded, you should be going to the river more often than not—even if it's bottom pair! Let's look at another example. Say you have A-8 offsuit under the gun in a ten-handed game. What should you do? If you said fold, you'd be correct. How about the same question in a four-handed game? If you said fold again, you couldn't be more wrong. With only three players to act behind you, the chances of you running into kicker trouble are less, and the possibility that you have the best hand is greater. If an ace flops, that makes it even less likely that you are up against an ace with a better kicker.

Suited Connectors

The problem with hands like 6-7 suited is that if you don't improve your hand, you have virtually no chance of winning the pot in a showdown. The way limit hold'em is being played today, having a hand that can win in a showdown is even more valuable. You can blame some of that on internet poker. Since players can't pick up physical tells while playing poker online, they tend to call more often when there is a reasonable chance that you are bluffing, hoping their small pair or ace-high will pick off a bluff. Despite that, you shouldn't completely rule out playing suited connectors. Remember, you need to play more hands shorthanded anyway.

I'm not suggesting that you avoid playing these hands, just that you play them for different reasons. For example, in a shorthanded game, you don't really want to limp into a five-handed pot with the 6-7 of hearts. You can still play it, but if you do, raise it! Take the lead and try to represent a big hand on the flop whether you hit the flop or not. If you meet with some resistance, it's time to abort the mission and simply give up on the bluff before it's too late.

Blind Defense

By now, you should be able to guess that I advise defending your blinds fiercely when playing shorthanded. Don't be paranoid, fearing premium hands all the time. Shorthanded, your opponents will be raising will all kinds of junk, and there is no reason to think they have a great hand just because they raised.

For instance, say in a ten-handed game, you hold A-7 offsuit. The first player raises and all fold to you. Should you call, fold, or reraise? If you said fold, you're correct.

Same hand, same situation—only this time the raise came from the button in a three-handed game. Would folding still be correct? Of course not. In this situation you should lean toward reraising and sometimes just calling to mix up your play. A-7 simply figures to be better than the initial raiser's starting hand, and you want to reraise to take control of the hand. It's a decent hand that can win without improvement, but more often than not you would be happy to win it on the flop with a bet.

HEADS-UP PLAY

To some degree, you can throw the rulebooks out the window when playing heads-up. Now, anything goes; it is psychological warfare in its purest form. Your goal is to seek out your opponent's weaknesses and figure out a way to exploit them. How you do that depends on what those weaknesses are.

Pre-Flop Play

When playing heads-up, the button acts first before the flop but last on the remaining betting rounds. The button has the small blind, while the other player has the big blind. As we've stressed throughout this chapter, position is of paramount importance in Texas hold'em but especially when playing heads-up. This makes virtually any hand playable on the button. In fact, if you were to watch two world-class players play heads-up, you'd soon notice that both players see a large percentage of the flops!

The flop is usually raised by the button and either called or reraised by the big blind. The button raises because of his powerful position, and the big blind usually calls or reraises based on the merit of his holecards—unless he is holding one of the rare hands he folds.

If you decide to play on the button, which I suggest you do with over 75 percent of the hands dealt, you should come in for a raise. Limping in to mix it up is fine, but you can't go wrong with a raise. As the big blind, it's important that you respect your positional disadvantage. You should still defend your blind most of the time, but you don't want to get too carried away and end up overplaying your hand before the flop. When the button raises, you will be getting 3 to 1 on your money to call a bet. The button is two bets, plus the one you already have in the big blind. That's simply too good a price to pass up with most any hand you are dealt. Even J-6 offsuit is worth a call here.

Post-Flop Play

One thing we know for sure is that you will miss the flop more often than you will hit it. When you do hit a piece of the flop, it's usually correct to take the hand all the way to the river, depending on the action and the cards that come off on the turn and river. For example, say the button raises and you call the raise with K-6. The flop comes Q-8-6, giving you bottom pair and an overcard. You should never throw this hand away on the flop. It's very probable that you have the best hand, and even if you don't, you have five outs to win the pot, namely three kings and two sixes. In fact, if you flop this hand you should probably bet right out or go for the check-raise on the flop. Depending on your opponent, you may even decide to simply check and call on the flop, but that could potentially give your opponent the free card he needs to beat you. The best play here would be check-raising, followed closely by betting right out, and lastly check-calling. Folding is not an option. If you are waiting to flop better than that, you simply aren't going to beat anybody playing heads-up.

Playing Against a Passive Player

I could easily substitute bad or weak player for passive player in this section's title. A passive player is your ideal opponent heads-up. Against a player like this, you should be able to take full control and win all the pots where both you and your opponent miss the flop. The player who wins the majority of these pots is generally the player that will get the money in the end.

If your opponent is folding too many hands pre-flop, you should be raising on the button 100 percent of the time—even with 7-2! Think about it, if your opponent isn't defending his blind with 10-6, K-2, 8-5, etc., raising with any hand on the button is probably enough to ensure a win. A pre-flop raise followed up by a position bet will force your opponent to either hit the flop or try to make a play at the pot. And who's to say that you can't hit the flop? Describing a player as passive in heads-up play is a more polite way of saying that he can't win.

Playing Against an Aggressive Player

Well, if you have a choice between Mr. Passive and Mr. Aggressive, you might want to avoid Mr. Aggressive and pound on poor old Mr. Passive. However, if you do find yourself up against an aggressive player heads-up, there are some things you should keep in mind.

Defeating a passive player by playing aggressively works, so we should assume that the remedy for an aggressive player would be to play passively, right? Wrong. Against an aggressive player you'll simply have to fight fire with fire and attack him with an array of weapons, the most deadly being the check-raise.

When you know that your opponent will bet almost any flop, the best way to take advantage is to check-raise him out of position, then raise him in position. If you can call, raise. When you feel like you have the best of it, take the lead and try to put in the last bet on every street, getting full value for your hand.

Sitting back and waiting to trap your opponent with a big hand simply doesn't work in limit poker. This is a viable strategy in no-limit because you can trap a player for his whole stack, but in limit poker the best you can do is maybe win an extra bet or two. In the meantime, while you are waiting to trap him, he's just picked up more than three or four bets from you with nothing! Remember, the winner of a heads-up pot will generally be the player who plays better in marginal situations.

Limit hold'em is all about pound, pound, pound. No fear.

OMAHA EIGHT-OR-BETTER

Bobby Baldwin

As one of the all time greats in any form of hold'em, Bobby Baldwin was a logical choice to be my limit hold'em collaborator in the original *Super/System*. Knowing the rare insight he brings to all poker games he plays, I asked him to shift gears and write a section on Omaha eight-or-better for *Super/System 2*.

Bobby, who serves as CEO of the Mirage Corporation and President of the multi-billion dollar Bellagio Hotel and Casino, told me he would do it on one condition. Due to the demands of his various positions, he asked to enlist the help of Mark Gregorich. I readily agreed, thinking that three heads are better than two and knowing Mark to be a top Omaha eight-or-better player. So Bobby supervised the writing and had the final word on the strategies you will find in the chapter.

Bobby left professional poker in 1978 after winning the World Series of Poker main event, and now he plays only in the ultra high stakes games. However, his analysis of Omaha eight-or-better can be used to win at any level of play. You are about to discover the powerful thought processes and poker strategies that put Bobby into the Poker Hall of Fame.

Special Acknowledgment To Mark Gregorich

This chapter could not have been completed without the special expertise and coordination of Mark Gregorich, who is regarded as one of the best Omaha high-low players in the world. In fact, in a 2001 *Card Player* magazine players poll conducted during the World Series of Poker, Mark was voted the #1 live action Omaha high-low player.

OMAHA EIGHT-OR-BETTER
by Bobby Baldwin

INTRODUCTION

Omaha eight-or-better is a newcomer on the poker scene. Discussion of the game wasn't even included in the original *Super/System*. It's hard to believe that a relatively new game could achieve such a loyal following so rapidly. However, it is now the game of choice for thousands of poker players in the United States and around the world. You can find games at virtually every level, from beginner tables to ultra high stakes games, in most major card rooms.

Probably the most significant reason for its popularity is its well-deserved reputation as an action game, because so many hands can be played before and after the flop. But there's a lot to learn before you hit the tables, so let's get to it!

BEGINNING OMAHA EIGHT-OR-BETTER

Before we begin a discussion of game strategy, here is a brief course in the rules of Omaha eight-or-better.

Betting
Like Texas hold'em, Omaha eight-or-better is a flop game. In fact, once the initial four downcards have been dealt, the play of the hand is identical to hold'em. The two players to the left of the dealer button post the small and large blinds. Action begins with the player to the left of the big blind who must call the amount of the big blind, raise, or fold. The action then continues around the

table to the big blind, who has last action before the flop.

After the flop, the player still in the hand who is seated closest to the left of the button acts first, as is the case with each successive round of betting. In most games with fixed limits, the pre-flop and flop bets are one size, and the turn and river bets are double that. For example, in a $2-$4 game, the first two rounds of betting must be in increments of $2 and the last two rounds in increments of $4. In $50/$100 games, the increments would be $50 and $100. The standard game features a maximum of one bet and three raises per round, although the majority of games in Las Vegas permit four raises.

When the Pot Is Split

Omaha eight-or-better is a **high-low split game**, which means the high and low hands each get half of the pot. There is always a high hand, which will receive some portion of the pot, but sometimes no low hand is possible because to make a low hand, a player must have five unpaired cards eight or below. For example, if the flop came K-J-9, it would be impossible for any player to make a hand of five unpaired cards eight or below. When there is no low, the high hand wins the whole pot. The best possible low is 5-4-3-2-A and is commonly referred to as a **wheel** or a **bicycle**.

Furthermore, in Omaha eight-or-better, straights and flushes don't count against a low hand. Thus, 6-4-3-2-A of hearts would be a 6-4 low, in addition to a flush for the high.

If two or more players hold the same high or low hand, they divide that half of the pot. Dividing half a pot in this way is called **quartering**. You will encounter this much more often on the low side of the pot.

You Must Play Two Cards from Your Hand

In hold'em a player is allowed to use one, both, or neither of the cards dealt to him in conjunction with the cards on board to make the best possible five-card hand. Omaha players, however, are forced to make their best five-card hand by using exactly two of their own cards and exactly three from the board—no more, no less. But many different combinations are possible.

You May Play Different Combinations for High and Low

In Omaha eight-or-better, you are allowed to make both your best high and your best low hand by combining two of your cards with three from the board. You may use different cards in each direction, or you can use a card for both your high hand and low hand. For example, suppose you have A♣ 2♦ 7♣ K♠ and the board is: 3♣ 4♣ 6♣ J♠ Q♦. In this case, you can use the A-7 of clubs for high (ace-high flush) and the A-2 for low (6-4-3-2-A).

Ranking of Low Hands

If you have played stud eight-or-better, ace-to-five lowball, or razz, you already know the ranking order of low hands in Omaha eight-or-better. The best possible hand is 5-4-3-2-A, and the worst qualifying low hand is 8-7-6-5-4. To determine whether or not you have your opponent beat, compare the hands in order of highest card to lowest card. Here is an example:

Your hand: 8-5-3-2-A.
Your opponent: 7-6-5-4-3.

Your 8 is worse than his 7, so your opponent wins this hand. It's also common for both players to share the board cards. For instance, with 8-5-4 on the board, one player is likely to edge out another by holding A-2 against A-3.

Hand Reading

All of these different possibilities can be quite confusing for new players and even experienced ones. It is not uncommon for even a winning high-limit player to misread his own hand in Omaha eight-or-better. If you are new to the game and unsure of what you're holding at the end of the hand, your best bet is to turn your hand over at the river and ask the dealer for assistance in reading it. With a bit of practice, though, reading your hand will become second nature.

Hand Reading Examples

The following are examples of some common situations that arise in Omaha eight-or-better—and some that are a little tricky. If you have trouble following some of them, try dealing out some sample hands and practice identifying each player's best high and low hands. Once you have sharpened your hand reading skills, you will be ready to move on to strategy.

Example One
Your hand: A-3-K-K
Opponent: 2-3-5-9
Board: 6-7-8-J-Q

This is a split pot, as your 8-7-6-3-A low edges out your opponent's 8-7-6-3-2, and his high hand, a 9-high straight, beats your pair of kings.

Example Two
Your hand: A-6-K-K
Opponent: A-4-8-8
Board: 2-3-4-5-J

With a wheel (5-4-3-2-A) for both high and low, your opponent scoops. You cannot make the nut low, because you must play both the ace and 6 in your hand, leaving you with only a 6-4-3-2-A for low. These cards don't stretch to make a straight, either, so you're stuck with just a pair of kings for high.

This may seem confusing, particularly if hold'em has been your primary game. If this were hold'em, you could play the ace to make a wheel, and the 6 to make a 6-high straight. But in Omaha eight-or-better, you must always play exactly two cards from your hand and exactly three from the board.

Example Three

Your hand:	A-3-5-6
Opponent:	3-4-J-J
Board:	A-2-3-4-5

You wind up with three quarters of this pot. The low side is split, as your opponent plays his 3-4 with the A-2-5 on the board, and you can play any combination of A-3, A-5, or 3-5 to make the nuts, the best hand. However, you can use your 6 and either your 3 or 5 to make a 6-high straight, which wins the high half of the pot.

Example Four

Your hand:	A-A-4-7
Opponent:	2-5-5-7
Board:	2-4-6-7-8

Another split pot. Your opponent wins the high with an 8-high straight, beating your two-pair hand of sevens and fours. However, your 7-6-4-2-A low is good enough to beat his 7-6-5-4-2. The low hand is somewhat tricky to read, as both players have low cards matched by the board. A low can still be made, provided some combination of five cards can be played without a pair. In Omaha jargon, you have a "live ace" for low.

Example Five

Your hand: A-A-4-7
Opponent: 2-5-6-K
Board: 2-4-7-8-9

This time, your opponent wins the whole pot. His 9-high straight beats your two pair, and his low is good as well. You must play an 8-7-4-2-A low, but your opponent can play a 7-6-5-4-2.

Example Six

Your hand: A-3-J-J
Opponent: 4-4-8-Q
Board: 3-9-10-J-Q

This hand is likely to send you shuffling off to the dice tables shaking your head. You have a set of jacks, but lose to a queen-high straight. Note that you also have a trey in your hand matching the trey on board, but you cannot make a full house, as this would require three cards from your hand. It is impossible in Omaha, as it is in hold'em, to hold a full house when there is no pair on the board.

Example Seven

Your hand: A♥ 2♣ 8♣ 10♦
Opponent: 3-4-5-8
Board: 6-7-9-J-K (four hearts)

You win this pot, but not with a flush. You must hold two hearts in order to make a flush, so the ace by itself is meaningless. However, the 10-8 in your hand produces a jack-high straight, barely edging your opponent's 9-high straight. No low is possible here.

Example Eight

Your hand:	A-2-4-J
Opponent:	4-5-7-7
Board:	3-3-7-J-J

You take another tough loss on this hand. Again, no low is possible, and the best you can do for a high is play the A-J from your hand with J-J-7 from the board, giving you trip jacks with an ace kicker. Be careful not to think you have a full house. It could turn out to be an expensive mistake. Playing his 7-7 with the 7-J-J on the board, your opponent does make a full house, with sevens full of jacks. Note that if you held A-2-3-J rather than A-2-4-J, you would have won the pot with a bigger full house.

Example Nine

Your hand:	2-3-3-Q
Opponent:	A-2-3-Q
Board:	8-8-8-8-9

So, you finally decide to take an inferior starting hand up against your opponent, and you emerge victorious. Do you see why? Since only three board cards can be used, you take 8-8-8 from the board and combine it with your pair of threes for a full house. The best hand your opponent can make, however, is 8-8-8-A-Q. By the way, any player holding two nines in his hand would have the nuts, as nines full of eights would beat all varieties of eights full. The second nuts? Two aces.

Example Ten

Your hand:	A-4-5-8
Opponent:	A-4-5-K
Board:	A-4-5-8-9

You win the entire pot. Your aces and eights nip your opponent's aces and fives. Neither one of you can make a low hand, as you must be able to play five unpaired cards. If there had been a low card on the board instead of the nine, both you and your opponent would be able to make some kind of low hand.

PRE-FLOP PLAY

Basic Pre-Flop Play

Starting Hand Fundamentals: An Overview

One of the great features of most loose lower limit Omaha eight-or-better games is that adhering to strict starting hand requirements will be enough to produce a profit. The reason for this is that in many of these games, six or more players see the flop, and in multiway pots, it takes a very strong hand—frequently the nut hand—to win. So knowing which starting hands are most likely to produce nut hands and strictly playing only these cards will give you a built-in advantage over your loose-playing opponents.

In a multiway hold'em pot, there are times when you should play a lesser holding, such as 7-6 suited, for example. Furthermore, in hold'em, hands such as A-K decrease in value as the number of players in the pot increases.

In Omaha eight-or-better, however, all hands are speculative, even more so than in hold'em. The more players contesting the pot, the more important it is that you hold a premium hand that can develop into the nuts.

While starting hand play can generate a profit in loose low-limit games, this will not be enough as you progress up the ladder. Nonetheless, being able to hold your own in a game during the learning process is a nice bonus. It makes for extremely cheap and potentially profitable lessons. As the limits get higher, it becomes more important that you have a mastery of all aspects of the game, as you will be facing more highly skilled opponents. But no matter how high or low the stakes, the players who have worked hardest to develop their games win the most money.

What To Look For in a Starting Hand

The Ace. It is of paramount importance that you remember this fact: Although Omaha eight-or-better is a split-pot game, the key to the game is winning the entire pot or **scooping**. With this in mind, you should select hands that stand a good chance of winning the whole pot. The key card is an ace, and few hands are playable without one. In fact, if you're just starting out, it's not a bad idea to routinely fold every hand without an ace in it. In doing so, you're not giving up much potential profit. A number of experienced players cling to the "Don't leave home without it" philosophy, and it serves them well.

Why are aces so significant? Not only are they required for the best low starting hands, they are also the highest card in the deck, providing the highest pair, two pair, three of a kind, flush, and straight hands. Why would you want to spot your opponents a card this powerful and versatile?

Middle Cards. If aces are at the top of the Omaha food chain, then middle cards are the lowest form of life. Hands dominated by middle cards—sevens, eights, and nines, and to a lesser extent fives, sixes, and tens—stand virtually no chance of scooping, unless there's no low hand.

Despite the fact that hands such as 6-7-8-9 produce many straights, the presence of these straights means that a low will be possible, and the pot is likely to be split. In order for no low to be possible, the board would have to contain three high cards. But that's trouble, too. For example, if the flop comes 10-J-Q, you have made your straight, but you could easily lose to a higher straight. Also, straights are vulnerable hands in Omaha, because any time a flush or full house is made possible by the board, it is quite likely that one of your opponents has one.

High Hands. Straight high hands such as 10-J-Q-K can win some nice pots when they connect perfectly with the board. However, these hands don't hit often, and sometimes the pot still gets chopped between you and an opponent with a low hand or the same high hand, typically a straight or two pair. Although this type of hand can be played at times, it is important to remember that it is a drawing hand that will usually miss and be folded on the flop.

So with high-only hands, you should look for certain situations, such as multiway pots, when you can get in for one bet and receive a good price on your investment. It's generally best to play this hand cheaply against a large number of opponents, in the hopes of winning a sizable pot should you connect with the flop.

Ace Companions. So if the best starting hands contain an ace, what cards make the best companions for the ace? Premium low cards are best, preferably a deuce, but ace-trey combinations are generally playable as well. The board will frequently pair either your ace, deuce, or trey, so having a third low card, 5 or below, is important as well. Before you go to war prior to the flop, make sure you have at least three cards to a wheel, including an ace and either a deuce or trey.

Since scooping is the goal, it's also important to have high-hand possibilities with your low cards. Two aces with a deuce or a trey hold two-way potential, as do suited cards. Obviously, it's best if your ace is suited, but even small suited combinations add to your chances of scooping the hand. Hands like A-2-3-9 unsuited are playable due to the presence of the three best low cards, but these types of hands will typically only win the low side. Moving down the ladder, low hands without an ace, such as 2-3-4-10, are only marginally playable, and hands such as 4-5-6-J are not playable at all.

Good Starting Hands

The following are a few examples of good Omaha eight-or-better starting hands:

A-A-2-x	A-A-3-x	A-A-4-5
A-2-3-x	A-2-4-K	A-2-5-6
A-3-4-5	A-K-Q-2	A-3-5-Q (double-suited)

Notice that all of the preceding hands contain at least one ace. Remember, if your hand doesn't contain an ace, there is one extra premium card that could be in the clutches of your opponents. In a full Omaha eight-or-better game, most of the deck is dealt, so you can expect most of the aces to be in your opponents' hands.

The Most Important Decision of the Hand

Of all the decisions made during the course of an Omaha eight-or-better hand, the choice of whether to initially play or fold is by far the most important. Seeing a flop with an inferior hand might seem like a relatively harmless decision, but it is a mistake that tends to lead to more costly mistakes.

Make this your Omaha eight-or-better mantra: Play only hands that have obvious potential of developing into the nuts.

A hold'em player might occasionally play an inferior hand or rags, but he will typically be hard pressed to continue after the flop. However, due to the four-card hands in Omaha eight-or-better, players seeing the flop with a raggy hand will frequently flop just enough of a draw to justify staying in—often incorrectly. As a result, instead of simply missing the flop and folding, a reckless player may find himself tied on until the river, chasing a draw that should not have been pursued.

Omaha eight-or-better is a perfect example of that old computer maxim GIGO: "Garbage In, Garbage Out." Starting with middle cards will produce lots of middle straights, which often either lose to better high hands or split with low hands. Starting with double-suited medium cards will produce flushes that often lose to bigger flushes. However, playing premium cards, such as suited aces with a deuce and/or a trey, allows you to make the nut low hand and gives you a chance to develop a high hand as well.

Remember your mantra about only playing possible nut hands. If you find yourself uncertain about whether a hand should be played or folded, it's generally best to fold. Being too creative with your starting hands is a liability in Omaha eight-or-better.

Raising Before the Flop

A common misconception is that it's wrong to raise before the flop. Many players—especially those that have played a lot of hold'em—feel that playing the flop is the key to the game and that only a minimal investment should be made prior to seeing the first three board cards. In hold'em, hands such as two aces are obvious raising hands, as they need not improve to win the pot. Omaha eight-or-better hands almost always need to improve to win, so many players consider this enough of a reason to avoid making a raise before the flop. Although flop play is crucial to success, there are numerous situations in which it is in fact correct to raise pre-flop. You will be making a mistake if you never raise before the flop in this game.

There are two reasons to raise a pot before the flop:

(1) To eliminate players and narrow the field;

(2) To build a bigger pot.

It is important to consider which of these effects your raise is likely to have. In the loose "no fold-em" games common at some of the lower limits, a raise might not narrow the field. If this is the case in your game, don't raise. This doesn't mean raising before the flop is incorrect in a no fold-em game; rather, a raise should be made only when you are looking to play a bigger pot against several opponents.

When is a raise likely to narrow the field? Typically, if the table is fairly tight or most of the players are trying to play decent starting hands, which tends to be the case as limits progress in size, raising will thin the crowd. The raise should be even more effective if no one has entered the pot yet. Also, if your opponents perceive you to be a tight, solid player, they may be less likely to call your raise. Poker games are almost always in a state of flux, so it's important to pay attention to how the game is playing. The addition or subtraction of just one player is often enough to dramatically alter the entire complexion of the game.

Hands that should be protected with a raise are those that fare best against fewer opponents. These include most hands with two aces, as two aces with any two other cards are a favorite against nearly all other hands in a one-on-one situation. Other hands that have both low and high potential, such as A-2-K-x, A-3-5-K, or A-2-Q-Q, play well against few opponents, although they also play fine multiway.

Holding an A-K combination frequently comes in handy in pots against only one or two opponents. When only a couple of players see the flop, the deck is often richer in aces than normal. This assumption is based on the tendency of Omaha eight-or-better players to play hands with an ace in them. If both you and your opponent are holding an ace and an ace flops, your king may wind up playing as a kicker, enabling you to win the high side of the pot with A-K. Also, you generally won't need as strong of a hand to win a heads-up pot, so flopping a king or kings up has definite value. Not unlike hold'em, the value of the A-K combination declines as more players contest the pot, since stronger hands—such as straights, flushes, or full houses—will typically be needed to win the high portion of the pot.

Great Omaha eight-or-better hands like A-2-3-4 can be raising hands before the flop as well, but for another reason. Raising in spots that are likely to produce a short field is a mistake with this sort of hand, due to its lack of high-hand potential. However, in a pot contested by several players, this hand is excellent. If a low hand is possible—and a low hand will be possible most of the time—you will most likely be holding the nuts. Due to this hand's high probability of making the nut low, go ahead and raise to build a big pot if several players have already entered the hand. Additionally, if your opponents seem to have no respect for raises, go ahead and raise regardless of your position. You should still get plenty of action.

Other good hands to raise with in multiway pots include A-A-2-x, A-2-3-x, and A-2-4-x, especially if your ace is suited. Being suited adds significant value to your high prospects, and nut flush cards play very well in multiway situations. It's okay to raise with just about any A-2 suited holding if several players are already in the pot. Your opponents will often make and overvalue smaller flushes. Even hands like A-3 suited are acceptable raising hands in very loose games, as you want to charge your opponents the maximum amount for playing inferior, low percentage hands.

Playing High-Only Hands

Properly playing hands with four big cards—by definition, nines or higher—is not an easy task in Omaha eight-or-better.

However, playing them selectively and skillfully will add to your profits.

By definition, a quality high-only hand contains four big cards, 9 or higher. Nines tend to taint the hand, as they will not stretch to form part of an ace-high straight. When a 9 is used as part of a straight, two problems exist:

(1) If a 9 helps make the nut straight, then either a low or a full house will be possible based on the board cards.

(2) If a 9 forms a straight with no possible low, then either a higher straight or a full house will be possible.

Hands such as K-K-J-8, Q-Q-6-7, and K-Q-J-3 are not playable in Omaha eight-or-better, as they contain too many uncoordinated cards. Think in terms of the number of decent combinations created by a hand, and it's easy to see why these hands belong in the muck.

There are, however, a number of good high-only hands. Here are some hands that are playable under many conditions:

K-Q-J-10	A-K-Q-10	Q-J-10-9
K-K-J-10	K-Q-Q-J	A-K-J-J
Q-Q-J-J		

In order to determine if it is correct to enter a pot with a hand comprised only of high cards, there are several variables to consider. On the positive side, high hands play best when you can play in an un-raised multiway pot, because you want to get a good price on your hand from the pot. In the case of straight-high hands, you will most likely miss the flop and be forced to fold. Therefore, if you can get in without much initial investment against several players, you are getting far better odds on your money than if you play against only one or two players for a raise. In some Omaha eight-or-better games, multiway unraised pots are the norm. If this is the case, calling with quality straight-high hands is acceptable from even the earliest positions.

However, in many games, it is difficult to foresee whether the pot will be raised or how many players will see the flop. If this is the situation, you need to use position to determine if a high-only hand is playable. In early position, you can't count on an unraised multiway pot, so you should fold.

In later positions, more information is available to you. If several opponents come in, then go ahead and play. If the pot will play out shorthanded, calling a raise with a straight-high hand is generally not a good strategy, but in a multiway situation, it is fine to play for more than one bet. Your hand will usually miss the flop (thus, too much is risked for too little reward in shorthanded raised pots), but when it connects, it will frequently make the nuts. This is often what it takes to scoop a multiway pot. High-only hands take down some big pots in Omaha eight-or-better and can be profitable if discretion is utilized when deciding whether to play them.

Although aggressive poker is winning poker, there aren't many situations in which raising with high-only hands before the flop is beneficial. In general, since you will fold on the flop a good percentage of the time, raising only hurts the price the pot is offering you. The hand has greater implied value if the flop can be seen cheaply.

When everyone has folded to you and you are in last position, it is tempting to raise the pot with four coordinated high cards. But this is usually incorrect. In a heads up situation, few Omaha eight-or-better starting hands have a significant advantage over any other. Thus, the blinds will be correct to call with marginal hands. There are some exceptions though, such as when the blinds play either very tight or poorly. If this is the case, then go ahead and raise.

One argument for raising with high-only hands in multiway pots is that with so many players in, most of the low cards are being used. This makes the deck rich in high cards. This perception is logical, but large fields often contain other players targeting the high-only end as well. This is assuming that the game is one in which players are entering pots with decent hands. Generally, in these types of situations the deck is actually rich in middle cards, as players have entered the pot with either high or low cards, or a mix of each.

If you're playing against observant opponents, though, it is important to raise occasionally with a high-only hand. Deception is the reason for raising, as it is important that your opponents not be able to read you like a book. In games with a great deal of turnover or those in which the players are inattentive, this play is unnecessary. However, if you consistently play with players who are familiar with you, it's necessary to mix up your style a bit. If your opponents know that you only raise with low cards, then they will figure out that they can bet you out of the pot if high cards come. You don't need to raise with high hands all that often in these games, but do it enough to make your raising hands less transparent.

Advanced Pre-Flop Play

The Situational Nature of Omaha Eight-or-Better

Hold'em and Omaha are such complex, situational games that basic pre-flop play concepts alone are not enough to make you a winner. No single strategy is adequate for every situation. To play optimally, you must develop a deeper understanding of the game, which will produce a more flexible strategy. Then you will have what it takes to make accurate decisions at the table. Over time, accurate decisions will translate into profits. This section highlights some of the key factors you should consider when deciding how to proceed with a hand before the flop.

Loose Games vs. Tight Games

It is important that you have a good grasp of the style of the game you're playing. Whether the game is mostly loose (with five or more players typically seeing the flop), or tight (three or fewer), should have a significant impact on your hand selection. In loose games, hands going high-only or low-only increase in value. With low hands such as A-2-3-8, scooping against any number of opponents will be a difficult task, although getting half the pot is very likely when a low comes. Since winning half is the most likely positive outcome, it stands to reason that the more players in the pot, the more money you should win with this hand.

If your ace is suited, there is real potential for making the best high hand, too. Again, this is not dependent on the number of opponents in the pot. If you make the nut flush with this hand, you will almost always win the high whether you have one or seven opponents, providing the board is not paired. Therefore, it is best to play this type of hand in a manner that won't shut out other players before the flop.

When you are playing in a tight game, hands including two aces and virtually any other two cards become hands to push pre-flop, since raising with them will likely narrow the field to one or two opponents. By definition, tight games are those in which opponents are playing only very good starting hands, namely those with an ace. Since you are holding two of the aces, it is unlikely that many opponents will call your raise.

Passive Games vs. Aggressive Games

Another important distinction to make is whether the game is primarily passive or aggressive. Passive games are those in which there is very little raising before the flop, and not much later in the hand either. An advantage of playing hands in late position is that you generally have a better idea of how much it will cost to see the flop, but this particular benefit becomes relatively unimportant in passive games. As a result, more decent hands are playable from early position in these games.

The reverse is true in extremely aggressive games, as the price of seeing a flop is often two, three, or more bets. Since the pots will be large, it is best to play hands that are highly likely to develop some sort of draw on the flop, allowing you to remain in the hand. In these games the value of one-dimensional hands decreases, as they generally miss the flop.

Although hands that can swing both high and low are always desirable, the importance of holding versatile cards is magnified when the pot is jammed before the flop. The more likely you are to flop a draw of some sort, the better prepared you are to play a pot for several bets. Some examples of hands that are versatile enough to play very well in games with lots of pre-flop raising, whether the game is tight-aggressive or loose-aggressive, include A-2-3-K, A-2-5-K, A-2-3-J, A-A-3-5, A-3-4-Q, and A-K-Q-2.

Pay Attention To Who Is in the Pot

Although it is frequently correct to raise with hands containing an A-2 or A-3, it is important to notice the quality of your opposition. If one or two solid players have already entered a pot and you decide to put in a raise with A-3-8-10 offsuit, your Omaha license should be revoked. Do you feel your hand is better than their hands? Most likely, they have low cards—and prettier versions than yours.

Being aware of when tight players are in a hand is important in deciding how to play low cards. In a game in which six loose players have limped in, raising with any suited A-2 or A-3 is an acceptable play. However, with some solid players already in the hand, it is probably best to raise only with premium hands, including A-2-3-x suited, A-2-4-6 suited, or A-2-4-K suited. This is another advantage of late position, as it is possible to get a read on what types of hands are likely to be out.

Knowledge acquired from observation of your opponents' raising standards is a valuable tool in playing effective poker. This includes understanding how their position and other factors, such as how they are doing in the game, will affect their standards. For example, if an extremely tight player raises, it is frequently correct to fold most A-3 hands, if the rest of the hand lacks quality—probably because it includes a 7, 8, or 9.

Your decision to raise, call, or fold before the flop can also be affected by the skill level of the players in the blinds, particularly the big blind. If the blinds are tight, solid players, it may be worthwhile to raise in late position before the flop with a hand that might only appear to have calling strength. These players are unlikely to give you any action after the flop unless they have you beat, so why give them a free opportunity to outdraw you? The more potential your hand has to swing both high and low, the better it is to make the raise.

On the other hand, players who play poorly after the flop are desirable opponents. Many Omaha eight-or-better players make the mistake of trapping themselves when they're in the blinds. They might be holding a hand that they wouldn't have called one bet with, but now have decided to chase some type of long-shot after getting a free peek at the flop. If the blinds are players prone to chasing middle straights or small flushes, then it may be best to just call and leave them in the pot. Against these players, the extra bets you are likely to win in the long run are justification for playing your hand in this manner.

Playing Two Aces Before the Flop

Hands with a pair of aces in them are so frequently misplayed that some additional discussion is warranted. First, it should be noted that hands containing two aces are not always playable, and the value of the hand is hugely dependent upon the number of players in the pot. Against one or two opponents, the strength of the two aces alone will frequently win the high side of the pot.

When several players are in, however, you will need to improve to win. This improvement will often come in the form of a low or a flush, so having low cards or being suited will add value to the aces in a multiway situation.

Hands with two aces and little else should generally be thrown away if several players have already entered the pot. Some examples of these trashy aces hands include: A-A-7-J, A-A-6-9, and A-A-8-K. If you are first in with this type of hand from early position, folding is probably the best option, unless the game is extremely tight. In this case, a raise will likely narrow the field enough that the aces will have a good chance of winning on their own strength.

Hands with double-suited aces, even those without other quality cards, always have enough high potential to justify seeing the flop. Playing this hand for one bet in most cases, rather than putting in a raise, is probably the best approach for three reasons:

> **(1)** If the hand does hit, it will likely make a nut hand. Thus, the more opponents in the pot, the more money you will win. Raising before the flop might knock out a hand that would have paid off your nut flush.

> **(2)** When the hand misses the flop, as it often will, the pot is small and you can easily fold.

> **(3)** Finally, you add a degree of deception to the hand, as two aces are perceived by many to be a raising hand. Should you make a full house, you may get unwarranted action from opponents who misread your hand.

If your hand features two aces and marginal side cards, you might sometimes prefer to play them for three bets before the flop instead of two. By putting in the second raise, you make it likely that the pot will be heads-up. This play might not work in some of the loosest Omaha eight-or-better games, but it should be effective in situations where players have at least a little respect for money. When a player to your right has opened for a raise, you can make it three bets with hands like A-A-6-8, hoping to make it heads-up. If it works, you will be in a good situation, holding both the best hand and position. Even fairly loose players will tighten up a bit when faced with calling two raises cold.

However, in the same game, if you are first to act with the same A-A-6-8, it is normally better to fold than open for two bets, because it's much easier for other players to call one raise than two. Therefore you will likely have to play this hand out of position against multiple opponents. Ouch!

There are times to raise or reraise with aces in order to build a bigger pot, rather than to narrow the field. When your hand includes a strong supporting cast, most significantly a deuce with any other wheel card, raising for value is a good play. This is particularly true if one or both of the aces are suited. Hands like A-A-3-4 or A-A-2-5 double-suited are great starting hands, worthy of capping the betting before the flop. Unfortunately, this type of hand is rare. In fact, you are more likely to be dealt four of a kind than the dream hand of A-A-2-3 double-suited. There are only twelve combinations of A-A-2-3 double suited available, versus thirteen ways to be dealt quads.

More Reraising Situations

The goals of a reraise are essentially the same as those of a raise—you either want to narrow the field or increase the size of the pot. However, putting in a third bet often tends to be an even more effective means of eliminating the other players. Hands that many players would happily call two bets with, such as A-3-6-9 or A-4-5-J, now go sailing into the muck. Even loose players may balk at the prospect of calling three bets with garbage.

So, if you feel your hand matches up best against only one or two other hands, a reraise may be used to set up this scenario. Remember, it's often possible to shut out opponents who must come in cold for multiple bets, but it's almost impossible to shut out opponents who are already involved.

Taking note of how the blinds play is important when weighing the possibility of making a reraise. In general, the better the blinds play, the harder you should try to raise them out. Fairly good players will routinely call one additional bet from the big blind with a large number of hands, hoping for a big flop. By forcing them to call two more bets, you reduce the price they get from the pot. This should convince them to fold most of the time. Another benefit you'll receive by making this play is that you sometimes will reraise with hands that don't appear to merit it, so it makes you more unpredictable in the eyes of your opponents. On top of that, you've enhanced this image while making a sound strategic play.

There will be times when you hold a premium hand and several players are already in the pot for a raise or two. In these cases, go ahead and reraise or cap the betting, since you are holding a hand that performs well against several opponents. Hands such as A-2-3-4, A-2-3-x suited, and A-2-4-K suited are good candidates for creating a large pot, as there is a high likelihood that the flop will be promising for you. It should be noted, though, that when some strong players are in the hand, it is likely that they hold hands similar in strength to yours. Reraising in this spot will lead to financial fluctuations rather than increased profits.

Raising When You're in the Blind

Due to the disadvantage of your position throughout the hand, it is generally not a good idea to raise before the flop when you are in either the small or big blind. When you do raise, it will almost exclusively be to build a bigger pot, rather than to narrow the field. The exception here comes when you're in the small blind, a player has raised the pot from a late position, and you reraise in an attempt to eliminate the big blind. For the most part, though, raising from the blinds should be reserved for premium starting hands such as A-2-3-x suited, which have enough value to overcome their positional handicap.

The Blind Structure and Playing the Small Blind

Most limit poker games feature a blind structure in which the small blind is half the size of the big blind. In these games, you should not call from the small blind with the poorest hands. While you will call with most hands, it is a mistake to automatically toss in the half-bet, as you'll get involved in some hands that don't have much nut potential. Be careful, because playing these hands might lead you into one of the numerous traps common in Omaha eight-or-better. As long as you aren't holding one of the worst hands, it is okay to loosen up a bit when calling the half-bet in the small blind.

Other games feature a two-and-three chip blind structure. In these games, it is acceptable to call nearly all the time from the small blind when the price is only a third of a bet. Save the chip with hands such as trips and trash like 2-2-6-K.

Defending Your Blinds

Sometimes you should base your decision of whether to play a hand on how your opponent plays. Calling a raise from the blind has far more value if the player or players in the pot play much worse than you. You can't take this idea too far in Omaha eight-or-better, because starting with the worst hand out of position is a lot to overcome. Nonetheless, you should consider it if your hand is decent. Additionally, not all raises are created equal—there is a big difference in the hand strength of a solid player raising in early position and that of a loose, reckless player raising on the button. If you are in the big blind and the pot is heads-up, a hand such as 2-4-6-8 can sometimes be folded against the solid player's raise but is a clear call against the speeder.

Another key consideration is the number of players in the pot, and the big blind is the best position from which to determine how many players will see the flop. You should have a good idea of which hands are worth defending against a large field and which have more value in a shorthanded situation. For example, hands such as 3-4-5-7 greatly diminish in value in a multiway raised pot, as it is likely the cards you are looking to flop—aces and deuces—are dead. This reduces your chances of making the nut low, and you'd have to be rather creative to envision other ways that this hand can make the nuts. Remember, you will often require the nuts to take down a multiway pot.

When playing heads-up, though, the hand has more value. For one thing, with everyone else folding, it seems more likely that there are still some aces left in the deck. Also, having a small flush draw adds value when playing heads-up, whereas making a small flush against five or six opponents is likely to be an expensive second-best hand. It is also reasonable to assume that the raiser probably has at least a couple of low cards. If a low hand is possible on the board, he might be **counterfeited**, meaning that the board has duplicated one of the low cards in his hand, rendering it useless to him. This will often allow you to win the low. If he's not counterfeited, his low hand might use cards that make you the best high hand, either two pair or a straight. Small two pairs can win when up against only one or two opponents, but are relatively hopeless against a large field.

While low hands like 3-4-5-6 and 3-4-5-7 play well against one or two opponents, high hands do not. Calling a raise with a hand like 9-10-J-Q from the big blind against only one player isn't as favorable as it seems. Unless the board comes with mostly high cards, it will be tough for you to win the whole pot. When high hands connect, they frequently make the nuts, which are just as effective in beating eight opponents as they are in beating one.

It's nice to have some type of low hand to fall back on when defending your blind against only one or two players. Low hands are the easiest draws to complete in the game, and they often serve as safety valves when your high prospects fall through. Even an emergency low such as A-8 is worth something in these situations.

When defending your blind in a pot with several opponents, it's key to have some cards that can make nut hands. Since you will be getting a good price to call, it is acceptable to allow your hand selection standards to dip a bit, provided you play hands capable of beating a large field. These types of hands may include cards such as A-x suited, 2-3-4-x, or three face cards, preferably suited or double-suited. It is still important to avoid playing middle cards, and any questionable hand containing two cards in that range should almost always be mucked.

Conclusion

Omaha eight-or-better is a game of many draws. If you have a good pre-flop strategy and play the right kinds of hands, you'll draw to hands that you actually want to make. Playing too loose will result in poker's greatest and most expensive frustration: making a lot of second best hands. This will burn up your chips. Only in rare circumstances should hands not containing an ace be played. It is also good to realize that even hands containing the key combinations A-A and A-3 should on occasion be discarded before the flop.

Keep in mind that the decisions you make before the flop will have a monumental impact on your results. Playing good starting cards should give you a fair chance to beat most low-limit games, provided that your opponents play too loosely. If you play too many hands, you will have little chance to win. As the limits get progressively higher, the players become more skilled and tend to become more aware of starting hand values, so the huge edge selective players hold at the smaller games begins to evaporate. Although a good foundation in hand selection and pre-flop play remains critical, it alone will not be enough to beat the bigger games.

PLAYING THE FLOP

Basic Flop Play

Once you have established that your hand is playable, the flop will present you with a whole new set of variables to consider. To be a successful Omaha eight-or-better player, you must become proficient in evaluating how the flop affects your chances of winning. Here are some general guidelines:

1. Playing for the Nuts

When deciding whether to remain in the hand, it is important to consider how many players are in the pot. The more players in the hand, the more important it is that you either are holding or are drawing at the nuts. This point cannot be emphasized enough! In a six- or seven-way action pot, typical of loose Omaha eight-or-better games, it will generally take the nuts to win. This means that you must flop the nut low draw, the nut flush draw, a set, a quality straight draw, or a made hand to remain in the pot. Nearly all other hands should be abandoned at this point. Most of the time, the best they will do is make a bankroll-busting second-best hand.

2. Protect the Pot or Let People In?

Once you determine that your hand is playable, the next decision is whether to play it in a manner that narrows the field or one that encourages action. Do you want to protect the pot or let people in? Since players have a propensity for finding some hope in their hand, it's hard to thin out the competition for a single bet. To narrow the field you usually need to make plays that will charge your opponents two bets to proceed. You accomplish this by raising a bet coming from your right, or by check-raising when you are in early position and feel a late position player will bet. Hands such as sets and straights are likely to be outdrawn, often by players with hands they would fold if faced with calling two bets. For example, most opponents will fold a small flush draw or inside straight draw after a raise, but will call a single bet. Raising with your made high hand may considerably increase your chances of winning.

On the other hand, some Omaha eight-or-better hands fare better with larger fields. Nut flush and nut low draws gain value when several players are in the pot, as the holdings of your opponents can develop into second-best paying-off hands. It is sometimes necessary to walk a fine line here, as building a big pot with premium draws is desirable, but it should be done in a manner that keeps your opponents in the hand.

3. How the Flop Affects Your Hand's Value

Remember that the object of this game is to scoop the pot. With that in mind, be aware that the value of high hands plummets when the flop contains three low cards, and the value of low hands decreases when the flop contains two or three high cards. Suppose five players see a flop, which comes 3-4-6 (two hearts). You are holding A-K-Q-J with the A-J of hearts. Although you are drawing to the nut high, this hand should sometimes be folded when facing multiple bets after the flop, as you are only playing for half the pot.

4. Pot Odds

When drawing, it is necessary that you have some idea of the likelihood of making your hand versus the price the pot is laying you. If, as above, you are drawing to the nut flush, even though you should end up with the best high hand about one time in three and the pot is giving you the correct price, you are playing for only half the money. The presence of a low hand on the board divides in half the price you receive on a high draw from the pot, generally making it unprofitable to stay with this type of hand.

Conversely, if you have a hand like A-2-6-8 and the flop comes J-Q-7, it is an easy fold. You need to catch consecutive low cards for half, or possibly a quarter, of the pot. Although you may catch a runner-runner miracle straight, this isn't a hand to chase.

However, if the 8 in your hand were a king or 10, this changes things considerably. While your hand still isn't great, you now have the chance to make the ace-high straight, which may enable you to scoop. The presence of this draw, along with your backdoor nut-low draw, is often enough to make this a playable situation, especially if the pot is large and it's only one bet to you.

5. Position

Your position relative to the betting is extremely important. When a bet comes from your immediate right, you must play tighter and pass on more draws, because you don't know if the players behind you are looking to go to war with their hands. If they are, it will become expensive to stay in. However, if you are last to act after the action has been made, and thus the pot cannot be raised behind you, you're right to call with many more hands. These principles apply to both of the previous examples. You don't mind paying one small bet on a marginal draw if the pot cannot be raised. Out of position though, the same hand must be folded to a bet, given the threat of additional action.

Hand-Specific Guidelines

Playing Low Draws on the Flop. Since a high percentage of your playable hands in Omaha eight-or-better will contain an A-2 or A-3, the most common draw you'll develop is to the nut low. You shouldn't play this draw the same way all the time, though. There are times to play it fast, times to call meekly, and times to throw it away. Numerous variables influence this decision, including how the rest of your hand coordinates with the board, the number of players in the pot, and your position.

When playing a multiway pot that no one is interested in conceding, two important considerations factor into the decision of whether to play aggressively or passively. The first is whether your hand contains backup; the second is your hand's potential to win the high.

Having **backup** refers to holding a third low card close in rank to your two nut cards. If the board is 3-7-J, having a hand like A-2-4-K, or to a lesser extent A-2-5-K, may encourage you to play your draw more aggressively since you have the 4 as backup. Without the four, you have sixteen cards that make you the nuts. Of course, sometimes you will turn the nuts and get counterfeited on the river, which frequently will cost you half the pot. Holding that extra low card not only gives you twenty-one cards to catch, it also prevents you from losing if the river card counterfeits you. This makes your hand much stronger and provides quite a bit of incentive to build a bigger pot.

If you have a good chance to win the high as well, playing aggressively can significantly improve your chances of winning. For example, suppose that you are holding A-2-5-Q in a four-player pot with a board of 3-8-10. It is highly unlikely that you will win the high. If none of your opponents has an A-2, the pot is laying you even money on future bets, as you only get your own money plus one of your opponents' bets back should you make a low. Now, suppose you hold the nut flush draw as well. Since you have a chance to scoop, you can factor into the pot odds the bets from all of your opponents, so playing aggressively will have much more value.

When you flop both the nut-low draw and nut-flush draw, especially if you have backup for low, you should try and get as much money into the pot as possible. Although you can simply raise an opponent's bet, you may want to just call on the flop if the bet is coming from your immediate right. With such a big draw, you don't want to knock anybody out, so play your hand in the way that gets the most money to the center, without eliminating too many players. Other big draws may include hands like A-3-5-J with a flop of 2-4-Q.

When you have a chance to win only the low and your draw doesn't contain backup, it's often best to just check and call. The main exception to this rule is if you think a bet gives you a reasonable chance to take down the pot immediately. While this might be the case in some shorthanded pots or higher limit games, you're drawing dead if you think this will work in most loose Omaha eight-or-better games.

Occasionally, a situation arises in which it is correct to fold a nut-low draw on the flop. This usually occurs when the pot is small, and it's a bet and raise to you. Suppose you are holding A-2-K-Q, and the board is 7-8-9. Here you have virtually no shot at scooping—at best you can win half the pot, and you may be playing for only a quarter. With the absence of a backup card in your hand, this is clearly a fold.

When you play an A-3, you will frequently flop a draw to the second nuts. It's nice when the deuce pops right up on the flop, but it usually doesn't—it likes to wait until you are holding the A-2 to show its face. Drawing to the second nut low is one of the biggest drains on the bankrolls of Omaha eight-or-better players. Unless you are strongly convinced that no one is drawing at the nut low, this draw should be routinely mucked.

You can make an exception to this rule when you have the nut flush draw, a set, or top two pair with your second-nut low draw. This generally adds enough scoop potential to your hand to justify remaining in the pot. Also, if you have a hand like A-3-K-10 and the board is 4-5-Q, you may be able to see another card. This is because a deuce, in addition to making you the nut low, makes a straight that may enable you to scoop. Drawing at the second nuts is much better if your nut card lets you scoop the pot. Don't throw good money after bad if you have A-3-8-K and the board shows 4-7-J, however. With several players in, if you are fortunate enough not to be up against an A-2, it is a near certainty that another player will be holding A-3. If you draw to this hand, you will be lucky to wind up with a quarter of the pot.

Playing When You Flop a Set. Flopping a set in hold'em is a joyful occurrence. You are almost certain to have the best hand, and you can bet and raise with impunity, hoping for lots of action. Even when you don't fill up, you generally expect to take down a nice pot.

Unfortunately, such is not the case with sets in Omaha eight-or-better. Even when you improve to a full house (about 35 percent of the time), you'll often split the pot with a low hand. Also, since each player is dealt four cards, it is very likely that you will lose to a straight or a flush if you don't fill up. As a result, sets are at best marginal holdings, and at worst, a significant drain on your bankroll and enthusiasm.

The following guidelines should help you recognize when sets can be played profitably and when they should be folded. In the Advanced Flop Play section to follow, some of these topics are covered in greater detail.

(1) Playing for half the pot with a hand that is likely to be outdrawn is not a good strategy. When the board contains three low cards, it is difficult if not impossible for you to scoop the pot with a set. As a result, it is generally correct to fold, unless you

can play for one bet without the pot being raised behind you.

(2) Since you often have to make a full house to win half the pot, the size of your set matters as well. It is not uncommon for more than one player to fill up when the board pairs. Continuing with a hand like A-3-3-K and a board of 3-5-6 against several players is suicidal. It is possible that either a higher set or two pair is out there, so even if you *do* improve there is no guarantee you will win. If you held top set in this instance, folding would still be correct much of the time, especially when it costs you multiple bets to stay in the hand.

(3) When is the best time to play a set when the board contains three low cards? For example: The flop comes 7-3-2 of three different suits and you are holding 7-7-Q-K. Hopefully, you've found yourself in this pot because you received a free look in the big blind. While you have no shot at scooping against a few players, you do have the current nuts for high. Since three different suits are represented on the board, it is unlikely that a flush will beat you. However, the fact that you're only playing for half the pot means that you want to see the hand through as cheaply as possible, unless the board pairs. If a straight card comes on the turn, especially a 4 or 5, you will have to fold if you are faced with calling more than one bet, as the pot won't give you enough of a price to draw at just the high end. Since you will often be forced to fold on the turn, it is not in your best interest to play this hand aggressively on the flop.

(4) Cards like 3-6-J with two clubs can be a problem flop in Omaha eight-or-better. There are two low cards with a flush draw present, providing a number of draws. If you hold a hand such as J-J-Q-K with this board, your prospects are uncertain. Although you hold the current nuts, you are vulnerable from a number of different directions. In fact, if a low club comes on the

turn, you may have to fold your hand. Therefore, with boards like the one above, you might want to wait until after the turn card comes before betting the hand aggressively. This way, you can cheaply fold if disaster strikes. Also, if you catch a good card, you may gain extra action by not telegraphing your hand on the flop.

Raising might be correct though, if the player to your immediate right is the bettor. A raise might succeed in eliminating some of the draws posing a threat to your hand, thus enhancing your chances of winning. You won't eliminate the nut flush draw or a low straight draw such as A-4-5, but you might induce smaller flush draws to fold, enabling your hand to hold up as long as none of your opponents was drawing to the nut flush.

(5) The best time to flop a set is when the board comes with either two or three high cards, because high boards mean that no low is possible; therefore, you're playing for the whole pot. This has a significant impact on your pot odds, as the pot is essentially laying you double the price as when the board contains a low hand. As a result, it is generally correct to go to the river when you flop a set with a high board.

(6) The drawback with hands such as A-3-K-K when the flop comes K-Q-J is that you frequently need to fill up to win the pot. In Omaha eight-or-better, with several players in the hand, someone will have A-10 more often than you might think. Even though you may be trailing, it is okay to play aggressively here. For one thing, your hand may be good. Also, if you are behind, you will improve to a full house about 35 percent of the time. This means a bet is only unprofitable when you're up against precisely one player who has the straight.

(7) However, with the same flop of K-Q-J, you will have to consider folding your set if you have three jacks instead of three kings, particularly if several players remain in the hand. Against only one opponent who is likely to have a straight, it is correct to draw. But if you're facing a bet, a raise, and a call, it is likely that you're up against a larger set or top two pair, as well as the straight. Either way, this doesn't leave you with very many wins. Fold.

Playing Wraparound Straight Draws. Although there may not be an official definition of a wrap, it's really a straight draw with more outs than a common open-ender. For example, a hand such as 8-9-10-K and a board of A-6-7 provides thirteen cards to make the straight (four fives, three eights, three nines, and three tens). In Omaha eight-or-better, the vulnerability of straights and the frequent problem of running into an opponent with the same straight means that wrap draws are typically the only straight draws worth pursuing for their own sake.

Not all wraps are created equal. Key considerations are the likelihood of making the nut straight and whether your hand will allow you to scoop the pot. If you are in the big blind with 6-7-8-9 and the flop comes 2-4-5, your hand should usually be folded. Although many cards will complete the straight, you can only win half the pot. Also, if the board pairs or a flush card comes, it might kill your hand.

To further illustrate the difference between good and bad times to pursue straight draws, let's look at a couple of examples:

Example One
Your hand: 10-J-Q-K (red)
Board: A-10-6 (two clubs)

Although any jack, queen or king will make a straight, this hand is severely flawed. With the flush draw on the board, the danger exists that the card you need to complete your straight will also complete an opponent's flush. This effectively eliminates three of the nine possible straight cards, leaving only six safe cards to make your hand. Even if one of these six cards comes on the turn, your hand could still be in jeopardy. The flush can always show up on the river, or the board could pair. Furthermore, even if the straight wins, it will be exceedingly difficult to scoop this pot. Any low card will likely cost you half the pot, and even a safe face card that doesn't pair the board might hurt you. The presence of four unpaired high cards on the board makes it easier for an opponent to tie your hand. So, that means the only truly safe card is an offsuit 9.

Example Two
Your hand: 10-J-Q-K (red)
Board: 3-9-10 (offsuit)

Here is a situation where you can apply the gas pedal. This time, thirteen cards will make the nut straight, essentially creating an even money proposition with two cards to come. If you complete the straight with a jack, queen, or king on the turn or river, then no low hand will be possible. The absence of a flush draw on the flop also adds significant value to your hand, as all of your outs are clean. Bear in mind also that any jack, queen, or king not only makes the nut straight, it also creates the possibility of making a full house on the river. This can come in handy against a player holding a hand like A-3-3-4, as some of his supposed outs will make him the second-best hand. Should you make a full house on the end, it is likely that you will win extra bets from this player, who is probably reading you for a straight.

Slow-Playing

Slow-playing a huge hand is rarely an optimal strategy in Omaha eight-or-better for two reasons:

(1) Players will tend to call you down anyway, hoping to make whatever hand they are drawing at. It is a good idea to let them pay to draw dead, or close to it, if they're willing.

(2) Few hands are immune to all the potential draws in this game. If you flop the nut full house or quads in hold'em, it is a safe bet that you will win the pot. The main issue is picking a strategy that allows you to win the most money. The problem with this in Omaha eight-or-better is that two running low cards can come, costing you half the pot—unless three high cards flop. So ordinarily, even four of a kind should be bet aggressively, as it is important to make the low draws pay for the privilege of splitting the pot with you.

If you do decide to slow-play a big hand, don't give your opponents the chance to outdraw you by giving them free cards. When slow-playing, you are hoping that your opponents will improve their hands enough to give you action, but not enough to beat you. Here are some examples to illustrate this point:

Example One

Your hand: A-2-4-K
Board: K-4-4

Here, it is best to play the hand aggressively on the flop. Don't give players with hands like 9-9-10-Q a free opportunity to spike a miracle card.

Example Two
Your hand: K-K-Q-J
Board: K-4-4

This time slow-playing is, again, a bad idea, but for a different reason. Although your high hand is not in jeopardy, by checking you might allow opponents to develop low draws, potentially costing you half the pot. Sometimes checking on the flop is a good idea if the pot is very small, since you shouldn't mind risking half of a small pot to gain some bets on the turn from opponents who develop low draws. However, it is almost always a mistake to do this in pots that were raised before the flop.

Example Three
Your hand: A-2-K-K
Board: K-4-4

In this example, not only do you have the high hand more or less wrapped up, you also have the best possible backdoor low draw. So, if you don't feel you'll get much action by betting the flop, then slow-playing will probably add value to your hand. If the players in your game are likely to automatically call on the flop anyway, then go ahead and bet.

When the Board Is Paired
The complexion of a hand changes drastically when the flop contains a pair. In pots featuring several players, a full house will likely be required to win the high hand. As the number of players in the hand increases, so does the likelihood that someone has flopped trips or better. This means that unless you also have a quality low draw, you should fold straight draws and anything except nut flush draws in multiway pots.

Proceeding with lesser high draws is a trickier proposition against a smaller field. Although it's dangerous to play flush and straight draws, you will be playing far too tightly if you automatically fold every time the flop brings a pair. Applying some card sense to this situation should help you make more accurate decisions. For example the presence of two eights on the board should not elicit the same degree of fear as two aces.

If the card that pairs on the board is a key card in Omaha eight-or-better, it is likely to have hit one of your opponents. When it doesn't appear probable that the pair helped another player, it becomes more correct to continue with other draws. In fact, you can sometimes bet a flush draw into a paired board, inducing your opponents to fold out of fear that you flopped trips or a full house.

When you hold two aces in your hand against a small number of opponents, a paired board often is a good thing. It is generally a good idea to play the flop aggressively, both to cut down on the competition and to try to find out if your hand is the best. The presence of the pair makes a straight or flush—common ace-killers in Omaha eight-or-better—less likely. Also, the pair on the board gives you the nut two pair, which will frequently win the high against a small field. However, if the pot is a family affair, someone will usually have trips. In this case, two aces should be folded if there is any substantial action.

Advanced Flop Play

Here are some additional tips for playing hands on the flop. These focus more sharply on topics already discussed and deal with a few additional issues that come into play more often at the higher limits.

Creating Extra Outs

In Omaha eight-or-better, sometimes you have a hand that seems to be heading in one direction, but winds up winning part or all of the pot with a different hand that you made almost by accident. This is one reason why playing quality starting hands is important. Not only do they produce more good hands and draws on the flop, they also tend to be more easily rerouted into winning backdoor hands.

The ability to recognize when you may be able to develop some secondary draws to fall back on should your primary draw not materialize is a valuable skill. Its value is based on the fact that if you see an opportunity, you may be able to create some extra wins for your hand by making a timely bet or raise. Consider the following example.

Example One

Flop: Q-J-2 (two clubs)
Scenario One: Your hand: A-3-4-10 (nut clubs)
Scenario Two: Your hand: A-5-6-10 (nut clubs)

Note that in both cases, your only immediate draws are to the nut flush and nut straight. However, both hands also have a backdoor low draw. Assuming that five players are in the hand, if the player to your right bets and you are next to act, what is your best course of action in each scenario?

In Scenario 1, a call is clearly the correct play. You don't want to eliminate players when all your draws are to the nuts. Whether you make the nut flush, ace-high straight, or catch two running low cards, any hand you make will be the nuts in one direction or another. Therefore, the more players in the hand, the more money you should make. You might consider raising for value with your draw, but not until everyone has called the initial bet. Raising in this situation will tend to eliminate players likely to make second-best hands and pay you off.

Although your high prospects are essentially the same in Scenario 2, the fact that you have a weak backdoor low draw is a good reason to raise the bettor. Raising may cause players to fold hands such as A-4-5-J or A-2-3-6, with which they would likely call one bet. As a result, even if you miss the flush and straight draws, you might still win half the pot if two low cards come, because your raise on the flop drove out the stronger backdoor low draws. By thinking ahead and realizing all the ways a hand can develop, you can sometimes play a situation more aggressively than normal in order to create some additional winning cards for your hand.

Of course, choosing whether to raise or just call in this type of situation depends on the size of the pot, the style of your opponents, and the previous betting that led to the situation.

Folding the Nut Low

There are times when you will make the nut low on the flop but realize that it doesn't have much value. You then have a decision to make regarding whether to stick it out until the end or fold. It may seem absurd to fold the nuts—and it usually is—but there are some instances when it would be the right thing to do—typically, when a previously small pot is now being bet aggressively.

You don't want to throw away the nuts if the pot is large or if it's inexpensive to stay in the hand. However, if your hand is something like A-2-K-J and the flop is 6-7-8 (two flush cards, not yours), and the other three players in the pot start betting and raising like maniacs, it may be time to reassess your involvement. For one thing, you are likely playing for a quarter of the pot, especially if you know some of your opponents are very solid players. Also, any ace or deuce that falls on the turn or river will likely turn your hand into a loser. If you are relatively certain that another player also has the nut low, you really aren't giving anything up by folding. The cost of the small bet already invested in the pot is offset by the potential for winding up with nothing if you get counterfeited.

Nevertheless, it isn't a good idea to fold the made nut low very often. Sometimes it may seem like you're only playing for a quarter, but you'll get a pleasant surprise on the end when the other players turn over high hands. This possibility alone should be enough to keep you from folding the low nuts most of the time. It might also be better to stay in the hand if the pot is already large, or if it's multiway. Also, the presence of a backup low card in your hand should be enough of a reason not to fold the nut low.

Sets When the Board Is Small: To Play or Not To Play?

In multiway pots, with a flop of three low cards, sets should usually be folded. It is a mistake to play sets aggressively in an attempt to protect them, as they can only win half the pot and will frequently be outdrawn. A better approach is to treat a set as you would a drawing hand, and play or fold based on the price the pot is offering you. If one player bets, four players call, and you are last to act with a hand like A-4-4-K and a board of 2-4-6, it is okay to call and see another card. Here's why:

(1) The pot cannot be raised behind you.

(2) You are receiving a favorable price on the hand.

However, if the first player bets, the second raises, and the others fold around to you, folding is clearly the right play. Why? Because in order to proceed, you'll have to call two bets cold and face the possibility of a reraise by the initial bettor. This eliminates all value from the situation, because instead of calling one small bet to perhaps win half of a decent sized pot, you are now faced with putting in multiple bets while playing for half of a three-way pot. Furthermore, with both a bet and a raise, it is more likely that one of your opponents has flopped a straight. Thus, you will need to improve your hand to win the high.

In tighter Omaha eight-or-better games, sets have more value. Suppose you have A-2-2-Q and the flop is 2-3-8. Against a large field, this hand can be flung into the discards without hesitation. However, if you are playing the pot heads-up, this is a better-than-average flop for your hand. Even though a low hand is possible, your opponent doesn't necessarily have one. He may have something like A-3-10-10, in which case you have him beat. It is important to play these situations aggressively. You figure to have the best high hand, which may be good for a scoop. Another point worth noting is that your aggressive play may encourage a single opponent to relinquish a hand with a made, albeit rough, low such as A-3-7-K. This major victory could not have been won by checking. If your opponent raises you, then you can revert to calling mode for the rest of the hand, as his raise probably signifies a made low.

Manipulating the Size of the Pot

One of the most common and aggravating perils of Omaha eight-or-better comes when you flop a nice high hand or high draw and play it aggressively, only to see two opponents make their low hands on the turn and promptly go to war. You are then faced with the unpalatable prospect of calling several double-sized turn bets when the low portion of the pot is already spoken for. It's painful to give up the hand because of all the money already in the pot, but it's equally painful to watch your stacks erode as you pay for your draws.

Fortunately, there is a method you can employ to make playing the turn card less agonizing. It can be used primarily when you have a high hand and two low cards appear on the flop. For example, suppose your hand is A-3-J-J, and the flop is 3-5-J with a flush draw. Although you have the current nuts, your hand is not that strong. If any low card comes on the turn or river, it will cost you half the pot, or all of it if someone makes a straight. Also, there is a flush draw present.

This is not a time to manipulate the size of the pot by playing your top set aggressively. Should one of the many potential horror cards appear on the turn, the fact that you helped keep the pot small by not betting or raising on the flop enables you to make an easy release of your hand if faced with too much action.

Another benefit to playing this way is that you make it harder for your opponents to gauge what you're holding. If the board pairs on the turn, your opponents probably won't give you credit for having the nut full house, since you didn't play the flop aggressively. This might enable you to win some extra bets if one of your opponents feels his trips or smaller full house is the best hand.

Consider the following scenario. All four opponents check to you in last position, and your hand is A-K-J-10 with a nut flush draw (hearts). Then the flop comes 3-5-9, two to the flush. Since many turn cards will render the hand unplayable, you check rather than bet the nut flush draw. The turn is the perfect Q♥. An alert, aggressive opponent bets out, two other players call, and you raise with the absolute nuts. The aggressive player reraises with his smaller flush, and you wind up scooping a big pot when the board pairs on the end. It could probably be argued that checking on the button induced your aggressive opponent to overplay his hand on the turn, as he refused to accept the fact that a player holding the nut flush draw could check the hand in last position.

You should manipulate the size of the pot fairly often in such situations. However, it is important that you don't hurt your chances of winning the pot with this play. In hands with small fields, you can sometimes win the pot right on the flop with a bet. If you believe you have a decent chance of winning the pot immediately, it's better to go ahead and bet than to wait for a safe turn card. Also, when the player to your immediate right bets and you're holding a high hand such as a set, you should probably raise in an effort to narrow the field. Checking or calling with a set is best when a raise won't get anybody to fold.

Bluffing When Trash Flops

Although Omaha eight-or-better has a reputation for being a game in which bluffing is nearly impossible, there are some good situations in which to give it a shot. One of the more common bluffing opportunities arises when high cards flop, particularly if the board is paired. Since most players play low cards, it stands to reason that a high flop will likely miss everyone's hand. Betting into boards such as 10-10-7 is often effective against a small number of opponents, preferably three or less (with more players, it's likely that you will run into a legitimate hand). This play can be made from any position, and if you are raised, it is probably best to fold, rather than to attempt to create some justification for clinging to the hand. It is most effective against tight, unimaginative players who will automatically give you credit for a hand when you bet.

One thing to be aware of if you are playing in a higher limit game is that perceptive opponents will not only make this play themselves, but will be aware that you might attempt it. These players could be capable of raising you with nothing, which puts you in a rough spot. It is far easier to raise with nothing than to call with it. You must either modify this play or abandon it against these types of opponents.

Here is another example of a play you can use. Say your hand is A-2-4-10, and the board reads J-J-Q. Only you and the blinds are in the pot, and the small blind bets the flop. The big blind folds, and now you call with nothing but an inside straight draw. You aren't calling on the strength of your hand, but on the assumption that your opponent has very little. If he checks to you on the turn, you can bet and expect to win the pot. However, it's probably best to fold if he bets again and you don't catch a king, as another bet probably signifies a legitimate hand. It will be difficult for him to bluff a second time into this board after being called on the flop.

Conclusion

There is a lot to think about when the flop is laid on the table in Omaha eight-or-better. When in the heat of the game, you probably won't have time to correctly consider all of the factors discussed above, but you should be aware of them and strive to apply as many as possible. With that in mind, here are a few questions to ask yourself after looking at the flop:

(1) How much of the pot am I playing for?

(2) What price is the pot laying me, based on my potential to make the best hand and the portion of the pot I can win?

(3) What implied value does my hand possess? That is to say, how much additional money can I win if the right card comes? Will the other players in the pot pay me off? Is there an aggressive player on my left, meaning there's a chance to check-raise the field? Will the low hands bet and raise aggressively if I make the high? And so on.

(4) If I call, can the pot get raised behind me?

(5) Does my hand play better against more or fewer opponents? Can my hand be played in such a way as to create a favorable situation against one or the other?

PLAYING THE TURN

Basic Turn Play

Give Up Some Marginal Hands

Because the size of the bet doubles on the turn, many marginal hands that were worth one bet on the flop must now be abandoned. Also, a low hand will frequently be possible by the time the turn comes, and this cuts in half the odds the pot is laying you to draw at a high hand. Hands such as top two pair and sets lose their chance to scoop the pot when the board shows three cards to a low. This is particularly true when several players are in, as someone will almost certainly have a low. These hands must be played with extreme caution, as the turn can be an expensive round. With a less than premium hand, you can wind up investing a lot of chips with little chance for a return on that investment.

Often, one or two players are holding the nut low, another player the nut high, and a raising war begins. If you are in the pot with a draw of some kind, it is time to really question staying involved. It's generally not a good idea to pay multiple bets on the turn to draw at half the pot, unless you have a chance to scoop. Suppose you have A-2-5-5, and the board is 2-4-5-K. If there is a bet and a raise to you, give up this hand. Your set is no good, and the best river cards can only gain you half the pot.

It is also correct to fold this hand when the player to your right bets and there are players yet to act behind you. It is unlikely that your hand is good, as the bettor is representing a straight. Furthermore, the pot can still be raised. This hand is another example of a situation in which you can draw for one bet if you are in last position—but you must fold when you don't know what drawing may cost. Getting stuck in the middle of raising wars in Omaha eight-or-better is among the most costly errors players can make on the turn. You need to be aware that any time a low hand is possible and several players are in the pot, it is likely that there will be at least one raise on the turn.

Playing Strong Hands on the Turn

Usually, in order to win the most money with strong hands on the turn, you should raise if someone else bets, or bet when it's checked to you. One of the best situations in Omaha eight-or-better is when you own half the pot and are drawing at the other half, commonly referred to as a freeroll. You cannot lose the whole pot, and you have the potential to scoop.

For example, say you are holding a hand such as A-2-3-10, and the board is 4-5-8-Q (two of your suit). Note that although you might get quartered, you are guaranteed to win the low side, and pairing up any of your low cards makes you a wheel, which might be good for a scoop. Plus, this hand features the nut flush draw. With a hand this strong, you should pump the pot, as there is plenty of upside with virtually no risk.

Even if your hand is only good enough to win a quarter of the pot at this point, raising is the correct play due to the hand's high potential. If three or more other players are in the pot, you won't lose money if the pot gets quartered, unless it is one of those rare times that two of your opponents share the nut low with you.

Against two other players, you should still be aggressive with your freeroll hands, even if you feel one of your opponents has the nut low as well. It's a good low risk investment that can produce excellent returns if you make your high hand. Here's an example from a $10/$20 limit game to illustrate:

Your hand: A-2-3-10
Board: 4-5-8-Q (two flush cards)

One opponent, Player A, bets and another, Player B, calls. If you raise and get quartered, your raise costs you $5 (as all three players pay $20, totaling $60, of which you recoup $15). If you raise, make the flush, and get three-quarters, your raise makes you $25 ($20 x 3 = $60, of which you get $45).

Risking $5 for a chance to win $25 is a good investment in this spot, since the odds of your making a flush are better than 5 to 1 against—35 to 9, or about 4 to 1. However, in real life the odds are even better than that. Sometimes you will catch an ace or deuce and scoop the pot because an opponent with A-2 gets counterfeited. Also, a 3 or a 6 will make you a straight, which may be good for the high. So a 3 will get you half the pot, and a 6 is worth three quarters. Plus, there is always the possibility that you have the only low hand. Due to their limited liability and great upside, these types of hands should be played as aggressively as possible.

Knocking Out the Competition

When the turn comes and the size of the bet doubles, players might begin to develop a greater respect for their chips. At this point in the hand, the pots often are pretty large, so it is in your best interest to protect your hand as much as possible. Opponents are more willing to pass without a strong hand when faced with calling two bets cold. Marginal hands with which opponents will likely call one bet but fold for two include most two-pair hands, as well as some small flushes, small straights, and second- or third-nut lows. It is often in your best interest to raise opponents with these types of hands out of the pot.

Often, an opponent holding a hand like A-3-6-Q will bet into a board showing 2-5-8-K. If you are next, holding A-3-8-9, and you raise the initial bettor, it may persuade the rest of the field to fold hands like A-2-8-10 or A-A-6-J. By raising, you are attempting to isolate one other player who you feel is also likely to have the nut low. With a bit of luck, your high hand may trump that of your opponent, giving you three-quarters of the pot. This play should be made often, and it is another example of a situation with little risk but significant upside.

Making it expensive for others to stay in the pot is also important if you hold a vulnerable high hand, especially if your hand is the nut flush. If no low or pair is on the board, it should be obvious that the nut flush is a hand to be bet and raised at every opportunity. However, suppose you have A-K-Q-J, the board is 3-4-5-8, and you have the nut flush. If a player bets into you, it is pretty clear that the most you will be able to win is half the pot. With this in mind, you might be tempted to just call, allowing some additional players into the pot to create extra profit.

The danger of playing this situation passively is that it allows players with two pair or sets to draw at you cheaply. If the board pairs on the river, you might lose multiple bets. It is likely that the player who bet the turn will also bet the river, and you will be faced with the grisly task of calling with the nut flush when the pot might get raised behind you. It's generally best to go ahead and raise on the turn. You'll still get action from any player holding an A-2, which doesn't pose a threat to your hand. If opponents with two pair want to call your raise and draw at half the pot, that's their prerogative. In fact, they should probably be placed on your Christmas card list.

You may want to put the brakes on with lesser nut high hands, though. For example, say you have 9-10-J-Q, and the board has 3-6-7-8 (two flush cards); or you've got A-4-K-K, and the board shows 3-4-8-K (two flush draws).

In both examples, even though you have the current nut high, your hand is in much greater jeopardy of being outdrawn than in the previous example when you were holding the nut flush. To compare, in the nut flush example, only ten cards could beat you if your opponent has a set; by comparison, with the straight shown above, there are the ten potential full house cards that could beat you, plus the additional flush cards. For the example in which you have three kings, sixteen cards create a straight possibility for your opponents and about half the deck completes a flush draw.

While it may seem even more crucial to raise in an effort to protect these extremely vulnerable hands, the problem is that opponents holding low cards are often holding the draws that can beat you as well. Thus, raising them out will be impossible, and they are likely to put in a reraise if they have the nut low with a flush draw. Contrast this with the nut flush example, in which any player holding two pair or a set is unlikely to also have a good low hand, as this would require a precise use of all four cards. With that in mind, it is normally best to just call with a lesser nut hand, hoping you don't get beaten, rather than make a futile attempt to narrow the field.

When You Only Have the Nut Low

It is common in loose, passive Omaha eight-or-better games typical at the lower limits for players to make the nut low and then check if their hand lacks high potential. But that's the wrong play. For one thing, if several players are in the pot, there is value in betting the hand. Winning half the pot will still be profitable, and so will receiving a quarter if five or more players are in.

Perhaps more significant is the possibility of winning the pot with a bet. This might be next to impossible in very loose games with several players in the pot, but in hands contested by fewer players, it is not that uncommon for everybody to fold to a bet when the low arrives. Even if you don't have a pair, it's a good idea to bet your nut low. Doing so in smallish pots might prompt your opponents to fold their high hands and draws, since they'll realize their chances to scoop have vanished. They might not want to risk calling turn and river bets to find out if their marginal two pair is any good. Passive Omaha eight-or-better players cost themselves a lot of half-pots by failing to bet their low hands aggressively.

Advanced Turn Play

As we have seen, playing aggressively on the turn has its benefits. Here are some additional opportunities to use aggression to your advantage.

Turning Good Draws into Better Draws

On the turn, the more cards there are that can make you the best hand on the river, the better off you are. So, there are times when raising with a draw on the turn might increase the number of outs for your hand.

Take a hand such as A-2-10-J (A-10 flush draw) with a board of 4-5-J-Q (4-5 of your suit). The player to your right bets, and you are next to act with three or four opponents behind you. At first glance it appears that a call is clearly the best play here. Additional callers enhance the values of your nut low and nut flush draws, and it's unlikely that your one pair of jacks is the best hand at this point.

While calling is a reasonable play, you should at least consider making a raise in this spot. Raising might cause hands such as A-3-8-K, that would certainly call one bet, to fold. This could open up the possibility of winning the pot if a ten comes on the end, making you two pair. Sure, you've only added three cards to your list of outs, but your decision to invest an extra bet with your big draw might have increased your chances of scooping.

The larger the pot, the more valuable it becomes to create extra outs for yourself, and you can do this by investing an extra bet or two and thinning the field. By the way, the draw mentioned above is big enough by itself to cause you to consider raising for value. You have sixteen low wins, plus the flush cards, the kings, and possibly the other two jacks.

Semi-Bluffing the Turn to Set Up a Bluff on the End

Omaha eight-or-better games that don't fit into the "no fold-em" category, most notably higher limit games, provide some good bluffing opportunities for the astute player. Often, it's more convincing if you set up a bluff on the river by betting a drawing hand on the turn, with the intention of following through if you miss your hand. This is commonly referred to as **semi-bluffing**, since you have two ways to win. Although you must fire two big bets into the pot to set up a bluff, your bets have equity because even if your opponents don't fold, there's a possibility that you will make the best hand on the river.

With more than two opponents, bluffing is dangerous because it is far too likely that you will run into the nuts. When a small number of opponents are in the pot, preferably no more than two other players, that's the best time to bluff. Also, it is effective to semi-bluff if you can represent a specific hand that materializes on the turn. The play works best when you have not been aggressive up to that point in the hand.

Here's a good example of just such a play: In the small blind, you call with 2-3-4-7 and see a flop of A-8-10. With three players in the pot, you check and call a bet, suspecting that the bettor has aces-up. The turn card is a queen, making a straight for any opponent holding a J-9 or K-J. While it's possible that one of your opponents has one of these hands, it is by no means a sure thing. This is a great opportunity to semi-bluff. You can either bet your hand, or you can go for a check-raise if you believe your opponent will bet his aces-up again. On the river, you must bet regardless of what card comes—unless it's an ace, which will almost certainly make someone a full house. If no low comes, your opponents will be hard pressed to call with any hand other than a straight. If a low does come, you'll win part of the pot anyway. In fact, if your opponents are convinced that you have a straight and fold two aces or two small pair, you might make your low hand and scoop the pot with seven-high.

There are two things to consider before making this play:

(1) Do not to try it against chronic calling stations, players who tend to call with a huge variety of hands, even weak ones. Opponents like this will want to see if you have your straight.

(2) You absolutely must have the nut low draw when attempting to semi-bluff in this fashion. When a low draw is on the board, it is a mistake to semi-bluff with only high draws to flushes and straights, since the low is too likely to show up on the river. Because of this, you will probably be called by anyone with a decent low hand. Your opponent might call your bluff with a low hand and wind up scooping the pot with one small pair or a similar hand.

PLAYING THE RIVER

Basic River Play

It is a common but incorrect belief among Omaha eight-or-better players that the river largely plays itself. There are a number of factors that indicate otherwise.

Paying Off

On the river, you'll frequently have to decide whether to call a bet with a marginal high hand or a weak low hand. Perhaps you flopped a set, only to see a flush arrive on the river. While it is certainly possible that you are beat, there is also a chance that the bettor is going for low and your set is still the best high hand. If you cannot decide which way an opponent is going in the hand, it is far better to call and possibly lose one bet, than to fold and risk giving up half the pot. It's called **paying off**, and you do this when the pot odds are good enough to make you call even though you think you have the losing hand.

Hand Reading

As your poker skills develop, you will become more proficient in reading your opponents' hands, which will allow you to make more accurate decisions on the river. Reconstructing the betting can make hand reading easier. For example, if a player that had raised the pot before the flop now bets the river when both a flush card and a third low card hit, it makes sense to read him for a low hand. This makes it easier for you to call with your set or two pair. In this situation, the bettor might show you the nut low and a flush, but that's just the nature of poker.

Position

Another element to weigh when debating whether to call on the river is the action yet to take place. If there are quite a few players behind you, you will need to tighten up a bit and pass more of your questionable hands. In the previous example, for instance, even though the bettor might not have a flush, if there are still four players to act behind you, it's a pretty safe bet that one of them has you beat and will also call.

Paying attention to the players to your left before you act will sometimes allow you to use their tells to save a bet or make a big call. If you can see that your opponents are preparing to fold, it makes it easier for you to call. Also, say an opponent grabs raising chips before it is his turn to act. Often this is an act, but it is sometimes a reliable indicator of the strength of his hand. It is nice to play against opponents who consistently give away their hands before it is their turn to act, particularly if they are sitting to your left.

Getting Counterfeited

Although you can play your made nut low hands more aggressively when you have a backup card, you sometimes will find yourself in the pot with just the bare nut low. In these cases, there are six cards that will counterfeit you, which means your hand could be killed on the river nearly one time out of seven (six out of forty-four unseen cards). Since this is such a common occurrence, it is good to have a game plan for dealing with it effectively.

Getting counterfeited won't always cost you the pot, and it is important to recognize when your hand is still good. If you are holding the nut low with a wheel draw, and you get counterfeited, then a player who has not been aggressive now bets, you are almost certainly beat. For example, say you are holding A-2-K-Q, the board is 4-5-8-Q, and the river is a deuce. If a player who has been calling to that point, bets—you are in trouble. There isn't much else this player can be betting other than a straight, so it is almost always safe to fold. The exception is when you are playing against a tricky, sophisticated opponent, who is capable of betting an A-6 here, hoping your A-2 got counterfeited and that you will fold a better high hand than his.

In a larger field, say more than three opponents, someone will often produce a better two card low hand when you get counterfeited. But in pots with only two or three players you might still win the low, so it is important not to fold too quickly. Rather, gauge the chances that your opponent's bet signifies a high hand. If you think this is the case, you might be able to play your live ace or deuce to win the low. Also, it's possible that your new high hand will be good. If you already had one pair, you now have two pair, which might win the high against a small field. Omaha eight-or-better players are notorious for moaning all the way to the bank in situations like this, complaining even as they catch the very card that wins them the pot.

Playing Three-Way Pots on the End

It is very common for there to be exactly three players left in the hand at the river, so it's important that you learn how to make accurate decisions in this situation. Following are some general guidelines that should be helpful.

1. When You Are First To Act. If you have the best hand, bet! This seems obvious, but you'd be surprised how often players check the nuts. In Omaha eight-or-better, playing for a check-raise on the river is generally a bad idea, unless you know for certain that an opponent will bet a worse hand. Unless they are bluffing, Omaha players tend only to bet hands that are the nuts or close to it on the river. So, if you attempt a check-raise with the nut high, you are likely to only coax a bet out of an opponent if he's holding the nut low. Nothing is gained from this maneuver. However, if you bet, an opponent might call with a worse high hand.

Sometimes a bet on the river will win you not only the side of the pot you have locked up, but the entire pot. If you are holding A-3-4-Q, the board shows 2-5-8-10-J, and you are positive that your opponents don't have you three-quartered, you should bet with just the nut low. A bet will often cause an opponent to fold a busted hand like A-2-K-Q (nut flush draw), even though he has you beat for high. Also, hands like A-4-6-7 will pay you off with the second-nut low, and you will be able to scoop them with the nut low and A-Q high. Although you won't get results like these every time, it should be clear that being aggressive has a lot of value.

2. When the First Player Bets and You're Next To Act. Here is a situation in which you must be willing to stick your neck out a bit. When the board contains three to a low hand but not a wheel possibility, and you have a marginal hand in both directions, you need to either raise or fold. Calling is a mistake, as it opens the door for the third player to call behind you. With a weak two-way hand, it is important to eliminate the other player and play heads-up against the bettor, hoping to win in one direction or the other.

Suppose the board shows 3-4-8-J-Q, and your hand is A-3-4-7. With bottom two pair for high and A-7 for low, it's unlikely that you will get a piece of the pot against more than one opponent. However, it will be difficult for a single opponent to scoop your hand heads-up, as he must use all four of his cards to beat you both ways. If you raise, the third player might fold a better two pair or better lows such as A-5, 2-5, and A-6.

Lean toward folding if the board contains a five-card low straight or a flush possibility. It will be easier for a lone opponent to scoop you in this case, plus there is the increased possibility that you will be reraised, meaning you'll have to risk three bets with the play rather than two. For example, if the board is 3-4-5-8-10 (flush) and you hold A-3-5-7 without having a flush, any opponent with A-2 has you scooped, as does one with a flush and a slightly better low than yours.

A completely different situation arises when the first player bets, and you are next to act holding the nut low and a very weak high hand. Here, the debate is whether to raise or call. If you know that the bettor has your high beat, calling is clearly the right play. You don't want to eliminate the third party and are fishing for the over-call. However, things are seldom this black and white. It is a big mistake to just call with the nut low, only to find that the original bettor was betting the nut low with no pair himself. Now, the third player might call with a marginal high hand and win half the pot, chips that would be heading your direction had you raised. Therefore, it is best to raise most of the time if you are holding the nut low with a high hand of one pair or better, unless you think the original bettor can beat your high hand.

When you make this play consistently, you should be prepared to receive a flurry of hate mail in the form of dirty looks and sarcastic comments from your opponents. Sometimes you will raise and the third player will be holding the nut low himself, so you wind up getting quartered while the initial bettor wins the high. This third player, disgusted at your raise, might mutter something to the effect of "How could that idiot raise with just the nut low? What did he think I had?"

It is true that if you regularly raise in this situation, you will sometimes cost yourself money, either because you get quartered or because you raise out the third player when the initial bettor was going high. However, it is also true that this play will occasionally win you the high half of the pot. The question is whether the fractions of bets you lose when you're wrong outweigh the half-pots you win when you are right. This play doesn't have to work out very often for you to show a profit, so you should use it any time you feel it has even a small chance of succeeding.

Here is one final scenario pertaining to three-way pots when your hand is the second to act. If you have a hand of A-3-5-K (king-high flush) with a board of 4-6-8-10-J (making your flush), you hold the second-best hand in each direction, which is a good, but not great situation in Omaha eight or better. It is best when you are the one doing the betting, since anyone that can beat your high hand would surely bet, and it is likely that the nut low hand would bet as well. Nevertheless, second-second is usually good enough for at least half the pot. In this case, if the first player bets, it likely signifies that he has you beat one way or another, so there isn't much point in raising. A worse hand behind you will fold, but a better hand will call or reraise, since the only better high or low hand is the nuts. Also, if you raise, you risk the possibility of a reraise from the original bettor.

3. When You're Last To Act on the River. If you only have the nut low and it's a bet and a call to you on the end, it is an easy, comfortable play to just call. This is not necessarily the correct play, though. Although you will lose money by raising if you only get a quarter of the pot, you are costing yourself even more money in the long run when you just call and get half. Here is why: Assuming a $10/$20 game, so the last bet is $20:

> (1) If you raise and win only a quarter of the pot, splitting the low side, you lose $5 on the raise ($20 x 3, you get back $15).

> (2) If you raise and win half of the pot, you win $10 on the raise ($20 x 3, you get back $30).

What this means is that you are getting a price of 2 to 1 on this raise. For raising to be incorrect, you must be quartered more than two out of three times. This will not be the case, especially if you refrain from raising when you are reasonably sure another player has the nut low.

Essentially, any time you have a reasonable doubt as to whether another nut low is out there, you should raise. Most players do the opposite in this spot. They will just call, feeling that they might be quartered. In fact, they should raise, because they might win half the pot.

When a sophisticated player is in the pot with you, you need to be aware that he may use some of the plays discussed here. He may not always hold what he is representing. He might raise on the river in an attempt to knock you out of the pot, rather than raising just on the strength of his hand. This happens more at the higher limits, though, and a river raise in smaller Omaha eight-or-better games nearly always signifies a nut hand.

If one of these tricky players is in your game and attempts to knock you out, you might call a raise from him on the river with a weaker-than-normal hand, such as two medium pair.

However, don't forget that the original bettor may have you beat, and might choose to reraise. This is a difficult situation to play correctly, and it draws on all your skills as a poker player.

Advanced River Play

Value Betting

When you bet for value, you do so because you believe you have a better hand than your opponents and may be called by one with an inferior hand. You do not, however, have the nuts, and there is a possibility that you'll be beaten. You bet because you feel that it will be profitable in the long run and that you will be called and win more often than you will be called and lose.

One major consideration is whether or not your opponents tend to bet for value. Some players seem to bet only the nuts on the river, so discretion must be exercised in betting medium strength hands against them. Just because one such opponent checks to you, it doesn't mean he isn't holding a very strong hand, so you must value bet less frequently.

Other players will pay off anything and everything. They might go home broke, but they won't go home curious. Against these types, bet any hand that you feel has a better than even-money chance to be the best hand. Since a player like this might call with as little as one pair, it is often a mistake to check hands like two pair if it is checked to you, even if bigger hands such as straights or flushes are possible. If an opponent like this tends to bet their good hands and you have anything decent at all, you can safely assume that if he checks, you have the best hand. So go ahead and bet it for value.

When you play against a mixed bag of players, you must exercise good judgment in betting for value. Some tricky players will try to check-raise on the end if they make their hands. When these players act before you and a scary card hits the board, you should think twice before betting.

Also, sometimes an extremely tight player will check the

best hand on the end. If this player has been betting throughout the hand, his check shouldn't be misinterpreted as a sign of weakness. Maybe his right arm got tired. Or maybe a card came that slightly weakened his hand. For example, he may hold something like A-3-10-J (ace-high flush) with a board of 4-5-7-Q-Q (nut flush). Although he has the nut flush and second nut low, the fact that the board paired means that he can still be beaten, so he checks the river. There are quite a few Omaha eight-or-better players who play in this fashion, particularly in the smaller games. If you can recognize them, this will help you avoid betting hands like A-4-K-K (king-high flush) for value when they are in the pot and have shown some strength.

Position has a huge influence on how often you can bet for value. This is one of the most important benefits of acting last in the hand. For example, suppose you hold A-2-3-Q (nut flush) in a four-way pot, and the board shows 4-5-9-J-4. The pot is fairly large, and you have what is possibly the best hand. Against more opponents, it would be more likely that someone has the full house. In a heads-up or three-way pot, your hand is most likely good. But in this case, you're not sure. If you had to act first, you would likely check, fearing a raise from a full house. However, if you have last position and it is checked around to you, betting for value is usually the best play.

Another example of how position can win you extra bets on the river is if you are holding A-3-Q-Q, and the board shows Q-J-7-5-K. Once again, if you are first to act and several players are behind you, you should probably check, as it is likely that one of them has made a straight. But if you are last and it is checked to you, go ahead and bet your three queens for value. You will probably be called by anyone with kings-up, a smaller set, and possibly some worse hands, too. It is also possible that someone made a straight, and is planning on check-raising you. Remember that you don't need to have a lock to bet.

Catching Bluffs

When deciding upon the most profitable course of action on the river, you will occasionally have to choose between betting your hand for value and checking to induce an opponent to bluff. This decision must be made when there are players remaining to act behind you. Basically, if you do not believe you are likely to be called by a worse hand, or if you have very aggressive players behind you, it is often best to adopt a strategy of checking and calling. This can even be done with very strong hands.

For example, say you have A-3-5-K, and the board comes 2-6-6-J-K. It is likely that your kings-up are good in a pot with a small number of opponents. However, it is unlikely you will be called, except by a hand equal to yours or possibly a jack. This is another situation in which checking to an aggressive player has some value. If you check, he might try to steal the pot, hoping that you have missed your low draw and will now fold to a bet.

Against a calling station, though, betting for value is probably best. Being aware of your opponents' playing styles is worth many bets in this and similar situations.

Using Scare Cards To Your Advantage

Sometimes the texture of the board cooperates to make it more likely that your bluff attempt will be successful. Players tend to pay off in Omaha eight-or-better unless the board shows a strong hand that they believe one of their opponents holds. For example, a board of A-K-Q-J makes it very difficult for an opponent to call if he is not holding the straight. However, it is very possible that no one has the nuts, and this very well could be one situation in which you will get credit for a straight if you bet.

The very idea of bluffing into a four-card straight board is not one that occurs to many players. Attempting to bluff here is a great play because by the time you get to the river, the pot should be large enough to give a good price on stealing it.

Therefore, this play needs to work only occasionally for it to show a nice profit.

Four cards to a wheel, such as A-2-4-Q-3 (or 5) is another scary board that might be worth a steal attempt, as long as no one has shown very much interest to this point. It will be difficult for anyone without a wheel to call you. As with the previous bluff, this play needs to work only a small percentage of the time to be profitable. However, this play is a bad idea when the board is 2-3-4-5-x, as at least one player—including you—should have a wheel.

When you are going for low and the board trips up on the end, it is worthwhile sometimes to take a stab at the pot against a relatively small number of opponents. There is a good chance that no one will be holding a pair, and most opponents won't call a bet with just ace-high when trips are on the board. You can check down hands like A-2-3-K or A-2-5-Q, since your high kicker might win the pot for you. However, if you are holding something like A-2-3-4, you have no chance to win unless you bet.

Although a bluff attempt is sometimes the only way you can win the pot, it is still important that you exercise some discretion. If you consistently try to bluff the river, your opponents will recognize this and start calling you down. The more astute ones will check their big hands to you, knowing you may try a bluff. Also, it doesn't matter how scary the board is, some opponents just have to see your hand. Have some respect for your chips, and don't fire in bluffs when calling stations are in the pot.

With that in mind, Omaha eight-or-better pots are typically large enough on the river to justify a bluff attempt into a scary board. If you are selective and execute these bluffs on pots with two or fewer opponents who are trying to play well, you should show a profit.

Conclusion

The most important concept to take with you from this section is that aggressive play gets rewarded. With that in mind, remember to make raises that can help you win half the pot, and to bet aggressively when you are holding the nuts. Also, don't forget to bet for value when you believe you hold the best hand, and keep some bluffing plays in your repertoire. The large pots in this game allow you to err on the side of aggression, as your bets don't have to be successful every time to turn you a profit.

BONUS TOPICS

This section will cover some related topics and provide more in-depth commentary on material already discussed.

Playing 2-3, A-4, and Similar Hands

Many Omaha eight-or-better players regularly play hands in which 2-3 or A-4 represent their best prospects for low. While these hands should not be played automatically in a full-handed game, there are times when you should see the flop with them. You will cost yourself some profitable opportunities if you automatically fold these hands.

Position influences when these types of hands become playable. It is probably best to play 2-3 and A-4 hands when you are near the button, as you can more accurately gauge when an opponent has you beat for low. Also, if a few good players have already entered the pot, you'll know your low draw is assuredly not the best. Additionally, the cards you need to flop—aces in the case of 2-3, and deuces and threes in the case of A-4—are probably not live. Therefore, folding is usually the right move.

Sometimes the field will fold around to you in a late position when you have a hand like 2-3-4-7 (suited). In the case of the 2-3-

4-7, it is likely that the ace you need to make the nut low is quite live in the deck, which makes your hand more playable. Also, you will have position on the blinds. A raise is probably your best play, especially if the blinds are tight players who will fold without a strong hand. Calling is fine if there are loose players in the blinds. However, if it's folded around to you on or near the button and you are holding A-4-6-8 (suited), you should probably raise rather than call. There are three reasons for this:

(1) You have one of the aces in your hand, making it less likely for one of the blinds to have a good hand. This may increase your chances of winning the blinds.

(2) You're unlikely to make the nut low, and raising may cause an opponent with 2-3 or A-4 to fold.

(3) The blinds are also likely to fold hands dominated by middle cards, which increases the high potential for your own middle cards.

If a late position player has opened the pot for a raise, and you are next with a hand like A-4-5-K or A-4-K-Q, you should consider reraising, hoping to play the pot heads-up. Unless your opponent has two aces, your hand has a good chance to win the high. Although your opponent likely has a better low draw, you hold better high potential. You also have position, which should allow you to steal the pot if your opponent doesn't connect with the flop.

When several players are in, hands containing 2-3 or A-4 might still be playable. Generally, you want to play these hands for only one bet, though, and it is important that your other two cards have some value. Hands such as 2-3-4-6, 2-3-Q-K (suited), A-4-6-Q, and A-4-10-J are probably worth a call when several players have limped in front of you. However, hands like 2-3-7-10, 2-3-9-K, A-4-8-K, or A-4-7-9 belong in the muck.

Having Backup Cards for Low Help

How helpful is having backup cards for low help? The short answer to this question is: very helpful! Take a look at the following figures:

(1) When you flop the nut low draw without a backup card, you will complete the hand about 57% of the time.

(2) However, you will pair your low draw (be counterfeited) nearly 25% of the time on the turn and river.

(3) You will make your low draw on the turn about 34% of the time, and then be counterfeited on the river 13% of the time.

(4) When you flop the nut low draw with backup, you will complete the hand 70% of the time.

(5) Only 3% of the time will both the turn and river counterfeit your hand when you have backup.

These numbers clearly demonstrate why having extra low cards in your hand is so important. Since you will be counterfeited nearly 25 percent of the time when you only have a two-card low-draw, it's questionable how aggressively you can play. The added value of the additional low card permits a far more aggressive approach. Another bonus of the backup card is that you have far greater straight potential. For example, with a board of 4-5-K, there is a huge difference between holding just an A-2 (four cards to complete your straight) versus an A-2-3 (thirteen cards to complete your straight).

Why Kings-Up Is the Best Two Pair To Flop

Besides the obvious fact that kings-up beat queens-up in a showdown, there are other good reasons to consider kings-up to be the only two pair in Omaha eight-or-better that is of much value. First, since a king is a high card, its presence on the board makes it more difficult for a low hand to be made. Although aces-up would be the best two pair, when an ace is on the board it is far more likely that the pot will be split with a low hand.

Since kings are the highest cards in the deck other than aces, it is unlikely that they will lose to a better two pair. Specifically, it will take a better kings-up hand to beat them. As a good Omaha eight-or-better player, you will generally have an ace in your hand when you flop kings-up, so if the ace then hits, you will now make the top two pair. Although top two pair is a dicey hand against several opponents, it should win a good percentage of the time against a small field.

A major problem with two pair is that there will nearly always be a straight possibility when the board is unpaired. In fact, in order for no straight to be possible, there must be a king, a queen, or both on the final board. This grants a little extra value to kings-up or queens-up.

A hand like A-4-10-J with a flop of J-10-6 is in trouble even though it is most likely the best hand on the flop. There are lots of dangerous turn cards, and even more peril waiting on the river. Any overcard produces the possibility of someone making either a straight or a higher two pair. (This won't be the case if you flop kings-up, because the straight could still beat you, but a higher two pair will not.) A low card provides a temporary reprieve, as your two pair is still likely to be the best hand. However, every low card creates an additional straight draw of some sort, and every river card in the deck that doesn't pair the board creates the possibility of a straight. These types of hands have a chance against a few players, but are in trouble if you are unable to narrow the field.

Playing Shorthanded

Playing shorthanded Omaha eight-or-better—that is with four or fewer players—is dramatically different from playing in a ring game. Probably the most distinct change is in the values of starting hands. In a full game, few hands without an ace are playable. Of these, most are hands with four high-cards. If you're playing shorthanded, however, you cannot afford to sit and wait for great starting cards. Not only do they not come around very often, they don't win with the same percentage as premium hands in other games.

Premium starting hands in full games are so valuable because they can improve to make nut hands, which is frequently what it takes to win the pot. In a shorthanded game, however, you generally don't need to show the nuts to win. High hands, such as any two pair, or lows as weak as the fourth nuts will often get the money. This allows you to play a broader range of hands.

Hands such as 3-4-5-6 (double-suited) are trash in ring games against several players, but are well above average in a three- or four-handed game. In a shorthanded game, you are looking for versatile hands more than simply nut potential, and the above hand is a poster child for versatility. Even a low hand as weak as 3-4 or 3-5 might be good enough in a shorthanded game, as your opponents won't necessarily have A-2 or A-3. Against a full table, though, someone is more likely to show you a better low.

The necessity of holding an ace in your hand is less pronounced in a shorthanded game. This is not to say that aces aren't still the best cards in the deck. It's just that, typically, aces are required to make nut hands—lows or flushes, in particular—and the need to make the nuts is not as great.

How does this fact affect your decision-making? Mainly, it means that versatile hands such as the aforementioned 3-4-5-6 (double-suited) become much more playable, and hands such as A-2-2-8 become more marginal. The fact is that while A-2-2-8 may make the nut low, which is good enough to win half of a pot, it will be hard-pressed to scoop without some miracle board such as 3-4-8-8-Q. It is important to look at a hand's scoop potential, and hands with little chance to scoop should be approached more conservatively in shorthanded games. If you take half of a pot heads-up, you make no money (except for half of possibly forfeited blinds), but if you take half of a multiway pot, you do make money. So, you should be much more reluctant to play low-only hands shorthanded.

One type of hand that becomes more playable in shorthanded games is a big pair with two low cards. For example, hands like A-7-K-K (either suited or unsuited) should be folded in a full game. But this is usually a raising hand in a four-handed game. In a three-way pot, the kings may very well win the high even if you don't improve them. And although A-7 is not much of a low draw, it is good to have it for backup should the kings get beat. Don't underestimate the value of any low draw in your hand when playing shorthanded, because frequently none of your opponents will end up with a low.

CONCLUSIONS

Although there is a lot to consider when playing Omaha eight-or-better, the game doesn't have to be that complicated. If you can learn to play quality hands in good position, you will avoid being confronted with too many difficult decisions. It is crucial to remember that in multiway pots, it frequently takes the nuts to win. Therefore, you have to be able to quickly recognize whether your hand has nut potential. And if it doesn't, you should usually fold.

In pots with three or fewer players, hands such as two pair or mediocre lows have some value. This permits you a bit more leeway in your starting requirements. Again, position is important. The later you act, the better idea you will have about the number of opponents you'll face and how strong their hands are.

You'll benefit from keeping in mind the concepts discussed in this section as the hand plays out. It is good to remember, though, that every situation is slightly different. The wide variety of variables, such as how your opponents are playing, the size of the pot, the number of opponents in the hand, and your position, mean that every Omaha eight-or-better problem is unique. You must make the best decision you can, based on the information available to you.

Realize that poker is a dynamic game, in which your decision-making has to adapt to constantly changing conditions. As you gain experience, you will learn to better assess the game, which will allow you to make good decisions. The concepts discussed in this section should help speed up your learning curve.

Omaha eight-or-better is a great game, because it presents a greater number of challenging decisions than any other form of poker. And now you know how to make those decisions profitably.

SEVEN-CARD STUD
HIGH-LOW
EIGHT-OR-BETTER

Todd Brunson

The old saying, "The apple doesn't fall far from the tree," is certainly true when it comes to my son, Todd Brunson. In 1989 after three years of college, studying to be a lawyer, Todd stunned me by announcing that he wasn't going back to school for his senior year. "I want to be a professional poker player," he explained. We had never talked much about gambling in my household, and I didn't even know that Todd knew how to play poker. It turned out he had been playing in the area around his college, Texas Tech in Lubbock. He had gotten fairly proficient and decided he liked it more than his studies. So at the age of 20, Todd started his career as a pro.

It soon became apparent that he had the skills to win. When he was 21, Todd won first-place at the $200,000 main-event in the Diamond Jim Brady tournament at the Bicycle Club in Los Angeles. It was the first of nine career wins in big tournaments.

Todd had an uncanny ability to remember things, even as a young child. I've always thought that a poker player's greatest gift is the ability to recall past hands and events, and I'm sure that his amazing knack for vividly remembering the past has helped him a lot.

Allow me to exercise my bragging rights by telling you a little story about Todd. I always knew that he was a great hold'em player, but he supported my belief in spades this past year in the two biggest games I've ever heard of. A brilliant businessman came to Vegas to challenge the world's best poker players. It was clear to me that his strategic capabilities extended beyond business and into poker. He wanted to play so high that his poker challengers needed to pool their money just to accommodate him. For ten days this wealthy executive battled different players to a standstill, a very rare feat for someone who doesn't practice day-in and day-out. We were all impressed.

Then Todd sat down to play him heads-up in a "friendly little game" of $50,000-$100,000 Texas hold'em. On the first day of their two-day match, Todd won $7 million. He slipped a little bit on the second day, tallying only $6.5 million more. I'm certain this game will become a part of poker folklore.

Todd's winnings in that Texas hold'em game were over $20 million. He also plays daily in the world's largest ongoing poker game, in which he is one of the most consistent winners. But, although his strengths at hold'em are unquestionable, his insights into seven-card stud eight-or-better are perhaps even more remarkable. That's why I've chosen him to write this chapter. There's no doubt in my mind that you'll be hearing the Brunson name in poker for years after I'm gone.

SEVEN-CARD STUD HIGH-LOW EIGHT-OR-BETTER
by Todd Brunson

INTRODUCTION

Seven-card stud high-low split eight-or-better to qualify for low, commonly known as eight-or-better, is found in home games and casinos throughout the world. In seven-card stud, each player is dealt three cards to start, two down and one up. This first upcard is called the **doorcard**. There is a round of betting, then three more upcards are dealt to each player with a round of betting following each card. Each player then receives his final card, known as **seventh street** or the **river**, which is dealt facedown. A final round of betting follows.

Throughout this chapter, I'll use examples to identify each player's cards. The first two cards shown will be the players initial two hole cards and the next one, two, three or four cards are the upcards. A final seventh card will either be shown by itself to the right of the four upcards or grouped with the first two downcards.

In many cases, your opponents' holecards will be represented by x's, meaning they are hidden or **buried**. Here's an example where all cards are shown:

You:	K-9	6-2-3-K	7
Player One:	2-3	A-J-5-3	2
Player Two:	J-J	5-J-Q-7	9

This example shows the three downcards together plus the x's representing unknown cards held by the opponents.

You:	A-2-A	5-8-7-10
Player One:	x-x-x	Q-4-6-9
Player Two:	x-x-x	A-5-8-J

During tournaments, there are many lower-limit ($5/$10 to $15/$30) and middle- to high-middle limit ($30/$60 to $200/$400) games where less experienced players can be found. Unfortunately, they seem to dry up when the tournament ends.

In the bigger limits, straight eight-or-better games are rare, but usually they are an important part of the composite that makes up the mixed games. If you have any aspirations of rising to the top in poker, you must learn all the games, especially eight-or-better. It's almost always included in the mixed games.

If you're unable to find low-limit training games in your area, you might need to get experience in medium-limit games. Granted $30/$60 or $50/$100 are extremely high limits to start out on, but besides this book, experience is the most important weapon in your poker arsenal. While smaller eight-or-better games are not popular in Las Vegas, they exist in your local card rooms and on the internet. Entering smaller buy-in tournaments is another good way of gaining experience without putting too big a strain on your bankroll.

One bit of good news on the bankroll front: Your swings should be much lower in eight-or-better than in many other forms of poker. First, you'll play fewer starting hands. And second, of the low hands you start with, you will usually get out of the pot early, or find yourself with a playable low draw after four cards. In this case, you'll make a low the majority of the time, which will win you at least half of the pot. As you follow along, remember that the lowest exposed card is forced to start the betting by making a token blind bet.

Once you find a place to start your eight-or-better career, read and memorize the concepts in this chapter, then just try and keep it simple. Unlike many other forms of poker, in eight-or-better, you usually have to show down a hand. This means, don't try and get too fancy too quickly. At first, keep it simple and play very straightforward poker. The time to make plays will come, but first you must know how to recognize the proper situation. My advice: Be patient!

For this book, I have picked what I feel are the eighteen most important concepts needed to master eight-or-better. The following is the most important of all the concepts, not just in eight-or-better but all split games. So, I'm going to start my chapter with this rule.

CONCEPT 1:
SCOOPING—THE PLATINUM RULE

The object of the game is winning the whole pot, also known as **scooping**. Of all the concepts I'll cover in this section, this one is the most important. I can't emphasize this point strongly enough. You've heard of the Golden Rule? Well since this is twice as important, I call it my **Platinum Rule**. When you are deciding whether or not to enter a pot or proceed to the next street, you should always ask yourself, "Can I scoop this *whole* pot? Or am I playing for half?" If you are only playing for half, strongly consider folding. There are exceptions to this rule, and we'll cover these later in the chapter, but always keep this rule in mind. Tattoo it into your memory.

Just as the continental divide separates the eastern and western United States, this concept separates mediocre players from great ones. Extremely smart and successful people play this game for decades, learn the ins and outs of the game, and then forever break even—or lose. This concept simply eludes people for some reason. Learn and practice my Platinum Rule and you will have a leg up on some more seasoned veterans.

CONCEPT 2: THREE BIG OR THREE LITTLE, BUT NEVER THREE IN THE MIDDLE

Three Big

If you're playing a pair, you'll want the biggest pair. Never play catch-up like you might in stud high. Two jacks with a king kicker against a raiser with a queen up is a good spot in stud high, but usually not in eight-or-better. There are two reasons for this. First of all, in stud, there's a real good chance that the raiser doesn't actually have the two queens. A three-flush, three-straight or a smaller pocket pair are actually more likely. Therefore, a call with jacks in stud is usually a sound play. This is not so in eight-or-better though. When a queen comes in with a raise in eight-or-better, he will usually have what he's representing, a big pair. This is a much more straightforward game than straight high.

A second reason you won't want to play less than the biggest pair in eight-or-better is that you will most likely pick up at least one hitchhiker going low. Now, not only are you a dog to win the high half of the pot, there's a good chance the low half will be gone, even if you manage to draw out on the queens. And you also need to consider the fact that the low hitchhiker may make a straight or some other hand that beats you.

So, like I said in the beginning of this concept: Always try and start with the biggest pair.

Three in the Middle

Avoid split nines, tens, and even jacks or queens on third street if you have overcards behind you. There are two exceptions to this rule, and they both come into play on rare occasions:

(1) There's nothing higher than an 8 on the board; or

(2) You are low with split eights or another low pair.

In the latter scenario, you would simply revert to seven-card high strategy and play underpairs with a kicker higher than your opponent's upcard.

Three Little

The three little cards component of this concept is basically self-explanatory. All three of your starting cards need to be below an eight. However, just because all three are below an eight doesn't mean it's a playable hand. You will usually need some type of high potential to accompany your low. This leads to our next concept.

CONCEPT 3: STARTING LOW HANDS

Three Suited Babies

The mother of all low starting hands is the three suited "babies." **Babies**, for the purpose of this section, are aces through eights. If your hand contains an ace or a three-straight, so much the better. This hand is only surpassed in value by a **rolled-up hand**; that is, three of a kind. When you have three suited babies, the more opponents still in, the better. If you are the first to enter the pot, raise as you normally would. If it has already been raised and there are players behind you, just call—don't shut out any customers. If you are last to act with no players behind you, go ahead and put in the extra raise, a move that might disguise your hand to less experienced players. More experienced players may put you on this hand, so the extra raise definitely has a drawback. Play it by ear, but when you are undecided on the correct play, lean heavily toward raising.

No-Gappers

The next best starting low hand is the three-straight. In this game, **no-gappers** are obviously the best option because there are eight possible cards that would give you an open-ended straight draw to go with your low draw—in other words, a monster. These hands include: 6-7-8, 5-6-7, 4-5-6, 3-4-5, 2-3-4, and especially A-2-3. You also have eight cards to give you a gutshot to go with your low draw. Not exactly a monster, but not too shabby, either.

The 5-6-7 and the 6-7-8 are especially good combinations against strictly high hands. With the 6-7-8, you can catch a 9 or a 10 to improve your hand but still keep that new strength completely hidden from your opponent. The 5-6-7 can also catch a 9 that will never look like a good card to your opponent. For example:

Example One
You: 6-7   5-3-9
Player One: K-Q   K-Q-9

In this example, Player One would most likely bet out on fifth street, thinking you caught bad. You now have an easy raise, having eight outs (four aces and four twos) to split, and eight more outs (four fours and four eights) to scoop the whole pot, not once, but twice—on sixth street and the river.

Example Two

You:	6-7	8-4-10
Player One:	K-Q	K-Q-9

Again, Player One will assume that the 10 was a bad card for you. In reality, you now have two chances to hit twelve outs for low and eight outs to scoop the whole pot. For you, a raise is even easier in this situation since you have four more outs for low than in the first example. Notice that you could also catch a 9 on fifth street with the same results.

One-Gappers

The next subset of hands are the **one-gappers**: 5-6-8, 5-7-8, 4-5-7, 4-6-7, 3-4-6, 3-5-6, 2-3-5, 2-4-5, A-3-4 and A-2-4. Except for the hands with an ace, you can catch four cards that will give you an open-end straight to go with your low draw. As with the no-gappers, eight cards will give you a gutshot. For instance:

Example One

You:	3-5	6
Player One:	x-x	8

In this example, if Player One raised coming in, you would simply want to call. Granted, if you and your opponent are both going low, you have the best low draw. But if he has split eights or a buried overpair, you would be well behind in the hand. Also, regardless of his holecards, you can't even beat the 8-high.

If you catch an ace, 2, 4, or 7 on fourth street, you'll want to raise Player One, regardless of what he catches—the one possible exception being if you caught an ace and Player One breaks into open eights. If both you and your opponent catch bad, you should call. This is one of the rare situations in eight-or-better where you could consider calling, even if you catch bad and your opponent catches good. There are two reasons for this:

(1) Obviously, your opponent can catch bad on fifth street while you catch good, making you the favorite to win the hand.

(2) Even if he catches good again, you can still hit sixteen cards (an ace, 2, 4, or 7) to put you in good shape against his two most likely hands—a made 8-low or a pair with an 8-low draw. If he has an overpair in the hole that aren't aces, you're in really good shape.

If you hit bad again on fifth street, don't even consider calling, regardless of what he catches.

Two-Gappers and Double-Gappers

The final subsets are the two-gapper and the double-gapper. **Two-gappers** and **double-gappers** are about the same in value. The double-gappers are: 8-7-4, 8-5-4, 7-6-3, 7-4-3, 6-5-2, 6-3-2, 5-4-A, and 5-2-A. The two-gappers are 8-6-4, 7-5-3, 6-4-2, and 5-3-A. These hands are fairly good, but the ones without an ace are still marginal. You should usually call one bet on third street with the marginal ones, but not two.

Your strategy would change only if both opponents go high, or if one is high the other has an 8-up, and you have three cards smaller than the 8. The reason being: If you make your low, it will probably beat his 8-low. Also, although it is fairly difficult to make straights with these hands, it's not impossible.

Both the two-gappers and double-gappers have twelve cards to catch to pick up a low draw and eight cards to pick up a gutshot straight draw to accompany the low draw. They need to develop early in the hand, especially in multiway pots. Say you have one of these hands in a multiway pot and you only catch the low draw without the straight. If it appears that you have the worst low, don't get stubborn. Get out. Here's an example:

Example One

You:	8-4	7-2
Player One:	x-x	6-4
Player Two:	x-x	Q-9

In this example, we should assume that Player Two has split queens or some other high hand. As you have no high possibilities, you have to fight with Player One for the low. Assuming Player One didn't pair, the only possible situation where you could have the best low draw would be if Player One had exactly 7-8 in the hole, which is highly unlikely. Even if that were the case, you would still only get the low about 60 percent of the time.

Most players will at least take one card here. Don't bother—save that extra bet. It may not seem like much now, but a few of these expert saves, tacked on to the rest of your tally at the end of the night, can turn a break-even play into a nice win, or keep what would have been a bad loss into a small one. Remember, every bet counts!

Ace and Two Babies

Next in the hierarchy of starting low hands is an ace with any other two low cards that won't make a straight. This hand often will have the best low draw, with the added potential of hitting the ace at anytime throughout the hand. It may not even be necessary to pair the ace against another low hand; it may win you the high all by itself. For example:

Example One

You:	A-3	6-7-4-9	K
Player One:	3-6	8-7-10-Q	2

Notice that not only do you have a board lock on the low end, but the ace-high gives you the best high as well. This results in a scooped pot—the two sweetest words in all of poker, along with "You win," "I give," "I missed," and "That's good."

Remember, the ace with two babies that aren't both wheel cards can be a great hand. It should be played very aggressively early on. You don't want any middle pairs hanging around to steal your high half of the pot, and if you have the ace-up, you can get rid of even big pairs right away. Consider this example:

Example Two

You:	4 -6	A
Player One:	5-6	4
Player Two:	K-J	K

In this example, you can probably get the kings to fold on third or fourth street if you catch good. The trick is to keep the heat on. Raise the bet on third street or reraise if it gets completed in front of you. But this is a tricky hand, and getting rid of the kings is only half the battle here.

You still have Player One to deal with—that's the other half of the battle. Now that you're heads-up with the best high and the best low, a scoop looks easy. But looks can be deceiving. If you make a low, it will be best almost 55 percent of the time, and Player One's 4-5-6 will wind up with the best high a little over 55 percent of the time. Net result? The 4-5-6 is about a one percent overall favorite against the A-4-6. I know this is hard to believe, but it goes to show you the strength of the straight potential with a 4-5-6. This shows that you're better off getting 49.5 percent of a heads-up pot with some dead money in it, than 32 percent of a three way pot. So try and get those kings to fold!

Hands with an 8

On a final note in this concept, I'd like to touch on eights, because you're in jeopardy almost anytime you have one in your hand. This point is so complex that Concept 12 is totally devoted to it, but I still wanted to touch on it here. When you start with an 8—be it in a straight draw, with an ace and another baby, or even when you have the proverbial monster of three suited babies—your hand is almost always marginal. This is true unless you are only up against a high hand. Remember, an 8 loses to all other low hands except other eights.

If your 8 is the upcard in your starting hand, be very careful. You might even want to fold on third street against a scary board. Your opponents might be able to force you out with a worse concealed 8 of their own, knowing that with an 8-up, you've got your hands tied. If your 8 is concealed, your opponents can't see your weakness, which will probably stop them from jamming you out of the pot.

I'm not suggesting that you pass all hands containing an 8. Just keep these factors in mind and don't get married to the hand. These are marginal situations that take years of experience to handle correctly. Now that we've covered all the low playable hands, let's move on to the high hands.

CONCEPT 4: THE VALUE OF BIG PAIRS

If you've ever played seven-card stud high-low split with no qualifier, you're used to throwing away big pairs in almost any situation, because it's nearly impossible to scoop a pot with these starting hands. Conversely, in seven-card stud high-low with an eight-or-better to qualify, these hands have great value. Why? Here's the difference: In eight-or-better, players must qualify for low. If your opponent fails to do so, your high hand will scoop the entire pot. With a qualifier in play, your opponent can't freeroll with his unmade hand. For instance:

Example One

You:	3-4	6-7-J-Q
Player One:	K-K	9-2-7-9

If you were playing without a qualifier, you would have the low half locked up with your jack-low—the best low hand Player One can make is a king—and you would be freerolling with your gutshot. However, playing with a qualifier for low, you now have to catch the 5 to hit your gutshot for the scoop, or an ace, 2, or 8 for a low. You go from a huge favorite to a huge dog as we shift between the two different games.

Aces

Obviously, aces are the best pair to start with in any game. In split games, aces have the double bonus of being both high and low. Therefore, aces combined with a low card is a monster that ranks up there with the three suited babies. Which hand is better, though, is a close call. In a multiway pot, I'd take the three suited babies, but in a heads-up pot, the aces with a baby is clearly the best hand you can have other than a rolled-up hand.

So, how to play this monster? Play it very straightforward. Raise or reraise right away. Make the scoop much more likely for yourself by narrowing the field. In the previous section, I explained that it's best to play your ace-up with two babies in the hole very aggressively, and this is why: Your opponents will be confused by the way you play both hands similarly. And due to the deception you used earlier, they'll often die with their kings or queens.

Aces without a small kicker should be played in much the same way. Exceptions can be made or mixing up your play can be done after you've accumulated enough experience. In the meantime, you must know your opponent and how he will play his hand. Don't get too tricky with good players who will recognize what you are doing and find a way to make your play come back and bite you.

Here's a play that should usually be used against novice or overly aggressive players: If you have split aces and a big card raises in front of you, just call. You can also limp in from early position if there aren't too many low cards out. After slow-playing on third street, check-call if you catch high, but bet out if you catch low. This will give your opponents the impression that you have a strictly low hand. Hopefully you will catch high on fifth street and can get in a check-raise. But once you have three low cards showing, the jig is up. Play the hand out accordingly, by simply betting out the whole way. Almost no one will fall for a check-raise against an ace and two other low cards.

Other Big Pairs

After aces, it's all downhill from here. Kings and queens still have value, but much caution must be used when playing them. If an ace raises in front of you, muck them immediately. Yes, your opponent might only have two cards under an 8 to go with it, but so what? If he does have the aces you're screwed, and even if he just has a low, he can still hit the ace any time throughout the hand.

So keep this in mind: When up against an ace, big pairs degenerate into nearly worthless hands. Also, they don't play very well in multiway pots. Heads-up against a smaller pair, a low not containing an ace, or a straight draw are the ideal situations, which brings us to our next concept.

CONCEPT 5: NEVER HAVE THE SECOND-BEST HIGH HAND

I've already touched on this point, but it is so important that you avoid holding the second-best high hands, that I wanted it to have its own section. As I stated earlier, don't play underpairs without a real good reason; for example, a drunk is playing every hand and raises with a king and you have split jacks with an ace. This is still an iffy proposition unless you can get it heads-up between the two of you.

Another time you may want to play the second-best pair is if it's buried and you have a big card up. You can probably scare the best hand out of the pot and either win it right there, or get heads-up with a low draw. Example:

Example One

You:	J-J	K
Player One:	x-x	2
Player Two:	Q-9	Q

In this example, Player One would bring it in and Player Two would probably raise. A reraise would make Player Two think you had the best hand with split kings, instead of the buried jacks you actually have. Player Two would now almost certainly fold. You used the power of your upcard along with a little deception to bluff out the best hand.

Other high hands that aren't too good are three-flushes without little cards and three big connected cards. These are great hands in stud, but in eight-or-better? Forget about it.

CONCEPT 6:
MISCELLANEOUS STARTING HANDS

We've covered the high and the low starting hands; now let's discuss hands that have value in both directions, specifically small pairs with ace kickers, small pairs with baby kickers, and three-flushes with two babies.

Small Pairs with Ace Kickers

I know I've said over and over that you should never have the second-best high hand, but I also said that there are exceptions to rules, and this is one of them. A pair below eights with an ace kicker has a lot of value against a big pair other than aces, and it also has the added value of its two low cards. If heads-up against a big pair, this hand should be played out until the end, unless your opponent's board gets real scary, that is, he pairs his doorcard. If you catch small, there's a good chance that you will get a free card or two along the way; take them, and don't bother trying to bluff until you make something here.

If there is a hitchhiker in the pot who is going low, beware. You're now second best in both directions. Very dangerous! If you and the hitchhiker both catch good, proceed with caution. If you catch good and he catches bad, get rid of him if you can. If he catches good and you catch bad, take an early out , or "E.O.," in dealer lingo. Throw your hand away before you get put in the middle. If you call on fourth street, you'll almost certainly be in that vulnerable position.

Small Pairs with a Baby Kicker

A small pair with a baby kicker is a much more marginal hand. Preferably, you'll want a two-straight with your pair, and you'll need to catch good here right away, no matter what the circumstances. A possible exception would come into play if you were heads-up against another low card and you both caught bad. By **catching bad**, I mean a 9 or higher. If you're lucky enough to hit an ace right off, play it aggressively. If you're even luckier and make trips right away, bet out, and if you then catch bad on fifth or sixth street, go for the check-raise. Don't get stubborn with this marginal hand. Don't even play it if you don't think you can pass or take your free cards when appropriate.

Three-Flush with Two Babies

Finally, there is the three-flush with two babies. If your upcard is a 9, 10, or jack and a bigger card raises, you'll probably want to pass immediately. Your hand will be too obvious to your opponents, and you're less likely get paid off if you make your hand. When you have the three-flush with the biggest card up, play it aggressively, representing that pair. You'll give yourself an extra chance to win if your opponents catch bad or make small pairs. Also, when you wind up making a low, no one will suspect it. Example:

Example One

You:	2♥ 3♥	K♥ 5♦ 6♥ Q♠	8♥
Player One:	4♦ 7♥	8♣ 5♠ 10♠ 6♦	J♠

If you came into the pot with a double raise on third street, Player One will never give you credit for a three-flush. Your hand is so well disguised that Player One can't help but lose many extra bets with his 8-high straight.

Now, if you start your three-flush with a low card and not-so-low card buried and a low card up, your play should be much simpler. Don't try to get fancy here, just make it look like any other low. You might even improve into a flush draw and be forced to fold with this kind of hand. Here's an example:

Example Two

You:	3♥ J♥	5♥ Q♥ 9♦
Player One:	x-x	6♦ 2♠ 5♣
Player Two:	x-x	K♠ A♣ 8♦

In this hand, Player Two will most likely bet. You would call here and hold your breath, hoping Player One paired along the way and won't raise. If he does raise, Player Two will certainly reraise, and you'll have no choice but to fold, knowing Player One either made his low or is representing that he did. This is another time when my Platinum Rule comes into play: Never play for half.

If you still don't understand the Platinum Rule this perfectly illustrates its importance. The low half is already gone and you are an underdog to get the high half. Would you like to draw to a flush under these circumstances? If you answered yes, please come find me in the top section of the Bellagio and sit in my game.

Three-Straight with a 9-High

I'm going to include one more scenario that rarely arises. Say you have the lowest card and you have a three-straight with a 9 and two other cards 8 or below, such as 7-8-9, 6-7-9, 6-8-9, or even 5-6-9. These hands are only playable against high hands without low possibilities. While these hands are usually unprofitable in straight-high seven-card stud, the chances of backing into a low and salvaging half the pot make them worthwhile in eight-or-better. Never get involved with these against a baby.

Now that we've covered starting hands, let's move on to how you'll want to play them on later rounds.

CONCEPT 7: PLAYING BIG PAIRS

Against One Opponent

When playing a big pair, you will usually be the only player going high and will be up against either one or more low hands. Let's start with the single opponent going low.

When playing a big pair against one player who starts with a baby, you should check if he catches another low card that can give him a straight or a flush draw. If he bets, only call him; but if he catches a big card—a 9 through king, or another low card with many gaps—you should bet.

Example One

You:	K-10	K-6
Player One:	x-x	8-3 offsuit

You should go ahead and bet in this situation. Although Player One has probably picked up a low draw, his board is very weak for high. Make him pay to draw. Also, the three might have paired Player One, in which case he has few low possibilities and a much worse high hand than you. On fifth street, check-call if Player One catches a third baby and bet if he catches big.

Example Two

You:	K-10	K-6
Player One:	x-x	4-5 offsuit

Unlike the first scenario, you should definitely check when faced with this situation. The reason for the check is that Player One easily could have picked up a straight draw as well as a low draw, making him the favorite. A call is still definitely warranted, however. Remember, he may have paired or started with a pair or three-flush. As in the previous example, check-call on fifth street if Player One catches a third baby and bet if he catches big.

Example Three

You:	K-10	K-6
Player One:	x-x	2-7 suited

Example Three is not as clear cut as the first two, but a check is still the best option. Player One will almost always bet when checked to, so the street gets bet anyway and a small amount of deception is gained by your check. If Player One did pair sevens on fourth street, then catches bad on fifth, he may call you down with his sevens because of your check on fourth street.

Also, in Example Three, if Player One started with the mother of all low hands, three suited babies, you are a monster dog. Even if your opponent has only three suited cards, because of his low draw, he still has a big advantage over you. Play conservatively here and check-call.

Once again, if Player One catches a third baby on fifth street, check-call, and if he catches big, bet.

However, if Player One catches a big card that is suited to his first two, you should definitely check here. You can call, but if your opponent catches another suited card on sixth street, you'll probably have to fold—unless you have two pair. If Player One catches another low on sixth street that is offsuit, you should use a crying call here and on the end. If Player One catches another suited baby card, you should fold and run screaming from the table.

Disregarding the suits, if Player One makes four open babies in any of these examples, it's probably best to fold a pair of kings. Remember, it's going to cost two big bets to see the hand out, not just the one put in on sixth street. If you have improved to trips or kings-up, you will just have to hold your breath and check-call on sixth and seventh streets, hoping for the best. You're not breaking the Platinum Rule here because at this point, the best is still a scoop, as Player One could have made two pair and missed his low, or he could have started with a buried pair or a three-flush.

Against Multiple Opponents

Let's move on to the second and trickier half of this concept: Playing the big pair against multiple opponents going low.

When holding a high pair against multiple opponents going low, don't put extra bets in on third street unless you feel that you can narrow the field by doing so. Wait until fourth street, when some people catch bad, to put the pressure on.

Example One

You:	K-9	K
Player One:	x-x	4
Player Two:	x-x	6
Player Three:	x-x	2

Let's say that in Example One, you complete the bet and are raised by Player One, only to be called by Players Two and Three. As I stated earlier, you should just call here and see what develops. Now let's say the next round of cards looks like this:

You:	K-9	K-10
Player One:	x-x	4-7
Player Two:	x-x	6-J
Player Three:	x-x	2-J

Now is the time to weed out the field. Bet out, knowing that Player One will raise you. If Player Two or Three is stubborn enough to call the double bet here, go ahead and really punish them with another raise and make them pay to draw. It will rarely happen that players catch bad and call multiple bets once an opponent catches good, but even a so-called expert recently wrote that he would call a cap with A-2-3 on fourth street in this spot after he caught a big card. That's a terrible move because that player would then have the worst high and the worst low. Calling would be suicidal.

Now, let's say the hand develops as follows instead:

You:	K-9	K-10
Player One:	x-x	4-7
Player Two:	x-x	6-5
Player Three:	x-x	2-5

Proceed with extreme caution. Check, and if it's two bets back to you, get out early and save those bets. Even for one bet you may want to concede the hand here and now, rather than getting sucked down the tube. Remember, big pairs play well against one low hand but poorly against multiple low hands.

This basically sums up concept seven but I want to touch on one other situation briefly. What do you do when you pick up a hitchhiker who is also going high when you have the big pair?

Example Two

You:	Q-7	Q
Player One:	x-x	4
Player Two:	x-x	J

The first thing you need to ask yourself is, what kind of player is your opponent? Would he play two jacks here? Would he play a three-flush here? Hopefully for your sake, the answer to either of these questions would be yes. But if I happen to be Player Two, the answer is no, and you are in for a world of hurt. I may have an ace-baby suited, but chances are I have a concealed high hand. Again, in this situation, you should fold and run screaming from the table. This leads us into our next concept.

CONCEPT 8:
PLAYING A CONCEALED HIGH HAND

When you play a concealed high hand such as rolled-up trips, buried aces, or a buried pair bigger than anyone else's upcard, play your hand according to what your upcard represents. In other words:

(1) If you have a high card, raise as you normally would with a big pair.

(2) If you start with a middle card, raise. If a bigger card reraises you, just call until you get to bigger betting on future streets.

(3) If you catch low, represent a low hand and play accordingly. If heads-up against a high hand, you might be lucky enough to catch bad on fifth street. This will allow you to raise and get a double bet in on a big bet street.

(4) If you catch what appears to be a bad card in a multiway pot, allow yourself to be put in the middle, never showing strength, which would tip your hand.

If you are fortunate enough to start with a rolled-up hand and make quads on fourth street, remember this: In seven-card stud-high, you should almost always check this hand on fourth street. No matter how obvious it may seem, you want to give your opponent a chance to make something or some kind of draw to call you with.

Conversely, in stud eight-or-better, you want to bet out right away, no matter what. If your opponent is going low, bet whether he catches good or not. Make him pay to draw to his low, especially if he's trying to backdoor it. Also, even if it appears he is going low, he may also have a concealed high hand and might be able to continue.

CONCEPT 9: DISPELLING A LONG-HELD MISCONCEPTION

This is an extremely important concept, not just in eight-or-better, but in almost all forms of stud. Curious yet? Okay, let me break it down for you.

You're playing in an eight-handed stud game and a very tight player raises with an ace-up. Since your such a good player, you throw away split kings. Now say the same scenario arises again, only this time two players have aces showing after three cards. The same player raises, and then you reraise him, knowing it's less likely anyone can have aces since you're looking at two of them. Smart, right? Wrong. While an ace is gone, making it less likely a single player would hold aces, the fact that you're up against two players showing an ace makes it more likely that you'll be facing aces in at least one spot. Still confused? Let me break it down further.

Situation One

One opponent has an ace-up. What are the chances he has split aces or rolled-up aces? We multiply three unaccounted for aces by 39 other unknown cards and get 117 combinations of holecards that include a single ace.

$$3 \times 39 = 117$$

There are also three combinations possible in which one of your opponents has two aces in the hole for trip aces.
$$(3 \times 2) / (2 \times 1) = 3$$

That makes 120 total combinations that give your opponent aces or better (117+3). There are 861 total combinations of cards (42 unknown cards x 41 still unknown cards divided by 2) that your opponent could have in the hole. So the player with an ace up has aces or better 120 out of 861 times, 13.94 percent of the time, meaning he is a 6.18 to 1 underdog.

Situation Two

Two opponents have an ace-up. How often will one have aces or better? Now we have four holecards between the two players. Let's calculate by multiplying the number of unknown cards remaining as each card gets removed in order to derive the total number of holecard combinations.

$$42 \times 41 \times 40 \times 39 = 2{,}686{,}320$$

We divide the total number of unknown cards by 24 holecard combinations (4 possible first cards x 3 possible second cards x 2 possible third cards x 1 possible fourth card) to eliminate the possibility of counting the same hand more than once when the cards are in a different order. This leaves 111,930 combinations of buried cards that your opponents could have.

$$2{,}686{,}320 \ / \ 24 = 111{,}930$$

Using the same formula, we can calculate the number of scenarios in which exactly one of the four opposing holecards will be an ace. Multiply the number of non-aces among the unknown cards, 40, by 39 and 38, then divide that number by 6 (3 x 2 x 1) to eliminate the possibility of counting differently ordered but equal hands twice, and you get 19,760 combinations of one ace and three non-aces among the four opposing holecards.

To determine how many combinations exist in which two of the holecards will be aces, multiply the combination of both remaining aces, 1, by the number of combinations of two non-ace cards among 40 unknown non-aces, which is 1560 (40 x 39). Then divide that by 2 (2 possible first cards x 1 possible second card) to get 780 combinations of two aces and two non-aces among the four opposing holecards.

That makes a total of 20,540 combinations (19,760 + 780) out of 111,930 total in which you'll be facing at least a pair of aces from your opponents' hands. This means you'll bump up against aces or better 18.35 percent of the time. It's only 4.55 to 1 against that happening, making the threat greater than when you face a single ace.

Okay, enough with this complicated stuff, just remember: If there are two aces out, it is about 24 percent more likely that someone has split or rolled up aces than if there is only one ace-up.

CONCEPT 10: RECOGNIZING THE NUT LOW

In all forms of poker, especially in eight-or-better, it is very important to know when you have a **board lock**, meaning that it is impossible for any opponent to have your hand beat at that point. You don't want to be raised out of a pot when you have a board lock. Let's look at an example (all hands offsuit):

Example One

You:	A-4	2-5-7
Player One:	x-x	7-6-2
Player Two:	K-K	4-9-K

You have a board lock for low with your 7-5 low and, as no one has a straight or flush possible, Player Two has a board lock for high. Again, it's imperative to recognize when you have the best possible hand, whichever direction you are going. You obviously don't want to be raised out with the best hand, and you don't want to miss any bets either.

I'll add that just because you have a board lock doesn't mean you should keep raising as you may still be a dog if all the cards aren't yet out, even if you have the nuts at the time.

Example Two

You:	8-7	6-2-3
Player One:	A-2	3-4-10
Player Two:	K-Q	K-J-J

Notice that Player One has a 10-up and would need another low card to form an 8-or-better low. You have a low already made, meaning you have a board lock. Should you keep raising here? Absolutely not. You must hit runner-runner in order to make a high (about 20 to 1 against), and you are actually a dog on the low side by a few percentage points. Of course, you don't know that he has perfect low cards buried, but he's most likely drawing better than you are, so don't push it, because you're most likely playing for only half the pot. You would even fold if you could see his holecards.

Valuing a Lowball Hand

The proper way to value a lowball hand is from the weakest cards, not the strongest. For example, an inexperienced player might not know that 3-4-5-6-8 beats A-2-3-7-8 because he might start counting from the bottom of the hand, 3-4 or A-2, instead of the top, 8-6 or 8-7. But as you and I know, the 8-6 hand is obviously a better low than the 8-7. Similarly, a 7-6-5-4-A, a 7-6 hand, obviously would be better than an 8-4-3-2-A, an 8-4 hand. Notice that the hands are referred to by their two weakest cards. An A-2-4-6-7 would be called a 7-6 hand, as would a 2-3-4-6-7. But weaker players might not know right away that, in a showdown, given that the worst three cards, the 7, 6, and 4, are all identical, the first hand would win since the 2 is lower than the 3.

Although it may seem unnecessary to most readers with a background playing ace-to-five lowball, I want to take time out to make sure everyone is so comfortable with the low hand values that they don't have to give it a second thought at the table. To do this, I created the following chart to show the ranking of all the qualifying lowball hands. The chart reads from top to bottom, left to right, from the weakest low hand (the 8-7-6-5-4) to the strongest (5-4-3-2-A, the wheel).

87654	87632	8753A	86542	8642A	76543	7643A	7432A
87653	8763A	8752A	8654A	8632A	76542	7642A	65432
87652	8762A	87432	86532	85432	7654A	7632A	6543A
8765A	87543	8743A	8653A	8543A	76532	75432	6542A
87643	87542	8742A	8652A	8542A	7653A	7543A	6532A
87642	8754A	8732A	86432	8532A	7652A	7542A	6432A
8764A	87532	86543	8643A	8432A	76432	7532A	5432A

You can use this chart to help you recognize when you hold the best low possible, given the cards that are in play.

Playing the Second-Best Low Hand

Although having the second best low hand is not a spot you want to be in, it is sometimes unavoidable. This is nowhere near as bad as having the second-best high hand. Why?

First of all, you'll often know for certain when a player is going high. For instance, if an opponent with a king-up raises into multiple opponents on third street, he's definitely telling you that he's going high. On the other hand, when that same player raises into multiple opponents on third street with a 3-up instead of a king, he may be rolled up or may have a big pair in the hole. Then again, he may not. In the former situation, you know for sure which way your opponent is going; in the latter you don't. You can't simply muck all your low hands for fear of being up against a better low. That's especially true when you may be the only one that's actually going low. Also, just because you're going low, that doesn't mean you might not wind up with the high end of the pot. It's much easier to improve your low hand into a high hand than vice versa.

Take K-K-4 for example. With this starting hand, you must catch four runners to make a low. Meanwhile a hand like 5-6-7 obviously has great low potential. The difference between the two hands is that the 5-6-7 can easily develop into a high hand by making either a straight, two pair, or possibly even a flush— enabling it to scoop the entire pot! Here are some more examples to drive the point home.

Example One

You:	5-6	7
Player One:	K-K	3
Player Two:	K-J	K

Here, Player Two comes in for a raise, you call, and Player One reraises. While this looks scary from the outside, this is actually one of the best spots you can ever occupy in eight-or-better. While another player has a low card up, you are actually up against two players both going high.

Example Two

You:	5-6	7
Player One:	8-5	3 all suited
Player Two:	K-J	K

In this example, the action comes down the same way and again you fear you have the worst low. But once again, you are in good shape. While Player One is also going low, he isn't raising on the power of his low draw but on his two-way draw. You have the best low draw along with some pretty good potential for high.

Example Three
You:	5-6	7
Player One:	A-2	3
Player Two:	K-J	K

While in the first two examples you were in good shape, in Example Three you are up against it. But even though you have the worst high and low draws, you can still draw out in either, or both, directions. Part of the beauty of poker is that the best hand at the outset doesn't always win. If it did, I would be sitting by myself up in the Bellagio poker room instead of being swamped with customers.

Try not to make having the worst low hand or draw a habit. On the contrary, try to be drawing better than your opponents the majority of the time. Just keep in mind that this is not always possible, and remember that you can't play poker scared. Aggressive usually, cautious sometimes, scared never!

Let's look at one more example:

Example Four
You:	2-4	7-5
Player One:	x-x	K-Q
Player Two:	x-x	2-3

In this situation, you may think you are drawing to the second-best low, and you probably are. Although you might be tempted to fold, you shouldn't. You should take a card here. Your hand still has straight potential and you may out-draw him for low anyway. An ace will give you a very good low and a 3 or a 6 will give you a decent low with a gutshot straight draw for dessert. Player Two may also have an 8 or a worse 7 (7-6) in the hole, so keep the faith.

CONCEPT 11: PLAYING LOW HANDS

In eight-or-better, how low hands are played is much of what separates the experts from the merely good players. Much of eight-or-better is fairly obvious to an experienced player, and many of the situations that call for the expert plays I've covered, and will cover later, rarely arise. Conversely, low hands will be a constant part of your game, forcing you into decision after decision. Let's start off by addressing how to play these hands as they develop.

Don't make a habit of jamming it or putting extra money in the pot with mere low hands on third street. Complete the bet or just call if someone has already done so in front of you. Hands such as A-2-6 or 2-3-4 are fine starting hands and can develop into monsters, but much of the time you will simply catch bad and have to fold.

If you do catch bad on fourth, should you call and see fifth street? This depends on your opponents' boards, your position, and how many bets went in on third street. The following examples illustrate the importance of position and your opponents' boards:

Example One

You:	3-4	5-J
Player One:	x-x	6-7
Player Two:	x-x	K-9

In example one, you must definitely fold right away, even if you put two bets in on third street. The reason for this is that if you call Player Two's bet, Player One will definitely raise. Then Player Two will raise again putting you in the middle and forcing you to call at least two, and probably four more bets to stay in the hand. You will almost certainly get jammed out of the pot if you call, so save that bet.

Example Two

You:	3-4	5-J
Player One:	x-x	6-Q
Player Two:	x-x	K-9

Can you guess what the action will be in Example Two? Even if Player Two were Stevie Wonder, he would still bet out into these two boards. Call, cross your fingers, and say a quick prayer. Again, you must catch good immediately to continue with the hand. If not, ditch it.

Getting Quartered

For Omaha eight-or-better players starting to play stud eight-or-better, remember this: In Omaha, getting quartered is a very real fear, even when you have the nuts. A pot gets **quartered** when one player has the high and two players have the same low, or vice versa. When this happens, the two players with the same hands—usually the low hands—wind up with only one quarter of the pot and actually lose money if they are two of the only three still in. In Omaha eight-or-better, getting quartered happens a lot, even when you have the nuts, because players get to play two cards out of the four in their hands and share three of the five community cards. This makes it considerably more likely that two players will wind up with the same hand.

But in stud eight-or-better, this almost never happens, because you have to play five cards out of your hand and you share none. Therefore, when you have a board lock in stud eight-or-better, go ahead and cap it on the end, don't stop raising as you would in Omaha eight-or-better. For example:

Example One

You:	A-2	5-7-8-Q	3
Player One:	x-x	6-7-8-Q	x
Player Two:	x-x	A-8-K-9	x

Okay, here you have a 7-5, unbeatable against these two boards. The best Player One could have is a 7-6 low and the best Player Two could hope to muster is an eight perfect (8-4-3-2-A) not good enough, unfortunately for your opponents. Keep the pressure on here. Raise and reraise until the cows come home. Although you can't scoop, you have half locked up for sure.

There are times, however, when should not raise even when you obviously have the best low draw. There are two reasons:

(1) You don't want to knock anybody out. You want full value.

(2) If you miss, you wind up with nothing anyway. You lose the minimum as well as disguise the true strength of your hand.

Let's look at an example that illustrates these points:

Example Two

You:	2-3	5-6
Player One:	x-x	K-Q
Player Two:	x-x	A-7

In this example, you have a multiway pot with only a low draw and a gutshot straight draw for high. You want to make sure it stays a multiway pot, so don't raise the obvious high hand out of the pot. When Player Two bets out, just call him. You will accomplish little by knocking out Player One, as Player Two has you beat for the high hand right now anyway. If you are lucky enough to complete your straight, you'll want as many victims in there as possible, so let him live.

If you raise Player One out, there are times when you will get scooped instead of winning the high with a small pair. When this happens, take a deep breath and take solace in the fact that you played your hand correctly. You don't have to win all the battles, just the war.

CONCEPT 12: BEWARE THE 8

When playing your low hands, be extremely careful any time you're drawing to an 8 and other opponents are going low. In fact, unless you have a straight or flush draw, or an ace in your hand to go along with the 8, you shouldn't even be in the hand to begin with. Hands like 2-3-8 might look good, but ask yourself, "What am I hoping to make with this hand?" Remember the Platinum Rule! Even when you have the straight potential, whatever low you end up with won't be very good. Here's an example:

Example One

You:	8-2-10	7-4-3-10
Player One:	4-5-J	2-6-Q-7
Player Two:	2-8-A	A-3-6-9

This is what you can expect to happen when you play these hands. Since you're drawing to the worst low, you'll probably wind up with the worst low. You started with no high potential, so you got what you deserved. Hands such as 2-3-8, 2-4-8, 2-5-8, 2-6-8, 2-7-8, 3-4-8, 3-5-8, 3-6-8, and 3-7-8 are all unplayable unless you're in a multiway pot against strictly high hands. Although they have no eights, 2-3-7, 2-4-7, 2-5-7, and 2-6-7 are usually unprofitable, even when you are the low card or bring-in. Don't fall into the trap of playing mediocre one-way hands.

Would you buy a business that was losing money and had little potential to change that? Of course not. Even if you got a cheap price on it, it would still be a losing proposition. It's the same when you are the bring-in: Just because you can buy this lemon of a hand at a discounted rate, don't fall for it. Dodge the trap and save your money. Here's an example:

Example Two

You:	8-4	2-6-9-J	5
Player One:	K-6	K-J-6-2	9

Let's say you are the low card and have to bring it in. You did manage to get your money back, so it was worth it, right? I hope you said "Wrong." If not, reread this chapter, then take a five-minute time out in the corner and think about your answer.

Why were you wrong for chasing? You had to call the completion of the bet on third street, a small bet on fourth, and big bets on fifth and sixth to make your low. What did you accomplish by taking all this heat? You got your money back, almost all of which you could have kept anyway—and half the antes and half the bring-in—at no risk, by mucking your hand on third street. That means that in a $200/$400 game, you risked $1,150 to win a profit of $225. And you were an underdog to get that. In many poker games, you sometimes have to take a stand. Eight-or-better is not one of those games. If you like to get stubborn, stick to limit hold'em or stud high. eight-or-better is a game of discipline and patience.

CONCEPT 13:
KEEPING TRACK OF THE UPCARDS

Keeping track of the upcards is important in all variations of seven-card stud, but it is imperative in eight-or-better—especially when it comes to the babies.

If you are going high and there are a lot of low cards out, you know it will be more difficult for an opponent to complete his low draw. Likewise, if he were showing three clubs, you need not worry nearly as much if three or four clubs were seen in other players' hands on third street. It's best to remember each card by suit, but if you can't, try to remember all the low cards as well as any duplicates in other people's hands and whether there are many cards of one suit out.

Upcards and Hand Reading

One of the beauties of any stud game is that you can get an idea of your opponent's hand by his upcards. In eight-or-better, you can usually tell who's going high and who's going low and make your plays accordingly. Keep in mind that low hands can develop into high hands and, to a lesser extent, vice versa. Take this situation, for example:

Example One

You: 7♣ 6♣ 5♠ 8♦ Q♥ J♥ 2♣

Player One: 2♦ A♦ K♦ J♦ 5♣ 7♦ 4♥

Notice that Player One started with a big card up, caught a card suited to his first card, and then followed that with two babies. This is a very deceptive hand. It looks like he is strictly high but he wound up with a decent low, and actually scoops you. These situations are rare, but they do occur, so keep them in mind. Remember that the cards you've seen will help you decipher your opponent's hand. The following scenarios, though, are much more common:

Example Two

You:	3-4	7-5-K-3	5
Player One:	Q-7	Q-2-10-4	9

Example Three

You:	3-4	6-2-J-9	5
Player One:	Q-7	Q-2-10-9	9

In Example two, you started out going low only to stumble into two pair, winning yourself the pot, as Player One failed to improve his pair of queens. In Example three, Player One improves to two pair, only to lose to your straight. This is why it's usually correct to check your high hand on the end against a player going low. If he missed everything, you won't get paid anyway. If he has a small pair, he will most likely fold. If he made a low, you won't win anything anyway, and if he made a high that beats you, you'll lose it all. Lastly, if you each made a high hand—most likely two pair—and you check, your opponent will almost always bet, hoping to get paid off by one pair (unless, of course you have an open pair on board). So you see, the end gets bet anyway—you just risked much less.

Recognizing When an Opponent Pairs His Holecard

Another advantage to remembering all the upcards is that it will help you recognize when someone has paired his holecard. Let's say a good player calls a double raise with a five-up, and there are two sixes and two deuces out on third street. Now, that player then catches a 6 on fourth street and a 2 on fifth street to go with his 5. There is only one 6 and one 2 left in the deck, so chances are he didn't pair either. From this you can deduce that this player likely made a straight or at least a very good low with a straight draw. Thanks to the additional information you gained by remembering the upcards on third street, you could muck a big pair here.

Let's look at an example where you can tell someone actually did pair his holecard:

Example One

You:	3-4	2-5-J
Player One:	x-x	K-J-8
Player Two:	x-x	5-7-8

Let's say Player One bets and Player Two just calls. What could Player Two have? A low without a straight? Impossible.

He would raise to get you out. A 9-high straight? Again, he would have to try to raise you out and get the scoop. An 8-high straight? Possible, but highly unlikely. With the worst possible low, any other low hand would beat his, unless he improved, so he would want to get the low draw out. So what does Player Two most likely have? He either started with some kind of high hand, which is still unlikely since he didn't attempt to raise the low draw out, or he has made a pair.

Knowing this, what is your best course of action? Provided no aces or sixes were out on third street, this hand definitely warrants a raise. You've got eight cards to scoop and five or six to take half the pot. If you make your low, you know he will need to hit runner-runner to beat it, as he is drawing to an 8-7 low—if he even has a low draw at this point. Here's another example:

Example Two

You:	4-5	7-8
Player One:	x-x	K-Q
Player Two:	x-x	2-6
Player Three:	x-x	4-6

In this scenario Player One bets, Player Two raises, and Player Three folds. What should you do? Most likely, Player Three paired his 6 since he folded right away. Player Two also has a 6 showing, meaning that there is probably only one 6 left in the deck. Not only is a raise the wrong play, a call here is tough as well, since you almost certainly have the worst low draw with little hope of developing it into a high hand.

I would definitely still take a card on fourth street for one bet—but not for two—hoping both that Player Two catches bad and that I catch good, or maybe even snag that miracle 6. Note: Although Player Three folded on fourth street, the 6 did not necessarily affect his hand. He may have started with split fours, a pocket pair, or a three-flush and failed to catch a fourth card of that suit. So, there is still a fair chance that there are two sixes left. But pairing the sixes is simply the most likely scenario that would make Player Three fold.

Blockers

In the previous example, the 6 is what's known as a **blocker**. Recognizing when blockers are out can enable you to get in extra raises you normally might not be able to make. These situations arise in all forms of stud. They are more important in eight-or-better than stud-high, but not as important as in razz, which is another name for seven-card stud ace-to-five lowball. In razz you can go from an underdog to a huge favorite, depending on the other cards that are out.

Let's look at another example that illustrates the effect of blockers:

Example One

You:	5-5	5-2-3-7
Player One:	x-x	7-6-4-A

To emphasize the point, let's say the last 5 was out on third street. In this situation, you should not only raise Player One, you should put four or more bets in, depending on who your opponent is. If you make any low, even an 8-low, you can raise with almost no fear of being scooped. In order to scoop, Player One would need to make a better low hand—assuming you hit yours with a 6 or an 8—and have three sixes, sevens, or aces to go with it.

CONCEPT 14:
ELIMINATING THE COMPETITION

No, I don't mean killing off the other good players, although, if a few were suddenly whacked, the rest would probably fall into line. Just kidding—put your gun away.

In the previous section, I talked about not raising, or smooth-calling, to keep a third opponent in the pot. In this concept, I will talk about raising in order to limit the field, which will maximize your chances at scooping the whole pot. Often, when hands develop and boards start looking scary, you can use this to your advantage by representing something that a player holding a high hand would be afraid of, so you could bluff him out.

So, if you're in a three-way pot with the best low and a weak high that has a chance to beat your other opponent who is also going low, a raise to force out the high hand might enable you to scoop the whole pot. For example:

Example One

You:	A-2	4-3-J-6
Player One:	x-x	K-Q-4-3
Player Two:	x-x	7-6-5-10

If Player Two bets here, a raise might knock out Player One. If that happens, your A-J might be good for high. If the A-J isn't good enough, pairing the ace, jack, 6, or maybe even one of the babies might earn you the scoop. This probably would not have been possible if Player One had stayed in for the showdown.

But if Player One does get stubborn and stays in, it's great value anyway, as you have the nut low and are assured of getting at least half.

Another time to knock out an opponent is if you have the worst low or low draw and only you know it. Take this scenario:

Example Two
You:	7-8	4-5
Player One:	x-x	8-6
Player Two:	x-x	K-Q

In this example, if Player Two bets out, a raise might get Player One to fold. Why do you want him to muck here? He probably has the best low draw but doesn't know it, as your 7 and 8 are buried. This is the kind of situation you want to be in—three cards to come with a low draw and a straight draw, even if it is just a gutshot, against a strictly high hand. One last example:

Example Three
You:	3-4	6-7
Player One:	x-x	5-J
Player Two:	x-x	K-10

Player Two will certainly bet out here, and you must raise. Why? For value, for one thing. As we just discussed, this is a great spot to be in. However, the main reason you'll want to raise here is to force out Player One. "Why?" you ask. You're thinking, "I have the best low draw, maybe I should let him hang around." No, absolutely not! It would be easy for him to catch good while you caught bad, and then you might wind up with the worst low draw.

I see fairly good players just call here on a regular basis. This is a horrible play. These are the spots you're waiting for. This is the time to divide and conquer!

CONCEPT 15: STEALING THE ANTES

Ante stealing is not as intricate a part in stud eight-or-better games as it is in many other forms of poker, especially in full games, mostly because the low card is almost always below an 8, so any player with such a card has one-third of a playable hand showing.

As in other games, if you're going to try to steal the antes, you obviously need to be in late position. If there is an ace or multiple low cards behind you, don't even think of trying it. Your best chance is when you have an ace-up, and there's nothing but middle cards behind you. The reason being, even if one of your opponents has a split middle pair, he will probably muck it when an ace raises in front of him. Here are three examples.

Example One

You:	K-J	A
Player One:	x-x	10
Player Two:	x-x	9
Player Three:	x-x	4

Example one is the situation you're looking for to steal the antes. Remember, the lowest card on board in the first round of betting—the 4 held by Player Three—is forced to start the action by making a token blind bet, so basically, your only concern is whether or not the low card has a hand.* If he does, he probably will not reraise you anyway, but just calling here gives you another shot at stealing this pot. This arises when you catch good on fourth street and he doesn't. He'll probably give up right there and you will get the pot. If you both catch good and you are on a cold steal, say with two paints in the hole, give it

---

* For betting purposes on the first round, the ace plays as the high card, not the low.

up right there. Don't go down with the ship; just check and muck with a coy smile.

Example Two

You:	9-4	J
Player One:	x-x	K
Player Two:	x-x	9
Player Three:	x-x	4

This is another good spot to try to pick up the antes. If you can get by the king, the 9 is probably out unless he holds an overpair. Play the way I just described against the 4. The most important thing to remember is that you should throw your hand away immediately should the king, or anyone else for that matter, reraise. Don't throw good money after bad.

Example Three

You:	9-2	J
Player One:	x-x	A
Player Two:	x-x	8
Player Three:	x-x	4

I put in this last example just to make you feel smart. If you can't recognize that this is a bad spot to try to steal, hang up your guns and mask. You'll never make it as a thief.

CONCEPT 16:
DEFENDING AGAINST THE STEAL

Once again, this is not a very common situation in eight-or-better. Be sure your timing is right and don't overuse this play. When a loose and aggressive player, especially one on tilt, raises in late steal position with a low card, what do you do? If you feel he may be stealing, you should probably reraise him with any hand that you would normally just call with.

You don't want to give the thief a free chance to win the pot, which is exactly what he'll do if he catches good and you catch bad with only one bet each in the pot on fourth street. On the other hand, if you each have two bets in on fourth street, the pot is now big enough to justify a call even though you might be behind. Remember, if he started with a bad one in the hole, you're not behind—you're even.

That reraise on third street is a kind of insurance against the luck of the draw. You now double your chances to stay in the pot by forcing yourself to see an additional card on fifth street. Also, you are compounding his mistake for him; if he had the bad one buried, he's now putting in two bets with that bad hand. If you find yourself on the other end of this situation, don't call, hoping for some miracle. Get out immediately and save that extra bet.

Let's look at some examples of this technique.

Example One

| You: | 2-3 | 5 |
| Player One: | x-x | 5 |

In the first example, Player One raises in late position. Often, you would just call in this spot. However, if you suspect a burglary is in progress, reraise and bring this thief to justice.

Example Two

| You: | A-8 | 5 |
| Player One: | x-x | 7 |

The same goes for this example, only this time the ace you hold makes the reraise much easier. Reason being, even if Player One has a legitimate hand, you will probably still have him beat for high with your ace. The play in the second example can be used much more than in the play in Example One. In addition to defending against the steal, it can be used to push around weaker players, to establish a loose, confident image, or just to mix up your play. It would be a much better hand if your other two cards besides the ace were sevens or lower.

Example Three

You:	6-J	5
Player One:	x-x	6

Finally, in this third example, when Player One raises in late position, just fold, even if you are the low card and feel strongly that he is on the steal. Get out now! Don't try and get fancy or out-play him. If he's bad enough to raise here, he will hang himself later on, so save those extra bets for that time.

CONCEPT 17: AN ADVANCED PLAY

As seldom as the last two concepts occur, this scenario comes into play even less frequently. But, rare or not, this play, if executed properly, can have such powerful repercussions, I felt it deserved it's own section. As with the last concept, be sure that your timing is right and don't overuse this play. Here we go!

If you start with a monster on third street and cap it in a multiway pot, put in a raise on fourth street to back down an opponent going high, which will keep you from getting put in the middle if you catch bad. This can be used in any poker game, but works by far the best in stud eight-or-better. Let's look at a couple of examples:

Example One

You:	2♣ 3♣	4♣ 10♥
Player One:	x-x	7♠ 4♦
Player Two:	x-x	K♦ J♥

In this example, after third street is capped, Player Two will bet out. If you call, Player One will most likely raise. Then, Player Two will definitely reraise, Player One will go to four bets, and Player Two has an easy decision in capping it. With a hand as big as yours, you can't go out. You also want to put the minimum amount of money possible into the pot at this point.

The solution? Instead of just calling, raise. If Player One paired, the raising will stop right here, saving you three bets. If not, Player One will go to three bets and unless Player Two is a beginner, he will just call, saving you two bets.

Example Two

You: 2♣ 3♣ 4♣ 10♥
Player One: K♦ J♥
Player Two: 7♠ 4♦

Similarly, in this example, Player One will bet out and Player Two will raise unless he paired—and there's a good chance he will raise even if he did pair. Once again, if you just call, Player One has an easy decision to raise, and you're looking at a capped pot. And once again, the solution is the same. A raise will freeze Player One and cause him to just call. If Player Two did not pair, you'll still have to call another raise from him, but four bets are better than five.

Not only do you save these extra bets, the beauty of the play is the deception it provides you. Both players will put you on a high hand, and the opponent that's going high will be scared to put a bet in the pot throughout the hand. Meanwhile, since you've put in so many bets, your opponent going low will never give you credit when you make your low, often putting too many big bets in on the end. I've often used this play and had both players so confused that they checked all the way to the river. With these free cards you can backdoor all kinds of hands, such as straights, flushes, lows, and even two pairs or trips.

Before we move on, I want to once again emphasize that this play should not be used on a regular basis. It should only be used after a lot of bets have gone in on third street, adding the equity required to make this successful.

CONCEPT 18: PARTING THOUGHTS

In conclusion, I want to tell a short anecdote. This final story has to do with all forms of poker, not just eight-or-better—even all of life for that matter. Although it doesn't pertain only to the game that I covered in this chapter, I wanted to include it in a book as great as *Super/System 2* for posterity's sake.

Let's say you went to a pet store and saw a dog you fell in love with because of its bark. Would you then take the dog home and yell at it and tell it that it was stupid for barking? Would you try to teach the dog how to meow or moo instead? No, of course not. Doing so would be unreasonable and ridiculous.

You would probably say a person who did this was irrational or even crazy. However, if you look for games with bad players, then get in the game and yell at them and tell them that they're stupid when they play badly and beat you, isn't that the same thing? Isn't that crazy? Dogs bark. That's what they do.

This is tantamount to what bad players do—they lay bad beats on people. You wanted to play with them because they play bad. So, you have no right to get mad or make speeches when they do play bad and wind up beating you.

Don't try to teach a dog to meow and don't try to teach bad players how to play good. It's their money and they can play it as they like. Also, think about how fussing at bad players makes you look. If this bad player has enough money to play crazy and loose in the same game you're trying to win in, how can you call him a sucker? I find nothing more amusing than when a player of modest means tells a recreational player worth many millions that he's a sucker. (A few years ago, I heard Phil Hellmuth, who didn't have a lot of money at the time, tell Larry Flynt that if he kept playing that way he'd go broke.)

As the old saying goes, if you can't handle the heat, stay out of the kitchen. Find a kinder, gentler poker game with less maniacs and more stable players. You will probably win less, but you might manage to hold on to your sanity a little longer.

Keep in mind that I'm referring to comments that will be taken seriously. Good-natured joking and ribbing—or giving the needle, as we say in poker—is part of the game. It provides a sense of camaraderie not found in most other forms of gambling. So don't be afraid of poking a little fun here and there. In fact, a little needling will keep many players coming back who normally wouldn't do so. Just keep it good-natured.

Remember, the point of playing games is to have fun, and poker is the greatest game ever created!

POT-LIMIT OMAHA HIGH

Lyle Berman

There was only one possible choice of a writer for the pot-limit Omaha chapter—world-renowned businessman and the greatest pot-limit Omaha player in the world, Lyle Berman. While his game is geared for ultra high-stakes poker, Lyle was the first player to really crunch the numbers of the game and has calculated statistical charts that were the first of their kind.

An all-around poker player, Lyle has won three gold bracelets at the World Series of Poker: one each in limit Omaha, no-limit Texas hold'em, and deuce-to-seven lowball. When *Super/System* first came out in 1978, Lyle bought a copy and let it gather cobwebs until 1983, when he finally read it. That year he won $10,000—not in poker, but in a craps game—and decided to kick back by entering a $100 buy-in poker tournament at the Stardust.

"I didn't win the tournament, but I found that I enjoyed playing poker more than shooting craps," he told me. "And from that point on, I was hooked."

Always a quick study, he won the pot-limit Omaha event at the Super Bowl of Poker at Lake Tahoe the very next year. In 2002 Lyle was awarded poker's highest honor when he was inducted into the Poker Hall of Fame.

Ironically, as great a player as he is, Lyle's legacy to the poker world will not be his exploits at the table, but rather the popularity explosion poker has enjoyed thanks to the World Poker Tour on television. Had it not been for his backing and participation in the management of the WPT through his company, Lakes Entertainment, a generation of new players might never have evolved. Millions watch the innovative and exciting poker program that offers peeks at the players' hole cards and follows the action through expert play-by-play commentary. Along with Benny and Jack Binion, Lyle Berman will go down as one of the founding fathers of the new world of poker.

POT-LIMIT OMAHA HIGH
by Lyle Berman

INTRODUCTION

People used to think of no-limit hold'em as being the biggest game in town, but there aren't many high-stakes no-limit hold'em games anymore, outside of tournaments. Today, the version of Omaha played for high only, which is the subject of this chapter, is the highest-stake pot-limit poker game played in the world. That alone should make this chapter the most colorful and exciting in this book!

Big Omaha games played at fixed limits are rare, but when pot-limit poker is played, Omaha high—often referred to simply as Omaha—is where the action is. It's the professional's choice. Professionals often choose to play at tables where a variety of different poker games are dealt. In this environment, you might see fixed-limit Omaha played with $1,500/$3,000 blinds during the big tournaments. These can be bigger than the $100/$200 pot-limit Omaha games, because more money will trade hands.

Years ago I read a chart of starting hands and I assigned points to them according to the flop. What my point-count showed is that at the end of the day, there are no monster favorites in Omaha like there are in other games. For example, in hold'em, if you have two aces and someone is playing a pair against you, your aces are a 4 to 1 favorite. In Omaha, no hand is a 4 to 1 favorite. That's why there is so much action to the game and why you can take a lot more flops than you can in hold'em. In simple terms, you're not always getting the worst of it. If two reasonable hands are dealt, it is rare for one to be a 60-40 favorite over the other.

THE GAMES I PLAY

The big pot-limit Omaha games I play with my friends occupy a unique niche in poker. We play high-stakes games with blinds from $50/$100 up to $1,000/$2,000, with or without a **cap**, which is a predetermined amount of money that a player can lose in one hand. Frequently in Omaha, great hands come up and players have to put in all their chips. So knowing whether or not your game has a cap will affect your strategy.

For example, if you have a substantial amount of money on the table in a game with no cap, you have to play more cautiously. You can't afford to take the turn with a bottom or middle set, so you don't want to play the low or sometimes even the middle pairs. We don't often play this way, because players tend to quit the game when they're winning and have a pile of money in front of them. And believe me, we don't want people quitting, because at the stakes that we play, the pool of players isn't very large. On the other hand, if there is a cap, bottom or middle sets may be worth the risk to play. So having a cap not only makes the game less volatile, it also creates a lot of action. We don't want someone to lose all of his money on one hand, so we almost always play this way.

Without the Europeans, who join us during the World Series of Poker and the big tournaments at Bellagio, pot-limit Omaha games with $50/$100 blinds and higher are rare. But this doesn't mean that you can't find profitable games at lower limits, especially at multi-game tables.

Generally, when multi-game poker is spread, we play eight hands each of Omaha, limit seven-card stud eight-or-better, no-limit hold'em, and seven-card stud. At our big game during a recent Bellagio tournament, we played seven games: no-limit hold'em, limit hold'em, no-limit deuce-to-seven lowball, limit triple draw deuce-to-seven, limit seven-card stud, pot-limit Omaha, and limit Omaha eight-or-better.

It's a challenge to play multi-game poker, and it does keep some people out of the game. Almost nobody excels at every game, but there are specialists who are great at one game and decent at another. We're not looking for this type of player. We want people who will play all the games and are great at some, just okay at some, and hopefully terrible at others.

Sometimes we structure our multi-game sessions to fit the tastes of players. For example, Sammy Farha, who came in second at the 2003 World Series, doesn't play all the games, but he does like to play a few of them. He'll play Omaha eight-or-better, triple draw, and pot-limit Omaha, so when he joins us, we play the games he likes because we enjoy gambling with him.

Whether you seek to play pot-limit Omaha at these stakes or at more modest ones, keep in mind that you need to know about caps and that you might find yourself in situations where you'll need to play other games as well.

OMAHA VS. HOLD'EM

What sets pot-limit Omaha apart from hold'em is that in Omaha, each hand is comprised of four cards, two of which you must use in combination with three cards from the board. If you're playing in an eight-handed hold'em game, there are only eight hands in play. But if you are playing an eight-handed Omaha game, everyone has six possible combinations, so there are literally forty-eight hands in play. So here are seven things you need to keep in mind when playing pot-limit:

1. The Nuts

The best possible hand is often out. That is, somebody has the nuts much more often than novices expect, especially if they are used to playing no-limit hold'em. When a player raises in pot-limit Omaha, especially on the end, he very often has the very best hand possible. For example, if there's a possible flush on the board and someone reraises at the end, he usually has the nut flush. The same goes for straights.

2. Bluffing

There is far less bluffing in pot-limit Omaha than there is in no-limit hold'em. Of course, players do bluff in pot-limit Omaha, but with so many hands possible, it's more difficult. You must be more cautious when you bluff because it is likely that someone will have the best hand or the best draw.

3. Starting Hands

With so many possible combinations, you can usually play more starting hands in pot-limit Omaha, if the structure is right. And if you hit certain hands, the payoff can be very good. You can play a little looser before the flop if you truly understand the game, interpret the flop correctly, and know which hands to play carefully, which to bluff with, and which to fold.

4. Drawing Hands

You can play a lot more drawing hands in pot-limit Omaha, but you should make sure you're drawing to the nuts most of the time. Some classic problems arise when you're drawing to less than the nut flush or the bottom end of a straight. For example, suppose there is a 10-5-4 on board and you have the 6-3 in your hand. This is not a very good drawing hand because you are drawing to the bottom or ignorant end. You will have the best hand if you hit the deuce, but if a 7 hits, you face the risk that someone has the 8-7-6-5 and has made the higher straight. Of course, you would always like to have the wrap straight draw with the nut-flush draw. Let's say that the flop comes with the 10♣ 5♣ 4♠. You have the A♣ 8♣ 7♥ 6♠ in your hand. You have six hands to draw to, all of which are pretty much in play.

As a general rule, if you are going to draw to a straight or a flush, make sure it's the best possible straight or flush—otherwise, it gets too expensive. If you have two opponents and each of them has six possible hands, you might think of it as having twelve hands out against you, not just two.

5. Volatility

Pot-limit Omaha is more volatile than hold'em. You're going to play bigger pots more often, and you'll seldom be a huge favorite in a hand. Many times, hands come up that both you and your opponent would still put all your money in the pot with—even if the cards were played face up. Typically, this happens when one player has the top set and his opponent has a big wrap or a wrap with a flush draw. In this scenario, if one player bets and the other raises, both players are going to play the hand, no matter which side of the raise they're on. It's basically a coin flip when you're in this type of situation, because the odds on the two hands are just about even money. You become the victim of the cards since neither hand is a big favorite over the other. It is harder to lay down coin-flip hands in pot-limit Omaha than it is in hold'em. You just aren't going to fold top set or lay down a flush and straight draw.

6. Backdoor Hands

Backdoor hands are made more often in pot-limit Omaha than in hold'em. And although you're primarily playing your main hand, you might also have a backdoor draw, because you have six hands rather than two. Suppose you flop two pair or a set with one of your flush cards also on the board. You and your opponent, who flopped top set, get all your money in on the flop. Then it comes runner-runner in your suit to make your flush and win the pot.

In other words, you have escape valves in pot-limit Omaha that you don't have in hold'em. In hold'em you have only two cards to start with, and sometimes there is no escape possibility—you're trying to hit two specific cards and that's it. The odds of two of your suit coming on the turn and river are about 23 to 1. But in Omaha, the odds are more in your favor. Let's say that I have A♣ 10♦ 2♣ 2♦ and the flop comes J♣ 7♦ 2♠. My opponent makes trip jacks and I make trip deuces. We get all our money into the pot. I still have about a 10 percent chance to make a flush if it comes club-club or diamond-diamond on the turn and river. Therefore my backdoor possibilities, my escape valves, are pretty important.

7. Implied Odds

Understanding implied odds is very important in both pot-limit Omaha and hold'em. In part, your implied odds in a hand take into account what you are going to be paid off with.

But you often cannot count on that payoff in Omaha. For example, if you're drawing to the nut flush and you hit it on the river, there is a strong chance that nobody is going to call you. Therefore, although you must be aware of your implied odds in Omaha, you must also realize that there's a good chance that you may not get called on the river if you make the nuts.

General Guidelines for Raising

Before we get into the advanced concepts, I want to give you some advice on raising. In the early stages of a hand—before and on the flop—you typically raise the size of the pot. Later on in the hand, you may choose not to bet the size of the pot. Clearly, when you have the best hand, you want to get your opponent to put in the maximum money to draw to his hand or get him to fold so that you can take the pot. Betting the maximum amount of money serves both these purposes quite well.

For example, suppose you have a set. The last thing you want to do is to make it profitable for an opponent with a flush or straight draw to call with one card to come, because he will be able to fire on the river if the board changes. And since you don't know for sure whether he is on a straight or flush draw, you will be at a disadvantage. In other words, you don't want to give him the proper odds to call your bet.

ADVANCED CONCEPTS

When we talk about advanced concepts for high-stakes games, it should be clear that some of these work in medium and low-stakes games as well. No matter how high or low the stakes, you'll profit from the pointers in this section.

The Best Hands To Play

When you have good hands, you're going to play most of them. I play the hands described in this section, and so does everybody else. Players like to debate whether A-A-K-K double-suited is a better hand than A-A-J-10 double-suited. I much prefer A-A-J-10, and I think that most other players do too. But it really doesn't matter which hand is better because you should play both of them. Of course, there's a big difference between hands that you can bet on after the flop, and those that you can't bet on because you went all-in before the flop.

I also like a hand with three connected cards and a suited ace, such as A♠ 8♣ 7♦ 6♠ or A♥ J♦ 10♥ 9♣. Three connected cards with one gap and a suited ace is also fine. With a hand like this, you're either going to be in the hunt, or you're going to throw the hand away. You can flop a very good hand, like a flush or a straight, or good draws to them. And many times you'll pick up a monster draw, such as a flush draw combined with a straight draw.

I like these hands because they're not trouble hands. If they're very good on the flop, play them. If not, throw them away.

A double-pair hand, such as J-J-10-10, is also good. When you're dealt a double pair, you will flop a set about one time in four. If you flop a set, you'll probably be in a very profitable situation. If you don't flop a set, you'll probably just fold.

You want hands in which all four of your cards are working together. If you have Q-Q-J-10 your hand is obviously superior to Q-Q-8-6. Suited cards look much better before the flop than after. If you don't have the nut flush draw, you really don't want to play them.

But suited cards do have backdoor possibilities. Sometimes, if you turn a set, you still have a chance to make a backdoor flush. Suited cards also are very good from a defensive standpoint. For example, say you have two hearts in your hand and you flop a set with two hearts on board. Your hand makes it more difficult for an opponent to hit his hearts if he is playing the ace-high flush draw. If you have a good hand independent of the flush draw, your flush draw can play defense, as opposed to offense.

For example, suppose you have the Q♥ Q♣ J♦ 10♥, and the flop comes with the Q♠ 7♥ 4♥. You have top set and a flush draw. With nine hearts to draw to, an opponent who has the nut flush draw is 1.81 to 1 to make the flush. However, since you have two of them, he has only seven hearts to draw to, making him a much bigger underdog to make it. You really don't want a heart to hit, so I call cards like these defensive hearts instead of offensive hearts. You already have the best hand, and you have cards he needs.

Dangerous Hands To Play on the Flop

If you're relying on making a flush that is lower than the ace-high flush, you're drawing to an inferior hand. Low suited cards may look good before the flop, but as soon as the flop comes, they diminish in value.

It is very dangerous to play top and bottom pair, bottom two pair, and less than the nut straight or flush draw. With small pairs, you can flop a set. But this can be dangerous because when you get beat with a set, you get beat expensively. That's why you don't play hands such as K-6-6-2, whether its unsuited, suited, or double-suited. You stay away from those types of hands.

Bad Hands To Play Before the Flop

A hand like Q-Q-7-2 is not good because you're really only playing one hand. You just don't have enough going for you. You might play this type of hand in position or in special situations, but in general, you have to play the odds. And the odds are that you need more than one possible combination. You need a tight hand, one that fits in a box without a dangler hanging over the edge. For example, when you hold 10-9-8-7, you have every combination working. But when you have 10-9-8-2, you have three combinations—10-2, 9-2, and 8-2—that don't have much going for them. I'm not saying that you would never play a hand like Q-J-10-2—the hand has some substance to it—but you wouldn't want to play 9-8-7-2, because it doesn't have enough going for it.

Position

Position is incredibly important in pot-limit Omaha, maybe more so than in any other poker game. Whether you play certain types of hands or muck them always depends on your position. You'll make more on your good hands and lose less on your other hands when you play them from the correct position.

Bluffing

There are some good bluffing opportunities in this game, though perhaps fewer than in other forms of poker. You'll pick up most of your bluffing opportunities after people have checked to you, indicating that they may have nothing. Every check represents either a lie or the truth and your challenge is to figure out which is which.

Most of the bluffing in Omaha happens on uncoordinated flops, and they usually are made by a player sitting in late position. Uncoordinated bluffs are often hard to defend. There isn't as much bluffing on the turn and river because so many different combinations are possible.

What You're Looking for on the Flop

In addition to completed hands, you're looking for nut flush draws, nut straight draws, sets, and top two pair, although the top two pair is often dangerous.

When it comes to straight draws, you'll probably want to play Q-J-10-9, because you're going to turn the top end, when you turn it. On the other hand, if you play small cards such as 6-5-4-3, you can very easily turn the bottom end of something. This isn't so good, because it's so much easier for someone to make the top straight in Omaha than it is in hold'em. For example, if you're holding 6-5-4-3 and 9-8-7 or 8-7-6 on the flop makes your straight, an opponent might be holding 8-9-10-J, giving him the higher straight. This is not to say that you never play a low sequential hand. If you're in the correct position, the pot has not been raised, and there isn't much action in front of you, you'll probably play that 6-5-4-3.

It isn't as important for your low cards to be suited as it is for your high cards, but suits are still good. Remember, you want suited cards for two reasons: (1) they have backdoor flush possibilities; and (2) they have defensive possibilities as blockers that make it harder for your opponent to make a flush.

Playing Big Pairs with No Connecting Cards

Even with the big pairs, like pocket aces or kings, you should care about your connecting cards, because you want something working with them. A player might easily throw away a hand such as K-K-7-2 before the flop, since there's no possibility of making the connecting cards work for him. I often play that hand, but tighter players will fold it without thinking twice. However, even I would not play K-K-7-2 for a big raise.

There are times when you might like to play a smaller hand such as 6-5-4-3 if the pot is raised in front of you. With small connecting cards, you can turn a straight or two pair. And two small pair becomes a monster when your opponent indicates that he has two aces or two kings and didn't hit the flop.

Don't Raise from Up Front

Never raise before the flop from a front position. This is a cardinal rule of Omaha. When you have to act first on subsequent streets, you're at a tremendous disadvantage. The better your hand, the bigger the disadvantage, because you'll want to protect it. Suppose you raise from up front with a very good hand that contains a pair of aces or kings. You don't hit the flop, but it looks innocent. Be careful here—there still are many possible draws to even the most innocent of flops. You're first to act and you want to win the pot, so you make a bet at it. Then somebody comes over the top with a raise. You've put enough money in the pot that you almost have to call. See the problem?

Pot-limit Omaha is a game that you don't like to play from up front. You're going to take flops with good hands, but you don't want to raise with them from a front position. One problem with raising is that you're advertising that you have a good hand. Typically, players don't want to raise with a low hand, so your opponents will have the tendency to put you on a high hand. Of course, you can be somewhat deceptive and raise with a drawing hand, but you must be prepared to call a reraise behind you. Also, when you raise from up front in pot-limit games, you're giving the other guy twice the ammunition to fire back at you. This can be particularly dangerous if you don't have a really top hand.

So here is a general rule: do not raise before the flop from under the gun or from the two blind positions, because you'll be over-committing yourself to your hand. It's much better to be committed from the backside, because players tend to check to the raiser on the flop. More often than not, when you have a big hand up front, you should limp. Most of the raising in pot-limit Omaha is done from the late seats. If you raised from behind and the flop is scary, you can take off a free card if you feel like it, whereas if you raised from the front, you have to declare what you're going to do before anyone else acts. The bottom line is that you're simply putting too much money at risk when you raise from up front.

Here's a situation where you might think about making an exception and raise from up front. Say you're playing $50/$100 blinds and each player has $100,000 in front of him. If you raise $200 from up front, an opponent can call $200 and raise $500. That isn't too terrible. You have $700 in the pot and you still have $100,000. Or if you're playing $50,000 cap, you still have $49,300 to go.

We have one player in our game—I'll call him Joe—who plays a different brand of Omaha than anyone else. Joe literally raises eight of nine hands. It's unbelievable. But we have a small structure in the game that Joe plays. It's $50/$100 or $100/$200, and he's raising $500. Even if somebody comes back at him, they're only going to raise him $2,000, and since he still has a long way to go to reach the $50,000 cap, he doesn't mind the action.

The point is this: before you raise, remember that you could get closed out of a hand if somebody with aces came back at you, although aces generally are never more than about a 3 to 2 favorite over any other hand.

Reading the Board on the Flop

Reading the flop is critical in Omaha. You have to know what is the best possible hand and what is the best possible draw. This is an elementary concept for experienced players, but it's quite easy to miss a straight possibility on the board or to think that you have the best straight draw when a higher one is possible. It's also important that you be able to identify the cards that your opponent needs in order to call the flop. Ask yourself, "What are the possibilities out there, and what might my opponent have?"

Suppose the flop comes Q♦ 10♦ 7♣, and you have two black queens in your hand. If you bet and someone only calls, you can pretty much infer that your opponent has a straight or flush draw. If he had both, he would probably raise. And if he had an underset, he would probably reraise. So, if you have a set or top two pair and somebody calls your bet, there is a high probability that he is on a draw. Your job is to guess what hand might have made him call your bet.

Now let's take a look at another situation in which reading the flop is critical. Suppose you have pocket threes, and the flop comes J-7-3 rainbow, giving you trip threes. You raise and someone reraises. Most people would not reraise you with an inside straight draw such as 10-9-8-x or 6-5-4-x. So, if there isn't much out there and you get reraised, you can pretty much infer that your opponent has the top set, unless he's bluffing. If there isn't a big draw possibility on board, then it is more likely that the raiser has top two pair or a set. So, this might be a good time to fold your bottom set.

Here's an example from a hand that actually happened in a big pot-limit Omaha game with a $75,000 cap. The pot was raised and reraised before the flop. Five players—David Grey, Chip Reese, Johnny Chan, Jay Heimowitz, and I—put in $15,000 each to see the flop, a very rare occurrence.

The flop came Q-7-5 rainbow. I had the 8-6-4-x, so I had the bottom straight wrap. I bet $60,000 to try to pick up the pot, and David called with essentially the same hand that I had, the low straight wrap. Chip was next and he called with the 9-8-6-x, the high wrap, much better than mine. Johnny had raised the pot before the flop with two aces, and with three of us already in on the flop, he called, thinking he could still win the hand if he caught an ace. I think he also had a backdoor flush draw.

Then it was Jay's turn. He had pocket queens and made top set on the flop. Now he has all these guys in the pot with him and he's sitting there with trip queens! The next card off was a 6, which gave David and me the bottom end of the straight and Chip the top end. When a blank came on the river, Chip won the hand and $375,000.

To this day, that is one of the biggest pots we've played in our game. And it's a good example of why you don't want to put your money in with the bottom end of the straight. This reminds me of the old saying about a guy who owned four farms: He lost three of them drawing to inside straights and lost the fourth one when he made it.

Another interesting hand came up a few years ago in a tournament. I've got two aces in my hand, and the flop comes A-10-10. A fellow leads at the pot, and I call. At this point, I don't know what he has. He could have a hand or he could be bluffing.

A blank comes on the turn, he leads at it again, and again I call. Now I know he's not bluffing—he has a hand. And there are only two hands he could have: quad tens or tens full of aces.

Another nothing card comes off on the river and he leads at it a third time. Now I know for a fact that he either has 10-10 or A-10. Since there is only one way that he could have 10-10 and two ways that he could have A-10, it's 2 to 1 he's got A-10. I just call with my case chips, because I'm thinking that if he had 10-10, he would not have led at the pot. Usually it's an automatic check when you flop four of a kind, because you want to let somebody catch up. But not this time. He had 10-10. And I had a very nice view from the rail.

Picking Up the Pot on the Flop

Most of the bluffs in pot-limit Omaha come on the flop rather than on the turn or river. It's usually easier to pick up the pot on the flop from behind—that is, from late position—although you can also pick it up when you're in the lead or early position. In fact, it is even easier to bluff on the flop from late position in Omaha than it is in other games because with four cards in your hand, you're more likely to flop something. When there are few possibilities on the board—that is, no flush draws and no wrap straight draws—it is easier to bluff than if the board were coordinated in some way. Flops like J-7-3 and Q-5-2 make it easy to pick up the pot.

But sometimes the opposite is true. When there's a very scary board, you can sometimes pick up the pot because nobody wants to commit. Let's say that the board comes with three diamonds, and everybody checks to you. You might take a stab at it, representing a made flush. If nobody else has anything, they'll often just give it up.

It's possible to pick up the pot with a bluff on the turn and river, but that's much harder to do than picking it up on the flop. If a player calls on the flop with a drawing hand, he will usually call on the turn as long as the board doesn't change dramatically—that is, as long as it doesn't pair or show a third suited card. Suppose the flop comes K-10-7. You bet, someone calls, and a deuce comes off on the turn. If you bet again, you can be pretty sure that you will be called again.

Draw Only To the Nuts

This concept is incredibly important in Omaha: When you're drawing to a straight or a flush, draw to the nuts or don't draw. Although this isn't true 100 percent of the time, it is at least a 98-percenter. Even if you're drawing to the nut flush, you're only going to make it approximately one out of three times anyway, so why draw to the non-nuts? It's simply a bad play.

Of course, there are times when you might draw to a non-nuts flush, but only when you have other possibilities working for you, for example, when you have other cards in your hand that might help you win the pot even if you don't make the flush. Suppose you have the K♥ J♦ 10♥ 8♣, and the flop comes 10♣ 7♥ 2♥. You have the second-nut flush draw, a gutshot straight draw, plus the possibility of making trips or two pair. You aren't 100 percent sure where you're at in the hand, but the hand has enough value to warrant taking a card off.

If you hit your draw, you don't want someone else to hit it bigger. Suppose the flop comes 10-6-5 to your 7-4-x-x. If an 8 comes, you will make your straight, but someone with 9-9-8-7 will make a higher one. Nor should you draw in the hopes of making two pair if most of the cards that will make a second pair for you could make a straight for someone else.

If there is a flush draw possibility on the board, putting too much money in the pot is dangerous when you are drawing to a straight, because the possible flush takes away 25 percent of your cards. Three bad things could happen: (1) you miss your straight; (2) you make the straight with a card that gives your opponent the flush; or (3) you make a straight on the turn with one card to come and your opponent makes the flush on the river.

Of course, there are always minor exceptions, times when you might think about drawing to the non-nuts. For example, suppose a guy raises before the flop, and you know that he only raises with big pairs. You flop the bottom wrap straight draw. You have clear insight into the type of hand that your opponent has, so you have good reason to think that a small straight draw might be good. Since you're pretty sure that he doesn't have the top wrap, you might draw to the lower straight. But if you don't have a clear read in heads-up action like this, you draw to the nut flush or the best straight—or you don't play the hand.

Playing the Nut Straight from Late Position

Here's a hand that I played some time ago that illustrates an important concept. I was sitting on the button with 9-6-x-x, and the flop came 8-7-5. A player led into me and I just called, for two reasons:

(1) His bet implied that he had a made straight.

(2) If the board paired on the next card, I could probably take the pot away from him by betting, thus representing a full house.

Equally important, if he had the second-nut straight, as I suspected, raising on the flop would have told him that I had the best hand, and he might have folded. But, if I just called on the flop, he checked the turn, then I bet, he'd have no idea what I was holding. Do I have the nut straight? The second-best straight for a tie with him? Do I have two pair or a set that I'm betting because I don't think he has the straight? As it turned out, he checked on the turn, I bet the pot, and he called with all the money he had on the table. As I suspected, he had the 6-4, and I won the pot. Judging from the way he played, I knew that this particular player would have folded if I had raised him on the flop.

When you play with strong players, they will often bet at the pot with less than the nuts. If you have the best hand and raise behind them, it's very easy for them to throw their hands away. In other words, top players are not reluctant to fold a hand if they think they are beaten. Here's an example: I was playing in a game with David "Devilfish" Ulliot. I bet, he called, and off came a card that made the second-best straight for me. I checked, and he also checked behind me. Had he bet, I think I would've thrown my hand away. Nothing came on the river to change things, and again I checked. This time, he bet. I had a very hard time putting him on the nut straight since he'd let a free card come off with one to come. After all, I could have had a set or two pair, in which case he was giving me an absolutely free draw to a full house. So, I paid him off. Turns out, he had the nut straight. I lost.

You can make a similar play with the nut flush. Let's say that the flop comes with three hearts, giving you the ace-high flush. An opponent checks, you bet, and he calls. On the turn, nothing significant comes off. Now's your chance to make a sophisticated play: If he checks, check right behind him. That way, he'll think that his king or queen flush is good. On the river he might bet right into you, or if he checks again and you bet, it might appear to him that you don't have the nuts and he might call. This strategy gives you a way to get paid off on the hand.

When playing against very good players, it is occasionally wise to check on the turn with the absolutely best hand. In essence, you delay betting in order to make more money at the end.

Playing Cautiously with the Nuts

When I first started playing back in the '80s, I lost my first big pot in a game where I flopped the best possible hand. It was against Bobby Baldwin, and we both had the nut straight, but he also had a heart draw. When a heart came on the river, he won a very large pot. This taught me the lesson that in Omaha having the best hand at the moment doesn't always make you the favorite.

Omaha is one of those rare games in which you sometimes need to exercise caution when you're holding the absolute best hand on the flop. One of the most perilous situations you can get into is when you flop the nut straight with a flush draw on the board, and somebody raises you. Let's say that the board comes 8♣ 7♣ 6♥, you have a 10-9-x-x in your hand, and your opponent raises you. Two bad things can happen:

(1) At the very least, your opponent has also flopped the nut straight with perhaps an overcard that could make a higher straight. If he has the J-10-9, and a 9 or 10 falls, you will lose the hand to a superior straight.

(2) You might be up against the same straight—in which case you might win very little by splitting the pot—not to mention a flush draw, two pair, or a set, and you'll lose a great deal of money if your opponent hits.

The point is that experienced players in big-limit poker would be very cautious about reraising with only a naked nut straight. They need more than that in order to raise. So when you bet and a good player raises, there's a good chance that he has you tied and also has outs to a better hand.

Here's an example from a $50,000 cap game I played a while ago with Joe and another player that I will call Bill. Bill had been killing the game, winning a lot of pots. Two deals before this particular hand was played, Bill had showed his cards on the river. He had a hand that was the second-best possible, a hand that almost anybody would have bet in this scenario. But Bill elected to just show it down, thus telegraphing to everyone how cautiously he was playing.

Now, two hands later, the flop comes Q-J-10 with two clubs. Bill checks, Joe bets, and Bill raises. If I had been Joe, I would have thrown my hand away at that point and lost about $4,000, because there was no question that Bill had the nut straight with a flush draw. But not Joe—he raised the $50,000 cap. Off came a club on the turn, and Joe lost his $50,000. This is another example of how a previous hand can affect your play as the game goes forward, and again why you should be very observant of your opponent's play at all times.

One interesting point to make about the play of this hand is that it shows how a very good player can make money against a mediocre player. I would have lost $4,000 playing this hand, but Joe lost $50,000 and thought he had been very unlucky. He wasn't unlucky at all—he simply played the hand horribly. If the flop comes Q-J-10 with two flush cards, giving you the nut straight and you get raised after you've bet, it is almost an automatic fold. Why? Because very few players in our high-stakes game would put in a lot of money with a naked A-K on that flop. Perhaps at lower limits, less advanced players would play differently.

I once had the same type of hand in a tournament, except that the flop came 9-8-7. I bet with the nut straight, and there was a raise and a reraise behind me. "This straight can't be any good," I said to myself as I threw it away. As it turned out, however, one guy had a flush draw and the other one had a set. Neither one of them got there, so I would have won a humongous pot. But the point is that in Omaha there are situations when throwing away the nuts is obviously the proper thing to do—usually when you have the nut straight and it's pretty clear that an opponent has the same hand, plus a draw to a flush or a bigger straight. This doesn't happen when you have the nut flush because nobody can make a better flush.

The question of risk versus reward is very relevant in this type of situation. In the hand that Bill and Joe played, Joe had very little money invested in the hand, only about $4,000, and he had to either make it $50,000 or fold. Now that's a big difference—put in $46,000 more or fold! The risk-reward ratio just wasn't there. The question is, "Is it worth the risk of going broke to the hand?"

Most of the time when you bet, you make a small commitment to the pot, but you may have to put in ten times that amount to see the hand through. Obviously, you don't just routinely throw away the best hand, but many times you might want to check the nut straight on the flop when a flush draw is possible and wait to bet it on the turn if the board doesn't change. This strategy is more typical of an un-raised pot, because there isn't a lot of money in it yet. If there's been a substantial raise before the flop, you have a little more incentive to play the hand because there's more money in the pot.

Everything in poker is risk versus reward. Suppose you're playing in our game with $500/$1,000 blinds and a $75,000 cap. Three people have limped in, so there's three or four thousand in the pot. The flop comes Q-J-10 with two clubs. You have the A-K with nothing else. Everyone checks to you, and you bet $4,000. Then somebody comes over the top and raises $12,000. You know that on the very next card, he's going to bet $36,000. And then the board might change on the river, and you won't know where your opponent is at in the hand. Do you want to risk $71,000 more in order to split—at best—an $8,000 pot? The answer is no.

Chess is the ultimate think-ahead game. Top chess players think seven or more moves ahead. In poker you must similarly think two or three moves ahead. Sometimes you're even thinking two or three hands ahead, laying the foundation for a play you're going to make in a future hand. Knowing this, think back about the hand I described between Bill and Joe, when Joe lost $50,000 to Bill when he only needed to lose a few thousand on the flop and ask yourself if you would have folded Joe's hand.

Implied Odds

The concept of implied odds is important in all types of poker. **Implied odds** is a ratio that weighs the amount of money risked by betting against the amount of money that can be won if you hit your hand and get your opponent to pay you off. For example, if you bet $10,000, hit your overfull, and figure to win $90,000, your implied odds would be 9-1 (betting $10,000 to win $90,000).

So when deciding whether to call, bet, raise or fold, you make a risk-reward calculation based on your odds of winning, how much you will get paid back, and how big the pot is relative to that sum. That is, you look at the implied odds of the situation. In limit poker, it's a lot easier to calculate your implied odds because of the structure of the game. For example, suppose you're playing $1,000/$2,000 limit and you have a flush draw on the turn. You know that it's about 4 to 1 against making the flush. The pot is already $12,000, and your opponent bets $2,000. You're getting 7 to 1 odds to make a flush, so it's a slam-dunk to call the bet. Your $2,000 bet could turn into $14,000 or even $16,000 and up if the pot is raised on the river.

Pot-limit is much different, because many times you'll put your money in, even though the current pot odds aren't in your favor; but you do so hoping that the odds will improve later in the hand. For example, let's say that with one card to come, you have the nut flush draw. Again, the odds are 4 to 1 against your making it. If there's $5,000 in the pot and somebody bets $5,000, you're only getting 2 to 1 pot odds if you call. You can't possibly call unless you believe that you'll get called for a $15,000 bet if you make the flush on the river. If you think all this will happen, you'll be getting 5 to 1 implied odds (betting $5,000 to win $25,000) on your money in a 4 to 1 set up, so that's a good reward. For this play to work, though, you have to know your opponents and really believe they'll call.

Generally speaking, if someone bets and you call, your opponents will put you on a draw. Then if the board changes and you make that draw, it's harder to get paid off because they'll suspect that you've got it. It's what we call the reverse-play odds, meaning you can't necessarily expect to get paid off. You have to know your opponent and his frame of mind at the time. Is he winning or losing? Is he frustrated?

All of these variables go into the formula of how you play implied odds. And that's why they can be deceptive. In fact, implied odds can be deceptive in two ways. (1) They can fool you into thinking that you are going to get paid off, and that you therefore should call; and (2) they can fool you into thinking there's no way you'll get paid off, so you shouldn't call. You're simply making an educated guess.

How important are implied odds in tournament play? They're important, of course, but they aren't always as important as they are in cash games. In tournament play, even if the implied odds are good enough to bet, you might bomb out of the tournament if you lose the hand. Therefore, even if the implied odds are in your favor, you might not want to risk taking a draw when someone makes a large bet that would require risking the last of your money. On the other hand, you have to win some money to stay in the tournament, so it's a dilemma.

Playing with a Pair Showing on the Board

When the Board Pairs on the Flop

It's Omaha 101: When a pair comes on the flop, everybody plays very cautiously. I think it is almost a cardinal rule that when a pair appears on the flop in Omaha, you're not going to try to make a flush or a straight.

In hold'em, when there is a pair showing on the board, chances are slim that one of your opponents has a full house, so drawing to a flush or straight isn't always bad. But when there's a pair on the board in Omaha, it's all too likely that someone has flopped a full house or has a good chance of making one with the same card that you need to make your straight. If the flop comes 8-7-7, for example, and you have J-10-9-x, the person who has a 7 in his hand may very well also have an 8, 9, 10, or jack, which are connecting cards.

The one exception to this rule comes into play when you feel strongly that your opponent is playing aces or kings, and you have either the nut flush draw or the nut wrap to a straight.

Suppose your opponent raised before the flop, and you're almost positive that he raised with aces, which often happens—this is another reason why you don't want to tell people that you have aces by raising before the flop. Then the board comes 8-7-7, and you have J-10-9-x. Your opponent bets into you. What do you do? If you can't guess what he has, you'll probably have to throw your hand away. But if he reraised before the flop—and most reraises come from players who have pocket aces or big cards—you might very well play the hand.

The Overfull. When there's a pair on board, you can also make an overfull house or an underfull house. If the flop comes A-7-7 and you have pocket aces, you have the overfull. Naturally, this is the best position you can be in. Furthermore, you should bet, looking to catch someone who has a seven in his hand or even better, an A-7, the underfull.

Or suppose the flop comes 8-7-7 to your pocket eights or K-7-7 to your pocket kings. In either case, you want to bet or raise immediately, trying to get as much money in the pot as you can. You're looking for someone who has a 7 in his hand to give you some action. You could also check, hoping that someone with a 7 will bet, allowing you to reraise him.

The Underfull. It's hard to make money with an underfull. If you have pocket deuces, for example, and the flop comes 7-7-2, you're in jeopardy. If someone plays with you, chances are he has a 7. You have a wonderful hand on the flop, but unless a deuce comes off on the turn, you're in a lot of trouble. If you can raise and get a lot of money in early, you're justified in playing the hand. But if you raise and there's still a whole lot of money left to play, you'll have trouble even calling one big bet after another card comes off. In Omaha, many people, including me, play small connectors such as 4-3-2-2. While small pairs can make you a lot of money in the right situation, they aren't particularly good hands to play in Omaha, and they can get you into a lot of trouble. Of course, it always depends on what hand you put your opponent on.

When the Board Pairs on the Turn or the River

When the board pairs on the turn or the river, there's a good chance that someone has made a full house. You must be cautious about playing an underfull in these scenarios. Suppose the board comes Q-8-7 and you have a pair of sevens in your hand; someone bets and you call. Off comes an 8 on the turn, so the board now reads Q-8-7-8. You have the underfull, and you're in jeopardy. When you make an underfull on the turn or river, you have a hand that is very hard to get paid off with, especially on the river.

If the board pairs on the river, you should rarely if ever raise with an underfull. It's okay to bet, but if you get raised, you're beaten unless your opponent is on an absolute bluff. Essentially, if you're 99 percent sure that you have the best hand but the only hand that you know your opponent will call with will beat you, then you should not bet.

An underfull is a hand you can bet for value, but if you get raised, be aware that the only hand you can beat is a bluff. A good Omaha player won't raise with straights or flushes on the river when there's a pair on board. If he thinks you're bluffing, he might call with a straight or flush, but he won't raise.

I'm not saying that you shouldn't bet an underfull. If a man bets on the turn with a straight or flush possibility on board, then he checks to you when the board pairs on the river, you're probably going to bet your underfull. Just be cautious about calling a raise on the river. I have laid down many an underfull on the river against a raise.

Playing Two Pair

In general, the only two pairs that are any good in Omaha are the top two. Top and bottom pair, and bottom two pair are extremely vulnerable. It is very difficult to win a lot of money with them, but it's easy to lose a lot. As a rule, they aren't worth playing for two reasons:

(1) You can easily be beat by top two pair or a set, in which case you have very few outs.

(2) Even if you have the best hand, it may not look very good as soon as another card comes off.

In Omaha, an important question to ask yourself when you are holding two pair or just about any hand, for that matter, is, "What card do I need to help my hand, and how much will it help somebody else?" For example, in a recent shorthanded game, the flop came 10-6-2. With sixes and deuces, I was 90 percent sure that my hand was good at the time, but as soon as one card comes off, what good would it be? Unless I caught a 6 or a 2, any card that came off the deck would have put me in jeopardy. So, I threw it away.

In Omaha, playing even the top two pair can be less profitable than you think. Here's an example from a game I played. I had tens and nines on a flop of 10-9-2. A player I'll refer to as "Al" led at it, and another player called. I wasn't willing to raise with my top two pair because it would have put me in too much jeopardy against this type of board. I called, but I was still very leery because if any card from a 6 to a king came off, my hand would be vulnerable. The turn card was a 5, which probably helped no one. I checked, and Al bet $11,000. The third man called the bet with all the money he had left on the table. I still thought that I had the best hand, so I raised $30,000, thinking that Al was on some type of draw and I had the best of it. Al folded. When we turned our hands up, the third man had the same hand I did and we split the pot.

Top and Bottom Pair

When hold'em players come into an Omaha game, they often think that top and bottom pair is a very good hand, as it is in Texas hold'em. But it's a very poor hand in Omaha, except when you believe your opponent has aces. In Omaha games, a reraise—not the original raise—generally means pocket aces. Generally, a player with anything less than aces won't reraise, because he realizes that he will be vulnerable if he runs into aces and might wind up looking at a bet that he can't even call. Therefore, when you know that a player has reraised with aces (as in the example below), top and bottom pair look fantastic.

I rarely raise with aces, but I have been known to make exceptions to my rule. In a side game that my friends and I played during a recent World Poker Tour event, somebody raised $8,000, and Chip Reese called. I thought he had raised $10,000, so I tried to reraise $35,000 with my A-A double-suited. As it turned out, I could only raise about $28,000, and Chip called my reraise. The flop came K-J-8. Chip flopped jacks and eights and moved in. Had I not reraised before the flop, Chip would not have called after the flop with just jacks and eights. But he knew for a fact that I had aces—I might as well have shown it. There was a slim chance that I could have had A-K-K-Q double-suited or a similar hand, and with a king on the board, he was taking a little risk. But the point is that his jacks and eights became a very big hand exactly because he could put me on aces. And that's why it's usually best not to raise with aces in Omaha.

Top Two Pair

Top two pair is playable in many situations, but it's still a dangerous hand. Flopping top two pair against a board like Q-7-2 is best, because there aren't many hands that could be drawing to that board. With a hand like A-K-Q-7, that flop doesn't look so bad, since your queens and sevens have a chance to improve. This is much better than flopping top two pair on a board of 10♣ 9♠ 2♠, because you are vulnerable to straight and flush draws.

Or suppose the flop comes K-J-8, as it did in an earlier example. If you have kings and jacks, you have a vulnerable hand because the next card off could complete a straight for an opponent. A lot of people will call a bet on the flop with a straight or flush draw, so two pair must be played very carefully.

A two-pair hand plays better from a late position because after the cards come off, you see what your opponent does in front of you without having to commit yourself. So you can duck a scare card if you want. On the flop, your opponent won't know where you're at in the hand, so if he checks, you can check behind him. Or you could get most of your money in before the turn card comes so that you don't have to make any guesses.

Playing Double Pairs: My 25 Percent Rule

I mentioned earlier that I like to play hands such as A♣ 9♦ 8♠ 7♣, with the ace suited, because they don't get me into a lot of trouble. I also like to play two-pair hands, and sometimes I'll raise with them, even if they're smaller pairs like nines and sixes or eights and fives. The rationale behind raising before the flop with two small pair is that you have a lot of deception going for you. When you raise, people put you on big pairs or big cards. If the flop comes something like J-8-5 and you have pocket fives, they don't put you on trip fives because you raised before the flop, so they're going to play their two-pair hands.

Not only is this type of hand deceptive, it has the potential for making a little more money if you make your set. Obviously, it's easier to make money with good hands in raised pots than in unraised pots. However you can't carry things to the extreme— deuces and threes aren't particularly good hands. You could flop a set and still not be happy about it.

My 25 percent rule is simply a reminder that you will flop a set one out of four times when you start with two pocket pair. It's pretty much, "No set, no bet," unless an accidental straight combination leaves you in contention. Your raise represented a big pair, so if the flop comes J-6-2 unsuited, you might take a stab at the pot if you miss.

Playing Aces

I think that more money has been lost with a pair of aces in Omaha than has been won. Unlike in hold'em, where they hold up more than 50 percent of the time, aces generally have to improve to win in Omaha. If a straight is possible on the board, anything less than a set of aces is a tough hand to play. If you raised before the flop and then a pair flops—it comes 7-2-2, for example—you're vulnerable because you're almost forced to bet. Anyone who has a deuce knows that you probably have pocket aces, and he is going to come over the top of you, so you're already playing a big pot. However, if you didn't raise before the flop and it comes 7-2-2, you can make a stab at it. Then if you get reraised, you can throw your hand away. It's harder to do that when you've committed to the pot before the flop.

There is a downside to raising before the flop. Even if your opponents know that you're aggressive and might have raised with any four cards, you're still putting yourself in jeopardy because you're forcing yourself to bet marginal hands on the flop that you normally wouldn't bet. If you raised before the flop with pocket aces, you would have to bet on the 7-2-2 flop because there's just too much money in the pot to leave it laying out there.

Now suppose the flop comes 7-2-2 in an unraised pot and everyone checks around to you. You might make a small stab at it, and if you get raised, you would probably throw it away. Or you might want to let one more card come off for free and see what happens. But remember that since every player has six hands, it's very easy to hit gutshots or make a set with a small pair, so it's extraordinarily dangerous to give free cards.

To recap, unless you're an extraordinarily aggressive player who raises all the time, you should not usually raise with aces before the flop. One could even make an argument that you should never raise before the flop with aces, because even if you're a good player and your opponents can't put you on aces, the fact that you put so much money in the pot forces you to defend your aces over very risky flops.

Put simply, a reraise with aces almost screams at your opponents, "I have aces!" And once you've told people that you have aces, bottom two pair and top and bottom pair look good to them, and any set looks like a monster on the flop. Almost as important, a hand that flops one pair with nine cards to make two pair looks pretty good to your opponents. For example, let's say that I just call an opponent's pre-flop reraise with 10-9-8-7 and the flop comes 7-5-2. I know that he has aces, but I figure that I have a pretty good hand. In order to beat him, I need to catch a 10, 9, or 8 to pick up a second pair, a 6 to make a gutshot straight, or a 7 to make trips. There are four sixes and two sevens, plus nine other cards—fifteen outs total—that I could catch to beat him, so I'm about even money to win. My opponent's aces are vulnerable in this situation. Of course, if I didn't know that he had aces and he bet on the 7-5-2 flop, I would be more careful.

Any time you advertise that you have aces, unless you can get three quarters or more of your money in the pot, just call and wait to see what happens on the flop—even if you're normally an extremely aggressive player.

Playing a Drawing Hand

Drawing hands are a big part of Omaha. You can turn monsters that are favorites over sets. It's easy to turn nut flush draws, nut flush draws with a straight draw, or a wrap with a flush draw, all of which are dangerous hands for your opponents to draw against. If somebody bets into them, many players, including me, will raise with big draws such as a flush draw with a straight draw or maybe two pair with a flush draw.

If you have a drawing hand and you've been given a free card, it's dangerous to bet on the turn, especially from late position. If you bet it, you're giving someone the opportunity to come over the top for all his money. If you get most of your money in on the flop, it's fine; but if you make a small bet on the flop and get called, and nothing happens on the turn, then it's a good idea to check and wait to see what happens on the river.

Another reason not to bet a good draw from a late position is that you can be a little more deceptive. Let's say that you have the nut flush draw with one card to come. You bet from the late position with a club draw and get called. Then a club comes on the river, giving you the nut flush. Your opponent is going to put you on a flush because the board looks dangerous. In other words, it will be harder for you to get paid off. Now, suppose you check the turn and a club comes on the river. Your opponent might check and call when you bet. The point is that you can be a little deceptive by checking a big drawing hand rather than betting it.

Don't Give Free Cards

In hold'em, when you have a big hand, you want your opponent to catch up a little, so you'll get paid off. Therefore, if you are far ahead in the hand, you don't mind giving away a free card. In Omaha you rarely want to give your opponent a chance to improve and catch up with you. For example, if the flop is A-7-7 and I have pocket aces, I would bet because I'm **trolling for a 7**. This means I make a bet and hope someone with trip sevens calls. I'm setting a trap. If none of my opponents has a 7, I'm not going to make any money. But if somebody has one and takes the bait, I stand to make some pretty good money.

When you give free cards, there's a chance that an opponent with a pair will catch a two-outer to beat you or that he'll make a gutshot straight, which happens often. Also, remember that a lot of backdoor hands are possible in Omaha. Backdoor flushes, in particular, don't always have to be the nuts to win the pot. So, if you have a hand on the flop, you should usually bet it.

Also, sometimes you have to be prepared to throw the hand away. Let's say that the flop comes J-8-2 and you have top and bottom pair. Everybody checks around to you, and you bet it, mainly because you don't want to give a free card. You want to pick up the pot right there. If you get raised, it's pretty easy to throw it away. If you get called, you have to be cautious from that point onward.

This doesn't mean that you shouldn't bet this type of hand; you're still trying to pick up a pot with a little bit of something. If you just sit there and say, "I can't bet these marginal hands," you aren't going to win in Omaha. You take stabs at pots, but you're also prepared to fold if you get raised. Another factor to consider if you're betting these hands as well as your good hands, such as top set, is that your opponents may not be able to put you on just two pair.

Betting When You Can't Call

Many times you make bets in Omaha that you cannot call if you get raised. This often happens when you make a bet in order to avoid giving a free card. But you should still go ahead and bet because if you don't, you're just too vulnerable and you're not going to pick up many pots. To win at Omaha, you must pick up some small pots.

Raising To Protect a Hand

Suppose you have top two pair or a set, and you want to get some money into the pot. The flop comes 10♦ 9♣ 2♣. You have the A♣ 10♠ 10♥ 4♣. Even though you have top set and the nut flush draw, your hand is still vulnerable to a straight draw. Suppose an opponent has a K-Q in his hand, you let a free card come off, and he catches a jack. Many times, he'll have a wrap and call your bet, and you'll lose. It's one thing to lose when you've put money into the pot, but it's something else to give him a free card and lose.

Playing the Turn

If you're going to call on the river, you might as well raise on the turn—this is a fundamental concept in pot-limit and no-limit poker, especially when your game has a cap. Let's suppose a person bets into you on the turn. Although you have a calling hand, you don't know if it's the best one out there, but you're planning to call on the river with your last money anyway. In this case, you might as well raise, because if you just call, you're giving him a free shot. For example, let's say that there's a possible flush on board, you have the king-high flush, and someone bets into you. If you've made up your mind that you're going to call him on the river, don't wait for him to bet it again, because he might not—go ahead and raise. He might have two pair or three of a kind, and he's probably going to call the raise. With this play, you're going to make more money if you win at the river, and if you lose, you'll still only lose the same amount. There are two exceptions to this rule. If you are planning to call on the river, you should not automatically raise the turn if:

(1) you think he's bluffing and you have such a good hand that you want him to bluff into you again; or

(2) you have a powerful hand that is far better than his good hand, so you don't want to scare him off.

By just calling in these situations, you're inducing your opponent to bet at the river.

Sometimes by raising on the turn you might even get people to lay down better hands than yours. Let's say that with a jack-high flush, you know that you're going to call on the river, and your opponent bets into you on the turn. If you move in on him in this situation, he might lay down a king-high flush.

Here's another story that illustrates this point: In a hand that I played with David Sklansky, the flop came K-Q-J-x. David bet on the flop, and I called him with three kings. On the turn, after no help came, he bet again. I had made up my mind that I was going to call him on the river, so I raised him. Well, guess what? He didn't have the A-10 for the nut straight; he had the 10-9—and he threw it away. By raising I told him that I had the best hand.

Playing the River

Playing the river is a very interesting aspect of Omaha. Here are a couple of pointers that may help you win more or lose less on the river. If you have the nuts, it isn't always the best idea to bet the size of the pot, because you're forcing people to play good poker. You're saying to them, "I have the best hand and I'm gonna bet all this money, so I suggest you drop." Well, guess what? They do just what you expect. If the pot is $40,000 and you have the best hand, there's nothing wrong with betting only $15,000 or $20,000. This is called **selling the nuts**. You make a moderate bet so you'll get paid off.

This play also sets up bluffs for you. If your opponents know that you'll sell the river with the best hand because they've seen you do it, a $15,000 bet on the river with a bluff has the same impact. In this sense, it's win-win. When you bluff and get called, you lose less. And you get paid off on your good hands a lot more often. Many people just can't stand the idea of throwing a hand away for a small amount of money—and that notion allows you to sell the nuts. In general, there is no reason to always bet the size of the pot on the river when you have the nuts, unless you're pretty sure that your opponent will call. A while ago I played a hand against a man I'll call Nate. There was a Q-J on the board, and I had an A-K-x-x in my hand. Nate made a big bet on the flop and then he checked on the turn. On the river came a 10, giving me the nut straight. My hand didn't look like the nuts to him because he knew that I would have raised him on the flop with a wrap. I bet the pot, about $40,000. Nate thought for a long time and then threw his hand away. In retrospect, I regretted betting that much—I wish I had bet about $20,000 to make it look more like a bluff, in which case he may have called.

Here's a play that works better against average players than top players: Let's say that you have the second or third best hand, like a straight that's not the best available, and you don't know where your opponent is at in the hand. Or maybe you make a queen-high flush on the river, but again, you're not sure where he's at. Don't make a full bet—toss in something small. You can throw the hand away if he raises, because he's probably got the nuts, and of course, you still might get paid off if he calls. But if you check and he bets, you won't know where he's at. If you try this play against good players, be aware that it can work the other way—they'll know what you're doing and will reraise you, knowing that you're going to throw your hand away.

Making an Educated Guess About Your Opponents' Cards

You can sometimes figure out exactly what your opponents' holecards are through inductive logic. Several years ago, Doyle, Roger Moore, and I played an interesting hand that illustrates this point. Doyle had A-A-x-x in his hand, Roger had a 10 with connecting cards, and I had an A-10-x-x. The flop came A-10-10. Doyle bet, I called, and Roger called.

At this point, I had no idea what Doyle had. He may have had a good hand or he could have been bluffing, but I knew Roger wouldn't call without a reasonable hand. Roger must have had either two aces or a 10 to have made the call.

Doyle led at it again on the turn, so I knew that Doyle wasn't bluffing—the flop was just too dangerous to bluff into again with two people calling. At that point, I should have thrown my hand away. Why? Because even if Doyle didn't have two aces, I thought Roger did. Unfortunately, I called. When Roger threw his hand away, I knew for sure that Roger had a 10, I absolutely knew it, because he called and then folded. At that point, I also knew that Doyle could not have a 10, since Roger had one and I held another, so he obviously had two aces.

On the river Doyle bet for the third time. There was just no hand in the deck that he could have other than two aces. Even though Doyle's last bet was relatively small, I showed him my hand of tens full of aces and threw it away. He made some unflattering remarks as he showed me his two aces. This hand clearly shows how good players are able to decipher an opponent's hand.

Although not as cut-and-dried as this example, a similar hand came up in a recent World Poker Tour no-limit hold'em tournament. I played my A-10 badly, but this time I won a big pot with it. Sitting in middle position, I raised before the flop with an A-10, Billy Grey called on the button, and an elderly player who was short-chipped called from the big blind. The flop came A-A-3. I bet $1,500, and Billy raised $3,500 more. I thought that maybe Billy had an A-8 or A-9 and was testing me to find out where he was at in the hand. But then the senior moved in with his last $7,000. At that point, I should have given credit to either player and thrown my hand away. What could I beat? Maybe I was just being naive in thinking that Billy had an A-8 and was probing the strength of my hand, and that the elderly gentleman had two kings. Of course, it just wasn't possible that the senior had moved in with his case money if he didn't have at least A-K or A-Q. I called anyway.

But as badly as I played it on the flop, Billy played it even worse on the turn when a 10 slid off the deck. I bet $10,000 with my full house, and he moved in $15,000 more. What did he think I was betting? Did he think that I would bet an A-K or A-Q at that point? Give me a break—this was a dry pot! The third man was all-in, and it was obvious that he had sent all his chips in with a good hand, so there was no point in my bluffing at the pot. What was I going to do, try to get Billy out so that I can lose to the third guy? Billy should have figured out pretty quickly that he had the worst hand.

As it turned out, Billy had 3-3 and the senior gentleman had A-3. True, I played it badly when I called on the flop, but they should have known that I wouldn't put $10,000 in on the turn if I didn't have something. If I hadn't hit my kicker, I would have checked and Billy would have bet. Then, realizing that Billy was betting into a dry pot, I would have given credit to the third man for an A-K or A-Q, and I would have folded.

In retrospect, I think that Billy may have been very tired after playing tournament poker for so many days in a row. In order to play poker well, you need to think well. I've found that when I get tired, I don't play cards well, I let the cards play me. If I'm just looking for a good hand, not out there thinking about everything, it's time to go to bed. Over the course of a week's play at poker, each simple mistake can cost you tons of money. Three of those mistakes during a trip can mean the difference between winning and losing.

FINAL NOTES

Playing Shorthanded

Shorthanded pot-limit Omaha is quite a different game than a ring game and requires different skills. A lot of people who play very good ring game Omaha can't play shorthanded, and vice versa. A friend of mine from Houston who plays super-aggressive is a much better shorthanded player because he raises virtually every pot. In a shorthanded game, that works because you aren't always up against quality hands. But if you continually raise in a ring game, you will often find yourself up against superior hands and will be taking the worst of it.

People bluff a lot in shorthanded play because, generally speaking, no one flops a good enough hand to call with. Additionally, the nut hand isn't out there nearly as often. I find that playing shorthanded is more fun than playing in a full game: You play more hands, and it isn't boring because as soon as you drop, another hand starts. Just remember that shorthanded Omaha requires a different set of skills.

What Separates Average Players From Top Players

I think that what separates average players from good players is the amount of money average players lose with pocket aces before the flop and with full houses. If you overplay your aces before the flop, and if you're not capable of laying down a full house—especially an underfull—when it's pretty obvious that you're beat, you're going to lose big pots playing Omaha. If you play enough Omaha, these big hands will mean the difference between winning and losing, so you have to play them in such a way that you won't lose a lot of money. And when you play an underfull, you must be careful not to over-commit to the pot, even in shorthanded games.

Let me tell you a little story just to show you how dangerous these hands can be. In a shorthanded game, a player I'll call "Don" and I each had a little bit of money in before the flop. The board came K-K-10, and although I had a king in my hand, I just checked. Don bet around $3,000. I thought he was bluffing, but as it turned out, he had two tens. I called, off came a four on the turn, and I made kings full of fours. He bet $10,000, and I raised him his last $10,000 to put him all-in. Since we were playing shorthanded, it was more difficult for Don to get away from his hand. He called, showed down his tens full of kings, and lost all his money.

This example just shows you how easy it is to lose a big pot with an underfull. Don couldn't have won as much money with tens full as he could have lost if I made kings full.

In this example, if I'd held something like K-Q-5-4, I still would have seen that flop. That's not an absolutely premium starting hand of course, but when you're playing three- or four-handed, you can play almost any four cards. That is, you'll have a little more latitude in your starting hands as long as you play well on the flop, turn, and river. Again, it's risk-reward—for example, if you're playing $200/$400 blinds and there is $50,000 or $60,000 on the table, you can take a lot of flops for $400 if the payoff might be $20,000 to $30,000.

Lyle Berman's Killer Cards Chart

In the late 1980s, I was twiddling my thumbs in my condo in Vail, forced by the crummy weather to stay inside all day. Sitting in front of the fireplace, I started to wonder what a killer card is worth in Omaha. For example, suppose you have a set or two pair and your opponent is drawing to a straight or a flush. If he makes his straight or flush on the turn, you could still kill him on the turn or the river by making a full house for the best hand. Or, you could make your full house on the turn, and he would be drawing dead.

I knew that killer cards were very valuable, but I didn't know exactly what they were worth. All I had with me was a calculator, but I was able to come up with a formula that generated the chart below, which has never before appeared in print. If I were given just a basic calculator today and forced to stay put in a room for a week, I wouldn't bet that I could recreate this chart. I believe it is perfect.

The chart shows how many wins you have, assuming that you're the dog, the person who does not have the best hand. When you have a set, you actually have two calculations to consider—one on the turn and one on the river. You have seven cards to kill with on the turn. In other words, you have seven cards that will make a full house or four-of-a-kind, and if you don't make it, you have three more because the river can pair that card as well. So you have seven and then ten, for seventeen outs or killers.

The chart shows the 41-card percentages for Omaha. We are concentrating on the 41-card percentages, and the eight killer columns to the right apply to Omaha. The fourth column shows what each killer card is worth in Omaha (it's very similar in hold'em) and extrapolates from there. Basically, the chart shows that in order to be 50-50 against a set, you really need seventeen outs twice. This is significant for Omaha, because most people think it's thirteen or fourteen, as it is in hold'em.

LYLE BERMAN'S KILLER CARDS CHART

Number of cards that hit hand	Hold'em: % success with two cards to come (45 cards unknown)	Omaha: % success with two cards to come (41 cards unknown)	Subtracted value of each "killer" card	1 kill card	2 kill cards	3 kill cards	4 kill cards	5 kill cards	6 kill cards	7 kill cards	8 to 10 kill cards
6	25.2	27.4	0.8	26.7	26.0	25.2	24.5	23.8	23.0	22.3	21.2
7	29.0	31.6	0.9	30.7	29.9	29.0	28.2	27.3	26.5	25.6	24.4
8	32.7	35.6	1.0	34.6	33.7	32.7	31.7	30.7	29.8	28.8	27.3
9	36.4	39.5	1.1	38.4	37.3	36.2	35.1	34.0	32.9	31.8	30.2
10	39.9	43.3	1.2	42.0	40.9	39.6	38.4	37.2	36.0	34.8	32.9
11	43.3	47.0	1.3	45.6	44.3	42.9	41.6	40.2	38.9	37.6	35.5
12	46.7	50.5	1.4	49.0	47.6	46.1	44.6	43.2	41.7	40.2	38.0
13	49.9	53.9	1.6	52.3	50.7	49.1	47.6	46.0	44.4	42.8	40.5
14	53.0	57.2	1.7	55.5	53.8	52.1	50.4	48.7	47.0	45.2	42.7
15	56.0	60.4	1.8	58.5	56.7	54.9	53.0	52.2	49.4	47.6	44.9
16	59.0	63.4	1.9	61.5	59.5	57.6	55.6	53.7	51.7	49.8	46.8
17	61.8	66.3	2.0	64.3	62.2	60.1	58.0	56.0	53.9	51.8	48.8
18	64.6	69.1	2.2	67.0	64.8	62.6	60.4	58.2	56.0	53.8	50.5
19	67.2	71.8	2.3	69.5	67.2	64.9	62.6	60.2	57.9	55.6	52.1
20	69.7	74.4	2.4	72.0	69.5	67.1	64.6	62.2	59.8	57.3	53.7

TRIPLE DRAW

Daniel Negreanu

Triple draw lowball is a relatively new game, which means nobody has a lifetime of experience. I figured that a young player could have as much expertise in triple draw as anybody. At age 29, Daniel Negreanu has proven himself to be the best under-30 player in the world. I had heard that he was good, but I didn't realize just how good he was until I played at his table in two tournaments. He has a tremendous table presence; you're always aware of him—a good indicator of a world-class player.

Daniel's record in tournament play rivals that of much older players. At the age of 23, he started his tournament career by winning the first event he ever entered, the pot-limit hold'em championship at the World Series of Poker. In 1997, after winning back-to-back limit hold'em titles, he won the Best All-Around Player award at the World Poker Finals at Foxwoods Casino.

He won the no-limit hold'em tournament at the Taj Mahal in Atlantic City in 1999 and the Best All-Around Player award at the L.A. Poker Classic at the Commerce Casino the next year. In 2003 Daniel was awarded his second gold bracelet at the WSOP when he demonstrated his versatility by winning the S.H.O.E. event, which alternates seven-card stud, hold'em, Omaha, and seven-card stud eight-or-better. That brought his tournament wins to a total of 26 from 1997-2003.

Lately, Daniel has started playing more live cash games, but if he ever redirects his energies back to tournament play, I won't be surprised if he someday holds the record for tournaments won and finds himself with more WSOP bracelets than anyone in history.

Daniel's 2004 credentials confirm my opinion of him. He made five final tables at the WSOP, won a championship bracelet in limit hold'em, and took the Best All-Around Player award. He won the 2004 Championship Poker Tournament at the Plaza Hotel in Las Vegas, was second in the Party Poker Million III limit hold'em event, third in the no-limit hold'em Caribbean Adventure Cruise, and second in the WPT Player of the Year race. He also won the 2004 WPT tournament at Borgata in Atlantic City.

Pretty impressive stuff and there are still three months left in 2004, as this book goes to press.

TRIPLE DRAW
by Daniel Negreanu

INTRODUCTION

In recent years, triple draw has steadily increased in popularity. In fact, these days you will rarely find a high-limit game at the Bellagio in Las Vegas that does not include some form of triple draw. Typically, tables that are $200/$400 and higher are mixed games, so in order to participate you'll have to learn the fundamentals of several forms of poker, including triple draw.

In this chapter, we'll cover the deuce-to-seven form of triple draw. It is the more widespread and intricate of the two most common triple draw games, the other being ace-to-five lowball. Most of what you'll learn here applies to ace-to-five as well, but near the end of the chapter, I will go over the key differences between the two games and the necessary adjustments you'll need to make when moving from one to the other.

There is a common misconception among some high-limit players that triple draw is nothing more than a game of pure luck. That's simply not the case. While luck plays a role in any given hand, playing correctly will minimize any dangerous swings that luck may bring, and skill will prevail.

Triple draw has caught on so quickly because of the allure of action and big pots. Typical triple draw pots are larger than those generated by a hand of Omaha high-low, for example. You'll also notice that when you add triple draw to a mix of other games, it tends to liven up everyone's play.

Triple draw is an action game, no question about it. You'll need to have your seat belt on at all times. To better prepare you for the bumpy ride, this chapter will give you all the tools you'll need to become a winning player. I'll provide you with a basic set of principles that, if followed closely, should be enough to enable you to beat almost any triple draw game in the world.

HOW TO PLAY THE GAME

Before we get into any strategy discussion, it's important that you understand the rules of the game, as well as how the betting works. The rules are rather simple: You are dealt five cards facedown and can choose to draw as many cards as you wish, up to three times. You can stop drawing at any point, which is more commonly known as **standing pat**.

In deuce-to-seven triple draw, the winner of the pot at the showdown is the player with the worst poker hand. For example, 2-3-4-5-7 with no flush is the worst hand in traditional poker but the best hand in deuce-to-seven. Straights and flushes count against you in deuce-to-seven, so 4-5-8-9-Q would actually beat 2-3-4-5-6, a straight. Also, in deuce-to-seven, an ace can only be used for high, and not for low. This leads to the rare case of the worst traditional poker hand winning. Since an ace is always high, 5-4-3-2-A is not a straight, and it beats any pair or other ace-high.

The rules for ace-to-five are slightly different. The best hand in ace-to-five is simply A-2-3-4-5. Flushes and straights don't count against you, and an ace is considered a one. In this game, the winner of the pot is the player with the five lowest unpaired cards. So A-2-3-5-Q would beat A-2-2-3-4. If, by the river, the two remaining players both have a pair, the lower pair wins. For example: A-A-5-6-9 would beat 2-2-3-4-5.

TRIPLE DRAW LOWBALL

The Deal

The deal is similar to hold'em, with a button, small blind, and, of course, a big blind. Since there are so many drawing rounds, this game can only be played six-handed; otherwise you would run out of cards too often. It is possible to play the game seven- or eight-handed, but only if players sit out on every deal. When playing seven-handed, the player to the left of the big blind is forced to sit out one hand. Eight-handed, the players in first and second positions sit out.

Betting

In some areas of the South, they play spread-limit, meaning that in a $100/$400 game, you can bet from $100 to $400 at any time, but the more popular betting structure is fixed limits. If you are seated in a $200/$400 triple draw game, the small blind posts $100 and the big blind $200. If you are first to act, you can fold, call the $200, or raise it to $400. Every player after you has the same options: fold, call, or raise. Once that action is complete, there is another betting round, also in $200 increments, after the first draw. After the second draw, the bet doubles. You can now bet or raise $400. Finally, after the third draw, the bet is once again $400.

So there are four betting rounds in total. In a $200/$400 game, they would be:

(1) $200 before the first draw;

(2) $200 after the first draw;

(3) $400 after the second draw; and

(4) $400 after the third draw.

Now that we've got that out of the way, let's look at what types of hands we should be starting with.

Starting Hands

First and foremost: Don't leave the gate without a deuce. In deuce-to-seven triple draw, the lowly deuce is more powerful than any other card. Your goal in deuce-to-seven triple draw would be to make a seven, and in order to do so, you must have a deuce in your hand. There are four possible sevens, all of which contain a deuce:

(1) 2-3-4-5-7 (known as a **wheel** or **number one**, for obvious reasons, and equivalent in ranking to the A-2-3-4-5 wheel in ace-to-five.)

(2) 2-3-4-6-7 (known as **number two**)

(3) 2-3-5-6-7 (known as **number three**)

(4) 2-4-5-6-7 (known as **number four**)

While 3-4-5-6-7 gives you five cards to a seven, it also makes a straight that can't be used in deuce-to-seven lowball. So obviously, most starting hands have a deuce in them.

Pat Hands

If you are dealt a **pat hand**—a good hand that requires no discarding or drawing on your part—you want to protect it by putting in every bet you can. Any pat seven is a monster, and while a pat eight is great, it is also vulnerable. For the most part, if you are dealt a pat seven or eight you won't be drawing at all, and depending on the action, you'll probably see the hand through to the end.

Once you've decided to stay pat with your seven or eight, there is no need to slow-play your hand. Bet and raise at every opportunity before the draw and after the first draw. With a pat hand, smooth calling before the draw is pointless, since your secret will be out as soon as the dealer asks you how many cards you want. Once you say, "I'm good," your opponents will know that you have a seven, eight, or maybe a nine.

A nine, however, is more difficult to play. In some situations, it may be okay to stay pat with a nine, but in general you want to avoid even playing a rough nine. You'd be better off placing a hand like 9-8-7-6-4 in the muck than hoping it holds up in a multiway pot.

However, if you held something like 9-7-4-3-2, you would have a dynamite draw. You would discard the nine and have three chances at a seven. You are certainly a favorite to make at least a nine or better with a draw like this, since you'd have fifteen outs three times! That makes you a big favorite over a foolish opponent who stays pat with the same nine.

One-Card Draws

All seven draws and most one-card eight draws are playable, provided you don't have a straight draw. While 4-5-6-7 is only one card from making a seven, only the valuable 2 will help you. If you are in a multiway pot, there may not even be a 2 left in the deck to save you! Even if you are lucky enough to catch a deuce, your hand is far from unbeatable. If any other player makes his seven, the best you can do is tie.

Unless you actually have a wheel you always want to be heads-up. Of course, if you have a draw like 2-3-4-7, you should welcome as many players as possible. However, to avoid giving away information about the strength of your hand, you should always raise and reraise with any one-card draw you decide to play.

As I said previously, any good seven draw should be played aggressively, regardless of your position, provided you don't have a straight draw. To a lesser extent, if you decide to play a straight draw, such as 2-3-4-5, 2-3-4-6, 2-3-5-6, or 2-4-5-6, play it aggressively, too. While a 7 would be the perfect catch for any of these four hands, and an 8 would be welcome, the straight potential makes them slightly less valuable than the other seven draws.

While a one-card eight draw with no straight possible isn't bad, any eight draw with a straight possible is almost always unplayable.

Here are the one-card eight draws you can often play:

2-3-4-8	2-3-5-8	2-4-5-8	2-3-6-8
2-4-6-8	2-5-6-8	2-3-7-8	2-4-7-8
2-5-7-8	2-6-7-8	3-4-5-8	3-4-6-8
3-5-6-8	3-4-7-8	3-5-7-8	3-6-7-8

These hands are too good to fold. When playing them, though, be sure to target one opponent or pick up the blinds. Any time you play a one-card draw, regardless of its ranking on the strength chart, you should be raising and reraising before the first draw.

In fact, any hand you choose to play before the first draw should be raised. There are few situations where limping is correct. If your hand is strong enough to play, play it aggressively. If it's not, send it to the muck. In triple draw, your strategy before the draw should be similar to that used in limit hold'em before the flop—tight but aggressive.

Two-Card Draws

The majority of the hands you play before the first draw will be two-card draws. The following two-card draws can be played for any amount of bets before the draw:

2-3-4	2-3-7	2-3-5
2-4-5	2-4-7	2-5-7

All these hands give you an opportunity later to draw at one card at the wheel without the presence of a straight draw.

If you are dealt any of these hands, raise it. In fact, if you are in position, I would advise reraising. That way you can isolate one player while having position, which makes it easier to control the action.

2-3-4 vs. 2-3-7

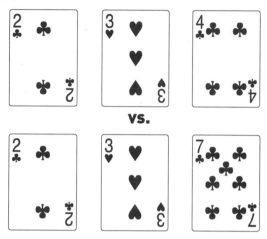

There has always been a great deal of debate over what the best starting hand is when drawing two. Is it the 2-3-4 or the 2-3-7?

Let me start by saying that it simply doesn't matter very much. You should play both hands the same way. The hands are so close in strength that wasting too much time talking about which is better is silly, but I'm going to do it anyway to illustrate the concept.

After running several simulations, I found the following: if the 2-3-4 ran against precisely 2-3-7, the 2-3-7 would be less than a 1 percent favorite. That makes the 2-3-7 the best hand then, right? Wrong. Against any other hand your opponent might have, the 2-3-4 would do better than the 2-3-7. Since you are rarely going to be in a situation where you hold 2-3-4 against precisely 2-3-7, I would say that the 2-3-4 is the best starting hand in terms of two-card draws.

You always want to be drawing from the bottom up. The smoother your draw, the more often you will win the pot when both you and your opponent make your hand. For example, if both the 2-3-4 and the 2-3-7 make an 8-7, the 2-3-4 can't lose! The 2-3-4 could make only 2-3-4-7-8, while the 2-3-7 would make 8-7s that look like this:

2-3-4-7-8
2-3-5-7-8
2-3-6-7-8

Notice how much stronger the first 8 is? With the 2-3-7 you'll often have to make a tough decision later as to whether or not you should draw to a 2-3-7-8 or throw the 8 away and go for the wheel. With the 2-3-4 you would simply keep the 8 every time.

Be Wary of the 6. There are four other two-card draw starting hands that should also be played in most situations. They are draws that contain a 6 that could still make you a 7-low. Here they are:

2-3-6
2-4-6
2-5-6
2-6-7

None of these draws can make a wheel, and the first three may actually cause you problems due to the presence of a possible straight. I would still advise you to play these hands in most situations, but you should fold them in the face of too much action, especially if the raises came from tight players.

Good Eight Draws. A good eight draw is one that could make **number five** (2-3-4-5-8), such as 2-3-8, 2-4-8, and 2-5-8—but again, be wary of the 6. If you make your hand with a 6 in it, you might lose to eights at the showdown. From early position, each of these hands can be folded safely. However, if you are in late position and no one has entered when it's your turn to act, you should raise with these hands. These hands are strong enough to defend your blind with as well. We'll learn more about blind play later in the section.

Trouble Hands Worth Playing

The following starting hands should only be played when stealing blinds or defending them:

3-4-8	3-5-7
3-5-8	3-6-7
3-4-7	4-5-7

These are trouble hands or trash hands, and they do much better in position and in heads-up situations. When dealt one of these hands, you often find yourself with either a bad eight draw or a straight seven draw. If you don't improve quickly with one of these hands, you should abort mission and throw them in the muck. Obviously, the one key card you are looking to catch would be the powerful deuce. As a general rule, you don't want to draw to a hand that needs a deuce to fill it—you should already have one.

Three-Card Draws

There are only two situations where you can justify drawing three:

> **(1)** Stealing on the button.

> **(2)** Defending your blind.

If you are going to draw three, one of the two cards you keep simply has to be a 2. Here are the hands worth drawing three on:

2-3
2-4
2-5
2-7

Notice we left out the 2-6. You are already on a steal drawing three; let's not compound the problem by drawing rough as well! It is usually correct to draw three out of the big blind with a hand like 2-3, as long as it only costs you one more bet.

Also, if no one has entered the pot, you can attempt to steal the blinds from the button with one of these three-card draws. The fact that you have position makes it likely that playing one of these hands will be profitable. After all, there is still a chance you'll win the blinds without a fight.

Since you are drawing three, chances are one of those three cards will help you. Any of the following: 4, 5, 6, 7, or 8 would improve a 2-3 starting hand enough to draw once more.

Four- and Five-Card Draws

Simple: Don't do it. The only time you should draw four is when you are the big blind in an unraised pot. In that case, keep a 2, 3, 4, 5, or 7, and discard the rest.

Playing from the Blinds

Playing out of the big blind can be very tricky. Though you will usually get excellent pot odds, if you start with rough draws, you will make rough hands and receive rough bruises to your bankroll!

You certainly want to stretch your starting requirements some, but if you go too far, you are going to be left with too many difficult decisions on later streets. For example, drawing two out of the big blind with a hand like 4-5-6 is just asking for trouble. What are you looking to catch? A deuce and a 7 or a deuce and an 8? Even if you catch this miracle draw, your hand is still not in the clear. Muck this draw and save yourself some major headaches.

The hands you should add to your playable list are the excellent three-card draws (2-3, 2-4, 2-5, 2-7) and some of the two-card eight draws (3-4-8, 3-5-8). Since you are being laid such great pot odds, you should also add the seven draws that don't contain a deuce (3-4-7, 3-5-7, 3-6-7, 4-5-7). With rough draws like these, you want to get to the draw as cheaply as possible. Calling one raise is fine; calling two raises is suicide.

Every once in a while you'll pick up a really strong draw in the blind, such as a one-card draw to a non-straight eight-or-better or a two-card draw to a wheel containing a deuce. If you are holding one of these and find yourself up against a late position raiser, you should punish him by reraising.

Small Blind vs. Big Blind. If everyone folds to you in the small blind, don't get carried away trying to steal the big blind's money. In fact, since you don't have position, you should play tighter than you would if you were the button. A good three-card draw—one containing a deuce and either a 3, 4, 5, or 7—is still playable. Against a loose, aggressive player you should probably limp with these weak hands, but if the big blind plays conservatively, you should raise it. Remember, the small blind acts first on all subsequent rounds of betting, so it's the worst position at the table. If anyone else has joined the pot, you'd need a solid starting hand to play from the small blind.

If you are in the big blind heads-up against the small blind, you should call one more bet with anything remotely playable. That even includes a three-card draw to a 3-4! There are many reasons why having position is so valuable when playing heads-up. That, in addition to the 3 to 1 odds you're getting to defend your big blind against the small blind, makes calling the right play with almost any three-card draw to a wheel.

Playing Against a Raise

If you are the button and are facing a raise, you should usually reraise and take the hand heads-up with the power of position. Hands like 2-3-4, 2-3-7, one-card draws, and pat hands are all strong hands that you don't want to fold. Take control by three-betting it.

If your hand isn't good enough to three-bet, seriously consider folding. If you're outside the blind, hands like 2-3-8 are good enough to raise with if no one has entered the pot, but not quite good enough to call a raise with.

Summary

Let me repeat this, because is so important: The deuce is the key card in this game. Most of the hands you choose to play should contain a deuce—there are few exceptions. You might see others drawing to hands that don't contain a deuce, but don't fall into that trap.

For the most part, you want to play strong hands that can make the nuts. When you are drawing smooth, you are going to make smooth hands when you hit. If you are drawing rough, you'll often be drawing to a loser or often even drawing dead!

Playing After the First Draw

Depending on the draw you start with, you'll generally want to bet and raise when you improve your hand and either check and call or check and fold when you don't. Again, it all depends on the draw you start with. If you were dealt 2-3-4-7 and were up against any player who drew two, you would bet whether you improved or not. In fact, it would be fine to bet without even looking to see if you improved!

When You Miss

What to do when you don't improve depends on your position, the number of cards you draw, and the number of cards your opponents draw. If you draw one and your opponents draw two or more, you should always bet. In fact, anytime you are a card ahead of your opponents, it's safe to bet—with one exception. Here it is: if you draw two and don't improve, then are called by two players drawing three, you should check. Chances are that one if not both of them improved, so it would be wise to take the free card rather than risk being raised or check-raised.

When out of position and drawing an equal number of cards as your opponents, what you do depends heavily on whether or not you improve. Generally speaking, you should play the hand straightforward, betting when you improve, checking when you miss.

For example, in the small blind with 2-5-6-7, a late position player raises you, and you reraise. You draw one, as does your opponent. If you don't improve, betting would be silly. Your opponent will almost never fold here, but he will likely raise you if he improves. Sure, you may have a marginally better draw than he does, but that doesn't justify losing an extra bet if he does improve.

Even if your opponent draws to a 3-4-5-8, it wouldn't be a disaster if the betting round went check, check. In the best case scenario, you'll get a bet in as a marginal favorite. In the worst case scenario, you'll get two bets in as either a significant underdog or drawing dead, while your opponent is drawing smoother than you to begin with.

Now, if you are drawing two cards to a premium hand in a raised multiway pot, you should still call a bet whether you improve or not, since the pot is already sizeable. However, you should rarely call a bet and a raise if you don't improve your two-card draw, as you will likely find yourself up against either two one-card draws, a one-card draw and a pat hand, or two pat hands. If you do decide to call a double bet, you won't even know for sure whether it will cost you more to see your next draw. If the first bettor does have a pat hand, he will likely reraise, putting you in a horrible position—drawing two against a pat hand with two draws left.

When You Improve

When you do improve after the first draw, it's time to get aggressive. Whether you improve to a one-card draw or a vulnerable pat hand, you'll want to narrow the field as much as possible in multiway pots. Being aggressive in heads-up situations isn't quite as important. Let's look at an example.

You raise in first position with 2-4-7. You are called by the button and reraised by the big blind. The big blind draws one, while both you and the button draw two. Now you catch a 5 and a king. The big blind bets and it's up to you. Should you call or raise?

The correct answer would be raise. While it's true that you may be up against a pat hand, you'd still have two draws to make a seven or possibly an eight, depending on your opponent's hand. Forcing the button out is the most important thing. If you just call, he would be getting good enough pot odds to draw two cards. That's not what you want. You want to secure last position by chasing the button out, then take the hand heads up. If the big blind didn't improve, you'll have an even better chance against just one opponent.

What if you are heads up the whole time? Same scenario, except this time there is no third player. In this case, a raise wouldn't be horrible, but calling would be better. Since you don't have to worry about knocking out a player, you can simply call here and draw to your hand cheaply. The one key drawback to raising is the risk of your opponent making his hand. It would then cost you three bets rather than one to outdraw him. As I mentioned earlier, you may be giving up a little value since you have the better draw, but that won't make up for the times you pay extra against a made hand.

Keep the 8 or Draw To the Wheel?

This is probably one of the most difficult decisions you'll have to make in a triple draw hand. When drawing to a hand like 2-3-7, should you keep the 8 after the first draw and draw rough, or discard it and draw to the wheel?

The reason it is such a difficult decision is because it depends on several variables, including the number of opponents, the number of cards your opponents need, your position, and the discards you made.

Number of Opponents. The more players in the pot, the more you should lean toward discarding the 8 and going for the wheel. The problem with keeping the 8 with more opponents drawing is that it will get beat too often by an 8-6, an 8-5, or a seven.

If you are up against just one opponent, you might decide to keep the 8, but you should consider other factors, like the number of cards your opponent is drawing and your position.

Number of Cards Your Opponent Is Drawing. If your opponents are drawing three or more, you should keep the 8. They need a lot of help, and if you make an 8-7 here, it will usually be good enough to win. If you go to the deck and again draw two, you will be giving them a better shot of getting back into the hand. Draw to the 8-7 and punish them for their loose play!

Position. Position is extremely important. When you are out of position, you won't have the luxury of knowing how many cards your opponents are drawing. Also, if you are out of position with a rough draw, you may even get outplayed on a later street. As a general rule, when out of position you want to be drawing to the nuts or as close to the nuts as possible. Although 8-7-3-2 may be a good draw, it's far from the nut draw. The best you can do is make **number ten**, 2-3-4-7-8.

Conversely, when you are in position, you have more control over your opponents. So, in effect, you can play their hands rather than yours. If you draw one to the 8-7 and your opponents are still drawing two after the first draw, you'll often win the pot whether you improve or not. Therein lies the value of position.

Discards. We are going to cover this subject in greater detail near the end of the chapter. But for now, we'll say that generally, the more paired wheel cards you have in your hand, the stronger the hand. While 2-3-4-K-Q and 2-3-4-3-4 appear to be the same draw (2-3-4), the latter is a much stronger hand. Why? Because that extra 3 and 4 might be cards your opponent is looking for but can now no longer catch! Additionally, it makes it less likely that you will pair. Furthermore, if your opponent holds 2-5-7, your discard makes it less likely that he will make his draw now that two of his cards are dead.

So how does that apply to keeping an 8? Simple. The more paired cards you have, the more you should lean toward keeping the 8.

Making an Eight on the First Draw

When you start out playing triple draw lowball, you are usually going to stay pat if you make an eight at any point. Once your reading ability improves, however, you will be able to break an eight and draw to the seven under the right circumstances. An 8-7 can be broken, but if you make an 8-6 or better, you're better off staying pat. Being in position will also play into your decision of whether or not to break an eight. How so?

If you are holding 2-3-6-7-8 and an opponent in front of you stands pat after the first draw, you have to ask yourself, "What can I beat?" Would your opponent stay pat with a nine here? Or could he possibly have a worse 8-7?

In this case, with an opponent standing pat in front of you, you will usually break the eight, since you have such a smooth draw to a seven (2-3-6-7). If no one yet has stood pat, you should stay pat until further notice.

Playing After the Second Draw

When To Check

After the second draw, you should always check to an opponent that is one card ahead of you. For example, if you are drawing two and your opponent is drawing one, you can even check in the dark. Or if you are drawing one and your opponent is pat, again you can check in the dark. In these situations, you won't be risking a free card because your opponent will surely bet. If your opponent doesn't make this normally automatic bet, then he will often give you a free card.

If after the first draw, both you and your opponent draw one and you fail to improve to a pat hand, you should probably check, especially when out of position and most of the time when in position. Even if you feel like you have the best draw going into the last card, it is usually only a slight advantage, so it's probably best to avoid the possible check-raise.

When To Bet

You should always bet if you are a card ahead, regardless of your position. If you have a one-card draw versus an opponent with a two-card draw, you should bet whether you improve or not. If you are pat and they are drawing, again you should bet automatically. You simply can't give away free cards with just one draw left. If there is any chance you can win the pot here, you have to take it. If your opponent with the two-card draw doesn't get help, he might fold even though you are still drawing as well.

If both you and your opponents draw one going into the last draw, you should bet with any hand that you are going to stay pat with. If you make 9-7-6-4-2, you should bet and stay pat if no one raises you. With just one draw left, the nine is a favorite over any draw.

To avoid becoming too predictable, you might want to bet your premium draws in position with or without improvement. For example, you have 2-3-4-7-7 and have already discarded a 3 and a 4. Your lone opponent checks to you. In this situation, your hand is a big enough favorite over your opponent's draw that it's worth a value bet.

If you had this hand out of position however, you should still check despite the powerful draw you have. Your opponent isn't going to fold here; he'll either raise or call. If he does raise, you've now lost an extra bet and are probably an underdog to win the pot. This is an important concept to understand. When out of position, you need to think about minimizing your losses by avoiding marginal value bets. They have value when your opponent happens to miss, but when your opponent completes his draw, you give up way too much equity when he raises you.

In position, you should also bet some of your premium one-card draws for another reason. If your opponent is perceptive, he will know that you don't have a pat hand when you check behind him going into the last draw. If he has a hand like 2-3-4-8-10, he might decide to stay pat knowing that your hand is not complete. However, had you bet your draw, he would have a really tough time staying pat with a ten.

If you don't have a pat hand, you want your opponent to break the ten. The ten is a favorite over even 2-3-4-7-7. If you can get him to break the ten with a bet, your 2-3-4-7 will become the favorite over his draw to the 2-3-4-8.

When To Call

When drawing one to a wheel or any seven, you should always call one bet going into the last draw. In fact, sometimes you may even raise with a draw like this, but we'll get to that later. Let's cover situations where you would simply call.

If both you and your opponent draw one going into the last draw and you don't improve but he bets, you should usually just call. Your opponent's bet should tell you that he has a pat hand, so unless you have reason to believe he'd fold or break his hand to a raise, you should just call and try to outdraw him.

Also, if you draw two and improve to a one-card draw, and your opponent draws one going into the second draw, you should just call. If you get really lucky and make a pat hand, then you might consider raising.

There is one more interesting situation where calling might be better than raising. Suppose your opponent draws one and you, though still drawing two, have position on him. You find yourself with a hand like 2-4-6-7-8. Should you raise or just call?

Let's think about what may happen if you just call. If you call, your opponent will assume that you are still drawing at least one, if not two. If he makes a hand like 10-7-4-3-2 he will probably stay pat ahead of you. After all, a pat ten is a favorite over any draw. Now, if you smooth call, you've just ensured yourself the pot. Since there are no draws left, you are protecting what's in the middle. In a sense, you're tricking your opponent into thinking he has the best hand because you didn't raise.

So what would have happened if you raised? Well, you'd certainly be taking the best of it, as your pat eight is a favorite over his wheel draw. The problem is, you don't want your opponent to be drawing live at all! If you raise and force your opponent to break the ten, he'll now be drawing live to a five, six, or even an eight. Why risk the whole pot to get in one extra bet in on the turn? You might even be able to win that bet on the river when the pot is secured. This play is a valuable weapon that has to be added to your arsenal if you want to be a winning triple draw player.

Finally—and this should go without saying—you should just call when you are a card behind. If you improve from a two-card draw to a one-card draw, but your opponent was already on a one-card draw, you should simply be a caller. If you are up against a player who was already pat and you are on a one-card draw, you should usually just call unless you have reason to believe he has a weak hand, in which case you may choose to raise. There is more on that in the next section.

When To Raise

The most obvious reason to raise is that you have the best hand. For the most part, with a seven, 8-5, or even 8-6, you should raise since you probably do have the best hand.

In a multiway pot, it's even more important to raise with one of these pat hands in order to put pressure on those opponents trying to outdraw you. They surely will call one bet drawing to a wheel or a good eight, but for two bets you may be able to get them to lay it down, depending, of course, on the players.

Even when heads-up, you should raise with a seven or an 8-5, then follow through with a bet on the river. Hands ranked one through five are difficult to outdraw. Your opponent can't possibly have too many outs if he is still drawing. Even if your opponent is drawing to a 2-3-4-7 against your 2-3-4-5-8, he can only win the pot with a 6 or one of three remaining fives—a total of seven outs. If your opponent has a pat eight, chances are he won't break it, thinking you might be making a play at the pot.

Making a Play at the Pot

What do I mean by making a play at the pot? Sometimes if you have an excellent draw, you might be better off spending an extra bet, hoping to force your opponent to break a pat hand, rather than just calling in the hopes of outdrawing him. For example, say you are on the button with 2-2-3-7-7. Your opponent raises before the first draw, and you reraise him.

Now your opponent draws one and you, of course, draw two. Your two new cards are a 4 and another 2, giving you a wheel draw, 2-3-4-7. Next, your opponent bets. Because of your position, your strong draw, and the valuable discards you've mucked, you decide to raise it. Your opponent calls and decides to stay pat.

Right there you can assume that your opponent doesn't have a very strong hand. If he did, he probably would have reraised once more. Also, since you have seen three deuces and two sevens, it's a lot more likely that your opponent has a hand like 3-4-5-6-8 or even 3-4-5-8-9.

On the second draw, your opponent is pat and you draw one to the wheel. This time, you catch another 7! Unless your opponent has both the case 2 and the case 7, he doesn't have a pat seven. Your opponent bets. What should you do?

It all depends on your read of your opponent. You have a pretty good idea as to the strength of his hand, most likely an eight or a nine. Will your opponent fold? Will your opponent come off of a nine and draw? If you think there is a reasonable chance that the answer to either question is yes, then go ahead and raise.

By investing one more bet, you may either win the pot right there or go from an underdog to a sizeable favorite. If it doesn't work out, it adds more deception to your game at little cost, deception that you can exploit later. After all, you have one more draw and could still make your hand.

In order for a play like this to work, you have to know your opponent. If you know him to be stubborn enough not to break or fold, save your money. However, if he is a thinking player, he'll ask himself, "What can I beat?" Since you played the hand so aggressively before and after the first draw, a thinking player would know that you have a strong draw. If he is looking down at 3-4-6-8-9, what could he possibly break and draw to? He has to simply hope and pray that you are making a play *and* that you will miss on the last draw. Based on all of this, a thinking player may decide it's not worth seeing the hand through and fold. Remember, though, do not try this play against a calling station. Trying to bluff a bad player will make you the fool.

Check-Raising

There are times when you'll be able to get in a check-raise after the second draw. Often, this happens when you are one card behind going into the draw, either drawing two to your opponent's one or drawing one while your opponent stays pat. Anytime you make your hand in this situation, you should be able to check-raise. After all, if your opponent is playing properly, he'll bet to keep from giving away a free draw.

Your check and your opponent's bet here should be automatic. You could even check in the dark, and your opponent would probably bet in the dark, but I wouldn't recommend doing this if there are novices in the game. While it's obvious to you and the other experienced players that these bets are automatic, a novice may not grasp it. So if there are rookies at the table, at least pretend to look before you check.

If you happen to make a good eight or a seven, check-raising is probably a good idea. These hands might already be dead, but there is an excellent chance that your opponent is still drawing. Playing a rough eight or a rough nine is a lot more difficult, and check-raising with either one is risky. If you're out of position, you might lose a lot of bets with a rough hand. And as you already know by now, you should try to avoid losing the maximum with rough hands, especially out of position. So with these hands, you generally will have to make a decision between checking and calling, then staying pat; or checking and calling, then drawing.

In order to make good decisions here, you have to pay attention to tells, as they are extremely valuable in this situation. Watch your opponent closely. Is he shuffling his cards, looking for the one he's planning to discard? Or does the way he is holding his hand look like he is staying pat? This isn't easy, but the best players read these situations very well.

If you aren't able to pick up any tells at all, I would advise staying pat with a nine or better and hope your opponent draws. If your opponent raps pat behind you, you are in deep trouble. If he bets the river, you should probably fold—unless you have reason to believe he would bluff here.

Now, don't get me wrong—in this situation, you can check-raise with any eight or nine. It's not a terrible play at all. In fact, by doing so, you'll definitely get a better idea as to whether or not you should call a river bet. For example, if you check-raise with a rough nine and the player behind you calls and raps pat as well, your hand is no good. Plain and simple. You can safely fold to a river bet. If he draws, then great! Now you'll just have to hope he misses.

When you're holding rough eights and nines, check-raising and check-calling are both viable options, and both should be used from time to time. There is value in either play. Check-calling allows you to minimize your losses, while check-raising may even force your opponent off a better hand! For example, if you check-raised and stood pat with a 2-3-4-8-9, your opponent may decide to break a hand like 2-3-6-7-9, which has you beat. That would be fantastic, regardless of the final outcome.

As you've probably noticed, there is more play on the second draw than any other street. Similar to the turn in hold'em, play on the second draw separates the great players from the rest of the pack. How strong a triple draw lowball player you become depends a lot on how well you're able to master the art of playing the second draw.

When To Fold

There are several situations where you should fold, even with one draw remaining. If you are still drawing two with only one draw remaining, you should usually fold to a bet, especially out of position. The only time you should consider drawing two going into the last draw is when you have position, you think your opponent is still drawing, there is a lot of money in the pot, *and* you have made valuable discards. Otherwise, it's just too difficult to make a hand drawing two with just one draw left. Even 2-3-4 is an underdog to beat K-Q-J-10-8! Amazing, but true.

Here's another situation where you should consider folding: say you are up against a pat hand drawing to a rough eight. If your opponent stays pat after the first draw and you are holding 2-6-7-8, for example, two things need to happen for you to win the pot:

(1) You would need to make your hand.

(2) You would need to be drawing live.

Since your opponent stayed pat after just the first draw, chances are he has at least an eight made, so you will be drawing dead here too often to make calling correct.

You should also consider folding when you make either a rough eight or nine and get raised after the second draw. The only way your hand could be playable is if your opponent is making a bluff-raise and is still drawing. For example, you make a 2-3-7-8-9 and bet against one lone opponent who raises you. You could stay pat and hope he is bluffing; you could draw one and hope that an 8-7 will be good enough to win; or you could take the safe route and simply muck your hand. Which course of action is the best depends on your read of your opponent.

Finally, you should fold when facing two bets going into the last draw, even when drawing to the nuts. This bit of advice may come as a shock to some, so let's look at the reasoning behind it. With one draw left, you have 2-4-5-7 on the button. In front of you, it's bet and raised. Fold. You know that a 6 will give you number four—a strong hand, but one that still might not be good enough considering the action in front of you. This leaves you needing a 3 to give you the nuts. Considering that you are facing two players who obviously have five low cards apiece, what are the chances that all four threes are still live? Not very good. In addition, there's always the chance that the first bettor will reraise once more. All of a sudden, your monster wheel draw doesn't look so hot now, does it?

When To Stay Pat

We know for sure that a pat jack is a small favorite over any draw. Even a hand like J-10-9-8-6 against 2-3-4-7 with one draw left is a 55 percent favorite. From this, can you assume that you should always stay pat with a jack or better with one draw left? Not quite.

Heads-up. If you are heads-up with position and know that your opponent is drawing, then, yes, you could consider staying pat, even with 2-3-4-7-J. However, if you are out of position and don't have the luxury of knowing whether or not your opponent is drawing or staying pat, that changes things dramatically. In this case, you should always draw.

Even after your opponent draws one card, you should probably draw one as well when you figure you're drawing better. That's because you have almost as big an advantage in the one-card versus one-card match-up as you do standing pat—assuming you just showed down the results without betting. In addition, you'll have the opportunity to gain ground through the final betting, considering your superior draw and the fact that you'll act last.

The opportunity to make more money outweighs your slightly diminished chances of ending up with the better hand. So it's usually correct to draw a card. In doing so, you'll also rule out the possibility of being bluffed out by an inspired opponent. Again, it's interesting to note that in a showdown situation, where there can be no future betting, the jack is the favorite over any draw, and it's correct to stand pat with such a hand.

As you see, this is what makes position so important in triple draw. With position in a showdown situation, you would know for certain that the correct play is to stand pat behind an opponent who drew one, hoping he missed.

Multiway Pots. What happens when you add a third player to the mix? How does that change things? Let's look at an extreme example:

YOU (20%)

PLAYER A (40%)

PLAYER B (40%)

In this case, both player A and Player B would win the pot approximately 40 percent of the time, meaning that your pat jack will win just 20 percent of the time. Not good. Let's look at a more typical example:

YOU (33%)

PLAYER A (37%)

PLAYER B (30%)

While that's not too bad—the jack will win its fair share of pots—let's look at what happens when we draw:

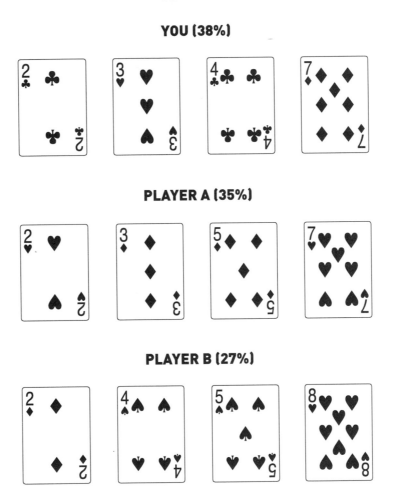

YOU (38%)

PLAYER A (35%)

PLAYER B (27%)

As you can see, you'd do much better by drawing. So what hand becomes a favorite over two other people drawing? The answer is a nine:

TRIPLE DRAW

YOU (42%)

PLAYER A (29%)

PLAYER B (29%)

Again, as in the previous examples, position is paramount. If you know both of your opponents are drawing, it makes staying pat an easy decision. However, if you are out of position and unsure whether your opponents will draw, it makes things much more difficult. That's why it's important to bet if you make your hand out of position. That way, if no one raises you, chances are your nine is the best hand and you can safely stay pat. While you might get the same information by checking, you'd also be giving your opponents a free ride against you.

When To Break

This is where the game becomes a little trickier because the correct decision is heavily dependent on your read. As you gain more experience with the game, it should become easier.

If you are a beginning player, I would advise you not to out-think yourself. Basically, you should stay pat anytime you make an eight or better. As your reading skills improve, there will be times when you'll want to break an eight and go for the wheel.

But keep in mind that 8-6 or an 8-5 should never be broken. If you hold one of these hands and are reasonably sure that the hand is no good, you're better off folding rather than breaking. Only a 7 could help you, and if you think the eight is no good, that leaves only three remaining sevens for you to catch. If you do lose with an 8-6 or an 8-5, there probably wasn't much you could have done about it. Tough beats happen often in this game; you've got to keep your cool.

Now an 8-7 is a different story. With the 8-6 or the 8-5, most hands that have you beat already are extremely difficult to outdraw. Breaking an 8-7, however, gives you a decent chance to outdraw several hands that have you beat, such as any rough 7, 8-5, 8-6, or better 8-7. For example, let's say you have an 8-7-6-3-2 with one draw left, and based on the betting, you think your opponent has a better hand. Unless your opponent is bluffing, if he raises you going into the last draw, he probably has a better hand.

By drawing to the 2-3-6-7, you have as many as eight possible outs to beat any eight (any 4 or 5). As I said earlier, this is a difficult decision to make, and you have to be pretty certain before you make it. Breaking an eight when it is already the best hand is a statistical nightmare! If your opponent bet at you with a nine or bluffed you and is still drawing, how nice it would be to have that eight back! That's why I suggest that beginning players play it straightforward and just take their lumps when they get beat with an eight.

Summary

After the second draw you learned that you should always check when you are a card behind, or when you are out of position drawing an equal number of cards as your opponent and you don't improve. You also learned that you should always bet when you are a card ahead—as when you are drawing one and your opponent is drawing two. You should also bet when you improve your hand and your draw was equal, regardless of your position.

You should call when you think you are drawing live. You should also consider sometimes calling when you have position and plan on staying pat, hoping to trap your opponent into staying pat ahead of you with a weaker hand.

You should raise when you have a strong hand and want to get more money in the pot. You should also raise to knock others out of the pot when you plan on staying pat with a vulnerable hand. In perfect situations, you should occasionally raise with some of your strong one-card draws, hoping to either make your opponent fold or break a made hand.

You should fold when you are still drawing two, and also when you think you may be drawing dead. You should also consider folding some of your rougher pat hands if you are raised.

Heads-up with position, you should stand pat with a ten or better if your opponent is still drawing, and even with a jack if it's a showdown situation with no more betting possible. In a three-handed pot, you should always stay pat with a nine or better if your opponents are still drawing.

You learned that breaking an 8-6 or 8-5 is a no-no. However, if you have an 8-7 and are reasonably certain that your opponent has you beat, you may consider breaking. If you are a novice player though, I recommend staying pat with any eight to avoid being outplayed by more sophisticated players.

Play on the River

Generally speaking, the river is no time to get fancy. The pots are usually so big by the river that bluffing becomes difficult. Most successful bluffs in deuce-to-seven triple draw start well before the river.

When Both You and Your Opponent Are Drawing One

In this situation, you rarely should bluff. Since the pots become so large, your opponent will likely call you with as little as a king. However, there are certain situations where a bluff could be profitable. You would have to have:

(1) The right table image; and

(2) The right opponent, one who makes laydowns.

Bluffing with an ace, king, or queen is just silly. You'll get called virtually every time your opponent has you beat, and you will "bluff" your opponent when he makes a pair that you can beat anyway.

I suggest that you only bluff when you make a big pair and have virtually no chance to win in a showdown. Even a pair of deuces can win in the showdown when your opponent also pairs. I suggest bluffing with pairs four and higher, and even then I would only advise you to do so every now and then. It will only work if your opponent makes a pair smaller than yours. Even then, I have seen people call bets on the river with pairs as high as 6-6!

The river is the time for value betting and not for bluffing. With so many bets in the pot, all you have to do is catch an occasional bluff to make calling correct. You should *always* call a bet with a jack or better and call most of the time with a queen through a pair of deuces.

You should also value bet hands as bad as a jack. As you

learned previously, a jack is a favorite over any one-card draw, so you should bet it when you make one, regardless of your position. Since your opponent will likely call you if he makes a queen, king, or ace, or even a small pair, there is value in betting the jack.

The only drawback comes when you get raised. In that case, you would have to go with your read. More often than not, your opponent won't raise you with a 9, 10, or a jack, but he might do it with an 8 and certainly will with a 7.

When Your Opponent Is Pat and You Are Drawing Out of Position

If your opponent is pat and you are drawing one out of position to 2-3-5-7, what should you do if you catch 4, 6, 8 or even a 9? As is true with most poker situations, it all depends. All four of those hands can likely beat your opponent if he stayed pat going into the last draw, but you might not always want to bet them.

Against the right opponent, you might want to go for a check-raise with the seven or the eight. It depends on how aggressive your opponent is and whether or not he would bet a nine or a ten on the river once you've checked.

The safer play is to simply bet right out, hoping to be called by a worse hand and not raised by a better hand. After all, your opponent could have anything from a seven all the way up to a jack.

This is another situation where a bluff might work. What if you paired sevens? An opponent might fold jack, ten, or even a nine in this spot. After all, he knows that you know he has a pat hand, yet you are still betting into him. Normally that means you must have made your hand and are looking to get paid off. A good player might decide to save the last bet, giving you the opportunity to steal a nice-sized pot.

It's important to understand that this play won't work as

well if your opponent stayed pat on or before the first draw. If your opponent does that, it usually signifies a good nine, an eight, or a seven. Your bluff probably won't work if he has any of these hands.

When Your Opponent Is Pat and You Are Drawing in Position

Being in position gives you more information about your opponent's hand. If he checks the river, it's less likely that he made a seven, eight, or nine, and more likely that he made a ten, a jack, or worse. Again, that is assuming that your opponent only rapped pat on the last draw. If he rapped pat earlier in the hand, he probably has an eight or better, or possibly a nine.

If your opponent bets the river, you should not raise unless you have a premium hand. An 8-6 is right on the borderline. Against more aggressive opponents, you can raise with an 8-6, but against a more conservative opponent you should give him more credit and just call.

If your opponent checks the river, you should value bet any eight or better, and sometimes bet your better nines. Your opponent's check doesn't necessarily mean he has a bad hand, especially if he stood pat earlier. He might be looking to check-raise or collect bullets, hoping you bluff off your money. It's customary for a player to check an eight in this spot and simply look to call if you bet. It's also customary for a player to check a seven to you, looking for the double bet, assuming you can't call if you miss anyway.

You want to bet an eight or better for value every time against a player who stayed pat after the second draw, but check your rougher eights against a player who stayed pat early in the hand. A hand like 2-5-6-7-8 isn't worth betting against a player who stayed pat early, but is a must-bet against a player who stayed pat on the last draw.

When Your Opponent is Drawing and You Are Pat Out of Position

In this situation you should check any nine, ten, or jack. If you had a rough eight before or after the first draw, you may consider checking as well. You opponent is probably drawing to beat you, and it may cost you two bets if he does. However, when your opponent misses, you will rarely get a crying call in that spot.

It is not a bad idea to check a wheel on occasion as well, looking for the double bet on the river. Your check might induce your opponent to bet an eight, at which time you can go for the check-raise with a seven. But most of the time, it is much safer to just bet right out and lock up one value bet if you can get it. Who knows, you may even be able to get in three bets on the river if your opponent raises you!

You should also bet with an eight if you stayed pat after the second draw. Your opponent might call you with a weak hand hoping to pick off a bluff, or he may make a nine and think it has a decent chance to be the best hand.

If you decide to check your pat hand on the river, be prepared to call a bet. Again, there is too much money in the pot, so it's no time to get cute. Unless you have an excellent read on your opponent's tendencies, you should be prepared to pay off one bet here.

When Your Opponent Is Drawing and You Are Pat in Position

By this point, the pot is so big that you should be hoping your opponent misses, giving you what's already in the middle. If you stayed pat after the first draw with an 8-7-6-4-2, you should check if your opponent checks ahead of you. Chances are, your opponent was drawing to beat such a rough eight, so if he makes an eight or better, he will either check and call, or even check-raise! The problem with betting such a rough eight in this spot is that a worse hand will rarely call you. Don't trap yourself by automatically betting here.

If you had made an eight on the second draw, you could make a case for betting it. Your opponent might call you with a nine or even a ten, trying to pick off a bluff. Again, you have to be up against a predictable opponent, one who doesn't check-raise the river and is a calling station. A calling station may even call you with a jack, just in case.

If your opponent bets into you on the river after you stayed pat, chances are he made his hand and you've been beat. By this time there are often so many bets in the pot that you better be pretty certain your opponents aren't going to bluff before folding.

Raising on the River

As a rule, you should never lose five bets on the river. If you are putting in five bets on the river, you better have precisely 2-3-4-5-7. While 2-3-4-6-7, number two, is a strong hand, if you put in five bets on the river with this hand, you'll lose.

Let's look at an example: You make a 2-3-4-6-7 after the first draw, but on the last draw your opponent bets into you. Of course you would raise here, but what should you do if your opponent reraises you? What could he possibly have to reraise you with? Most players would never reraise with an eight, so your opponent most likely has a seven. Knowledgeable players won't even raise with number four (2-4-5-6-7), so that leaves 2-3-4-5-7, 2-3-4-6-7, or 2-3-5-6-7.

You can beat one of these hands, tie another, and lose to another. The fact that you were reraised to three bets makes it even more likely that you are up against a wheel or number two. If you decide to make it four bets with your number two, you will probably win an extra bet against the number three, but you will lose two bets to the wheel. The best play here is just to call.

In general, you should only raise the river with a strong eight or a seven. Any other hand might be worth a bet or a call, but if you are raising, you better have the goods!

The Value of Pairs

While pairing your cards seemingly doesn't help you at all, the fact that you may have blockers against your opponent's draw increases the chances that you'll win the pot. Let's look at an example. Suppose with one draw left:

YOU (46%)

YOUR OPPONENT (54%)

Notice that the 2-3-4-7 is a significant favorite here. Now let's suppose that along the way you pair fives, sixes, and eights. What would that do to your chances?

YOU (52%)

YOUR OPPONENT (48%)

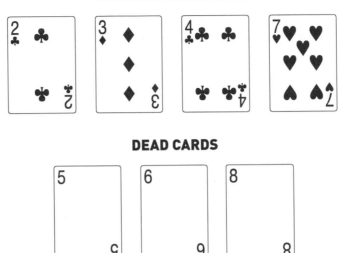

DEAD CARDS

Amazing. Even though your opponent appears to have the better draw, the fact that you've already burned three of the cards he would need makes your chances of winning the pot go from 46 percent all the way up to a 52 percent favorite!

Knowing that, you should understand why a hand like 2-2-3-3-7 is so much better than a hand like 2-3-7-K-K. It would essentially be the same draw (2-3-7), but your chances of winning the pot with the first draw will be much better than with the second draw.

So how do we use this information to our advantage? There are several ways:

(1) You are in position drawing two going into the last draw against a lone opponent who drew one. Your draw is 2-3-4, and you've already discarded a 2, two threes, and a 4. At this point you don't know for certain if your opponent is already pat, but because of your powerful discards, you can assume that it will be tougher for your opponent to

make a hand. Even if your opponent has 2-5-6-7 and is drawing one, you should still draw two based on the pot odds you are being laid. With the dead cards you burned, the 2-5-6-7 would only be a 57 percent favorite against your two-card draw.

(2) You can stay pat with a weaker hand. If you paired several cards, you can assume that some of the cards your opponent needs are now dead. That will make it more difficult for him to make his hand. In situations where you would normally break a pat nine or even discard an eight to draw to a wheel, making valuable discards should influence your decision. You might want to keep a hand you would otherwise fold, such as a pat nine or a one-card draw to a rough eight-seven.

(3) **Snowing** is a bluffing term that refers to staying pat before the last draw despite having a garbage hand. Let's look at an extreme example: Let's say you were dealt 2-2-2-2-3. Here you would have two options other than folding. You could draw three to the 2-3 or 2, or bluff the hand through. Since you have all of the powerful deuces, you know that your opponents could not possibly make a seven and would be hard pressed to make an eight. See below for a more in-depth look at this technique.

How To Snow

Snowing is something that you should do sporadically. If you do it too often it will lose its effectiveness, but not doing it at all will make you too predictable. If you get caught snowing again and again, you will get a few loose calls here and there, but that will also make this bluffing weapon useless to you. On the other hand, if you never snow, you won't get paid off like you should, and you will be giving up opportunities to steal some big pots. In order to pull it off, you need to have earned respect from your opponents without becoming predictable. As a general rule, snowing only when you have three deuces, three sevens, and so on would establish a decent snowing frequency.

There are several ways to snow, and I could go on and on about all of them. But if you have a good understanding of the ones I describe below, you'll do fine. As we learned in the last section, the information you receive from paired cards should heavily influence your decision of whether or not to snow. Generally speaking, snowing is more effective if you've stayed pat on the first or second draw. Staying pat so early in a hand represents strength. Finally, and as is the case with most poker strategies, this one works best when played in position.

So with the 2-2-2-2-3, you could raise it up and stay pat right off the bat. If you get any callers, you would be forced to bet the hand the whole way through and hope that your opponent doesn't make a hand he is willing to call you with.

Many times, when you stay pat right off the bat, alarm bells go off in your opponents' heads. They may suspect a snow and call you on the river to find out. To avoid this, you can draw one to your 2-2-2-2-3, and stay pat after the first draw. This approach is generally more believable and looks less suspicious.

If somewhere along the way, someone stays pat as well, it's time to abort the mission. You should fold to a bet or, naturally, draw if it's not bet to you.

I played in a game that illustrates a great way to send your opponents on tilt. In a $1,500/$3,000 game with Gus Hansen, I tried snowing a hand with 2-2-2-7-Q. Unfortunately, going into the last draw Gus stayed pat in front of me. It looked like the jig was up. Slightly embarrassed, I drew three cards. Gus bet right out, and I looked down at a 3-4-5. So obviously, I raised it! I caught not one, not two, but three perfect cards. Needless to say Gus didn't find the hand all that funny.

The point of the story is simple: When you get caught, abort the mission. Don't continue through with the bluff if someone else has stood pat as well.

There is another, more sophisticated snow play that often works: Say both you and your opponent are drawing one going into the last draw. Your opponent checks, and you make 3-3-4-5-7. Since your opponent checked, it's likely that he is still drawing. If you bet and stay pat, your opponent will have to assume you hit your hand. If your opponent misses on the river, you would continue with the bluff and hope that your opponent mucks. If he makes a jack, queen, king, ace, or a pair, he'll almost always fold.

There is one last snow play I'd like to share with you. Going into the last draw your opponent is drawing one and you draw two in position to a 2-3-7. Your opponent, being ahead one card, bets—as he should. Then you catch 2-2! If you call and draw, you would be an underdog to any hand, so what about raising and staying pat? If your opponent calls and draws one again, you can stay pat with your trip deuces and bet if your opponent misses. Now if your opponent stays pat anyway, then you'll have to abort the mission and try to get really lucky drawing two.

ACE-TO-FIVE TRIPLE DRAW

In essence, deuce-to-seven and ace-to-five triple draw are the same game with different hand ranking systems. The same rules apply, and the betting structure is the same.

The major difference is this: In deuce-to-seven, the best possible hand is 2-3-4-5-7; while in ace-to-five, the best hand is

A-2-3-4-5. Aces count as low (ones) in ace-to-five, and neither straights nor flushes count against you.

While these games are extremely similar, the correct strategies to use differ slightly for each. For example, snowing isn't as effective in ace-to-five as it is in deuce-to-seven. And although the ace is the most important card in ace-to-five, it isn't nearly as valuable as the deuce is in deuce-to-seven. Since straights and flushes don't count against you, it's much easier to make a strong hand, so bluffing is less profitable.

I'm not going to spend too much time on ace-to-five, as you should already have a good understanding of the concepts of triple draw from the deuce-to-seven section. However, I will give you some starting hand guidelines and go over some of the finer points of the game.

Pat Hands

Here's one big difference between the two games: in ace-to-five, a pat eight is a weak hand. If you are dealt 8-6-3-2-A, you would do better discarding the 8 and trying to make a good six. You would have three chances to improve and twelve cards to improve with, specifically fours, fives, and sevens. That makes you a favorite to improve on the eight. While eights will often win in deuce-to-seven, you'd have to consider yourself pretty lucky to win with an eight in ace-to-five.

A pat seven or better should be kept. You should play these hands aggressively, forcing your opponents to pay full price to outdraw you.

One-Card Draws

Below are all the strong one-card draws you should be playing, from strongest to weakest.

A-2-3-4
A-2-3-5
A-2-4-5
A-3-4-5
2-3-4-5
A-2-3-6
A-2-4-6
A-3-4-6
A-2-5-6
A-3-5-6
A-4-5-6
2-3-4-6
2-3-5-6

Notice there is no one-card draw to a seven. Drawing to a seven on the first draw is asking for trouble. A seven will win its fair share of pots, but often you will make a second best hand and lose a lot of bets. With a hand like A-2-3-7-K, you are better off drawing two to the A-2-3 than one to the A-2-3-seven.

Two-Card Draws

Here are the best two-card draws, from strongest to weakest, that can be played for any number of bets before the first draw.

A-2-3
A-2-4
A-3-4
2-3-4

In ace-to-five, it's extremely important to draw from the bottom up. While both A-2-3 and 3-4-5 offer you a two card wheel draw, if you miss the wheel and make a six or worse, it will often come down to the third, fourth, or even fifth card. If the A-2-3 and 3-4-5 both catch a 6 on the first draw, the A-2-3 draw would be way in front. In fact, a 4 or a 5 would shut out the other draw completely.

The hands above are the strongest two-card draws containing no 5 or 6, but they're not the only two-card draws you can play. The following hands, listed from strongest to weakest, are often good enough to raise with, but not necessarily good enough to come in cold for a double raise, if you're outside the blinds.

> A-2-5
> 2-3-5
> A-4-5
> 2-4-5
> 3-4-5
> A-2-6
> A-3-6
> 2-3-6
> A-4-6
> 2-4-6
> 3-4-6
> A-5-6
> 2-5-6

Depending on your skill level, you should consider folding the bottom half of this list to a raise. As your skills improve, you could think about expanding your list of starting hands to include 3-5-6, and maybe even 4-5-6 in steal position—although I still don't advise that play.

Three-Card Draws

The only time you should draw three is from the big blind, from the small blind for no raise, or on the button in an attempt to steal the blinds. The only three-card draws you should be willing to play are: A-2; A-3; and 2-3.

Flop and Turn Play

The flop and turn play advice I offered you in the deuce-to-seven section applies to the ace-to-five game as well, with the only adjustment being that you should make less plays in ace-to-five because there are less pure bluffing opportunities. Stick to a solid game plan and solid starting hands and you'll do just fine.

FINAL THOUGHTS

I'm a big fan of ace-to-five triple draw, especially when it is played in a mixed game that includes deuce-to-seven triple draw. People will often get confused and play the wrong game. Don't be that guy! If you are playing in a mixed game with both versions of triple draw, make sure you are alert and always know which game you are playing.

Often times, those players who are more accustomed to the deuce-to-seven version of triple draw really don't understand the hand strengths in ace-to-five. I've played in high-limit ace-to-five games with some fantastic players who stayed pat after the first draw with an A-3-4-6-9! In those same high-limit games, I often hear someone call out "six-four," only to find out later that they were playing deuce-to-seven!

If you plan on playing high limit poker, learning to play this game is an absolute must. The pots are bigger, and the fluctuations can be monstrous. Adding triple draw to the mix of games makes all of the games livelier, and since it causes such huge swings, it preys on the emotionally weak. Watch someone miss a couple of draws to the A-2-3-4, and you may soon see steam coming out of their ears! Before you know it, they are chasing that money in other games as well.

If you're going to play triple draw, be ready for an emotional roller coaster. So be strong, be smart, and be sure to buckle up!

Ace-to-Five—Deuce-to-Seven

Rank Comparison Chart*

Rank of Hand	Ace-to-Five	Deuce-to-Seven	Rank of Hand	Ace-to-Five	Deuce-to-Seven
1	5432A	75432	37	**8732A**	98543
2	**6432A**	76432	38	8742A	98632
3	**6532A**	76532	39	**8743A**	98642
4	**6542A**	76542	40	**87432**	98643
5	**6543A**	**85432**	41	**8752A**	98652
6	**65432**	**86432**	42	**8753A**	98653
7	7432A	**86532**	43	**87532**	98654
8	7532A	**86542**	44	**8754A**	98732
9	7542A	**86543**	45	**87542**	98742
10	7543A	**87432**	46	**87543**	98743
11	75432	**87532**	47	**8762A**	98752
12	7632A	**87542**	48	**8763A**	98753
13	7642A	**87543**	49	**87632**	98754
14	7643A	**87632**	50	**8764A**	98762
15	76432	**87642**	51	**87642**	98763
16	7652A	**87643**	52	**87643**	98764
17	7653A	**87652**	53	**8765A**	**10-5432**
18	76532	**87653**	54	**87652**	**10-6432**
19	7654A	95432	55	**87653**	**10-6532**
20	76542	96432	56	**87654**	**10-6542**
21	76543	96532	57	9432A	**10-6543**
22	**8432A**	96542	58	9532A	**10-7432**
23	**8532A**	96543	59	9542A	**10-7532**
24	**8542A**	97432	60	9543A	**10-7542**
25	**8543A**	97532	61	95432	**10-7543**
26	**85432**	97542	62	9632A	**10-7632**
27	**8632A**	97543	63	9642A	**10-7642**
28	**8642A**	97632	64	9643A	**10-7643**
29	**8643A**	97642	65	96432	**10-7652**
30	**86432**	97643	66	9652A	**10-7653**
31	**8652A**	97652	67	9653A	10-7654
32	**8653A**	97653	68	96532	**10-8432**
33	**86532**	97654	69	9654A	**10-8532**
34	**8654A**	98432	70	96542	**10-8542**
35	**86542**	98532	71	96543	**10-8543**
36	**86543**	98542	72	9732A	**10-8632**

(continued)

Ace-to-Five—Deuce-to-Seven

Rank Comparison Chart*

(continued)

Rank of Hand	Ace-to-Five	Deuce-to-Seven	Rank of Hand	Ace-to-Five	Deuce-to-Seven
73	9742A	10-8642	100	98542	10-9743
74	9743A	10-8643	101	98543	10-9752
75	97432	10-8652	102	9862A	10-9753
76	9752A	10-8653	103	9863A	10-9754
77	9753A	10-8654	104	98632	10-9762
78	97532	10-8732	105	9864A	10-9763
79	9754A	10-8742	106	98642	10-9764
80	97542	10-8753	107	98643	10-9765
81	97543	10-8752	108	9865A	10-9832
82	9762A	10-8753	109	98652	10-9842
83	9763A	10-8754	110	98653	10-9843
84	97632	10-8762	111	98654	10-9852
85	9764A	10-8763	112	9872A	10-9853
86	97642	10-8764	113	9873A	10-9854
87	97643	10-8765	114	98732	10-9862
88	9765A	10-9432	115	9874A	10-9863
89	97652	10-9532	116	98742	10-9864
90	97653	10-9542	117	98743	10-9865
91	97654	10-9543	118	9875A	10-9872
92	9832A	10-9632	119	98752	10-9873
93	9842A	10-9642	120	98753	10-9874
94	9843A	10-9643	121	98754	10-9875
95	98432	10-9652	122	9876A	J-5432
96	9852A	10-9653	123	98762	J-6432
97	9853A	10-9654	124	98763	J-6532
98	98532	10-9732	125	98764	J-6542
99	9854A	10-9742	126	98765	J-6543

*This chart compares hands by rank, not by frequency of distribution.

TOURNAMENT OVERVIEW

TOURNAMENT OVERVIEW
by Doyle Brunson

INTRODUCTION

Thanks to the recent media explosion taking place around no-limit tournament poker, learning how to play in tournaments is becoming more and more advantageous for every poker player. Tournaments are vastly different from cash games, because if you lose what you have in front of you, you are out of the tournament. You will come across many opposing strategies as you and your opponents wrestle with this fact.

There are very few players who've had substantial success in both tournaments and regular money games, and I'm fortunate to be one of them. I've had really good luck in tournament play over the years, even though I still prefer the cash games. So here are my thoughts on the tournaments.

THE FIRST DAY

Early Rounds

There are two basic styles of play in tournament poker: tight and loose. Of course, there is a lot of room in between, so there are really many different speeds you can use.

At the early levels of a no-limit tournament, I prefer playing extremely tight. I don't try to force the action. I just win what the cards allow me to win as safely as possible.

If you've read the original *Super/System* or the no-limit chapter in this book, you know that that goes completely against my way of playing no-limit hold'em in cash games. My main thought at these early levels is on the value of the chips, since their value now is much higher than it will be later on. If you advance far enough, the antes and blinds will exceed all the chips you have in front of you early in the tournament. Play the early levels, especially the first two levels, carefully and try to avoid the all-in, coin-flip hands.

Try to play small pots, raise a lot of pots with marginal hands, but be prepared to play very cautiously if you get called. You must have a better hand to call than to raise. For example, raise, but don't call, with A♥ J♣, 7♦ 7♥, K♥ J♦.

Be disciplined and be ready to lay down marginal hands. I once saw Phil Hellmuth, who has had great success in no-limit hold'em tournaments, lay down a K♦ J♦ to a Q♦ 10♦ 2♣ flop. He had raised the pot, bet at it on the flop, and got raised all his chips. It was early in the tournament and Phil passed, even though he had a draw at an open-ended straight flush.

This is something that would never happen in a cash game. I'm not sure I would have passed, but it was probably correct to do so, given that Phil expected to have even bigger advantages later. Needless to say, my opinion of Phil's no-limit tournament play went up several points after that hand.

Same Strategy

Remember, most of the players at your table, especially the professional players, have basically the same strategy. They know they have to advance to the next level, so they are extremely cautious. The amateurs want to play awhile, so they are usually playing tight to begin with. Sometimes you have a player at your table that throws caution to the wind and plays like a wild man, raising and betting every pot. You have to eventually take a stand, but the small blind structure allows you to get a quality hand before you challenge that wild man.

After the First Two Levels

If you can increase your chips by 15 to 25 percent in the first two levels, you have done well. After that, you must adopt more liberal standards. You can make more stabs at the limpers and at the antes and blinds. You should usually make a bet on the flop whenever you are the last raiser pre-flop, but be ready to put the brakes on if you get called. I don't usually advocate check-calling after the flop, but even with a very good hand, this is a safer way of playing at this stage of the tournament. It keeps you from getting broke.

You have to carefully evaluate your table, particularly if it isn't going to break for a while. You have to be aware of the size of the chip stack each player has. Remember, the short stacks are more likely to go all-in before the flop with marginal hands than the larger stacks. However, the short stacks can be pushed around more easily after the flop than the big stacks.

If it's apparent that your table isn't going to break, you want to seem as if you're unafraid to race by moving all-in occasionally. That is the best image. You try to wait for a favorable opportunity to go all-in, and you are almost always hoping not to get called. If I can double my chips the first day, I'm happy.

THE SECOND DAY

After the first day, you'll want to accelerate your play a little more. Not by a lot, because you have to remember that you can't win the tournament until the last day! But you have to accumulate some chips in order to have a better chance to survive the ante and blind increase. You need to be aware of your own chip count and your position in the tournament.

A few years ago, I had an early rush the second day and grabbed $70,000, which put me among the leaders. I had a fast table with several large stacks. On one hand, the player in first position opened, and the player in third position, who had about $50,000 in chips and two WSOP championship bracelets, made a large raise. I looked down at my hand and found two kings. I considered my position in the tournament and then threw them away.

I've always felt I made the right play, because I was probably either going to win a small pot or lose most of my chips. The player I laid that hand down to was Ron Stanley. He told me later that he had two aces, but he also told a friend of mine that my kings were good. Either way, I believe I was correct in throwing them away, because $70,000 was sufficient to get me comfortably through the next levels, and losing $50,000 would have been disastrous. Ironically, when we were down to twenty-three players, the same Ron Stanley broke me with pocket aces.

Here's one last thought about day two play: Just because you get short stacked, don't be suicidal late in the day. Remember that the blinds and antes increase again starting the third day, and in major tournaments the prize pools are so big that it's worth your time and effort to try to catch an early rush. To be in real contention you need four to eight times your original buy-in.

THE THIRD DAY

Entering the third day, even if it is a four- or five-day tournament, I am about ready to start playing as I play in the cash games. I have to remind myself, "Don't be afraid to go broke!" Perhaps I won't play quite as loose as I play the cash games, but now I'm prepared to take races on other close gambles in what I think are favorable situations.

Make no mistake about it, you have to be very, very lucky to win one of these major tournaments. It's impossible to play the entire tournament and always be a prohibitive favorite when the money goes in. So you can see the parlay that is required to win a large tournament. The players that continue to play very tight sometimes go deep into the tournaments, but seldom win. When they arrive at the later tables, they are short-stacked and facing a huge ante and blinds. They are forced to race for their chips before they are ready, so they are decided underdogs to the big stacks, who can better control their destinies. You need to take control of your table if possible. You can't help what is happening at the other tables.

THE FINAL TABLE

If you are lucky enough to make the final table, you need to evaluate your position. For example, if you have second-place chips and there are several short stacks, you might try to avoid any major confrontations until several players are eliminated. This depends on your financial situation and your desire to win the tournament. If you really need the money and you have a comfortable chip position, you can often assure yourself of a second or third place finish by playing carefully. That will result in a very nice payday in these ever-increasing large tournaments.

However, if your main interest is to win the tournament, this is a prime situation to really play aggressively and try to get closer to the leader or even overtake him. The difference in fifth place and first place is so huge that most players are just trying to hang on and can be pushed around in most pots.

My main objective has always been to win the tournament. Even before I was financially secure, I always did what I thought was best to achieve my goal of winning first place. You need to think about these things before you start a tournament and decide what is best for you. So if you are lucky enough to get to the last table, you'll be ready.

WILD CARD

There is one more thing you may need to consider. The ever-increasing number of weaker players entering the tournaments has added a new element in poker. I call it "two-card hold'em." These weaker players know that they can't compete with the better players and that they will get out-played in the latter stages of the hands, so they simply wait for two high cards or a wired pair and bet all their chips before the flop. I've seen this type of player go deep into the second and third day of the tournaments by doing this. I think Neal Furlong, a winner of the WSOP championship, mostly used this strategy.

I remember when Chris "Jesus" Ferguson was playing T. J. Cloutier in the 2000 WSOP finals. T. J., who I think is probably the premier tournament player in the world today, was whittling Chris away, chopping out the pots without having to gamble very much. Chris recognized this after a while and decided he had to force the action. So Chris made a comeback, and got even with T.J. in chips. Then Chris got A-9 and moved in. T.J. had A-Q and called. Then a 9 came on the flop and Chris won the championship.

Again, as in Hellmuth's case, Chris moved up in my opinion by a huge amount. He has proven it was no fluke by winning five bracelets at the WSOP. T. J. is the leading money winner in that tournament without ever winning the main event.

In closing, let me quote my favorite line from my limit hold'em collaborator, Jennifer Harman. "The winner of a heads-up pot will generally be the player who plays better in marginal situations."

If you are interested in how I recommend you play in the cash games and the later stages of the tournaments, turn the page.

NO-LIMIT HOLD'EM

NO-LIMIT HOLD'EM
by Doyle Brunson

INTRODUCTION

When I decided to create this all-new edition of *Super/System*, I pondered how much no-limit hold'em has changed in the past twenty-seven years. Players are more knowledgeable and aggressive today. And no longer do you have the luxury of facing half a table full of opponents who don't have a clue.

So, I sat down to revise this chapter, to bring it up to modern day standards. But you know what? I hadn't read my own advice for fifteen years, and when I sat down to examine it, I just kept nodding my head in agreement and muttering, "Damn, that's good!"

For you, this advice will be as profitable today as when I first wrote it. For me? Well, I've had to adjust my game. Most of my opponents have read this chapter in the original *Super/System*, and if I played that way, I'd be too predictable.

You don't have to play exactly the way I describe in this chapter. You'll probably want to pick your own style and modify these concepts to fit the games you play. Still, if you incorporate this advice, making it the soul of your strategy, the rest will fall in place.

I've added new thoughts and expanded some of the ideas, but the core concepts remain as valid and as profitable today as ever. So, here is my up-to-date advice, blending the previous tips and the tactics that will always win at no-limit hold'em with some new insights I hope will earn you extra money. Here's how to conquer any no-limit hold'em game in the world.

Ante Up

Now let's join the introduction from my original no-limit hold'em chapter. There's a story I've been hearing around poker games all my life. It's about a colorful player down in south Texas named Broomcorn. (Ever since I related this story about Broomcorn in the original *Super/System*, people have asked me time and again who was the real Broomcorn. He is the late Lawrence Herron from Houston.) Whenever someone in the game is playing real tight, the opposing players needle him by saying, "Well, you're gonna go like Broomcorn's uncle." The tight player perks up and responds sharply, "What do you mean, I'm gonna go like him?" And they say, "Well, he anted himself to death."

Whenever you find yourself playing a very tight and defensive style of poker, you'll be in danger of anteing yourself to death. As I've always said, the ante determines how fast you play in any poker game. Since you'll generally play in a normal or medium ante games, if you play an aggressive style of poker, you'll have the best of it.

That's the way I recommend you play, and it works. This is especially true in no-limit hold'em, which in my opinion is the Cadillac of poker games—and not just because it's my best game. Many of the world's best poker players, some of whom are only beginning to appreciate the great variety of skills you need to be a top-level hold'em player, agree with me. Although hold'em is similar in some respects to seven-card stud, there are enough differences to put it in a class by itself. It's truly a game that requires very special talents in order to play it at a world-class level.

Above all else, no-limit hold'em is a game where you have to be aggressive—and you have to gamble. One of the great things about hold'em is the infinite variety in the game. There are so many different combinations of hands and various plays in certain situations that the game never gets boring. Unlike other forms of poker, you can represent a lot of different hands in hold'em and put your opponent on one of several hands as well. It's a very complex game. You're forced to do a lot of guessing, as is your opponent.

Get in There and Gamble

If you want to be a winner—a big winner—at no-limit hold'em, you can't play a solid, safe game. My philosophy of play at no-limit hold'em is a simple one: Try to win big pots and pick up the small ones (win without a contest). It's a philosophy that necessitates a gambling style of play. My style.

Over the years, this style has fostered numerous comments from countless players about how "lucky" I am. I've been hearing that for years. The simple fact is that it's not true. Everyone gets lucky once in a while, but no one is consistently lucky. It takes more than luck to be a consistently big winner through the years, as I have done. It is something else. You'll soon discover what that "something else" is.

I appear to be a lucky player because every time a big pot comes up, I usually have the worst hand. There are good reasons for that. I'm a very aggressive player. I reach out and pick up small pots all the time. I'm always betting at those pots, hammering at them. And I don't want anybody to stop me from doing that. I don't want anyone to defeat my style of play.

And if I've got any kind of a hand, any kind of a draw, I bet. If I get raised, I don't quit. I go ahead and get all my money in the pot, if it's a reasonable amount, knowing I probably have the worst hand and am the underdog to win the pot.

Calling a Post-Oak Bluff

Sometimes I'll even call a very small bet in a big pot, knowing my opponent might be trying to pull off a **post-oak bluff** just to get a chance at a draw. But if I'm going to gamble like that, my opponent must have a lot of chips on the table. For example, say

I have a 10-9 and, with $10,000 in the pot, the flop comes 8-3-2. With a raggedy flop like that, my opponent—a tight player, let's say—might try to pick up the pot with a post-oak bluff of $1,200. Well that's a gutless bet, and I'll call it trying to catch a jack or a 7, just so I can get an open-end straight draw on fourth street. Of course, I'm hoping to catch a 10 or a 9, and I'm in a good position to pick up the pot on fourth street, whether I improve or not.

The tight player who made that weak bet on the flop is asking me to take his money. And in most cases, that's exactly what I'm going to do when the next card falls—regardless of what it is. I'm going to make a large bet into that tight player because I feel confident he's going to throw his hand away and not put his whole stack in jeopardy. As you can probably guess, I never make post-oak bluffs.

Aggression

I've built a reputation as an extremely aggressive player. And I don't ever want to lose that reputation. It's what enables me to pick up more than my share of pots.

In most cases, my opponents are afraid to play back at me because they know I'm liable to set them all-in. So when they don't have a real big hand, they let go of the pot, and I pick it up. The accumulation of all those small pots is a big part of my winning formula. It's the bonus I get for playing the way I do, and it's the secret of my success.

If I win ten pots where nobody has a big hand, ten pots with let's say $3,000 in them, I can afford to take 2 to 1 the worst of it and play a $30,000 pot. I've already got that pot covered thanks to all the small pots I've picked up. And when I play that big pot, it's a freeroll.

As I said a little while ago, when a big pot's played, I've usually got the worst hand. I'd say that when all the money goes in, I've got the worst hand over 50 percent of the time. Obviously, I wouldn't be able to overcome that statistic if I didn't always pad my stack by picking up all those small pots throughout the game.

Of course, I'm almost never completely out on a limb in a big pot. Whenever I make a substantial bet or raise, I've usually got an out. Betting with an out, that's what I call it. And it's the out I have that makes me appear lucky when I'm a dog in a big pot and wind up winning it.

There are other benefits to playing the aggressive way I recommend. You'll be able to break a lot of players because you're in there gambling all the time, and because of that, you'll get a lot of your real good hands paid off. Tight players don't get their real good hands paid off because they rarely make a move, so that whenever they do, their hand is an open book. And they almost never change gears and start playing loose.

But you'll be out there betting, betting, betting, all the time. Your opponents will see you're an aggressive player. They'll know you're out there trying to pick up all those pots, so they'll sometimes give you a little loose action. And since you won't always be out there with the worst hand, you'll break one or two of them. After that, they may be scared to get involved with you.

So your style of play will deceive and befuddle your opponents. They won't know whether or not you've really got a hand. They won't know whether you're going to set them all-in or not. And anytime you get your opponents in that confused state of mind you'll have an advantage over them.

Of course, you won't play every hand aggressively. Occasionally you'll slow down, and sometimes you'll completely stop and throw your hand away. You should never start out bluffing at a pot and keep bluffing at it without an out. For example, whenever I raise the pot before the flop I'm going to bet after the flop about 90 percent of the time.

If the flop comes completely ragged, and it doesn't look like anyone can have much of it, I'm going to bet at the pot and try to pick it up even if I don't have a piece of the flop. If I get called I'm usually going to give it up—unless I have some kind of an out—even as little as third pair or an inside straight draw. Sometimes, you can keep hammering on certain players and drive them off even when you don't have an out. But you're usually better off when you have some kind of escape hatch.

The reason I occasionally go ahead and put in all my money when I know I've probably got the worst hand deserves repeating, since it's so important for you to understand. I do it because I don't want somebody playing back at me and trying to stop me from being the aggressor. If I allow that to happen, it'll cramp my style. I'll no longer be able to pick up all those pots when nobody has a hand. And most of the time, nobody has anything decent. Somebody's got to get the money that's left out there. I want it to be me.

Small Connecting Cards

An example will best show you what I'm talking about. Let's say I raised before the flop with a type of hand that's one of my favorites: small connecting cards that are suited. I'm in the pot with one player who called behind me. At this point, I put him on a couple of big cards or a medium pair. That's all right. It's what I want him to have. Now, here's what'll happen if the following flop comes up:

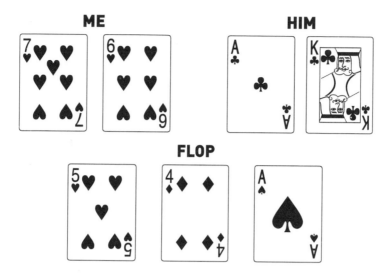

ME **HIM**

FLOP

With that flop, I'm going to lead right off and bet. If he plays back at me, I can now be quite sure he's got two aces or better. So, I'm about a 9 to 5 dog. The pot odds will compensate a little bit for that price, but it won't be laying me enough to put the rest of my money in. But I don't want that same guy, who might be a pretty good player, taking a J-10 and making that same play when I don't have anything. To let his play succeed, I have to throw my hand away and give him the pot. Because I want the pot, I can't let him succeed. I want him to fear me. I want him to have the opinion I'm going to defend the money I put out there. I don't want him to have any doubts about that, so I go ahead and put the rest of my money in.

In making that play on the flop, there's a good chance I can win the pot right there. Because I'm known to play any reasonable hand—and some unreasonable hands in a shorthanded high-ante game—I've really made it tough on him. I could've flopped a set of trips, two pair, or even the straight. I've put him on the defensive and he's got a lot of guessing to do.

It's not all that bad if he decides to call me because I've got an out. If I make my straight, I'm going to break him. And if I draw out on him, it will look like I got lucky again. Well, I did and I didn't. When I moved in on him, I was gambling to pick up the pot. When I didn't succeed because of his call, you might say I got unlucky. What's more, I am supposed to make my draws once in a while. In fact, in that specific situation I'll draw out more than one third of the time, by making my straight or back-dooring two pair or trips.

A very interesting thing about that particular 7-6 hand is that I'd rather have it than a 9-8. The reason is that when you flop a straight with a 9-8, you'll frequently find that somebody is on top of you. For example, when the flop comes Q-J-10, an A-K will have you nutted, and even a sucker who plays a K-9 will have you beat. I've flopped many a straight with a 9-8, but when a Q-J-10 falls, I'm always real cautious with the hand. Because people play the higher cards more frequently than the lower ones, you're less likely to be in trouble if you flop a straight with a 7-6 than you would be with a 9-8. I'll discuss the general category of small connecting cards in great detail a little later. As I previously noted, they're one of my favorite hands.

Double Belly-Buster Straight

Another of my favorites is a hand where you can flop a two-way inside or double **belly-buster straight**. It's one of the most deceptive hands there is, and I especially like it in no-limit. It has all the advantages of an open-end straight, but it's not as easy to read. Because it's so deceptive, I almost always raise with it when I can win a big pot.

For example, say you have a Q-10 and the flop comes A-J-8. As you can see, it's very deceptive because you can make a straight with a 9 or a king. What's more, if you catch a king and there's someone with A-K in the pot with you, you can see all the trouble he's in.

Since double belly-busters are such good gambling hands, you might find the following quick rule of thumb useful: It's possible to flop a double belly-buster with any two cards that are part of a straight, such as 7-6, 8-6, 9-6, and 10-6. Also, two cards with five gaps between them such as a Q-6 can also flop a double belly-buster draw. In the supplement at the end of this section you'll find a complete rundown on all the hands that have double belly-buster potential.

When you flop a double belly-buster draw, you should make careful note of which of your possible straights will be the nuts. For example, if you have a J-9 and the fall is K-10-7, both an 8 and a queen will make you a straight. However, only the 8 will give you the nuts. If a queen falls on fourth, someone with an A-J can beat your straight. So you must be careful—especially in no-limit play—and you must know how to read the board perfectly in order to recognize what hand is the absolute nuts. Practice at home until you don't make a single mistake. You'll learn quick enough if you get broke a few times with what you thought was the nuts but turned out to be only the second best hand.

Look again at the example above. A player with a J-9 could easily think he had the best straight when the queen fell until someone showed him an A-J for all his money.

An easy way to determine whether your straight is the nuts is by following some simple guidelines. You'll have the nut straight if:

(1) The high-end of the straight is made up with the highest card in your hand; or

(2) The high-end of the highest possible straight is already on the board.

Drawing to a double belly-buster is one of few situations in no-limit where you might be drawing to an inside straight that won't make the best hand. As I noted earlier, inside straight draws can be real good plays in no-limit hold'em because for a few chips you have the opportunity to win a very big pot. But you almost never draw to a single belly-buster straight that will not be the best hand if you make it. They're long-shot plays, so when you do make them, you want to be sure they're the nuts.

For example, let's say you held Q-J and the fall was 9-8-4. Now you might want to draw at that belly-buster, trying to catch a 10 or make a big pair (even in limit, but mostly in no-limit). You know if you catch that 10, you'll have a cinch hand. But if you held a 6-5, you'd never draw to it with that flop because there'd be two different straights that could beat you if you catch a 7, the 6-7-8-9-10 and the 7-8-9-10-J. If a man makes a straight with you, he's either got you tied or he's got you beat. So, you never draw to the dead-end of a single belly-buster.

Before you decide to draw to a belly-buster, you also want to be reasonably certain that your opponent is going to gamble with you if you do make it. I mean, drawing to a belly-buster is a good play, but only if you can win a big pot by making your long shot. So you want your opponent to have the best hand possible on the board. If the flop came 9-8-4, as above, ideally, you want your opponent to have three nines. You don't want him to have a pair of kings or A-9. You want him to have at least eights and nines, or better. You want him to have a very big hand. Your Q-J would be a very good hand against three nines. It wouldn't be as good against a pair of nines because it won't make enough money. Your opponent will release a pair far more readily than he'll release a set.

So if you can get in real cheap and have the potential to win a big pot, belly-buster straights are good gambles. But you also have to be very selective about the belly-busters you do draw to. You don't want it to be apparent to your opponent that you could've made a straight. In the illustration just used, you might not get the action you want if a 10 falls off on fourth street. The Q-J is actually a weak hand when the flop is 9-8-4. Your opponent might put you on a 7-6 and, when the 10 came, he might be very leery about calling a big bet you made. The straight possibility might even scare him off completely.

But if a possible straight wasn't so apparent when the 10 came off, you could probably win a lot of money. Let's say you had the Q♦ 9♦, and the flop was J-8-2. You might want to pick the 10 off there because that would be a very deceptive belly-buster draw. And inside straights like these are the ones you want to draw for to win a big pot because they aren't so obvious.

Bluffs

If you graduate from limit hold'em to no-limit, you might find yourself doing many things, in addition to drawing to inside straights, that simply won't work when all it can cost your opponent is another bet.

A good example of a bluff that has a lot of power to it in no-limit, but will rarely work at limit, comes when the board is one card off a straight on fourth street. Let's say there's an A-K-Q-J out there and your opponent bets. You've got a 10 in the hole, and since there's no flush possible, you've got the nuts. Your opponent bets, you raise, and he plays back. Now, there's no question he's also got a straight.

An unsophisticated player would move in on him right there because he knows he can't lose. But what good is that? He's only going to get a split.

However, adding some drama and a little acting to your play gives you a chance to win it all. You know you're going to call his reraise but you don't have to do it instantaneously. Take your time. Just stall around. Study the board real hard and shake your head several times making it appear as though you overlooked the possible straight. You could even pick up your cards slightly and make him think you're going to throw them away. Then put them back down and say "Okay, I'll call it."

With all your agonizing, he's got to give you credit for a set. You've made him think you're gambling the board will pair so you'll make a full. If the board does pair on the end, you bet him all your money. There's almost no risk to that play. You represent a full and many a time your opponent will throw his hand away. Of course, it's almost impossible to do in limit because all the guy has to do is call one bet.

Calling a Bluff

As you can see from the play just described, bluffing often involves a lot of art. But there's science to it also. There's even science to calling a bluff. The following pot I was involved in will clearly illustrate what I mean.

In a small ante no-limit game early in my career, I was on the button, so I limped in with a J-10 in the hole. There were two players in the pot in front of me. Here's what the flop looked like:

FLOP

As you see, I had a belly straight draw. Since there was no raise before the flop, I was reasonably sure neither of my two opponents had very strong hands. On the flop, the guy in the first seat made a reasonably sized bet (throughout these discussions, a reasonably sized bet means about the size of the pot), and the player in front of me called it. Both players had a lot of money in front of them, so I called as well.

The fourth card was the 2♠. They both checked on fourth street, and so did I. The last card was the 3♦. The board now looked like this:

FLOP   **4th ST.**   **5th ST.**

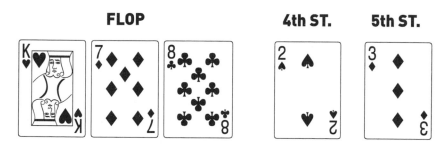

When all the cards were out, the guy in the first seat checked again. After he bet on the flop and then checked twice on fourth and fifth, I figured he had the top pair with a bad kicker. I felt the guy in front of me was drawing at some kind of straight and obviously had missed his hand. Much to my surprise, he made a real out-of-line bet on the end, far bigger than the size of the pot.

When he did that, it looked to me like he was clearly trying to steal the pot. I was also sure I had him high-carded. As I said, I felt sure he was drawing at a smaller straight than I was.

If I was correct in thinking I had been drawing at the highest possible straight, I knew I'd win the pot if I just called. I also knew the other player couldn't overcall because his hand wasn't strong enough.

So I called that out-of-line bet, and my analysis proved correct. The player with the pair threw his hand away and Johnny Moss, the guy who over-bet the pot, was drawing to a little straight. So I won the pot with a jack-high.

I didn't tell you that poker story because I won the pot with a jack-high. And you shouldn't remember it for that reason. It has a more significant message. I told you I felt neither guy had much of anything and explained why. Obviously, it was more than just a nebulous feel. I had played with both those guys often, so I used a certain amount of reasoning and a process of elimination. And a lot of it was based on recall of previous hands.

Recall

Whenever I use the word "feel," you should understand it's not some extra-sensory power that I have. It's just that I recall something that happened previously. Even though I might not consciously do it, I can often recall if this same play or something close to it came up in the past, and what the player did or what somebody else did. So, many times I get a feeling that he's bluffing or that I can make a play and get the pot. But actually my subconscious mind is reasoning it all out.

You build up a history of every player you ever played with, I mean everyone that you've ever done any serious gambling with. You've got some kind of information on them. It's there, buried in your mind. And you don't have to concentrate to get it out. When the time comes to use it, you won't have to force it. It'll come naturally.

All good poker players have tremendous recall. They reach back into the depths of their minds and remember what a certain guy did in a similar situation. A good player might not realize what he's doing and he might not know exactly what it is, but he feels when a guy is bluffing and knows he can make a real big play or make a super call. The vibrations are definitely there.

And what it actually is, is a sense of recall. If the same situation or a similar one existed some time ago, a good player knows exactly what to do in this one. It's usually a stress situation, when a relatively large amount of money is involved, that proves a player's recall ability.

There's another kind of feel you can have in a game that doesn't depend on recall. This type of feel depends on close observation of what's going on during a particular session. You acquire this feel when you notice that a certain player is really off his game and playing far worse than normal.

This happens all the time. A lot of players lose control and go on tilt after they get one or more big hands cracked. They become unglued, lose their composure. To recoup their losses, they start playing weak hands, and they play those hands bad-ly—very badly.

It's easy to capitalize on those situations. Let's say you're in a game with a high-ante structure, (a subject I'll cover in greater detail below) and naturally everybody's playing real fast. You played a J-9 and the flop came A-9-8. Normally, if you got played with, you'd be very concerned about that ace and also your kick-er. But in this case, you're in the pot with a player who's losing and, from what you've seen, he's playing very badly. You check on the flop, and so does he.

All of a sudden, you get a "feel" that all he's got is the third pair, a pair of eights. Since he checked, you feel he got some-thing, a small piece of the flop. He didn't bet because he wants to get the hand shown-down. If he had nothing he would've bet to try to steal the pot. And you know he doesn't have an ace. You know the worst that can happen is that he could also have a 9 and run you down, chase you. Well, what you want is for him to run you down with an 8, which is what you really think he has.

But you feel confident you're not wrong. If a rag falls off on fourth, you bet. You know he's going to call you, almost out of desperation because he's losing. So you make some money on fourth and also on the end. You know he's not going to show you a hand unless he gets lucky and pairs his kicker.

The very surprising thing about the previous discussion is that the player I was referring to as on tilt is actually a very good player. He could even be world-class. Of course, the super-stars of the poker world—those who I play against on a regular basis—are able to exercise far more control than the average player. Yet even a real good player has moments when he's playing considerably off his usual game. So you have to be observant and take advantage of such opportunities when they present themselves. You'll have many more opportunities to do that against the average player simply because they lose control far more often.

Categorizing Your Opponents

It is also extremely important that you be able to assess the quality of your opponents' play. You have to play very differently against strong players than you do against weaker ones. This is of crucial importance in no-limit.

Shortly, I'm going to go into considerable detail on this important subject because I've seen very good players fail to adjust their strategy when they're in a pot with a certain type of player. In fact, recently one of the best players I know made such amateurish mistakes that I wouldn't have believed it possible if I hadn't seen it with my own two eyes. But before I get into the specific details, I want to give you two general rules to guide you in this matter.

(1) Against a low-grade player: You simply make the obvious play. That is, you don't try to get fancy when you're in a pot with a weak player. You don't try to make subtle moves that'll be far beyond his capacity to understand or appreciate. In a word, you outplay him.

(2) Against a higher-grade player (someone who could be thinking along the same lines as you): You must mix-up your play. Sometimes you make an obvious play against a strong player—as you always would against a weak player—and other times you go at it another way and make a play that's not so obvious. Most of the time, you have to put a play on or out-maneuver a strong player.

In a nutshell, that's all there is to it. And it seems simple and logical enough. There are even very good players who know that that's what they're supposed to do, but knowing something and being able to execute it are two different things.

Playing Against a Weak Player

There was a particular player who entered a tournament for the first time and, almost immediately, it became obvious that he was a weak player. He was the supreme example of a calling station, a player who's next to impossible to bluff.

Even though I had never played against him before, it didn't take me very long to recognize the type of player he was. I've played with thousands just like him throughout my career. So I knew what to do when I was involved in a pot with him. More precisely, I knew what not to do. I was not going to try to bluff him. Not even once.

I quickly decided that if I was in the pot with him, I was going to show him a hand. And, if he got lucky enough to beat me, well, he was going to beat a hand. My mind was made up.

But there were other very good players in this tournament who tried to run over him, tried to force him out of a pot. They bluffed at him constantly and were rarely successful. If he had anything at all he looked 'em up. As I said, he was the ultimate calling station. He looked enough of them up to finish far higher than he should have. He was probably about a 1000 to 1 dog to finish as high as he did. The reason he did was simply because so many players—and some of them very experienced—just handed him their money. They literally gave it away to him.

What they should not have done is try to bluff him. It takes an idiot, in my book, to bluff at a man who you know is going to call you. You simply can't bluff a bad player because a bad player will call when he's got any kind of a hand and pass when he doesn't. It's clear-cut. You don't have to be an expert psychologist to figure out what he's doing. All you have to know is that if he's in the pot he's got something. And you're not going to get him out of the pot by trying to bluff him.

Above all, you don't want to gamble with that kind of a player. Forget about that. Show him a hand. You do very fundamental, even obvious things against a bad player—no tricks, no strategic play, nothing fancy. Play straightforward poker against a weak player.

For example, if a weak player raised the pot coming in, then checked it on the flop, and checked again on fourth street, I would automatically bet, regardless of what I've got, because I'd know he doesn't have anything at all. It's simple to outplay him because his actions tell me whether he's got something or not. There's no mystery about it.

I could also outplay him by adjusting my style to his. For example, I noted that I'm always stabbing around trying to pick up pots. I could still do that with a weak player in the pot, but I'd adjust my play because he's in there. For instance, I might raise him without looking at my hand. Now, here comes the flop and he checks. Well, I'm going to bet at that pot in the dark because I know he probably doesn't have anything, and I also know he's probably going to pass. He checked, didn't he? If he had something, he would've bet.

Of course, I might have to make a further adjustment. If he checked on the flop and then called me, I'd give him credit for something. If there's no straight or flush draw out there, he's probably got a small piece of the board. If he had a big piece he would've bet. If he checks again on fourth and calls me again, then I'd know I'm going to have to show him a hand on the end.

If I'm in the pot with a weak player and I flop a real big hand, say a set of trips, I would check it because I know that if he'd had anything, he would have bet, and I'd be able to break him anyway. Normally, I don't slow-play that hand. I always lead with it. But against a weak player, I wouldn't mind giving him a free card if he doesn't have anything, I want him to improve his hand. I want him to make something so I can possibly break him.

It's more difficult to outplay a strong player. You can't consistently do simple things against better players; you've got to put a play on somebody who knows what's obvious. And if I see him do something that's obvious, like I think he's trying to pick up the pot, I'll put a play on him and raise him with nothing because he might throw his hand away.

Since a good player will understand the obvious, I must try to deceive him. I'll even put a play on more than one good player. For example, if someone brought it in or raised it in an early position and three players just called it, I might make a big raise with nothing, trying to pick up that pot.

Against a good player, you'll have a lot more tools to work with and many different strategies to use. You're effectively restricted to a pickax and shovel against a weak player. Never forget that. Don't try to devise elaborate strategies to use against a bad player. They won't work against him. Use sophisticated plays against a good player. They'll work against him.

Another point you should note about weak players is that they come in several varieties. They're not all like the one I described above. Some are the complete opposite. There are some who check good hands and bet bad hands. They like to bluff, and they do it almost all the time. So, when you recognize a player like that, you keep on checking it to him and let him bluff his money off to you.

Note that I didn't say to check-raise him. You don't want to take the play away from that type of player. In fact, years ago, I rarely used check-raising. In the old days it was a weak play, and I used it only occasionally. I'd usually do it when someone seemed to be trying to take the play away from me. Perhaps, I might have checked it and moved in on him or something like that. But I didn't do it often.

Now that players are much more aggressive, it is easier to check-raise. But even today, check-raising isn't as integral a part of my philosophy as it is for many other professionals. I do it—you have to keep people in line—but I usually don't look for opportunities to check-raise.

However, I suppose I encounter more check-raising than the average player because I play so aggressively. If a player makes a hand, he'll check it to me thinking that I'm going to bet—and he's usually right. Most of the time, I will. So he checks it to me. And after I bet, he raises.

Surprisingly, if you employ my style of play at no-limit hold'em, you won't be in constant fear of getting check-raised. By playing aggressively, you might think "Well, they're probably going to get me this time" every time you bet. Even though you'll probably encounter more check-raising than most players, you'll be amazed at how many times your opponents keep throwing their hands away whenever you bet.

It all goes back to my basic style of play. My opponents know that if I've got any kind of a hand, any kind of a draw, and they do check-raise me, all of my chips—and theirs—are going to the middle. And because of that, they keep off of me. It stops them from playing back at me.

Not only does it give me, in most cases, an umbrella of protection against opponents playing back at me, and not only does it make my opponents fear me which in turn makes it easy for me to pick up numerous pots without a contest, but it has other advantages as well. I've already told you I also get a lot of loose action. This may seem contradictory—how can I pick up pots easily on the one hand and get a lot of loose action on the other? It's easy to understand when you realize that I pick up pots when nobody's got a hand. And, as I said, that's a big percentage of the time. I get this so-called loose action when somebody does have a hand. At those times, all the money is liable to go to the center. And when it does—as you now know—I've usually got the worst hand.

But I might also find a hand when I look down. And once in a while, it's the best hand. When I'm up against another hand at those times, the pot gets to be a mountain. It wouldn't be nearly as big if I weren't an aggressive player. I'd never get the action I do when I've got a hand if I were known to slow-play hands or do a lot of check-raising. That's why I rarely do those things.

The reason why being known as an aggressive player and constantly playing that way is the most profitable way to play poker is clearly illustrated by the following situation.

Let's say I flopped a big hand—a set of trips or even two pair. I'm first to act, and I'm in the pot with someone who raised before the flop. He's supposed to have a strong hand. He's probably got a big pair in the hole, bigger than anything that showed on the flop.

In this situation, there's a principle I always apply in hold'em: always make it a habit to lead into the raiser whenever I flop a big hand.

Most players will slow-play their hand in that spot or hope to get in a check-raise. When they do that, they're playing it wrong. By betting right into the raiser, you make him think you're either trying to take the pot away from him or you've got some kind of draw or a mediocre hand. Consequently, he'll almost invariably raise you. At that point you can get all your chips in. And it's tough for him to get away from his hand because he has so much money already in the pot. The raiser expects you to check to him on the flop. I mean, he knows you know he's supposedly got a strong hand. He raised coming in, didn't he?

When most players flop a set with a small pair or two pair with small connecting cards, they do the obvious. They check, waiting for the raiser to bet, and then they put in a raise. That's the wrong way to play it, because it gives the raiser an opportunity to get away from his hand at a minimum loss. But if you lead into him, he probably will raise, and then there's probably no getting away from it. He's all but committed to getting the rest of his money in the pot.

Even if it's a raggedy flop without a straight or flush draw, you should still make the same play. Perhaps even more so, because with three rags out there, a bet would indicate weakness rather than strength to most players. Since it does look like you're weak and trying to take the pot away from him, the average player will respond to your bet by raising.

The only risk you take when you play the hand this way is that the raiser might not raise you on the flop because he might not have a hand. However, he might have bluffed at it if you had checked, and you would have won the amount he bluffed.

It's far more probable that he does have a hand. He was the raiser. He's represented a hand. He's supposed to have a hand! Based upon that very reasonable assumption, I go ahead and lead into his hand. When compared to check-raising in that situation, it's the bigger money-making play, by far. I think it's one of the strongest plays in hold'em.

If you flopped a set in an unraised pot and it was a raggedy flop, you'd have to play the hand quite differently. Depending on what set you flopped, you might not even play it at all. You'll see what I mean in a minute. But the concept you should understand is this: In no-limit play, you must be very careful you don't lose all your chips in an unraised pot, unless you have the nuts at the point you go all-in.

Here's what I mean: let's say you and six other players got in for the absolute minimum, that is, you all limped-in for a $50 force, the blind bet. Everybody just called. Nobody raised—so the field wasn't weeded out at all. Now, a J-4-2 flops. You flop three deuces. In the previous situation—with this same flop—you should lead right into the raiser with your set. He's probably got an overpair and will raise as expected. But in the present situation, you must play it carefully. Very carefully. You flopped a hand that's easy to get broke with. There's nothing in the pot, and you don't want to get broke in a nothing pot.

The six people in the pot with you tried to flop the nuts for free. And one of them might have the nuts, or close to it. So if one of the players commits all his money when there's only a few hundred dollars in the pot, you better watch out. Your three deuces probably aren't any good.

You could be up against three jacks, but that's not as likely as three fours, since there was no raise before the flop. That's the hand you should be afraid of.

I'm not saying you shouldn't play the hand. I'm just saying that you have to play it carefully. Since nobody showed any early strength, you're not likely to be up against a big pair, but you could be facing another set. Nevertheless, if it's checked to you, you've got to bet it.

But you don't want to get broke with the hand because it was a nothing pot to begin with. If you get raised, your own judgment in the particular situation will have to prevail. With the third set, deuces, you might want to go on with the hand, but then you might not. With the second set, fours, you can't get away from it. Someone's going to have to show you three jacks. That's all there is to it.

Courage

An important point for you to remember is that in a judgment situation you're always better off sticking to your first impression. With constant observation of your opponents' play, you'll learn how to put them on a probable hand. Once you decide what a man's most likely to have—especially in no-limit—you should never change your mind. You'll probably be right the first time, so don't try to second-guess yourself. Have the courage and conviction to trust your instincts!

Having courage is one of the most important qualities of a good no-limit player. If you don't have it, you'll have to restrict your play to limit poker. You need courage in limit too, but not nearly as much as in no-limit.

Limit vs. No-Limit

A lot of limit players—and I'm talking about the very best limit players now—just can't play no-limit. They don't have the heart for it. What's more, they can't adjust to the complexity of no-limit play, and they find it very hard to go from limit which is essentially a mechanical game, to no-limit, one that takes into account everything. Only very special players can make that transition successfully.

You also have to have a different feel for no-limit play. I mean, you have to be right just about all the time, especially when your entire stack's at stake.

In limit play, you're not going to get knocked out of a game by one or two mistakes. You can make several mistakes in a limit game and still win the money if your opponents are making more mistakes than you are. With no-limit, make just one crucial mistake at any time and you can lose all your chips.

Muscle

It not only takes a lot of heart to play no-limit, it also takes a lot of muscle. You need muscle in limit too, but you need much more of it at no-limit. A strong no-limit player can keep slapping you around, just lean on you and keep leaning on you until you topple. Of course, that could happen in limit too, but again, not to the same degree.

The very best players I know are extremely aggressive players and that's what makes them great players. The more aggressive they are, the better they are. It's that simple. And I firmly believe that's what accounts for the difference between a very good player and a truly top player. It's the dividing line.

There's not a man alive that can keep leaning on me. I refuse to let somebody keep taking my money, and all the other truly top players are the same way. An aggressive player might do it for a while. But at the first opportunity I get, I'm going to take a stand and put all my money in the pot.

It's like that little boy who keeps sticking his head up and keeps getting slapped all the time. Well, sooner or later he's not going to stick his head up any more. So if a guy keeps going on and on and keeps pounding on me, then me and him are fixing to play a pot.

Like me, all the top players know you have to be extremely aggressive to be a consistent winner. You have to bet, bet, bet, all the time. If I find somebody I can keep betting at and he keeps saying "Take it Doyle," "Take it Doyle," well, I'm going to keep pounding on him. I'm not going to let up. And that poor guy never will win a pot from me. He'll have to have the nuts or the nerve to call me.

That's what most players do. They keep throwing their hand away. They're weak. They sit down and try to make the nuts on you. That's hard to do. So you keep whamming on 'em and whamming on 'em and you just wear 'em down. And sooner or later, you'll win all their money.

Perhaps now, you can see more clearly what I explained earlier. When a big pot comes up, I've usually got the worst hand. That weak player finally picks up the nuts and that's what I usually look at in a big pot. But I've already paid for that big pot with all the smaller pots I've won, so I'm freerolling with all that weak player's money and the money of all the others like him.

You can't do that against a truly top-player in no-limit because he's fixing to make a stand and play back at you. And that's the big difference between a merely good player and a great one.

Another important difference is that a real top player can win money with a marginal hand. A weaker player can't do that. Either they don't know how, or they're afraid to put any money in the pot in a borderline situation. They want the nuts or close to it before they'll jeopardize any of their chips. They don't want to do too much gambling, so they check a lot of hands that I'd bet for value.

Betting for Value

Betting for value is what it's all about. For example, if it came down to a tough situation on the end and a tight player had two pair but there's a possible straight out there, well, that tight player would probably check it trying to show the hands down. In that same situation, as long as I felt reasonably sure my opponent didn't have that straight, I'd be more aggressive. I want to make some money on the end. I want to get value for my two pair. So I'd bet and try to sell my hand for the most money I thought I could get. I never was a tight player, even when I first started to play. Experience has taught me a lot. Early in my career, I didn't know how to start at a pot and quit, like I do now.

I don't have to have the nuts to bet my hand on the end. If I feel like I've got the best hand, I'm going to bet it and get value for it. A more conservative player would check it on the end, and he'll get his check called. So he'll lose that last bet.

A very big part of winning consistently and winning big at no-limit is getting the other guy in a position where if he makes a bet he's actually jeopardizing all his chips as opposed to you jeopardizing all of yours. That has always been the key to no-limit play as far as I'm concerned. I want to force my opponent into a decision with all his chips on the line.

For example, if a guy's got $20,000 in chips and you lead off for $6,000 or $7,000, you're really betting him $20,000. He knows that if he calls that six or seven, well then, he's got to go for the rest of it. You're betting $7,000; he's betting $20,000.

On the other hand, if he bets me $7,000, the reverse is true. So, I always try to make the bet that puts him in jeopardy, not me. If he's right and I'm bluffing, he's going to move in with his $20,000, and I'm not going to call him. So he'll win $7,000. But if he's wrong and I've got a hand, he's still going to move in, but now he's going to get called. And he's going to lose $20,000. So he's laying me about 3 to 1, his $20,000 to my $7,000. I put the commitment on him. I make him commit himself. I'm not committed no matter what he thinks. That's the beauty of it. He's thinking about my bet and wondering how much more he's going to have to put in there.

It's an either/or situation. Either I'm bluffing, or I've got the nuts. And against me, he knows it could cost him $20,000—his whole stack—unless he throws his hand away.

And you'd be surprised how many times they say "Take it Doyle," "Take it Doyle." They just throw their hands away over and over and over again. I mean, even I'm surprised. I think to myself, "Well, he can't throw this one away." But I bet anyway. And there goes his hand—chunk! It finally gets to be mechanical with them. And I've won another pot.

I've stolen so many pots I can't begin to count them. And most of the time, I've actually had to force myself to bet. I'd be playing all night without one decent hand. Yet I'd win every pot because I didn't bet into the nuts. It goes on and on like that. I pick up a hand, and I've got nothing. The flop comes out there, and I've still got nothing. So I kind of have to hit myself to bet at it, because there's a guy I've been pounding on and pounding on. And all the time, I'm thinking, "How can he throw his hand away this time?" But I bet and away it goes. Chunk! One more time.

If he takes a stand and raises me, I go back to my basic philosophy. If I've got a hand, I'll go with it, even though I know it might be the worst hand.

By now, you should have a very good idea of how I play no-limit hold'em. I hope this somewhat lengthy introduction gave you a sufficient feel for my style of play, and I hope it will help you to understand how I play specific hands in various situations. I'll discuss those shortly.

However, when you read those discussions you should realize it's quite difficult to state exactly what I'd do with a specific hand in a particular situation. So many things are involved. No-limit hold'em is a very complex game.

Most of the things I say are an accurate reflection of what I'd generally do. But I might do something else or even the completely opposite depending on who's in the pot with me and whether or not I have position on him.

Always remember, no-limit hold'em is a game of position and people. There'll be a lot of times when only your good judgment will dictate the proper play. Often situations come up where a hard-and-fast rule will prove inadequate. Poker, especially no-limit hold'em, is not a game you can learn to play well in ten easy lessons. A thousand hard lessons might not be enough. There are simply too many variables involved.

Nevertheless, the lessons you'll learn below will go a long way in helping you to master no-limit hold'em. The general principles and concepts that I discuss will give you a far greater command of the game than almost all the players you could expect to be competing with. I wish I'd known all the general guidelines below when I first started to play. It would've made things a lot easier for me. That's for sure.

But before I get into how you should generally play specific hands, there should be a discussion of the ante, betting structure, bankroll requirements, and other considerations you'll have to take into account before you sit in on a no-limit hold'em game. So that's what I'll do now.

The Ante and Other Considerations

If I had to choose a particular size game that would be close to perfect for no-limit hold'em, it would be eight-handed, also known as a **ring** or **full game**. Of course, I prefer to play in a shorthanded game with about four or five players, because in a shorthanded game with a high ante, you're forced to get in there and play. You can't just sit there and wait for the big pair, A-K, or even small connecting cards. If you do, you'll go like Broomcorn's uncle. So a game like that suits my style just fine. It gives me plenty of room to muscle the game.

A full game with eight players is all right too. That's just about the right amount of players for a ring game where there'll be good action. I mean, there'll be people coming in the pots because they'll know they won't have to be looking at the nuts every hand.

However, when that eight-handed game all of a sudden turns into a ten- or eleven-handed game, well, the complexion of the game changes completely. What was once a relatively fast and loose game becomes a thing of the past. The players no longer get in there and play as often. The game begins to screw down real tight.

With eleven players, there are a lot more combinations out there on every hand than with nine players. So everyone stops playing borderline hands and starts waiting for the really good ones. In short, they don't do as much gambling, and the action really dries up.

Loosening Up a Game

Many poker games are like that, and they stay that way unless something happens to change the character of the game. More than anything else, the something that changes a tight game back into a loose game happens when one of the players starts giving a lot of action. As I've said, that's what I do. I'm known as an action player. It's an image I've always had. Because I give action, I get it.

I'll get into a poker game and almost from the very first hand I'll start gambling. I'll be taking chances—betting, raising, reraising, moving in. That'll stir up a game real fast. One player can do it. That's all it takes. And that player's usually me.

I don't merely talk loose, I prove I'm loose by my actions. You know the old cliché: "A first impression is a lasting impression." Well that first impression I create lasts throughout the session, even though I might change gears, say go from loose to tight to loose, several times during the course of a game.

Adjusting Your Speed

Being able to adjust your playing speed is a very important part of being a top player. There are a lot of reasons for this.

(1) You never want to get yourself stuck in an identifiable pattern. You must mix up your play. If you do, you'll always keep your opponents guessing.

(2) You want to create an image, the image of a loose, gambling-type of player who gives a lot of action. But it has to be the image of a good loose player, not the image of a fool who's throwing a party, giving his money away.

(3) Since you'll most likely get off loser if you play as I recommend and start plunging around (playing very loose) almost as soon as you begin to play, you'll have to gear down and start playing tight after you've laid the groundwork for your image. Then you'll start playing loose again, and you'll continue to vary your speed throughout the session.

(4) You'll also want to adjust your speed to the varying speeds of particular players. If there's a guy in the game who's speeding around, do exactly the opposite by gearing down and remember to play only solid hands against him. On the other hand, if you notice that a certain player is playing real tight, you can start bluffing at him.

(5) The game itself might dictate the speed at which you'll have to play. If everyone is playing real loose and all the pots are being jammed, start playing real tight. Conversely, when the game is so tight you can hear it squeaking, you should play loose and pick up all the pots you can.

(6) When players start dropping out of the game and their seats remain vacant, you have to move into high gear. As I said, you can't sit back and wait in a shorthanded game. If you do, the ante will get you because the good hands don't come often enough. So you must play, or you might as well quit the game.

(7) And of course, there's the ante. That's the main thing that determines how fast you play. Actually, the absolute size of the ante is not what's important. It's the relationship of the ante to the amount of money you have. A $10 ante in a no-limit game would be quite high if all you had was $500. But if you had $5,000, that $10 ante would be very low. In the high-ante game, you'd have to play pretty fast. You could slow down considerably in the low-ante game.

The ante and blinds is such an important factor in determining how fast you play, that the trouble and trash hands I later discuss would become big hands if you were anteing high enough. In fact, in the old days, that was the case in the World Championship Hold'em Tournament because of the way it was structured. It started with each player anteing $10, and there was a $50 blind. As the tournament progressed and players were eliminated, the ante and blind got higher and higher according to a predetermined time schedule until it was down to the final two players. At that point, each player anted $1,000 and blinded it for $2,000. If you sat around and waited putting that kind of money in every pot, you'd go faster than Broomcorn's uncle.

Today's tournaments are structured to be a lot faster than that. You've got to play almost every hand when you're anteing that high. At the very least, you've got to see the flop. So, it's really not all that surprising I won the 1976 and 1977 World Championships with trash hands. The only thing surprising about this is that the hands were almost identical both years.

In 1976, when I won $220,000, the last pot had $176,000 in it. I won that pot with the 10♠ 2♠. All it had on the flop was a pair of deuces, but I caught two running tens on fourth and fifth. Jesse Alto, a very experienced non-professional who owned an automobile dealership in Houston, Texas, was the man who came in second.

In 1977, the late Bones Berland was the young man who came in second to me. In the last pot with Bones, I had a 10♦ 2♥ and flopped a pair of tens. This time, I caught a 2 on fourth street—but I filled up with a 10 on the end. That last pot was worth $130,000 and I won $340,000 in the 1977 tournament.

Of course, in a normal ante ring game, I'd rarely play those hands. There's little reason to when the ante doesn't force you to play. A major exception is when I play a pot for the sole reason of trying to steal it. Then, it doesn't make any difference what I have. I mean, I could be playing the hand without even looking at my holecards. At such a time, I'd be playing my money, my position, and a particular player. My hand wouldn't matter. If I was forced to look at it because I got played with, I might find two aces, A-K, or trash.

People have criticized me for losing $580,000 with the Q-8 offsuit in the $25,000 buy-in final event at the Bellagio in 2003. Well, I've just explained to you how that happened. I was playing my money, my position, and a particular player—and my hand could have been anything. I hadn't made a pair the whole day, and I'd had to stay alive by stealing some pots, but on this particular play, my read was wrong.

You'll almost surely have to get some no-limit experience

under your belt before you'll be able to play a pot completely blind. So, in the beginning, I suggest that you restrict the way you play specific hands to the recommendations I make below. However, it's important for you to understand that those recommendations are what I would do in a normal or medium ante ring game. In different games you'll have to adjust your play as previously discussed.

In order to help you determine what constitutes a normal medium-ante game, you should use the following table as a guide.

Nine-Handed Game - Blinds Chart

Ante Size	$ Ante	Single Blind	Multiple Blinds		Buy-In*
			1st seat	2nd seat	
Very Low	$1-$5	$5-$10	$5-$10	$10-$20	$1,000
Low	$5-$10	$25	$25	$50	$2,000
Medium	$10-$20	$50	$50	$100	$5,000
High	$25-$50	$100	$100	$200	$10,000
Very High	$50-$100	$500	$300	$500	$25,000

*Twice the *minimum* buy-ins listed here would be much better. More than twice would be better still.

You wouldn't want to sit down with less than the minimum buys shown. As the footnote states, you should definitely consider buying-in for more.

Today, when I play in a game with two blinds of $300 and $500, I never sit down with less than $100,000. What's more, I like to have as much or more money than any other player at the table. If my stacks are not approximately equal to the guy with the most money, then I couldn't break him, could I?

And I practice what I preach. I start playing fast right away.

I've always played like that, even when I was just starting out. Back then I'd buy in for a thousand in a small no-limit game, and I'd usually get stuck that first thousand. Then, I'd pull up and start playing tighter, and I almost always got even or won.

About three out of four plays, I'd lose that first thousand, but on that fourth play, I'd get on a winning streak or a rush, and I'd more than make up for those first three losses. I mean, I'd be playing so fast and winning so many hands when I was rushing that I'd literally break every player in the game. Because as you know, whenever I hold a bunch of hands, I usually get action on them.

I've never won a bunch of pots watching the other guys play. If I'm making a bunch of hands or striking, I'm in there—I'm not on the sidelines. If you're going to have a rush, you've got to let yourself have one. You've got to sustain that rush. And to do that, you've got to get in there and play.

It used to be that after I had won a pot in no-limit I would be in the next pot, regardless of what two cards I picked up. And if I won that one, I'd always be in the next one. I'd keep playing every pot until I lost one. And in all those pots, I'd gamble more than I normally would. Nowadays, I still to try to observe this, but I've modified it because players are so much more aggressive.

If you don't play that way, you'll never have much of a rush. I know that scientists don't believe in rushes, but sometimes rushes can make you a fortune. There's only one world-class poker player that I know of who doesn't believe in rushes. Well, he's wrong, and so are the scientists. Besides, how many of them can play poker anyway? I've played poker for more than fifty years now, and I've made millions at it. A big part of my winnings came from playing my rushes.

If you want to take the money off, I mean, make a big score, then you've got to play your rushes. It's that simple. Not that there's anything supernatural about rushes, it's how your opponents perceive you when you're on one that's important. They are flat-out less dangerous. They pay you off more and challenge you less, and that translates into pure profit.

At this point, you should have a very good feel for my style of play. It should help you to understand and appreciate the things I'm going to say about the way I play specific hands, from before the flop on through each stage of play until all the cards are out.

In all the situations that I'll discuss below, an important assumption has been made: Unless otherwise noted, the way I'd play a specific hand at no-limit hold'em is how I'd play it in a pot against other top poker players and not the way I'd play it against a weak player.

The reason that assumption has been made is because, as you already know, against a weak player or a drunk you have to play quite differently. All you try to do against a weak player is make the best hand and then extract from him the largest amount of money you can. Just outplay him.

HOW TO PLAY SPECIFIC HANDS

Remember, the recommendations I make below are how you generally should play the hands discussed. That's the way I usually play them. But you should never fall into a pattern playing poker. I don't. I always vary my play. I try to mix it up as much as I can. I never consistently repeat my action on any hand. I don't play like a computer that's programmed to do the same routine over and over again. The high quality players I play against on a regular basis would easily detect a pattern to my play if there were any. So I never do the same thing with the same hand from the same position against the same player. I'm always changing speeds during the course of a game.

However, for your purposes, my playing recommendations

for a particular hand are a good way for you to play them until your opponents learn your style. When they do, you start shifting gears, up and down continuously, until there is no noticeable pattern.

I'm going to break the game down into four major and very broad categories as follows:

I. Pairs
II. Small Connecting Cards
III. Borderline Hands
IV. Trash Hands

How to play your hand when you have a pair in the pocket is going to be discussed first. That category will be sub-divided and discussed as follows:

a. Big Pairs and Big Slick: A-A, K-K, and A-K
b. Q-Q
c. J-J down to 2-2

I've grouped an A-K with a pair of aces and a pair of kings because it's a very strong hand. As you'll learn, I would rather have A-K than A-A or K-K. I'll discuss each of the hands as I would play them in a nine-handed game from an **early position** (first three seats), **middle position** (next three seats), and **late position** (last three seats). A medium-ante game is assumed, unless otherwise noted.

A-A and K-K

Pre-Flop Play

Early Position. With a pair of aces or kings in an early position before the flop, I would probably just call the blind or limp in, hoping that somebody raises it behind me so I can reraise.

Middle Position. In a middle position, if nobody in the early seats came in, I would play them the same way. But if somebody in the early seats did come in, I'd put in a raise of about the size of the pot.

Late Position. In a late position, I'd obviously raise with them and hope that somebody trailed his hand around to me, that is, slow-played his hand in order to reraise me. If he did, I'd play back of course, and I might move in depending on the circumstances. If I did play back with two aces or two kings and got about half my money in the pot before the flop, there's no question that I'd get the rest of it in on the flop, regardless of what came. Nothing could stop me. If my opponent didn't set me in on the flop I'd move it all-in myself, because there are too many ways I could outguess myself, and I'm not going to try. If I get either of those big pairs cracked, well, I'm just going to have to lose my money.

Conversely, a rare situation could exist where you'd consider throwing away two kings before the flop if you got raised. It's a hard hand to get away from, but if a real tight player, one so tight that he probably wouldn't make that kind of play unless he had two aces, moved in on you, then you might want to throw them away. Of course, you'd have to be almost certain about your man before you do that. One way I make this rare decision is to put myself in my opponent's position. I ask myself, "If I were him, would I reraise with two queens or less?" If the answer is no, I throw the two kings away.

I'm going to discuss how to play a big pair on the flop in a moment. But this is a good place to note that when you have two kings and there's a single ace on the flop, it's a complete judgment call as to whether or not you should go on with your hand. If you put your opponent on an ace, that's the end of the pot right there. If not, you play your two kings as if you had the best hand. Here are two particularly relevant hold'em probabilities:

(1) In a nine-handed game, when you have two kings, the probability that no other player has an ace is about 20 percent. Put another way, a player will have an ace about 80 percent of the time.

(2) If a player is holding two unpaired cards lower than kings, an ace will flop about 18 percent of the time.

The Flop

Regardless of your hand, the flop is where you'll make your most crucial decisions. It's the key point in the hand. It's where you put people on hands, decide what they've probably got. Usually, everything after the flop is more or less cut-and-dried.

Playing with No Help on the Flop. Of course, you put people on hands before the flop too, but on the flop, you're in a much better position to determine what a man probably has by the way he calls, whether he's drawing to a straight or flush and so forth. I play a pair of aces or kings very cautiously from an early position when there are three cards that'll make a straight or a flush on the flop. This is especially true if there are two or more people in the pot with me. The guys that called behind me are liable to have anything. In that position, they've either got a hand that could break me or I'll win a very small pot if I bet. So in an early position, a bell rings reminding me not to bet when I see three to a straight or flush on the flop and I've got aces or king in the pocket. Consequently, I immediately start playing that hand slow, and usually I just check in a front position.

If I'm in a late seat and somebody in the early seats had trailed in, I might go ahead and bet once. If I got called, I would immediately become defensive again with that hand. Anytime there are three cards to a straight or flush, I play the hand with extreme caution.

The quality of the possible straight that's out there also has a big influence on the way I'd play that big pair. If it came 9-8-7, 10-9-8, or J-10-9 and I've got two people in the pot with me, I immediately give it up. Almost any two cards that those two players have will fit into those flops somehow. They're either going to have a hand that's already got me beat or they'll be drawing to a hand that would make my hand no better than an even money shot.

If the flop comes 10-9-8 and one of your opponents has a Q-J, he's got the straight made. If he's got a J-10, he's got a pair with an open-end straight draw. He could catch a 7, 10, jack, or queen. There are thirteen cards in the deck that will beat me, namely four sevens, four queens, three jacks, and two tens, and he's got two shots at them. That makes his hand as good as mine at this point. In fact, he's almost exactly even-money to beat me, so I don't want to put myself in a position where I could get broke. I don't always give up the pot in that situation. I just play extremely cautiously. I don't just charge in and try to win the pot right there.

If just a J-10 falls, say the flop is a J-10-2, well, there I'd really play my two aces fast, because any combination of big cards would give my opponent some kind of hand. For example, a K-Q will give him an open-end straight draw; an A-K will give him two overcards and a belly-straight draw; and an A-J, K-J, Q-J, A-10, Q-10, or K-10 will give him a pair. So I'd go ahead and play my two aces in that situation. If he's got jacks and tens or better, well, more power to him. If you know your player, you'll be able to figure out what hand he's likely to have. You have to be logical in putting your opponent on a hand.

I'm not as leery of a three-card flush on the flop as I am of a three-card straight. With a three-card flush, there aren't as many possible hands that could beat me—although it's possible that your opponent has a pair and a flush draw if he's in there with you.

The first thing I'd do would be to see if either one of my two aces or kings matched the cards out there. If three hearts fell and I had two red aces, I would immediately play that hand. It's a big hand. But if I had the two black aces, or another hand without the A♥, I might be a little more hesitant to play it.

But if I did have the A♥, I'd play the hand fast on the flop. If I get called, I'm in a position to win it anyway. I know where the nuts are. That's one of the most important things about no-limit hold'em. If you can avoid it, you never want to get your money in dead.

For example, you don't want to be drawing for a flush when there's a pair on the board. Your opponent could have a full house. And you don't want to be drawing to a straight when another man could have a flush. If the board comes three hearts and you've got an open-end straight draw, you don't draw at that straight. You throw your hand away. All the top players try to keep from ever getting their money in completely dead.

If a pair and a rag flop and I had a pair of aces or kings in the pocket, I'd bet at that pot from an early position. If I got called, I'd proceed cautiously. I mean, when the next card was turned, I'd check it to him. If he bet, maybe I'd call it or maybe I wouldn't. It would depend on what I felt that he had. I'd know he's got something that he likes.

For example, if the flop is 6-6-2 and I bet and he calls, he's telling me he's got some kind of hand. He's probably got a pair in the pocket, anywhere from sevens to tens, or else he's got three sixes or three deuces. So I'd use my judgment at that point, and I'd be cautious again.

If there were a couple of players in the pot in front of me and one of them flopped a set of sixes, he'd probably check it to me. That's what most players do in this situation, check a set into the raiser. But as you know, that's the wrong way to play it. A strong player would know that the right thing to do is lead into you.

If it was checked to me and there wasn't a straight draw on

the board—say the flop was 7-7-2—I might check it as well and give a free card. I'd do that for two reasons:

(1) If he didn't have a hand, I'd want him to help his hand enough to continue playing. For example, if a jack or queen fell off on fourth street, it might pair him.

(2) I'd want to eliminate the possibility that I'd get broke if he does have a 7.

But if the flop was 6-6-2, I would bet because I wouldn't want a 3, 4, or 5 falling off and making somebody a straight. In brief, you don't give free cards if that free card could break you. If there's a possible straight or flush draw on board, you don't give a free card.

If I had two aces with a 6-6-K flop and it was checked to me, I'd probably check it back. If he's got a king, he's going to play it on fourth street, because by checking, you've made him think he's got the best hand. Plus, if he does have a 6, as before, you might be able to hold your losses to a minimum. A flop that's 6-6-5 is a lot different, because there's the possibility of a straight draw.

What it all boils down to is that with a pair of aces or kings, you're waiting until you get into what you think is a favorable situation before you really play a big pot. You're not looking to play a big pot if there's only a small chance you'll have the best of it or one where you're a big underdog.

In general, with those big pairs on the flop, you play them a little more aggressively from a late position than from an early position, but you should be aware that someone might be checking the nuts to you, such as three sixes in the examples used. You never worry about that. I've heard people say, "Well, I was afraid to bet because I was afraid he'd raise me." Never worry about getting raised. You have to go ahead and play. If it happens, it happens, and then you worry about it. Don't cross that bridge until you come to it.

You can't play winning poker by playing safe all the time. You must take chances. You must gamble. And you have to feel aggressive to play aggressively. That's my style of poker. And it's a winning style.

I've re-stated my general philosophy of play at this point because I'm discussing the play of a pair of aces or kings in the hole. In many cases, I play them slowly, but I don't slow-play them. That is, I play them cautiously. This is contrary to my usual style of play and to the way most people play them. Most players feel that aces or kings are so hard to come by that when they do get them they want to win a big pot. So they play them real fast. That's usually wrong, but there are exceptions that I'll discuss below. The fact is, with a pair of aces or kings, one of two things will usually happen:

(1) You win a small pot; or

(2) You lose a big pot.

The reason is that your opponent is not going to get a lot of money in the pot unless he can beat your big pair or has a straight or flush draw. In the latter case, as you'll see below, I'm going to make him pay to draw to his hand.

I also play two aces or kings slowly in the rare instance that a set of trips flops, say three sevens or three jacks. But this time I do it for somewhat different reasons. In this case, I want my opponent in the pot to improve his hand or catch up with me. So I check it, but just one time. I want to give him a free card so he can catch a pair or get a chance to bluff at it. It's tough to win anything in that spot by leading off unless you catch somebody with a pair in the pocket.

Of course, there's a small chance you could run into quads, but anyone who made that hand will let you know it by the way he puts all his money in the pot. It takes experience to recognize something like that, but it's just like any other situation where somebody's betting the pure nuts at you. You have to use judgment to evaluate it. After a while, you recognize it. As always, it boils down to reading people.

The one situation where I stand to lose a very big pot with a pair of aces or kings is when there are two to a straight or flush on the flop. For example, say there's a J-10-2 out there. If somebody bet at me, I'd move in a lot of chips. I could win the pot right there. If not, my opponent is really going to pay to draw to his hand. If I were first to act, I'd check, hoping I'd get the chance to raise it. This is one of the few times I check-raise.

If I get called, I'll probably put my opponent on a straight or flush draw. Of course, on fourth street I'll go ahead and bet again if a meaningless card or blank falls. Again, this involves a lot of good judgment, because my opponent might have been fortunate enough to make some kind of hand that would beat my two aces, such as jacks and tens. In that case, I'd go ahead and pay him off because, as I said earlier, I'm not going to try to out-guess myself.

If the board fell completely ragged, say a 10-6-5, I would bet from any position. As in all the hands I've discussed, there's always the chance that someone flopped a set. But again, I'm going to cross that bridge if and when I come to it. In this situation, I'd know if my big pair was beat, especially if I had raised with my hand from an early position before the flop. All good hold'em players would interpret that as a sign of strength. I mean, the first thing you usually give a man, especially a weaker player, credit for when he raises is a big pair. So if it comes a 10-6-5 and I had raised from an early position, the other players will think that I have a strong hand, possibly a big pair, which I've got. Then when I bet on the flop and get raised by somebody in a late position, it gets back to evaluating people again. You've just got to know your players. He's representing to you that he can beat a big pair. If he's a good, solid-type player, what else can he have besides a set of trips or possibly two pair? So you make up your mind right there whether or not to go ahead with your two aces or two kings.

Of course, it's possible that he has a pair of queens or jacks in a back position and didn't raise you before the flop, but that now on the flop he's decided to test you, because he's got an overpair. You might want to call his raise one time if it's not too big a bet. The next time, check it to him and see what he does. If he bets again, he's usually there.

Playing with Help on the Flop. Up to now, I've discussed how I'd play a pair of aces or kings on the flop assuming I didn't flop anything that helped my hand. Now I'll discuss the situations where I get some help.

If I flop a set, I never slow-play it. There is one exception to this rule, which I'll discuss below. But for the most part, I almost always come right out and bet, and I don't make just a nominal bet. I make an extra-large bet because you'll only win a big pot if an opponent flops something with you, puts you on a bluff, or tries to run you down. So, I really come out smokin' right there.

Earlier, I said that when you have a pair of aces and a single ace flops, there'll always be the possibility that the next card off will make someone a straight. For instance, look at the following situation:

FLOP A

With a single ace on the flop and anything 5 or under, there's always a draw to a 5-high straight. As in Flop A, if a deuce, trey or 5 falls on fourth street, it could make someone a small straight.

The same thing applies whenever there's a single ace on the flop with any card 10 or above.

FLOP B

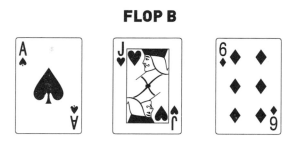

With Flop C, a king, queen, or 10 on fourth might give someone an ace-high straight. If there's no draw to a straight that includes an ace, then there'll be a draw to a medium straight because there'd have to be a two-card combination of the other four cards, namely a 6, 7, 8, or 9, as in the following example:

FLOP C

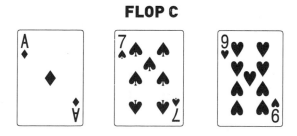

The straight possibility is more obvious with something like Flop C because there are seven different straights that can be made. If anyone has a J-10, J-8, 10-8, 10-6, 8-6, 8-5, or 6-5, they could make a straight with the next card off.

You should always keep this interesting discovery in mind whenever you see what appears to be a raggedy flop with an ace in it. The threat that someone could make a straight will always be present.

So when you flop a set of aces, you immediately go to betting, and you bet a large amount to prevent somebody from drawing at an inside straight cheaply. A good player will know it's worth it to take a cheap draw at a belly straight, and if he makes it, he can break you.

However, if you flop a set with two kings you could possibly give a free card if it comes ragged and there's no straight or flush draw. For example, say a K-8-2 falls. Now, you can give a card with that flop because you'd have the nuts as long as any card other than an ace, 8, or deuce fell. An ace might give someone three aces, and an 8 or deuce could possibly make someone four-of-a-kind. Realistically you shouldn't worry about quads, so you really want an 8 or deuce to hit the board on fourth street.

In the rare instance when you flop quads, say four aces, you're happy to have them, but you really don't have a very profitable hand. You've got the deck crippled. There's nothing left that your opponents can have. When you flop a hand that big, you just have to check along and maybe try to win a small bet on the end. Or, if you're extremely fortunate, you might get somebody to try to bluff at it. They just might try to pick up the pot by representing a hand. You could get lucky that way; but most of the time, you just play it very slow and take what you can get, meaning that you always bet on the end from any position.

Here's another situation where I almost always check: Say I flopped the highest possible full house, known as the **big full**. That's what you would have with two aces if the flop was A-3-3, or with two kings if it came K-7-7.

If you do have the big full, you'll have some leverage, so you could give them a free card in most situations (see below for the exception). After you check it once, you bet on fourth, hoping that somebody hit something there.

Whenever you've got a hand that's so big you've got the deck crippled or one that's very unlikely to get beaten, you should play it very slow on the flop for two reasons:

(1) You want to give your opponents a chance to bluff.

(2) You want to give them a chance to catch something if they don't bluff.

With a pair of aces or kings there's a chance you could flop a straight or flush draw. It would almost always be a gutshot straight draw, with the exception of a Q-J-10 when you had kings. In any case, if I flopped a straight draw, I'd be cautious with my hand. I could easily be beat at that point because any flop that would give me a straight draw could easily make my opponent two pair. I wouldn't fool with that hand. But if I've got the two red aces and three diamonds flop, well, as I noted earlier, that's a very big hand. I'd play that hand from the hip, and I'd be willing to put all my money in with it.

You should always remember that the flop is practically the whole game in hold'em. That's where your major decisions will be made. The play on fourth street and fifth street is pretty basic by comparison.

For example, on the flop, you put your opponent on a particular hand, and all your thinking follows from that. If you think he's drawing at a club flush, you bet. You must make your opponents pay to make their draws. If the club doesn't come on fourth street, you bet again. Obviously, if the club comes and you think your opponent made his hand, you check it. If you think you're beat, naturally, you check it. And if you think your opponent is drawing, you bet. That's the whole thing.

On fifth street, also called the river, if it looks like your opponent has missed his hand, there's usually no reason to bet any further. So you just show your hand over, or you check it and give him a chance to bluff.

That's no-limit hold'em in a nutshell, but as you know, it's a far more complex game than that. As you continue reading, you should be aware that my advice is intended to provide you with some general guidelines. I keep emphasizing this because it's so important that you understand it. There's not a single play that I'll always make with a particular hand. I'm liable to play every hand differently depending on the circumstances. The standards I have guide me in a general direction, as they should you. But sometimes, even I don't know exactly what I'm going to do until the situation comes up. Whatever my first feeling or impression is at the time, I'd go with that.

For example, I said I'd check my pair of aces one time if there were an open set of trips on the flop. On fourth street, if a man made a big bet, or if I bet and he moved-in on me, I'd probably go ahead and pay him off. If a man's lucky enough to flop quads when I've got two aces, he'd have to show me— unless I've got a lot of money in front of me and there's not too much money in the pot.

Let's look at a specific example, just, remember that no matter what I say now, I might do just the opposite if the situation calls for it. That depends on a lot of things, especially the guy in the pot with me. What do I know about him? So it's back to people again. Nevertheless, here's what I might do.

Let's say there's $20,000 in the pot. I've got $70,000 on the table. My opponent has $20,000, and he moves in on me. In that case, I'd probably pay him off if I knew him to be a player, as opposed to a rock.

However, if my opponent also had $70,000 and over-bet the pot by moving in his entire stack, well, then I'm not sure what I'd do. As I said, I'd go with my feelings. I'd look at him and then I'd decide. To start with, if he made a move like that I'd turn my hand face-up on the board. And I'd watch him real close. I'd want to see what his reaction was when I turned the two aces up. It would take a strong man not to show some kind of emotion. And from the emotion I saw, I'd judge whether he had quads or not. Then I'd react according to whichever way I felt.

Fourth and Fifth Streets

As I noted, you continue to bet your big pair on fourth street when it rags off and it doesn't look like it completed the straight or flush draw that showed on the flop. If your opponent wants to draw again, you make him pay for it.

If you flopped a set, you should also continue to bet on fourth even if it does look like someone might have completed a straight. You can't worry about it because you don't know which straight it is, if it was made at all. Just disregard any straight card and go ahead and bet.

But if a third flush card fell on the turn, then I'd probably check it. If someone bet, I'd call it, thinking that I'm probably beat but trying to make a full. I mean, I wouldn't know for sure that I was beat, but I'd call knowing there was a strong possibility I was. And I'd call a pretty big bet.

If the man moved all-in on me in that spot, I'd probably give him credit for the flush. Then whether or not to call is a matter of simple mathematics. Ten cards out of the forty-five left would help my hand, assuming the last ace is still in the deck, as are three each of the other three cards on the board that could pair and make my full. That means it's 35 to 10, or 3½ to 1, that I won't improve my hand. If the pot's laying me more than 3 to 1, I'd call. If not, I'd throw my hand away.

Of course, that formula only applies when you feel very strongly that your opponent has the flush made. If you think you could have the hand wrong and your opponent might have the second set of trips or some other hand, then you might call if the pot was laying you less odds. You could accept a smaller price because you have some doubts.

So much depends on your judgment in situations like that. This is especially true on the end. If I didn't make my full there and I was forced to call another bet, it would be completely up to my judgment.

When I discussed how I'd play my big pair when I flopped a full, I said that I'd almost always check it. I'd make an exception, though, if two of the cards on the flop were suited, or maybe even two to a straight. In that case, I would not check on the flop—I would bet. I'd be trying to get a man in there drawing to a flush and hoping that he makes it so I can break him. And if a flush card did come on fourth street, I'd bet, expecting and hoping to be raised.

I'd play the hand similarly if I had flopped a set and the board paired on the end, making my full and at the same time making a possible flush for somebody. Whenever you've got a full and a three-flush comes, it's exactly the situation you're looking for. You go ahead and bet—even an extraordinarily big bet—and you can break your opponent. You should not, by the way, bet as much with a three-card straight out there because your opponent may not have the nut straight. He may even be drawing. So in either case, if you've got him dead, you want him to play his straight if he made it or draw at it. And a very big bet might scare him off.

In the case where you flopped a set and the board pairs on fourth or fifth but there's no possible straight or flush out there—say the board is A♠ 6♥ J♣ J♦—you should lead with your full. Don't slow-play it. In fact, you should make a big bet, bigger than the size of the pot.

There's a good possibility that your opponent was calling you on the flop with the second pair or possibly the third pair. So when the board paired, it might've made him a strong hand, and you'd be in a position to break him. He'd probably play back if he made trips when the board paired. Also, knowing your aggressive style of play, he might think you're trying to represent his hand, and you might get a good play because of that.

But if a flush draw was out there on the flop and the pair on fourth didn't complete the flush, well, then I'd make a small bet, smaller than the size of the pot. I want him to call so he'll have an opportunity to make the flush on the last card.

But what if you don't make a big hand with two aces or kings? You'll have to play them very carefully in certain instances on fourth and fifth streets. For example, if there were three rags on the flop and then the board paired on fourth or fifth, I'd definitely slow down. This is not the same situation as when a pair came on the flop. When the pair shows after the flop, the possibility is much stronger that it helped your opponent. He's already called you on the flop, indicating that his cards fit into the community cards. His call clearly meant that he had something, so I'd be cautious again in that situation.

You are facing a somewhat different situation when there are four rags out there and the board pairs on fifth street. Exactly what I'd do depends on which card was paired and whether I had bet on the flop and on fourth. If the top card or possibly the second card paired, I'd suspect I might be beat. They'd be the two most dangerous pairs. If I had bet on the flop and on fourth street and the third or fourth highest card paired, I wouldn't be concerned.

Another time you should not be at all concerned is when the flop is say, 8-8-5 and then the third 8 falls on fourth or on the end. You just don't worry about quads. So actually your hand got stronger on fourth street. Before the third 8 showed, there was the nagging possibility your opponent had trips. That's far less likely now, and he's probably in there with an overpair.

A very tough situation could exist on fifth when there are four to a flush or straight, and you don't have any of it. With a big pair in that spot, it's back to judgment again. You have to evaluate what you think your opponent was drawing at and whether or not he's got one of the cards that would complete the straight or flush.

You should never bet in that situation. If he's first and he checks, you should just show it down. If you are first, you'd check it. If he bets, well, you're back to people. You'd just have to evaluate your player.

That situation brings to mind a play I often make. I've played a lot of pots against tight players when I've made a very weak call on fourth street, hoping the last card will make a four-card straight or flush on the board so I could represent the straight or flush by making a big bet. For example, my tight opponent has raised before the flop and I feel he has a big pair in the pocket. The situation might look like this:

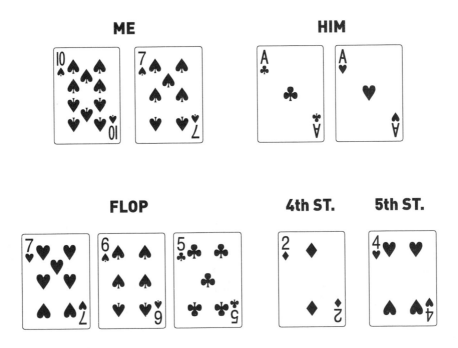

My opponent bets on the flop, and I call. The next card is the 2♦, and if my opponent bets again, I'll call—not because I think I have the best hand, but because of the tremendous bluffing opportunity I'll have if the last card is a 3, 4, 8, or 9. Any one of those four cards will mean the board is one card off of a straight. I'll almost certainly win the pot if, as in the example, a 4 fell on fifth and I represent the straight by making a substantial bet on the end.

There's also a chance that I'll catch a 10 or 7 on the end. I'd win a nice pot in that case as well, so I'm justified in calling on fourth street. I do a lot of gambling like that on fourth and on the end. And they're good gambles because I know a tight player wouldn't jeopardize all his money when one card would beat him.

It's not only tough for a tight player to make a call for all his money in a situation like that, it's tough for anyone to do it. But if you know your opponent, it does make it easier. If the straight or flush is made on fourth and fifth streets, a backdoor job, then you may want to reconstruct the play of the entire hand and try to determine whether that particular player would have gone as far as he did to make the hand. Of course, a lot of times a player will literally back into a hand like that. For example, he may have started with a small pair on the flop, picked up a straight or flush draw on fourth, and got there on the end without really trying.

With two aces or kings, you're going to have to use a lot of judgment when all the cards are out and your hand never got better. You'd have to go back to what you originally felt your opponent was drawing at on the flop and on fourth street. If you thought he made what he was drawing at on the last card, well, obviously, you'd check it, whether you were first or last to act. If you were first and you thought he was drawing at a hand and completely missed it, you'd still check. But this time you'd be doing it to give him an opportunity to bluff at it. If you were last and it looked like he missed his hand then he checked it to you, you'd just turn your hand over to avoid being wrong in your judgment. He's not going to call you if he missed his draw.

But if you put him on the wrong hand to begin with, you could get raised.

A-K

Before the Flop

A-K vs. A-A or K-K. I've already mentioned that I'd rather have A-K than either a pair of aces or a pair of kings. A lot of players will probably find that surprising. But it's not. You'll soon see why.

Of course, I know that an A-K would never outrun A-A or K-K if you played them against one another hot and cold. An A-K couldn't even beat a pair of deuces. I know from experience.

Once, on a proposition bet, I took the deuces and two other guys took the A-K. The proposition was to play the two hands against one another hot and cold. We simply dealt out five cards to see which hand would win more times. It was an even-money bet, and we bet $500 a hand. I won several thousand dollars before they quit. They weren't convinced the first time, so we did it two or three more times. They'd lose some money and quit. They'd go away, do some homework, come back, and then we'd do it again. And I'd beat them again.

But I'm not talking about playing hot and cold here. Now I'm talking about playing poker. An A-K is a better hand than two aces or two kings for two very important reasons:

(1) You'll win more money when you make a hand with it.

(2) You'll lose less money when you miss a hand with it.

And I can't think of two better reasons to choose an A-K over the very big pairs.

You can make more money with an A-K because it's a drawing type of hand as opposed to a made hand, like two aces or kings. I mean, you don't have anything with an A-K unless you hit something, so you can get away from it real easy. You're not tied on to it like you might be with a pair of aces or kings. And that's why you'll lose less money with it.

Furthermore, when you have A-K and you pair the ace or king on the flop, if your opponent is playing something like two connecting cards, it's much harder for him to make his hand than it would be if you had a big pair. For example, say you had two aces in the pocket, your opponent is playing a 7-6, and the board came 9-8-5, or any three cards that could help his hand, such as a pair and a draw. That one extra card considerably improves his chances of cracking your aces. On the other hand, say you have A-K, your opponent has 7-6, and the board comes A-9-8. In this case, he hasn't made anything yet because you've paired one of your holecards and now there are only two cards that will help him. Here's the exception to this rule: say the flop is three to a big straight with maybe two to a flush, like: A♠ J♥ 10♠ or K♦ J♦ 10♣. In this case, the ace or king helps both you and your opponent. Later on, we'll discuss why A-K is also a more flexible hand as far as how you can play it.

Suited vs. Offsuit. In the discussion to follow, the difference between the two hands is sometimes ignored. That is, I'm going to suggest playing them the same way. But you should always remember that A-K suited has more value than A-K offsuit and it can always be played a little stronger.

Anytime the cards are suited it's a somewhat stronger hand than when they're offsuit. This is especially true with A-K because you can make the nut flush. There's another big difference between A-K suited and A-K offsuit: with A-K suited it only takes three cards to make a flush. True, you can make one of two flushes with A-K offsuit, but it takes four cards to make either one. That's a lot harder to do. And even if you make the flush with the king, you might not have the nuts.

Flexibility. The reason why A-K is more flexible than A-A or K-K is that you can play an A-K in the lead or you can play it slow to raise with it. Also, I'd play A-K from any position for a reasonable size bet. And, on occasion, I'd get all my money in before the flop, as you'll see below.

Playing from Early Position. Specifically, in an early position, I'd raise the blind, bring it in, for whatever the normal bring-in is for that particular game. If I was raised, I'd probably call, although I don't like to call a raise with A-K, as most players do. I like to raise with it.

Playing from Middle Position. If I were in a middle position and someone else had brought it in, I'd just call with A-K. I wouldn't raise because I'd probably be raising just one man. I'd want at least one more player to come in.

Playing from Late Position. In a late position, I'd probably raise with it, especially if I were on the button.

Moving All-In. There are times I might even move all-in with an A-K. Let's say I brought it in from an early position, and a couple of people behind me just called. When it gets to the guy on the button, he raises. I'd think he was trying to pick up the pot since the two people behind me showed weakness. He's probably thinking the only person he had to come through is me, so I might move all here.

Or if I were on the button and three or four people were already in the pot, I might move all-in, trying to pick the pot up. At that point, I'd know that if I got called I'd probably be a slight underdog to a pair.

The Flop

As long as I don't help my A-K on the flop, I'm going to play the hand the same way regardless of whether or not the flop might've helped someone else. For example, if three rags, a pair, three to a straight or flush, or anything that does not help my hand flops, I play A-K quite simply. Barring one exception that I'll go into later, here's what I'd do:

(1) If I had been the bettor to start with or if I had been the raiser, I'd bet from any position.

(2) If I had called with A-K, I'd check.

(3) If there was a bet in front of me, I'd pass.

As I've already said, I play almost all my hands that way because if I was the bettor or raiser before the flop then I've represented a hand. So I'll bet on the flop regardless of what comes. I'll do it nine times out of ten.

You might have noticed that this is quite different from the way I'd play two aces or two kings. With either of those pairs in an early position, I'd check it if there were three to a straight or flush on the flop. Remember, I hear a bell ringing in that situation that reminds me not to bet. So if I've got a hand, like a pair in the pocket, I play it slow. But if I'm bluffing, I go ahead and play it fast, meaning I'll take one shot at it.

I do that because I know for sure I'm not going to go any further with an A-K if somebody plays back at me. If somebody plays back when I'm holding two aces or two kings, I've got a decision to make. But when I have nothing, I can bet A-K with confidence because I'm gone if I get raised. I just throw my hand away because there's nothing for me to think about. Now you can see why you're less likely to lose a big pot with A-K than with two aces or two kings.

When there's nothing on the flop that'll help me and I do go ahead and play the hand, I'll make a reasonable bet, somewhere in the neighborhood of the size of the pot. But as always, there are exceptions. On rare occasions, I'd revert back to the same philosophy I use with aces and kings. For example, if the fall was a J♥ 10♥ 9♥, I'd never bluff. I wouldn't even fool with the pot if only two of those cards were suited. You know somebody's going to have something. Here again, you have to use your judgment. It's an extreme situation.

This also explains why I'll bet on the flop 90 percent of the time but not every single the time if I played my hand strong before the flop. There are times when you know somebody must have flopped something. And bluffing at a pot in that situation will rarely succeed. So you just give it up.

If I get some help on the flop by catching an ace or a king, I'd make a reasonable bet at the pot from any position. The only time I might check-raise in this situation is when I had called in a middle position before the flop and the original raiser before the flop was behind me. When someone plays back at me in this situation I'll either move in or release my hand, depending on what flopped. In order for me to move in I'd have to think my opponent was drawing to his hand. For example, if the flop came A♣ 10♥ 9♥, I'd put him on a flush draw or maybe a straight draw, and I'd move in. Of course, if my opponent flopped three nines, he'd be in an ideal position to win a lot of money. It would look to me like he was drawing at a straight, flush, or both, and if he was lucky enough to have flopped a set, well, there's nothing magical I could do. I'd just have to go ahead and pay him off.

On the other hand, if it came off ragged, like a K♥ 8♠ 2♦, I might release my A-K, thinking that he possibly flopped a set.

If a pair of aces or kings flopped, giving me trips, and the other card is not one that'll give someone a straight or flush draw, I might check-raise. But I probably wouldn't because I like to lead with it. It's a very strong hand and as long as a pat hand, like a straight or a flush, can't be dealt off on the next card, I might give a free card in this situation so my opponent would have a chance to make something on fourth street. But I'd only give a free card if I were last to act. If I were first to act, I wouldn't. I would lead with that hand.

If I flopped two pair, aces and kings, I'd play them almost identically to trips. It's almost the same hand.

The important thing to remember is that anytime there's a possible draw on the flop, you should almost never check—you should almost always bet.

In the extremely rare case when I flop quads, I don't have any alternative, there's nothing else left, so I have to check it. If I bet, I could catch a man with a pair of queens or jacks, and he might accidentally pay me off. But realistically, I'd check it and hope that a 10, jack, or queen falls on fourth street and pairs someone. Then I'd bet hoping someone calls me with a full.

If a Q-J-10 flopped—giving me the nut straight—and I were the raiser, I'd lead again. Only this time it would not be a reasonable bet; it would be an abnormal size bet. I'd over-bet the pot when that flop came because somebody figures to have made something, like a smaller straight, possibly trips or two pair, or a pair and a straight draw. That's the type of hand most players move in with. So I'd probably get him to bet all his money, and he'd be almost dead.

If I were holding A-K and had called before the flop, I wouldn't slow-play it. I'd raise because the original raiser figures to have a hand that would fit the Q-J-10 flop. He could have two aces or two kings, three queens or three jacks, or a pair of queens with an ace or king kicker. He's liable to go all the way to fifth street if he has any one of those hands, and he'd get all his chips in the middle.

If the flop came J-10-2 and I have a belly-straight draw and two overcards with an A-K, I'd call a reasonable bet. I'd really be trying to catch a queen, because if I caught an ace or king, I'd have to be careful with it. An ace could make someone else a stronger hand than my own, say a straight or two pair.

But if I flop two of my flush cards when I have A-K suited, I have a very powerful hand. At that point, I'm a favorite over any overpair, with the exception of a pair of aces or kings. I'd lead with that hand, of course, and I'd also lead off and bet if I actually had a flush with A-K suited. I would not check-raise with my flush because my opponent doesn't figure to have made much on the flop. But he might call me with one pair, or he might accidentally have made a small flush. He might think I'm drawing to a flush, especially since I'm an aggressive player, and he might call me all the way through with just one pair.

Fourth and Fifth Streets

If I'm holding A-K and I make a pair on the flop, I'd play my hand on fourth and fifth streets almost the same way I'd play with a pair of aces or kings in the pocket. If I think my opponent made the hand he was drawing at, I'd check. If I don't think he made it, I'd bet.

However, I would make an exception if I thought I had my opponent out-kicked. That is, I might keep betting with A-K if I put my opponent on a hand that's a little bit worse than mine. For example, if I think he might've paired aces or kings with me but that he's got a smaller kicker, I'd bet the highest amount I think he'll call, hoping to sell my hand. I wouldn't try as hard to sell a pair of aces or kings in the pocket because he might've been drawing to beat them. If I've got A-K however, there's a good chance he's got the top card, an ace or king, paired with me but that my kicker or side card is higher.

The important point to remember is that unlike A-A or K-K, A-K is a drawing-type hand. It's therefore a much easier hand to get away from than the very big pairs.

Q-Q

I've put a pair of queens in a separate category for the simple reason that it's a hand that deserves special treatment. You'll soon see why.

When I get two queens in the pocket, I play them very carefully. I try not to play them too strongly from any position. Unless a good situation arises, I don't want to move in before the flop with two queens. A good situation would be one where I'm in a very late position, possibly on the button, and four people have called a raise in front of me. Here, I might try to shut them out by moving in. I'd use the combined strength of my pair of queens and my position.

If you're up against two aces or two kings with a pair of queens, you're about a 4 to 1 underdog. And if you're up against A-K, you're only a little better than a 6 to 5 favorite. When people go all-in before the flop they usually have one of those hands. So if you go all-in before the flop with two queens, your money is in a lot of jeopardy. If you get called, you're probably up against A-A, K-K, or A-K, in which case you'll be a big dog or just a small favorite. There are better spots to get all your money in.

That's not to say two queens don't have a certain amount of value. They do. They're considerably better than an average hand. But for the reason I just mentioned, I seldom raise back with a pair of queens from any position. But I will raise the blind a reasonable amount with two queens from any position if nobody else raised in front of me.

In a middle position, if somebody raised in front of me I'd just call, as I would with any pair. I'd just call with them in a late position, too. I wouldn't reraise, except in the situation mentioned above.

I also play two queens very slow on the flop, hoping to catch a third queen. If either an ace or a king comes on the flop, I'd play the hand as slowly as possible. If someone bets with any authority, I'd probably give him the pot. As long as an ace or king doesn't fall, I'd play two queens almost exactly the way I'd play two aces or two kings, and that includes the play on fourth and fifth streets.

In addition to the times when an ace or king flops, I'd play queens differently from two aces or kings when there's a flush draw on the flop. In that case, I wouldn't be eager to get all my money in. A man with a flush draw could also have an over-card, such as an ace or king. If he did, it would make his hand almost as strong as my Q-Q, as opposed to two aces or two kings against only a flush draw, either of which would be about a 9 to 5 favorite.

If you keep these differences in mind and make the right adjustments to your play, your approach with two queens on the flop, fourth, and fifth should be similar to your approach with aces or kings. In fact, you can play all pairs in the pocket in very much the same way, as you'll see.

Pairs Other Than Aces, Kings, and Queens

I'm going to refer to all the pairs from jacks down to deuces as small pairs, except when I name a particular pair. However, it should be obvious that the bigger the pair, the more valuable it is. And that principle extends all the way down to the very small pairs. That is, a pair of fours is better than a pair of treys for the simple reason that when the flop is 4-3-2, if someone flopped three fours he'd be a huge favorite, about 22 to 1, over someone who flopped three treys.

Furthermore, I mentally separate a pair of jacks, tens, or nines from the other small pairs and play them a little stronger. I do it simply because they are bigger pairs, and it's not unusual for three rags to fall. If that happens, you'll have an overpair. But if you've got two fives or two sixes, it's likely that the flop will have at least one overcard. And with an overcard out there, your hand is kind of dead, so you don't want to get too much money involved. Again, the higher the pair, the better, but I play them all as if they are small pairs.

Before the flop, with any of the small pairs except jacks, tens, and nines, I'd limp in. If somebody raised it from an early or middle position, I'd call it. I wouldn't reraise. I'd almost always take a flop with any small pair, hoping to flop a set so I could break somebody.

With a pair of jacks, tens, or nines, if somebody raised from an early position, I'd probably just call. But if it was raised from a middle or late position, I might reraise if I felt the raiser was weak. The reason I might do that is because the probability is good I'll have an overpair on the flop. In that case, I'd play nines, tens, and jacks just like I'd play two queens. The same strategy would apply.

However, I want to note a special exception I'd make in a very unusual situation. One of the reasons I like to play the small pairs from any position is because they give me an opportunity to slow down and not appear to be overbearingly aggressive when it might work against me. They also give me a chance to show a little respect for a particular opponent.

As you know, if I raise a pot before the flop, I'm going to bet on the flop about 90 percent of the time, no matter what it is. So if I raised the pot with two nines, I'd bet on the flop nine times out of ten. But let's say I'm in the pot with a guy I've been pounding on and pounding on all night long. And that guy's a real good player who I know is getting very tired of me pounding on him. I also know I've probably got him beat. But rather than bet him out of the pot, I'm going to purposely slow down against him. An example will best show you what I mean and explain why I do it.

Let's say I've got two nines and I raise my opponent before the flop. He calls. The flop comes 10-2-3, and he checks it. I check along. Another rag falls off on fourth street. He checks again. Now, I'm reasonably sure my two nines are the best hand. But I'm not going to bet it. I'll check along with him to show him some respect. The board's awful looking and I'm pretty sure he doesn't have any of it. I'm also quite sure that if I bet I'm not going to get called. So I don't bet.

It has nothing to do with feeling sorry for the man because if I thought there was a good chance he'd call me, I'd surely bet. But instead of pushing him out of the pot once more and getting him hotter than he is, I check along with him to cool him off a little. Remember, he's a real good player. And although I'm quite sure he won't call me, I'm not so sure he won't play back and put pressure on me when I've got a hand that can't stand much pressure.

What's more, if he doesn't put some kind of play on me in this pot, he could do it at any time. If I keep pushing him out of every pot, sooner or later he's going to stop sticking his head up, and I won't be able to slap him anymore. Then he's going to make me guess. I don't want that. I don't want him to start getting aggressive. That's the hardest player in the world to beat, a guy who you bet at and who's always playing back at you. That's exactly the kind of opponent I don't want to play against. I want all my opponents to be docile.

So it kind of cools him out when I just show down a hand. He knows that I know my two nines are the best hand. But by not betting them, I show him some respect. And because I showed the hand down, I've got him back to thinking that when I bet I'm either bluffing or I've got a hand I'm going to go with. He's back to guessing again. And that's exactly where I want him. I don't want to antagonize him to the point that he starts making me do the guesswork. It serves a lot of purposes to slow down in a situation like that.

A short time later, I might pick up another pair of nines, tens, or jacks in a very late position or on the button, and I might raise with it again. This time, he might play back at me. If he does, he'd get the pot. I'd give the pot to anyone who reraised me before the flop.

I'd never stand a reraise when I have a small pair before the flop. I won't take any pressure with them. If someone puts a play on me, I throw them away. But if I don't get reraised, I'm back to my basic style of play. If I were the raiser, I'd go ahead and bet on the flop. Just about any flop. If I raised with two tens and a 7-3-2 flopped, I'd bet for sure since I've got an overpair. However, the only time my pair is of any real value is when I flop a set.

Nevertheless, I'd still bet if I was the raiser, even if three overcards flopped. Even if I was sure a guy had a bigger pair on that flop, and even if I was almost sure I'd get called, I'd still bet. I'd be giving him the courtesy of a bet because there's an outside chance I could pick that pot up. And it wouldn't be a small bet. It would be a reasonable bet. He'd be looking for me to bet, and I don't want to disappoint him. It would hurt my table image.

I'll do that 90 percent of the time. In this case, I'll take one stab at the pot and if I don't get it there, I'll try to check it out from there on. I'd make an exception if I put a guy on a draw. In that case, he's going to have to pay to make his hand. If I got raised, I surely wouldn't go any further with the hand.

I play small pairs cautiously and try to win small pots with them. I won't put a lot of chips in the pot unless I flop trips. And when I don't make trips with a small pair, whenever I bet, I'm bluffing from then on.

Playing Small Pairs with No Help on the Flop

If I had called a raise before the flop and the raiser bet on the flop, unless I flopped a set, I'd probably surrender the pot. That's especially true if an overcard flopped. So right there, you can see the strength of being the raiser. He made me lay down my hand. That's why I like to be the raiser.

When you don't help your small pair on the flop, it's important points to remember these points:

(1) If you just called before the flop, you're through with them, and you don't put any more money in the pot from then on.

(2) If you raised with them, you should generally try to win a small pot by betting on the flop. But if you get called, you don't want to bet again on fourth and fifth, and you should try to play showdown without any more betting from that point on—unless you think your opponent is on a draw, in which case you continue betting.

(3) If you get raised, you throw away your hand.

Playing Small Pairs When You Flop a Set

It's a different situation entirely when you flop a set. That's what you played for. And you should play them fast. That's what I do, in almost all cases. I don't always raise with them, but I never check them. Needless to say, if I was the raiser and I flopped a set, I immediately bet right out. As you know, I wouldn't need a set to do that. However, I would make an exception if I was in the pot with a very weak player, and he was the only opponent I had. I'd check in this case.

Say I had called before the flop, then I flop trips. If someone checks it to me and there are people behind me, I'll always bet.

As you know, one of my favorite plays in hold'em is to lead right into the raiser with trips or even two pair, especially when I think he's got a big pair in the hole. I over-bet the pot right there, and if the raiser has what he represented, a big pair, he'll almost invariably go ahead and move in on me.

I'd make that play when I've got a small pair, say threes, and the flop is 10-7-3. I lead into the raiser, thinking he's got an overpair in the pocket. But a better flop would be one with a face card, say Q-10-3. Now the raiser's got to have some kind of combination with a flop like that. If he's got two aces or two kings and he's any kind of a player, he's got to raise. If he's got A-Q, he'll probably raise with that too. If he's got K-Q he'll probably call. If he's got a straight draw he'll call, and it's possible that he'll raise. So I lead right off into him. If he's fortunate enough to have my hand beat, well, again, there's nothing magical I can do about it. I'll have to pay him off.

If someone had called in front of me and bets on the flop when it comes like A-8-3 and I put him on a pair of aces, I'd probably play my three threes slowly. I wouldn't want to take him out of the lead.

Another time I start over-betting the pot on the flop is when I make the underfull, such as when the flop comes 9-9-4 and I've got two fours in the pocket. Well, I start making big bets right there because the only way I'm going to win any money with my hand is by catching somebody with a 9 or catching somebody with a big pair who calls or even raises me. I want to be sure there's enough money involved so I can win a big pot. And, to be sure of that, I've got to lead with my hand.

Note that you play the underfull different from the way you'd play the big full. If you remember, you play the big full by checking on the flop because you'd have the deck crippled. In this case, you want to give a free card to your opponent so he can catch up.

Are there times when you might release a set on the flop? Yes, but they're rare. It's very hard to turn this hand loose. However, there is a situation in which you might save some money. Say you have a small set, and you bet on the flop. There's a man in a late position who didn't raise it before the flop, so it's unlikely that he has a big pair in the pocket. Now, he makes a very strong play after the flop. I mean, he moves all-in and puts your entire stack in jeopardy. At that point, you might be able to determine that he's got a set, and you might be able to get away from your hand. But it's very difficult. In a high-stakes game, I almost never do it.

If you flop a set in a raised pot, it's practically impossible to get away from it. If the pot wasn't raised, conceivably, you could put a man on a bigger set than you've got. But if the pot was raised originally, it's just impossible to release a set.

If I raised it before the flop, then flop a set and get beat, well, my opponent is going to win a real big pot from me. If we don't get it all-in on the flop, we'll surely be all-in after fourth street.

Small Connecting Cards

Before the Flop

This is the hand I'm looking for when I play no-limit hold'em: small, suited connecting cards, such as 7♣ 6♣, 8♥ 7♥, and 5♦ 4♦. That's the kind of hand I want. It's my favorite. And when I get it, I want my opponent to have two aces or two kings and to believe that he should play them slow. If he does, he'll give me the opportunity to get a flop. And if I do, I can break him.

Exactly such a situation occurred in the 1977 World Series of Poker. It was definitely the most important and memorable pot of the tournament, bigger and more important than the pot I played with Bones, which I mentioned earlier. Not only did I win it, but I eliminated two very tough opponents. Here's what happened:

At this stage of the tournament, the ante was $200 and there were blinds of $300 and $600. Junior Whited had the big blind for $600. Buck Buchanan limped in for the six hundred. "Sailor" Roberts passed. Bones was next, and he made it $3,500 to go. I called, and so did Milo Jacobson. When it got back to Junior, he went all-in for $11,300. Buck was now looking at two raises: Bones's $2,900 and Junior's $8,400. He called, as did Bones. And so did I. Milo passed. It was a big pot already and destined to get bigger.

The flop was 5♣ 7♦ 7♠.

FLOP

Fourth street was A♠ and fifth street was 4♣.

4TH St.   5th St.

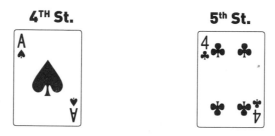

Junior was already all-in so Buck was first to act on the flop. He moved all-in with a huge bet. Bones passed, so it was up to me. Buck could've made his move and shut me out before the flop. He would've picked-up $26,500 had he done so. Now it was too late. I had him. There was no doubt in my mind about that. So I asked the dealer to count down his bet. It was $45,400. I shoved in four-and-a-half 20-chip stacks of $500 grays and four $100 black chips. I was the only one who had any chips left so we all turned our hands over.

BUCK   JUNIOR   ME

Buck had K♥ K♣, Junior had K♠ Q♥, and I had 7♣ 6♣. As you can see, when all the cards were out, the pot was mine. It was the only time in the tournament that two players were eliminated in the same pot—and two very tough ones at that.

In order to win that $142,500 pot, I had to gamble almost $12,000 with those small connecting cards before the flop. I'd do it again. I always do it when there's an opportunity for me to win a real big pot.

Buck and Junior had almost exactly the hands I thought they had. And when Buck made his move on the flop, I was certain he had a pair of kings or aces. He couldn't have had anything else.

If Buck had played his hand the way I recommend, he would've won a relatively small pot. As it was, he lost a big one, which is too often the case with two aces or two kings. If you recall, I stated earlier that with a pair of aces or kings in an early position before the flop, I would probably limp in, hoping somebody would raise it behind me so I could reraise. Buck got the first part right. If he'd followed the second part and raised Junior, I never would've played my hand.

That's the whole thing about the small connecting cards. I'll come in with them in an early or middle position. I might come in for the first bet or, as you've seen, even the second if I think I can win a real big pot. I probably won't raise with this kind of hand because I don't want to get shut out of the pot. If I raise and somebody else reraises, I probably won't be able to play it. Or if I have to call a double-raise cold, I probably won't be able to play it there either. There are always exceptions, but in general, I play the hand in order to get a flop with it.

For the most part, you don't want to put a whole lot of money in the pot with small connecting cards before the flop. It's best to take a lot of flops with these hands. You want to get a flop, hoping to make a little straight, a little set of trips, a little two pair, and so on.

With any two cards to a straight flush, connected or not—except for the top and bottom cards of a straight-flush, such as the 8♣ 4♣ or J♥ 7♥—I'd come in from any position. In a late position, I'd raise with them. When I come in with this hand in an early or middle position I'm really looking to get raised. In fact, I'm hoping someone has a big pair in the hole and raises behind me. Then I can put a relatively small amount of additional money in the pot, and if I get a flop, I can break him.

The beautiful part about having the small connecting cards is that if I don't get any help, I throw them away. If the flop comes 9-9-2, for example, I don't get involved with a 7-6. I'm through.

Normally, I wouldn't want to get more than 5 percent, maybe 10 percent, of my money involved before the flop with this type of hand. I'd only get as much as 20 percent of my money in with that hand if I was rushing. I wouldn't do it unless I was on a streak.

There are also times when I might raise from early or middle position with something like a 7-6. I noted that I generally just call. But if the tempo of the game were just right, I'd raise in an early or middle position.

For example, if I were winning a lot of pots, I'd do it. I said that I usually play the next pot after I win a pot, regardless of what position I'm in. And when I play that pot, I usually raise it. Also, if the game had tightened down to the point where everybody was playing the nuts, I'd shoot it up with a couple of small connecting cards.

Of course, you always try to keep from getting reraised with that hand. So, the ideal situation is when you think your muscle will keep anyone from playing back and will make your opponents think you've probably got big cards or a big pair.

I raise with this hand in a late position because I don't think I'll get reraised. Also, since nobody's raised in front of me, I'll be able to use some deception. I usually don't raise in an early position because I'd have to go through six or seven players without getting reraised. With a lot of top players in the game, that's not likely. Also, I like to be in the lead, and if I make something with it, I can take charge. So with players behind me, I usually call with it.

In this situation, I don't have to maintain my table image by betting on the flop when I'm the raiser. If I just called before the flop and somebody else raised, I very seldom try to pick up the pot or bluff into the raiser. The raiser commands respect. So when I miss that hand completely and somebody else raised it, well, it's his pot. That's why I generally like to be the raiser.

I don't like to raise with small connecting cards because when somebody has the hand I want him to have, such as a big pair, he's going to raise me back. That's one more reason I usually limp-in with them. When I limp in with this hand in an early position, I'm actually playing it like I would two aces or two kings, so there's also a bit of deception there. And if somebody raises in a middle or late position, I can pretty well put them on a hand—big cards like A-K, K-Q, or a big pair. That's what I'm looking to do. I want to be able to put somebody on a hand so I know what I'm trying to beat.

If you play in the style I recommend, very aggressively, you'll have to adjust your play in a small game. You'll probably discover that you get reraised more often when you raise in a small game than you will in a big game. That's been my experience.

Here's why: if I'm in a game where there's not much money on the table—say, everybody has $5,000 or $6,000—and I raise it $1,000, well, a guy with big cards is going to move in on me. It happens all the time in a small game. And when I've got a 7-6 or a 9-8 and someone bets the rest of his money at me, I can't call it. When I can't win anything if I get a flop, I'm not going to take two small connecting cards and try to beat two kings, A-K, and so forth. In a case like that, I throw my hand away. And because of that, I have trouble winning in a game where there's not much money on the table.

But it's a totally different story in a big game. If I raise it $3,000 or $4,000 and the other guy and I have a lot of chips on the table, he'll be a little more hesitant about raising me now because he knows there's a very good chance I'll play back. The guys I play with know that when I put my children out there, I don't like to let them drown.

But even if I do get reraised in this situation, it's all right. In fact, it's what I want. If he raises me $7,000 or $8,000 and I've got small connecting cards, I'll call now. If we've both got $250,000 in front of us, then I'm only putting in about five percent of my money. And it's worth it, because now I've got a chance to win something if I get a flop. I might be able to break him.

The Flop

Playing When You Miss Your Hand Completely. If I called in an early position with small connecting cards and I miss my hand completely, I give the pot up. I don't go ahead in that situation with that type of hand. I just surrender. The first loss is the best loss in a situation like that. But of course, if I was the raiser, I would go ahead and bet at the pot. As long as there wasn't something frightening out there like the Q♠ J♠ 10♠, I'm going to bet. And most of the time nothing frightening will be out there.

If I was rushing and had a 7♦ 6♦ in an early position, I'd probably raise it before the flop. Then, if the A♥ A♣ K♠ flopped, I'd bet right out. A flop like that wouldn't frighten me. Why? It's simple. My opponents don't know that I don't have A-K, A-Q, K-K, or any hand that would benefit from that flop. They don't know what I've got. In fact, if I raised in an early position on the pre-flop, they might think I have a hand with big cards.

If I had raised it from a middle position before the flop, I'd bet, unless someone bet in front of me. In that case, the pot is his. I'd know my opponent has something, and when I've got nothing with this kind of hand, I'm usually not going to try to make any great play, although occasionally I will bluff at it.

If I was a caller before the flop in a middle or late position and it was checked to me on the flop, I'd check along. As long as I didn't make anything, it would probably have to be checked to me twice, on the flop and fourth street, before I'd make a bet, which would be a bluff.

Of course, if I had raised it before the flop from a late position, I'd almost always bet, particularly if it was checked around to me. I'd bet even if the flop was A♥ A♣ K♠, as noted before, and it was probable that one of my opponents had an ace. I'd do it because I don't want my opponents to get out of the habit of checking to me. Since I was the raiser they expect me to bet. So I go ahead and make a courtesy bet for them. When I make that bet, I'm trying to do two things:

(1) Win the pot right there. And I will many a time because my opponents get into the habit of throwing their hands away.

(2) Maintain my aggressive image. As long as I do, they'll continue to check it to me.

That's the way I pick up all the pots I do. Of course, if I get check-raised, I'm out immediately. That's the risk I take. But a guy really has to have a hand before he'll put a play like that on me. So when he does, I let him have the pot. But they miss their hands more often than they make them. Because of that, I pick up more pots than I give up.

Fourth and Fifth Streets

Playing When You Miss Your Hand Completely. If I didn't improve on the flop, I wouldn't be in there on fourth street with small connected cards unless I was the bettor or the pot was checked to me and I checked it as well.

If someone had called my bet after having checked it to me on the flop, I would immediately put him on some kind of hand. If I thought he was on a drawing hand and it looked like he missed it on fourth, I'd bet again. If I thought he had a made hand—regardless of how weak I thought it was, even as weak as the third pair—I wouldn't try to make him throw away his hand on fourth if he called me on the flop and had, therefore, already committed himself to the pot. For example, say the flop was a K-8-2 and I tried to pick it up but got called. Well, then I'd try to check it out all the way through. At that point, I'd be giving up the pot at a minimum loss.

And, once again, if I thought my opponent was on a drawing hand, like two cards to a straight-flush, and I get check-raised after making another stab at the pot on fourth, I'm almost always going to give it up.

I'm never going to call a bet when I miss my hand completely, but in an extreme situation, I might play back at a guy who I think is putting a play on me. For example, if I was completely convinced a guy was trying to take the pot away from me, I'd re-play at him. But I'd have to feel strongly, about it before I'd jeopardize a bunch of chips in that spot.

My play on fifth street would be just like my play on fourth. If I'm still betting at the pot, I'd have to continue because it's almost impossible for me to win in a showdown. Assuming I didn't pair on the end, I'd have only a 7-high. Since I'd put my opponent on a draw on fourth and that's why I bet there, I'd have to feel that he didn't make it when all the cards were out. I'd also have to feel very strongly he wouldn't call my last bet. Naturally, if I felt like he completed his hand, I'd check.

This is a tough spot on the end, but you just can't leave all your money out there without one last stab at the pot. The key to what you'd do on fifth is very much based on your opinion of why your opponent called you on fourth. You'd have to feel pretty sure he was drawing, or you could get yourself in a lot of trouble.

You might find it difficult to continue betting your hand

when you know you don't have anything. You may think it takes a lot of courage to do that, and it does. But it's really just good poker. You'll discover, if you use my system of play, that your opponents will be scared to give you free cards whenever they've got a hand, because they know you might be drawing at an inside straight and betting with it. They know an aggressive player is liable to show them anything. Consequently, when they get a hand, they want to shut you out right then. They bet because they don't want you in the pot drawing at them.

So there are really two good reasons to play aggressively in this situation:

(1) If your opponents do have a hand, they'll show you right away. They don't want to keep giving you free cards.

(2) Your continuous betting makes them throw away borderline hands so you can pick up the pot when they don't have anything.

Quite simply, an aggressive player has by far the best of it.

Playing When You Make Something. I'm now going to discuss how I'd play small connecting cards when I flop something with them. The hand I'm going to use as an example throughout this discussion is a 7♦ 6♦. You'll learn how I'd play when I get:

(1) a poor flop (slightly helpful);

(2) a fair flop (moderately helpful); and

(3) a good flop (very helpful).

Poor Flop

When I've got a 7♦ 6♦ and a Q♠ 6♥ 2♣ falls, I'd consider that a poor flop to my hand, and I'd play it similarly to the way

I'd play if I got no help. However, there's one big difference. Depending on my opponent and, more importantly, how much money he had on the table, I'll gamble with the second pair—a pair of sixes, in this case—or even the third pair as long as the guy I was up against was sitting on a lot of checks. I'd do it even if I knew he had a pair of queens. If I thought I could break him if I caught another 6 or a 7, I'd call a reasonable bet and might even put as much as 10 percent of my money in the pot. I'd surely do it if I thought I could win a gigantic pot.

I might even raise. I'll always consider raising, whether I have caught a small piece of the flop, a pair of sixes in this case, or completely missed my hand. But that has nothing to do with the value of my hand. I'd do it because I detected a weakness in somebody or to take advantage of my position. Another difference in the way I'd play this hand when I got a little help on the flop and none on fourth or fifth is that I'd continue to bet on fourth if I was the original raiser. You'll recall that even if I missed this hand completely, I'd bet it on the flop as long as I was the raiser. But if my bet on the flop was called, I'd try to check it out from then on, unless I thought my opponent was drawing.

Now that I've gotten a little help on the flop, however, I'd bet again on fourth despite the fact that my bet on the flop was called. I don't like to keep betting when I'm on a complete bluff, but I do like to keep betting when I've got an out. In this case, I know that if I catch that other 6 or a 7, I'd likely have a stronger hand than my opponent. So I wouldn't show any weakness with my hand on fourth street. I'd go ahead and make a reasonable bet.

If I still didn't get any help on fifth street, I'd probably stop betting. If my opponent was drawing and he didn't make his hand, I'd know that my pair of sixes is more than likely good, so I'd check. And if they aren't good, there's no sense in losing any more money with them.

If I happen to get some additional help on fourth, such as a 7, well, then I'd make an oversized bet, one that's larger than what's in the pot. I'm always out to win a big pot, and now I'd have a hand to do it with. I wouldn't try to sell my hand for a small amount of money. I'd make a very big bet on fourth, and a very big bet on fifth.

If I didn't catch that 7 until the end, then I might try to sell it on fifth street for whatever I thought I could get.

Whether I caught the 7 on fourth or fifth, I'd play a hand this way only if I was the original raiser coming in and I stayed in the lead by betting on every turn of the cards.

Assuming I was a caller coming in and had checked and called on the flop, I'd play the hand differently if I caught a 7 on fourth street. If there was a lot of money in the pot, this is another one of the few times I'd check-raise. I wouldn't want to take my opponent, the original raiser, out of the lead, especially if I know the size of the pot will make him bet again on fourth and since he'd have no idea the 7 helped me. He'd surely try to shut me out, and when he bets, I'd raise him. I'd want to win the pot right there, because if a queen or deuce comes on the end, the board will pair, killing my two pair.

If I caught a 6 on fourth street, my strategy would be different still. The two sixes on the board would look very threatening, so my hand would be harder to conceal than if I caught a 7. So, even if I had been a caller up to this point, there's a good chance I'd take the lead and bet when the 6 hit. And even though the raiser should see that I might have three sixes, he might also think I am just representing them. If you didn't have a 6 in the hole, this would be a very good opportunity to bluff at the pot.

Fair Flop

Now I'll discuss how I'd play that 7♦ 6♦ if I got what I'd call a fair or moderately helpful flop—any three cards that gave me the top pair, an open-end straight draw, or a flush draw.

I play flush draws extremely slow because they're so obvious. When two of the same suit flop, I see so many players who are drawing to a flush move in on a guy after he bets. Occasionally, I do it too, because my philosophy is to protect my money and bet whenever I can. But it's usually a very obvious play. Most players will put you on a flush draw in that situation.

For that reason I like a straight draw better, and I play it fast. If I get that straight draw, well, I'm ready now. I mean, really ready. The battle is on. If I was the original raiser, of course, I'd bet on the flop. If I got raised, I'd play back and move all my chips in. If somebody bet in front of me, I'd raise 'em.

If I wasn't the original raiser, I'd check-raise. If the guy who raised it before the flop bet after I checked, I'd raise with most or all of my chips. I'd be the aggressor at that point and nobody would be able to take me out of the lead from then on.

As I said earlier, most decisions are made on the flop. I mean, that's where you steal pots. So I'd play my hand this way because this is a situation where I typically steal a lot of pots. I'd be bluffing with an out. I could win the pot right there. If I got called, I'd have a good draw—an open-end straight, which I'd make about 33 percent of the time—and a small chance to back-door two pair or trips.

Now, say the flop comes 6-4-2 or 7-4-2, giving me the top pair. In this case, I'd play it cautiously. I'm not going to fall in love with that hand, but I'll gamble a little with it. In other words, I'd check to the raiser, and then I'd probably call. If I were in a late position and hadn't raised originally, I'd call if somebody bet. But it would be a weak call, meaning that I probably wouldn't go any further with the hand if I don't get any help on fourth and somebody bets at me again.

One of the reasons I'd call on the flop is that my pair might be the best hand. Just because the other guy raised it originally doesn't mean he has a big pair in the pocket. So there's a possibility that I've got the best hand right now. I'd learn more from his play on fourth street. If I didn't help my hand and he bet again, I'd get rid of it pretty fast. I wouldn't invest a lot of money with that hand without any help.

But the main reason I'd call on the flop is the possibility that I could win a big pot if I improve my hand and beat a strong hand, such as two aces or two kings. And I check rather than bet because I might have the best hand and I don't want to get shut out by betting and being raised. Then, I'd have to throw my hand away. By checking, I could call a reasonable bet and try to catch a card. If I did improve on fourth, I'd play it from then on just like if I took a poor flop but got some help on fourth.

A good or even a great flop to a 7♦ 6♦ would be a pair with a straight or flush draw, two pair, trips, a straight, or a flush—even though it's a small one. With any good flop to small connecting cards, I play the hand as if it is complete, even if it's not. I'd lead with the hand in an early position, and I'd raise in a late position. I'd play the hand to get all my money in the center to start with.

Even if I flopped a pair with a draw, I'd use the same strategy since I'd have two chances to win it:

(1) I bet or raise and my opponent throws his hand away; or

(2) I improve and my bet or raise is called.

If you follow my advice here, you'll be in some jeopardy, even when you get a very good flop. But you're almost always in some jeopardy, so you can't worry about somebody having the nuts all the time. If you did, you would never get to play a pot.

For example, if you and your opponent both flopped a flush, yours will likely be the smaller of the two, and you'd be dead. In hold'em, there's no way you can draw out when it's flush-against-flush, unless you're drawing to a straight flush. But assuming you can't get a straight flush, you'll just have to lose your money, because you'll almost always have to pay your opponent off. It's one of the hazards of the game.

You could also flop the ignorant or low end of the straight. But this is also hazardous, since your opponent could turn a bigger straight. And again, if your opponent bet anything within reason, you'll have to go ahead and pay him. For example, if the flop was a 10-9-8 and somebody moved all-in on you, you'd be down to judgment. You'd have to know your opponent, and a lot would depend on how much is in the pot and the amount he sets you in for. If you've got $1,000 in the pot and he bets you $50,000 more, well, perhaps, you wouldn't go for it and you'd throw your hand away. But if you've got $1,000 in the pot and he bets you $2,000 more—all your money, or all his money—then you'd surely pay it off. If you're beat, you're beat. That happens a lot, by the way. And it's why hands like K-9 and J-7 are considered trash and shouldn't be played in a normal ante ring game.

Good Flop

If I've caught good on the flop, I'll already be committed to the pot, so I'll bet on fourth street, as long as I am first or it is checked to me. But as always, there are exceptions.

For example, if you flopped a diamond flush and another diamond came on fourth street, your hand would be almost ruined. All you'd have is a 7-high flush. At that point, you must check your hand and hope to show it down. If you can't show it down, you've got to throw it away if there's any kind of betting.

Or, if you flopped a straight and the board pairs on fourth street, you could be in trouble. Usually, that shouldn't stop you because if a man had flopped a set or two pair, he would've raised you. So if he made a full when the board paired, you'd have to pay him off. Another hazard.

As you continue to use my system of play, you'll discover the many advantages it has. The situation above is a good example. If the flop came 5-4-3, giving me a straight, my opponent would've let me know on the flop whether or not he had a hand, such as two pair or trips. If he's a good player he would, because he wouldn't want another card to fall that might be one card off of a straight. He knows if an ace, deuce, 6, or 7 comes on fourth, he's going to have to give the pot up. He knows I'll bet in that case, even if I don't have the one card that'll make the straight.

For that reason, all good hold'em players do most of their gambling on the flop, not on fourth and fifth streets. Occasionally, you'll see a big pot played after the turn, but in the majority of cases, all the money goes in on the flop. That's why the flop is the most crucial point in the game.

Earlier I stated that it's quite inconceivable to me that anybody could get away from their hand if they flopped a set of trips in a raised pot. At that point, I was talking about a hidden set, a pair in the pocket and one on the board. It's a different matter entirely when the pair is on the board and I have one of the matching cards in the hole. I've released a lot of sets in a situation like that. For example, say I have a 7-6 and the flop is 7-7-2. I bet and get called. There aren't really very many hands someone can call me with. So it's easy to release a set in this case, because when you get a lot of money involved you know the guy who's in there with you probably has a 7 also. This is especially true if he's the aggressor.

So you have to evaluate your kicker. I mean, what's it worth? The conclusion I usually reach is that it's not worth very much. If I really think he's got a 7 then I know the best I could hope for is a tie. Of course, I'm talking about a good player, and it's much more likely he's got me beat. He's probably in there with a 7 and a higher card that he could've flopped a straight with, such as an 8-7, 9-7, or 10-7. Another possibility is that he's got a high card, such as an ace or king, that's suited. He might have a 7-6, like I do, or a 7-5, the only likely hand I could beat. But it's almost inconceivable that he's in there with a 7-4, 7-3, or 7-2, although this last one would give him a full.

So when I got down into the hand and I gave him credit for the other 7 because he was showing a whole lot of speed, I couldn't continue playing my 7 with a small connecting card. And I'd release that set quite readily. I'd do it real quick.

When I have a set like that with a different kicker, I make another evaluation. If my kicker was slightly bigger, say a 9 or 10, I'd probably play it. If I had a suited ace or king, then I'd definitely go ahead and play it.

Of course, there are times when I might not release my hand after flopping a set with that 7-6. For example, say I raised with the hand before the flop, and everybody checks it to me on the flop. Then I bet, and one of my opponents plays back (check-raises). In this situation, I might go ahead with my hand, figuring that the guy is trying to shut me out. It's possible that he is playing back with an overpair or some other hand that he might not have raised me with before the flop.

On the other hand, say I held a 7-6 in late position and had called a small raise before the flop. Now, if the flop comes 7-7-2, I would not give the raiser credit for a 7. And I'd probably play my hand real fast trying to win a big pot.

Whenever there's a raise before the flop, there's a chance you can win a big pot. But in an unraised pot, it's hard to win a big one. Previously, I noted that you don't want to get broke in a nothing pot. I'm reminding you of that now because you might be tempted to try and win a big pot when you flop a set with small connecting cards in an unraised pot. You shouldn't. If I don't have anything in the pot to protect, I never jeopardize very much money without a real good hand. I don't go out of my way to win nothing pots.

Another important part of my playing philosophy I want to remind you about is this: You should constantly be trying to get as much value for your hand as you can. And the way you do that is by betting. That should be clear by now. You become a big winner at poker by betting, raising, and reraising—by playing aggressively. Of course, there are times you have to play defensively, when an aggressive strategy would be wrong because it could get you shut out of a pot. But in general, you want to be aggressive.

That means you can't let every card that hits the board threaten you. As I said, if you're always worrying about somebody having the nuts, you never will get to play a hand. This applies to all the hands I've discussed, but it's especially meaningful when it comes to playing small connecting cards when you get a good flop. That's what you're playing them for in the first place. So when you make something with them, you want to get value for them. So you should always apply this principle: If you're going to call, you might as well bet.

You should do that at all the stages of play, but it's particularly important on the end because you'll get paid off with hands that aren't what you thought they were. I mean, there'll be many times you'll put your opponent on a hand completely different than what he's got. I'm not Kreskin, and neither are you. You might think a man is drawing to a flush, but maybe he's got a pair, just one pair. He might have been running you down with a lot less than you thought he had. So, when a flush card hits the board on fifth street, it may not have helped him at all. I mean, you'll know he's got something when that flush card comes, either the flush you thought he was drawing at or some other piece of the flop. Or maybe he's got two pair and you've got a straight. You really don't know what he's got. But you've got a good hand with your small connecting cards, so you're going to pay it off anyway. Therefore, you might as well bet.

The only time I make an exception is when the board pairs on the end. Then I'll check it, and may or may not call, depending on how I feel about the situation. But assuming that doesn't happen, if I've made a real good hand with my small connecting cards, I'd go ahead and bet.

Although there are times when I might be a little concerned because I don't have the nuts, there will also be times when I do have the nuts. Naturally, in that case, I'll do whatever I think will get the most money in the pot. If I thought my opponent had a strong hand, I'd make a big bet. If I thought he had a weak hand, I'd try to sell my hand by making a smaller bet. I'll have to use careful judgment here, judgment about what I think he's got.

My decision on how much to bet depends on whether I made my hand early (on the flop) or late (on the end).

If I made my hand early, I'm not going to try to sell him anything. I'm going to try to break him.

If I made my hand late and I haven't been charged a lot of money to make it—say it was checked on the flop, there was a small bet on fourth, and I made the nuts on the end—well, then I'm not going to try to break him because he probably won't call a big bet. I'd try to sell my hand for whatever I thought I could get for it.

Those of you who are new to no-limit hold'em may not be able to appreciate how strongly I feel about the small connecting cards. And those of you who are experienced players are probably quite surprised. But that's where it's at, in my opinion. You have to use your good judgment when you play the small connecting cards. When you play them right, they're big money makers. And that's what no-limit hold'em is all about.

Borderline or Trouble Hands

You should commit to memory the list of trouble hands I list below. I call them trouble hands because that's exactly what they are, and I only play them in borderline situations.

Before I get to the list, it's important that you realize that trouble hands aren't necessarily unplayable if:

(1) They are suited; and

(2) They are dealt to me in a shorthanded game, one with four players or less. In a later section, I'll go over why in a shorthanded game, these trouble hands are actually big hands.

But in a ring game, these are hands you can lose a lot of money with, so you should play them cautiously. You don't want to jeopardize much money with them.

Trouble Hands (only when offsuit)

A-Q	A-J
A-10	K-Q
K-J	K-10
Q-J	Q-10
J-10	9-8

I call these borderline hands because I'd question calling a raise with them. If they're suited, I'll call a raise with them and take a flop. If they're not suited and I'm out of position, I won't call a raise. By out of position I mean that I'm in a middle position and a man in an early position came in raising. I'll pass these hands in that spot.

If I'm in a late position, the pot's been raised, and another man calls, well, then I'll usually call with them—but, I'll hear another bell ringing when I do. This time, that bell will be reminding me to play my hand with extreme caution, unless I get an excellent flop to it.

The reason why you have to be so careful with every one of those hands is that you might be up against a hand where you'd be almost dead. Most players consider A-A, K-K, or A-K to be the best raising hands, so there's a good possibility the raiser has one of those three hands. True, you can't always assume that, but it's always in the back of your mind. So, if you've got A-Q, A-J, or A-10, and you're up against A-A, K-K, or A-K, you've got a terrible hand.

It's extremely hard to win a big pot with these hands when you've called a raise. They're definitely trouble hands. You're much more likely to lose a big pot with them than you are to win a big pot. Even when I make a pair with them on the flop, I play them extremely cautiously, or about the same way I'd play a pair of aces or kings in the pocket.

For example, if I played a K-Q offsuit and the board came K-4-2, I'd be in a lot of trouble if the raiser's got one of the three big hands I think he might have. He'd have two aces, three kings, or a pair of kings, like me, but he'd also have an ace kicker.

Or, if I played a 9-8 and the flop was Q-J-10, I still wouldn't be too excited about my hand. Although I flopped a straight, it's the ignorant end of the straight. In addition, it is vulnerable to the high end of the straight, which would be made up by a very strong hand that everybody plays, A-K.

Something else you have to think about with the trouble hands is that when you flop a straight draw, it's not as easy to pick up pots with them as it is with other, stronger hands. You'll remember that when I flop a straight draw with small connecting cards, I play my hand real fast because I have two shots to win the pot. I can win the pot right on the flop because with small cards out there, it's less likely anyone else flopped a hand. And, if I do get called, I've still got a second shot to win it if I make my straight.

But let's say I'm holding K-Q and the flop comes J-10-5, giving me a straight draw. It's highly likely somebody else caught a piece of that flop as well, and I'll be less likely to pick the pot up if I bet. So I don't have two shots to win it anymore.

The same line of reasoning applies if you are holding K-Q and the flop comes Q-J-10, giving you the top pair and a straight draw. It's still not a good hand because if somebody has an A-K, the best you could be drawing for is a split.

Even when you flop a very good hand like two pair or trips, you could be in jeopardy. If the flop was K-K-2 to your K-Q, you could once again be in big trouble if someone's got A-K. The difference here is that you probably won't be able to get away from your hand and you'll have to go ahead and lose a lot of money.

The important point to remember about the trouble hands is when you do get a flop to them you don't want to get heavily involved. Just try to play the pot as cheaply as possible.

A minor exception to the above rule is when you flop a straight, as would happen if you are holding Q-10 and the flop is K-J-9 or J-9-8, for example. However, even when you have the nuts, as in this case, there's a chance you could lose the pot. If a queen fell on fourth, with the K-J-9 flop, you could lose to an A-10. And with the J-9-8 flop, you could lose to a K-10. So, you're not completely safe with some of these hands even when you flop the nuts.

For the most part, trouble hands, suited or offsuit, should be played the same way: slowly. However, trouble hands suited are much stronger hands than trouble hands offsuit, and if you flop a flush or a flush draw with a suited trouble hand, you can show some speed. For example, if you had the K♦ Q♦ and the flop was 10♠ 7♦ 2♦, you'd have a real big hand. Not only would you have a flush draw, but you'd also have two overcards. Or, if you had the 9♦ 8♦ with the same flop, you'd have a straight and a flush draw. Either situation would present a good opportunity to check-raise somebody if you were in an early position. If you were in a late position and somebody led into you, you could raise them. At that point, you're be back having two shots to pick up the pot. You might win it right there, or if you get called, you'd have a good hand to fall back on.

Trash Hands

With the exception of an ace or a king with any suited card, I consider any hand I haven't already discussed to be a trash hand. I put A♣ 8♣ and K♥ 4♥ in the same category as the small connecting cards and I play them approximately the same way. For example, if the flop was 9♥ 6♣ 2♣ and I had the A♣ 8♣, I'd have a flush draw and an overcard. If I was in the pot against two queens, I'd be about even money to win it. So I'd play my hand like I would if I had two small connecting cards that were suited, say the 9♣ 8♣. That is, I'd play it fast and try to win the pot on the flop, because once again, I'd have two shots to win.

But that's where I draw the line, with an ace or a king and another suited card. But when it comes to queens on down, if the two cards don't connect, I consider them trash hands—even if they're suited, such as Q♥ 4♥ or J♠ 6♠.

Hands with non-connecting and offsuit cards such as J♥ 5♣, 10♠ 3♦, 9♣ 4♥ are obviously garbage. But so are offsuit hands that a lot of people play because you can flop a straight with them, such as K-9, Q-8, J-7, 10-6, 9-5, 8-4, 7-3, and 6-2. I don't play these hands because even if I got the best flop I could to them—other than a full house—I could get broke by running into a bigger straight. Consequently, I never play a hand when I have the top and bottom cards of a straight, except when I'm in position.

I always make exceptions when I'm in position, even with the trash hands. For example, if I were on the button with a hand like A-8 offsuit, I might call a raise before the flop if enough people, say four, were in the pot in front of me and I didn't think there'd be any more raises. I might call a small raise and take a flop with a trash hand because it's a good percentage play. I'd be trying to make a full, trips, or two pair. But if I don't get a real good flop to the hand, I'll throw it away. I won't get involved and burn up a bunch of money with one of those trash hands. I'm not going to call any bets on the flop. I'll be raising or I'll be gone.

If I were in position, I might even raise with a trash hand. More than that, I might play it fast after the flop, too. Say the guys in the early positions threw their hands away, and someone in a middle position limped in. Well, if I were on the button, I'd be in position, and I'd raise it regardless of what two cards I have. And if it was checked to me on the flop, I'd bet regardless of what flopped.

Obviously, I wouldn't be playing my hand because of its value. Trash hands have no value. I might as well be playing with two blank cards in this situation because all I'm doing is playing my position and my opponent. Since he limped in, I'd assume that he's got a weak hand to begin with, and if he misses the flop, I'll be able to pick the pot up.

Other than the exceptional situations discussed above, trash hands are just not playable.

SHORTHANDED PLAY

A lot of times, you'll be playing in a full or ring game, and before the night is over, you'll find yourself playing shorthanded. As I already mentioned, you have to be able to change gears in this situation. You should play in the same basic style—aggressive—but you should realize that all the hands increase in value. This is particularly true of the big cards. And, in a shorthanded game, all the trouble hands become playable from almost any position.

In a shorthanded game, position is probably the most important thing. The reason is that you get to look at more cards and have to play more hands than you would in a ring game. You play your position more than your cards in a shorthanded game.

For example, when your game gets down to four-handed play, you need a better hand in the first two positions than you need in the last two. When you raise on the button, the other man has to act first, and that puts him at a big disadvantage. When the other man has to act on his hand first, it's a great equalizer.

So in a shorthanded game you'd play your position using the same theories you would in a full game, but keep in mind that the values of the hands go up a few notches. The trouble hands become better hands because you don't figure to be up against A-A, K-K, or A-K nearly as often as you might in a ring game.

You play more like you would with big cards. In a short-handed game, the bigger your cards are, the better hand you'll have. For instance, in a ring game, you might play two aces or two kings a lot slower after the flop because there could be a lot of people taking a flop to beat those big pairs. Whereas in a shorthanded game, two aces or two kings is a mountain of a hand and you can play them real fast after the flop. Consequently, these big pairs are much more valuable hands than they are in a ring game. What you're trying to catch in a shorthanded game is big cards in position.

INSURANCE

The practice of taking insurance is not as common today as when I wrote the original *Super/System*, however you still see it sometimes, and you should have a general idea of what deals are profitable.

Many times when you're playing no-limit hold'em a player will have all his money in the pot before the flop, on the flop, or even on fourth street. Since there are still cards to come and since no more betting can take place (if it's a head-up situation), both players will generally turn their hands over so that insurance can be considered. I say generally, because there is no rule that says you must turn your hand over, but such a request is rarely, if ever, refused.

Insurance is a side bet that's usually made between the two players involved in the pot or between one of the players involved and an insurance man who may or may not be an active player. The player with the hand that has the best potential to win the pot is offered or asks for some insurance as a way to protect his investment in the pot. But unless a mistake is made, it's always a bad bet. As it is in life away from the poker table, the insurance man won't be giving away anything. When he lays you a price on your hand, he'll be getting the best of it. The price you'll be getting will always be considerably less than the true price your hand is worth. The difference between the true value of your hand and the actual price the insurance man is willing to lay is his **vigorish**, also known as his **edge** or **commission**. I use the phrase "best potential to win the pot" because the best hand on the flop doesn't always have the best winning potential. For example, if the flop was 7♣ 5♦ 4♦ and you had the 7♦ 6♦, you'd be about a 2 to 1 favorite over an opponent with a pair of kings, say, the K♠ K♥.

There are twenty cards in the deck that could win for you with two shots to catch any one of them. Your straight-flush draw gives you fifteen wins, and the three sixes and two sevens that are still in the deck give you five more wins. Of course, the assumption here is that your opponent's hand doesn't improve.

Through the years, I've heard a lot of discussion about whether you should or shouldn't take insurance. My advice is to lay the insurance, but don't take it because the best potential hand always has to take the worst of it. For example, if you're a 3 to 2 favorite, the best you can usually get is 13 to 10 or maybe 7 to 5. So why take it? That's the advantage you're looking for to start with. If you take insurance, you're giving up your advantage. You can't argue with mathematical facts when you have the best of something. If you can lay 7 to 5 on a 3 to 2 shot, you should do it. But you shouldn't take 7 to 5 when you're a 3 to 2 favorite. However, I can understand if a man on a short bankroll considers taking insurance. I guess it would be okay to take the worst of it so you could stay in action. But if your bankroll allows, don't take insurance—lay it.

I used to talk about a related subject with a very big and successful gambler I've known for many years. He said, "If a man came in and offered to lay me 10 to 1 on the flip of a coin for all the money I had in the world, I wouldn't take it." He said he just couldn't liquidate everything he's got, all of his property and his cash. He wouldn't risk losing it all, which would be worth several million dollars. He wouldn't do it even if he thought he could get hold of a few more million.

But I'd do it. I surely would. I'd just have to. I couldn't pass up the opportunity to take 10 to 1 on an even money shot. I'd do it because I have enough confidence in myself that I'd be able to come up with more millions if I lost.

A FINAL WORD

Of course, I'm sure you understand that all the numerous possibilities have by no means been exhausted. No-limit Texas hold'em is a highly complex game. It's hardly possible and certainly not practical to attempt to discuss the enormous variety of situations that could occur. And as you now know, there are certain questions I wouldn't be able to answer definitively because many times, even I don't know exactly what I'd do until I'm faced with the problem. Regardless of what other books or other players teach, there is no magical formula for how to play poker. As I've said, at such times, I go with my feeling, which is really a rapid analysis of conscious and subconscious thoughts.

Nevertheless, I've given you a lot of white meat, sophisticated techniques and strategies that are known only to a few world-class poker players. The average player has never had access to the kind of information you've just read. First of all, nothing as comprehensive as this has ever been written about no-limit hold'em. Even if it were, unless it was written by someone who has played and consistently won at a world-class level for many years, it would not be worth much. In fact, it could even be harmful. Having no information at all is better than having bad information.

You should do quite well at no-limit hold'em now that you know almost as much about the game as I do. The rest is up to you.

HOLD'EM SUPPLEMENT

The following tables are contributed by Richard Englesteen.

DOUBLE BELLY-BUSTER STRAIGHTS

There is a fourteen-card straight continuum since aces may be used in a big or little straight.

A 2 3 4 5 6 7 8 9 10 J Q K A

You can flop a double belly-buster draw with any two adjacent cards from 3-4 to J-Q. In the cases where two flops yield a draw, the top example is of the form (the underscore lines represent "spaces" between the cards):

Top example in this form:	X_Y_ _ _Z
	(for example: 4-6-10)
Bottom example in this form:	X_ _ _Y_Z
	(for example: 6-10-Q)

YOU HOLD	FLOP*	YOU HOLD	FLOP*
3-4	A-5-7	8-9	5-7-J
			6-10-Q
4-5	A-3-7		
	2-6-8	9-10	6-8-Q
			7-J-K
5-6	2-4-8		
	3-7-9	10-J	7-9-K
			8-Q-A
6-7	3-5-9		
	4-8-10	J-Q	8-10-A
7-8	4-6-10		
	5-9-J		

There are 16 double belly-busters of this type.

You can flop a double belly-buster with any two cards that have one space between them. All flops have one of three forms:

X_YZ	(for example: 2-4-5)
XY_Z	(for example: 8-9-J)
X__Y__Z	(for example: 5-8-J)

YOU HOLD	FLOP*	YOU HOLD	FLOP*
A-3	4-5-7	7-9	3-5-6
			5-8-J
2-4	5-6-8		10-J-K
3-5	6-7-9	8-10	4-6-7
	A-4-7		6-9-Q
			J-Q-A
4-6	7-8-10		
	2-5-8	9-J	5-7-8
			7-10-K
5-7	A-3-4		
	3-6-9	10-Q	6-8-9
	8-9-J		7-10-K
6-8	2-4-5	J-K	7-9-10
	4-7-10		
	9-10-Q	Q-A	8-10-J

*There are 24 double belly-busters
of this type.

You can flop with a double belly-buster with any two cards with two spaces between them. The flop is always of the form: X_Y_Z

YOU HOLD	FLOP*	YOU HOLD	FLOP*
A-4	3-5-7	7-10	9-J-K
			4-6-8
2-5	4-6-8		
		8-J	10-Q-A
3-6	5-7-9		5-7-9
	A-4-7		J-Q-A
4-7	6-8-10	9-Q	6-8-10
	A-3-5		
		10-K	7-9-J
5-8	7-9-J		
	2-4-6	J-A	8-10-Q
6-9	8-10-Q		
	3-5-7		

You can flop a double belly-buster with any two cards with three spaces between them. The bottom flop is always of the form: X_ _YZ while the top one is: XY_ _Z.

YOU HOLD	FLOP*	YOU HOLD	FLOP*
A-5	3-4-7	6-10	8-9-Q
			4-7-8
2-6	4-5-8		
		7-J	9-10-K
3-7	5-6-9		5-8-9
	A-4-5		
		8-Q	10-J-A
4-8	6-7-10		6-9-10
	2-5-6		
		9-K	7-10-J
5-9	7-8-J		
	3-6-7	10-A	8-J-Q

There are 16 double belly-busters of this type.

With four spaces (e.g., A-6 or J-6) you can only turn an open-end straight draw.

You can flop a double belly-buster with any two cards with five spaces between them. The flop is always of the form: **XYZ**.

YOU HOLD	FLOP*	YOU HOLD	FLOP*
A-7	3-4-5	5-J	7-8-9
2-8	4-5-6	6-Q	8-9-10
3-9	5-6-7	7-K	9-10-J
4-10	6-7-8	8-A	10-J-Q

There are eight double bellybusters of this type.

There are eight five-card groups that with permutations yield ten possible double belly-busters. These groups all have the form: **V_WXY_Z**. All double belly-busters come up on seven-card segments of the fourteen-card continuum. The spaces, of course, appear in different sequences.

GROUP		GROUP	
I	A-3-4-5-7	V	5-7-8-9-J
II	2-4-5-6-8	VI	6-8-9-10-Q
III	3-5-6-7-9	VII	7-9-10-J-K
IV	4-6-7-8-10	VIII	8-10-J-Q-A

Using **GROUP III** as an example of the permutations:

YOU HOLD	FLOP	YOU HOLD	FLOP
(a) 3-5	6-7-9	(f) 5-7	3-6-9
(b) 3-6	5-7-9	(g) 5-9	3-6-7
(c) 3-7	5-6-9	(h) 6-7	3-5-9
(d) 3-9	5-6-7	(i) 6-9	3-5-7
(e) 5-6	3-7-9	(j) 7-9	3-5-6

Thus there are eighty possible double belly-busters (eight five-card groups times ten permutations). This is the same total yielded when you add the totals at the bottoms of each of the tables (16 + 24 + 16 + 8 = 80).

COLORFUL NAMES OF
VARIOUS HOLD'EM HANDS

A-A..American Airlines

A-K...Big Slick

A-Q..Doyle Brunson*

A-J..Ajax

A-10..Johnny Moss

A-8..Dead Man's Hand

3-A..Baskin-Robbins

K-Q...Marriage

K-J...Kojak

K-9..Canine

K-8..Kokomo

K-7...Columbia River

K-3..King Crab

Q-J..Maverick

Q♠-J♦..Pinochle

Q-10..Goolsby

Q-9...Quinine

Q-7..Computer Hand

J-6...Railroad Hand

J-5..Motown

5-10..Woolworth

10-4...Broderick Crawford

10-3..Weinberg

10-2..Doyle Brunson*

9-8..Oldsmobile

6-9...Joe Bernstein

3-9..Jack Benny

2-9..Twiggy

8-8...Little Oldsmobile

8-5..Finky Dink

3-8..Raquel Welch

7-6...Union Oil

5-7...Pickle Man

7-2...Beer Hand

6-3..Blocky

6-2..Ainsworth

4-5..Jesse James

3-5...Bully Johnson

2-4...Lumberman's Hand

3-3..Crabs

6-6-6..Kotch

4-4-4..Grand Jury

*The reason there are two hands named after me is because of what happened in the 1976 and 1977 World Series of Poker. In both years, I won with a 10-2. The A-Q has long been called "Doyle Brunson" in Texas because I try never to play this hand.

WORLD POKER TOUR

Steven Lipscomb

Steven Lipscomb learned to play poker from his devoutly Baptist grandmother for peanuts (literally) at a family reunion when he was eight. If he had known that one day he would be the catalyst for transforming the game into a televised sports phenomenon, he likely would have paid more attention.

When a childhood friend asked Steve, an award-winning film and television producer, to direct and produce a one-hour poker documentary for the Discovery Channel, it opened his eyes to the poker world and introduced him to the remarkable game of no-limit Texas hold'em. His affinity for the game and the knowledge he gained deconstructing the game for presentation to a wider audience helped Steve win the first poker tournament he ever entered.

Steve's foresight and love for the game led him to write a business plan for the World Poker Tour. Since that time, he has directed and produced hundreds of hours of poker tournaments and game-play for television. No one in the poker world has spent more time interviewing the great players and delving into the subtleties that make the game both simple and infinitely complex. His outside perspective, together with his knowledge of poker in general and tournament strategy in particular, have made him one of the great students of the game. And the poker world will never be quite be the same.

World Poker Tour
by Steven Lipscomb

INTRODUCTION

By nature, poker has no defined beginning or end. As Mojo Nixon once put it, "The best thing about the game is that you can't lose. As long as you still play, the worse you can be is behind." Little things like sleep, family, and medical necessities may slow the game down from time to time, but every poker player knows if a game breaks, there's always another one on the horizon.

Poker players are the most competitive beings on the planet, so it is no wonder that a form of poker that leaves only one player standing evolved out of the older, cash-game format. The new king-of-the-hill, survival-of-the-fittest, every-man-for-himself brand of poker has become known as tournament poker.

THE ORIGINS OF TOURNAMENT POKER

As far as anyone can tell, the first poker tournament was held in the spring of 1969 at the Holiday Inn in Reno, Nevada. One of the pit bosses threw what he called a Texas Gamblers Convention, inviting wealthy Texans to Reno to play poker. Legends like Jack Straus, Crandall Addington, Doyle Brunson, Benny Binion and his son Jack Binion attended.

Known for his ability to recognize and exploit marketing opportunities, Benny Binion staged a similar event at his casino in downtown Las Vegas the next year. He called it the World

Series of Poker and invited what he perceived to be the best poker players. After several days of poker, Benny asked those attending to vote on who they believed to be the best player, which was Johnny Moss. The next year, each player paid a fixed amount and played down to one winner, and Moss won again.

Over the course of the next thirty years, with the help of such poker luminaries as Jack McClelland and Jim Albrecht, Benny and his son developed a formula for tournament poker that is still used by most card rooms and casinos today. Tournaments tend to be a series of fixed buy-in poker events, from seven-card stud to no-limit hold'em, that take place over the course of two to six weeks, culminating in a championship event. Each event plays down to one winner.

TOURNAMENT POKER STORMS INTO THE MAINSTREAM

The format spread, and many card rooms and casinos across the country began holding poker tournaments with regularity. But by 2001, despite continued popular interest in the game, the poker business itself was in decline. Casinos were closing poker rooms across the country to add more lucrative slot machines. And more ominously, the poker population was growing older. The way esteemed tournament director Jack McClellan puts it "The problem with poker was that ten guys would die each year, and only one would walk through the door—and he was no spring chicken." But all that was about to change.

THE BIRTH OF THE WORLD'S FIRST POKER LEAGUE

In September of 2001, I conceived of and wrote a business plan to launch the NFL/NBA/PGA of poker, the World Poker Tour. A solid business team was assembled, composed of branding maven Audrey Kania, production stalwart Robyn Moder, and poker ambassadors Mike Sexton and Linda Johnson. In October we approached Lyle Berman, hoping that he would share our vision and help fund the Tour. Our mission statement was simple: "To launch the World Poker Tour and establish poker as the next significant televised mainstream sport."

Today, that statement sounds much less ambitious than it did at the time. But given the uncertain state of poker near the end of 2001, it was truly remarkable that Lyle and his company, Lakes Entertainment, pledged millions of dollars to help launch the world's first poker league.

POKER ON TELEVISION

From 2000 to 2001, I pitched televised poker to any broadcaster I imagined might air the game, including most of the entities now racing to get into the act. But before the World Poker Tour hit the airwaves, they quite simply did not believe that poker could garner an American audience. Their skepticism was well founded.

Poker had been broadcast on television for some time. Beginning in 1987, Jack Binion had hired production crews to film the World Series of Poker final event. He would then give the programs to ESPN for broadcast in exchange for some commercial spots. The result was something that only diehard poker players could stand to watch for long. The programs ran as filler in undesirable time slots and served as a constant reminder to all broadcasters that nine guys sitting around a table playing poker is not inherently interesting to watch.

It was not until 1999 that a poker tournament was filmed without a casino having to foot the bill. That year Mark Hickman, a childhood friend, drafted me to direct and produce a Discovery Channel documentary entitled "On the Inside of the World Series of Poker." The documentary introduced the poker world to a wider audience and rated well enough for the Discovery Networks to film the event the following two years.

But nothing could have prepared the poker community or television broadcasters for what happened when the World Poker Tour aired its first season.

TELEVISED POKER AND THE BIRTH OF THE WORLD POKER TOUR

The World Poker Tour, L.L.C., opened its doors on February 25, 2002, and quickly signed a who's who of high-class destination casinos associated with poker to exclusive, long-term deals. With no broadcast or cable network deal in place, the WPT promised that, if necessary, it would buy television airtime in order to prove that there was a market for televised poker.

The World Series of Poker declined to join the Tour despite the fact that no broadcaster had plans to film its tournament in 2002. Few people realize that, at the time, ESPN had not broadcast the WSOP for three years. And, as far as I can tell, no network had plans to shoot the WSOP that year.

In fact, two weeks before the World Series main event we received a call from Tex Whitson, who was running the WSOP for Becky Binion-Behnen. He asked if we could help him film the final table of the WSOP—without joining the World Poker Tour. The first WPT event was about to take place at Bellagio, so time simply did not allow us to help. Instead, we directed him back to the people who had filmed their events in past years. Once again, the casino paid for the production in hopes that it could be placed somewhere.

POKER GOES PRIMETIME

In early 2003, Doug DePriest and Steve Cheskin at the Travel Channel made the World Poker Tour an offer we could not refuse—a weekly, two-hour prime-time slot on the network and their commitment to establish Wednesday night as poker night on the Travel Channel year-round. As a result, we rejected an offer from ESPN to try the show on their air without a dedicated time slot. We strongly believed that the key to transforming poker into a televised sport was creating appointment television. And we were willing to buy airtime to prove it.

Though the show had yet to air, the WPT had already generated a remarkable amount of positive press, so ESPN wasn't ready to give up without a fight. The execs circled back again, offering six one-hour time slots. But with half of our thirteen episodes already in the can and contractual obligations to broadcast every episode at least twice, the WPT rejected the offer.

Having lost the WPT to the Travel Channel, ESPN picked up the 2002 World Series of Poker and broadcast it in the six one-hour time slots offered to the WPT. Once ESPN saw the ratings numbers achieved by the WPT in its first season, it rushed out to secure long-term rights to the WSOP, an arrangement that has served the network well.

The first episode of the WPT aired on the Travel Channel on March 30, 2003. Few in the poker community had any idea that their world was about to change forever. And none of it could have happened without the shared vision of everyone at the WPT, including Lyle Berman, as well as Doug DePriest, Steve Cheskin, and Billy Campbell at the Travel Channel. Also critical to the launch and success were important figures in the casino poker world, including Doug Dalton and Bobby Baldwin at Bellagio, Kathy Raymond at Foxwoods, Tim Gustin at Commerce, and Kelly O'Hara at the Bicycle Casino.

TRANSFORMING POKER INTO A SPORT

A lot of ink has been spilled discussing the WPT Cam that reveals players' holecards to the television audience. Poker players and journalists alike have pointed to this innovation by the World Poker Tour as the primary thing that revolutionized the game and made the broadcasts one of the most widely viewed series of events ever to hit cable TV. But if it were really that simple, it stands to reason that the BBC's *Late Night Poker* would have been picked up in the U.S. television market many years before. *Late Night Poker*, which predates the WPT, revealed players' holecards by shooting under the table, but they were unable to make a sale until after the WPT phenomenon—and by then, they were utilizing many other WPT innovations.

The truth is that the WPT Cam was part of a much larger package that transformed poker into a televised sports sensation. Production value was the centerpiece. The WPT transported an arena across the country and filmed six players with sixteen cameras instead of nine players with four cameras, as had been done before. But the production was just the beginning. It took us eight months to edit the first episode of the World Poker Tour. Working ten to fifteen hours a day, seven days a week, we invented a new language—graphic and otherwise—to translate poker into a televised sport.

THE GREATEST FORM OF FLATTERY

All newcomers to the televised poker market have copied our formula exactly, right down to the elements of our graphics pallet. When a player looks at his cards, his name appears on the bottom left-hand side of the screen with a shorthand graphic of his cards. The community cards appear beneath and near the holecard graphics, making it possible for the viewer to follow the game. A graphic on the top left-hand side of the screen shows the mounting pot size.

Another innovation, as important as the WPT Cam, was the introduction of "live fiction" to televised poker. Before the WPT, poker shows discussed how much time passed and/or how many hands were played when the audience was not watching. This put televised poker into the documentary category, making the event feel dated. The World Poker Tour changed all that and made each two-hour episode appear live. For the first time, the WPT created an experience that transported the audience into the game—making people feel like they were sitting in that seat, making million-dollar decisions on every hand. The result has captured the imagination of the American television audience.

Yet another major element of the WPT television package was the inclusion of bios to encourage viewers to pull for certain players. Plus, with the hard work and cooperation of Mike Sexton and Vince Van Patten, we completely overhauled the poker commentary to minimize "poker-speak" and make it accessible to a wide audience. Another key component was my partner Lyle's insistence on a two-hour format, which is almost unheard of in television land but necessary for us to explore the rich nuances of the game. All this is to say that, while the World Poker Tour did in fact introduce the WPT Cam to the U.S. television audience, the comprehensive package of innovative elements in the new WPT television format created the WPT poker phenomenon.

ANYONE CAN PLAY IN WORLD POKER TOUR EVENTS

The best part about this new league is that, unlike any other sport in the history of televised sporting events, anyone can play. You don't have to qualify. You don't have to practice six hours a day. You don't even have to be good at the game. If you want to have the experience of playing with the best poker players in the world for millions of dollars in prize money, all you need to do is buy or win your way into a World Poker Tour event. And with 40 to 60 percent of all WPT players coming from low-cost satellite tournaments, where they win their way into an event for as little as $30, truly anyone can play and win. Sometime during the season, we will be in your neighborhood. Although we expect to evolve further over the years, even as I write this I can say that from June to April, we make a millionaire a month—sometimes two, three, or more per month. After studying *Super/System 2*, my guess is you'll be motivated to enter a tour event or to try to qualify for one. If so, you can find out where and how to play at www.WorldPokerTour.com. The Great American Card Game has finally found a home on the World Poker Tour, and we look forward to dealing you in.

TIPS FOR COMPETING ON THE WORLD POKER TOUR: HOW TO BECOME A WPT CHAMPION

Once you make up your mind to take a shot at the big-time, the following sections will help you get ready for that rendezvous with destiny. Your first task is to ignore the intimidation factor. WPT tournaments are brimming with poker legends, but on any given day, if you know how to play tournament poker and the cards fall your way, you have a legitimate shot at walking away with the title. And when that happens, you will have forever earned the right to be called a World Poker Tour Champion.

Step #1: Be Mentally Prepared

Like any athletes, poker players must mentally prepare for every tournament they enter. New players often mistake the nature of a poker tournament entirely. They tend to see the contest as a series of hands leading to an inevitable conclusion—you win or you lose. That doesn't even begin to capture it. A poker tournament is a living, breathing, organic event. No individual hand matters—nor do players. You may get excited when you knock out Chip Reese, but I assure you, none of us will even want to hear the story next week. What matters is the tournament itself—and your place in it. Your only goal is to never find yourself without chips in front of you. That's it.

In order to have a shot at experiencing that simple pleasure, you will need to start thinking of a poker tournament in its entirety—whether it is a two-hour satellite or a multi-day WPT championship event. You need to understand the tournament structure, feel the ebb and flow of the event and recognize the critical moments that determine your place in that tournament. You will have to prepare yourself before the tournament begins. You will need to keep your head in the game for the entire duration of the tournament. And, you will have to find a way to cope with the good beats and the bad beats that will inevitably come your way. To do this, you will have to prepare yourself as a warrior prepares for battle—remove all mental obstacles between you and the final table that lies ahead of you.

Step #2: Know the Basics of Tournament Poker

This book is filled with the wisdom of some of the greatest players to ever play the Great American Card Game. I will leave the poker lessons to them. Suffice to say, you need to know how to play the underlying poker game at every level. There is no substitute for the knowledge that comes with experience and practice. The purpose of this section is to adapt your game to tournament poker. I will focus primarily on no-limit Texas hold'em—the game of choice on the World Poker Tour. But the techniques are applicable to any tournament.

It has become something of a cliché to point out that in tournament poker you cannot reach back into your pocket and get more cash. But that simple fact makes tournament poker unlike any cash game you have ever played. And it gives rise to the two most important things to remember when you play in a poker tournament. I call them poker mantras because I suggest you say them to yourself before you go to sleep every poker tournament night, that you chant them in the shower every morning, and remind yourself of them on every break.

Poker Tournament Mantra #1:
It Is a Game of Traps; Be the Trapper.

More poker tournaments are lost with big cards than with little ones—by a long shot. You might feel better on the rail talking about how you got your aces cracked, but the story is always the same from that side of the rail—you're out. That's all there is to it.

Your primary objective is to put yourself in a position to trap. You want a huge hand—three of a kind or better—with someone else at the table betting into you with what they think is a big hand. That is the best way to get chips and build a big stack in a poker tournament. What you don't want to be is the guy two hours into the tournament who is betting into someone else's straight with a big pair. That is how you manage to give up all those chips and leave with nothing. So, be the trapper!

Poker Tournament Mantra #2:
It's About the Chips.

Play your chips, not your cards. Remember, your goal is simply to keep and build those chips in front of you. You should always be aware of how many chips you have and how much you have at risk in a given pot. Any time you are about to invest a significant percentage of your stack in a hand, make sure you take the time to ask yourself:

(1) How much have I already invested in the hand and how big is the pot?

(2) What hands, including draws, are out there that can/might beat me?

(3) Am I willing to put the tournament on the line this hand?

You should not feel any time pressure. Great players like Men "the Master" Nguyen have long known that it is important to reflect on the big decisions—and they take their time to do so. Make sure to think through your tournament chip position. If you have not already committed too much of your stack to the hand, and you think you may be beat—or even that you may be in a 50-50 race situation—you have a decision to make. If you have the opportunity to make a bet at the pot, you may be able to take it down without a showdown. On the other hand, unless you're trapping, if someone has bet into you, it is probably time to pass and wait for a better opportunity. Why jeopardize the chips when you are not leading the charge?

The key is not to fall in love with a hand that you sense is a loser and throw away your shot at millions of dollars in prize money and a WPT title. Watching Phil Hellmuth play tournament poker is a remarkable experience. When he senses he is beat, he makes some huge laydowns, preserving his chances of staging a comeback. The exponential nature of betting in no-limit Texas hold'em makes such comebacks commonplace on the Tour.

Step #3: Make a Plan and Play to Your Strengths

Tournament poker has evolved significantly over the past few years. With all major events expanding to fields of hundreds or more players, participants are forced to adjust style and strategy, to adapt to the brave new world of televised poker. Young guns like Phil Ivey, Gus Hansen, and Daniel Negraneau have developed a super-aggressive style that either takes them out quickly or allows them to gather chips early. Once they have chips, they tend to use them mercilessly as weapons against the smaller stacks at the table, forcing them to make near all-in decisions every time they play.

Players like Howard Lederer, Dewey Tomko, and Jennifer Harman Traniello have used a solid approach to great effect. They tend to choose their spots, waiting for strong hands and milking them for all they are worth. Once they get chips, they tend to mix it up a little more, but they also seem to hold on to the chips they win, building gradually to the final table. It is important for you to figure out what kind of player you think you are and to create a plan of attack for the tournament, from beginning to end.

Step #4: See the Whole Tournament

There are three basic phases of a tournament—all defined by how much pressure the antes and blinds are putting on your chip stack:

> Phase 1 = Slight Pressure
> Phase 2 = Moderate Pressure
> Phase 3 = Significant Pressure

Good tournament structures are designed to slowly increase antes and blinds, giving strong players plenty of time to maneuver in Phase 1. But be aware that one unfortunate hand at the beginning of a tournament may put you in Phase 3 while most players are still enjoying Phase 1. And you may run well enough to stay in Phase 1 all the way to the final table. You should always be aware not only of what phase you are in, but also of what phase every player at your table is in, relative to their own chips. That will help you be aware of when you need to adjust your play, as well as when the other players may be opening up their game (i.e. playing weaker hands) out of necessity.

You will want to adjust the parameters for your own style of play, but here are some simple rules of thumb to go by:

> **(1)** Phase 1 (Slight Pressure): You have enough chips to play eleven to fifteen rounds, meaning you can pay antes and blinds for the dealer button to move eleven to fifteen times around the table.

> **(2)** Phase 2 (Moderate Pressure): You have enough chips to play eight to ten rounds.

> **(3)** Phase 3 (Significant Pressure): You only have enough chips to play seven rounds or fewer.

All major tournaments publish structure sheets. Pick up a copy when you register so that you can study how many chips you start with and how quickly the blinds and antes increase.

Phase 1

T. J. Cloutier calls Phase 1 "survival day." The idea is not to get yourself stuck in a hand that you don't control or can't get out of. On the other hand, you want to get as many other players stuck in your web as you possibly can.

The critical thing to recognize about Phase 1 is that it often lasts a long time, even days. If you never played a hand on the first day of a World Poker Tour event, you would almost certainly still have chips at the end of the day—despite the fact that the field would have narrowed significantly.

Think of Phase 1 as your opportunity to trap players and build chips. For a more detailed analysis of Phase 1 play, see Doyle's "Tournament Overview."

Phase 2

At various points in the tournament, either because you have lost chips or because the structure has escalated, you will begin to feel the pressure of the antes and blinds on your chip stack. If you are a solid player, you will probably want to wait for strong opportunities to take a stand, play a hand aggressively, and hopefully double-up or win a significant pot.

In Phase 2 it becomes more expensive to splash around with small pairs and trapping hands. Your goal should be to conserve chips while playing aggressively with a strong hand when you get it. This conservative approach may also give you the opportunity to bluff and rob blinds from time to time.

If you are an aggressive player, you might want to do exactly the opposite—open up your game, take more chances, and dare someone to chase you down. If your table image allows you to pick up lots of small pots, you might climb your way back up the chip stack ladder.

Phase 3

At some point in the tournament, you are likely to reach a spot in which your chips are low enough to make you fear extinction. This is Phase 3. What you want to try to avoid at all costs is letting your stack get so low that doubling up will not help or make a difference.

When you reach Phase 3, your inner poker spirit comes to life. As you get down to ten times the big blind, you will need to find a hand fairly soon that you are willing to take all the way. You need to put on your best Gus Hansen/Layne Flack/

Devilfish Ulliot impression and try to scrap your way back into contention.

But, again, you should never give up. If you have chosen a hand—and the flop manages to decimate that choice—and you don't think you have a prayer of buying the pot with your remaining chips, you may want to fold to give yourself one more shot. The old poker adage of "All you need is a chip and a chair" has been born out time and time again in tournament poker.

Pay Attention To the Ebb and Flow of the Tournament

It sounds strange, but there really is a flow to every tournament. Critical moments help determine that flow. The two most potent and recognizable of these moments are when players are on the bubble, which means everyone is in the money except for the next person out, and when players are on the television bubble, meaning the next person out won't be on television. I have seen play come to a screeching halt for six hours when seven guys are left and they all want to be on prime-time television. It is wise to keep track of when both of these moments are near and to decide how and if you want to take advantage of them.

In both cases, play slows because no one wants to risk going out next. Because the blinds and antes are often significant at this stage in the event, tournament greats like T. J. Cloutier counsel players to go on the offensive during these periods and gather as many chips as possible.

In addition to specific moments, you should pay attention to the overall flow of the tournament. There are times when your table—and even the whole tournament—will simply become more or less aggressive. Adjusting your style to counter the ebbs and flows will help you grow your chip stack.

A Word on Bluffing

There are two truths to bluffing in tournament poker. First, it is highly overrated. And second, it is absolutely essential.

My partner Lyle Berman and I have often discussed the frustration of playing solid poker for three days and then throwing off half of our chips with a stupid bluff.

The biggest danger is trying to bluff the wrong person—usually when you are tired. And it hurts every time. You should not feel like you have to bluff just to be cool or because you are bored. If you have lots of chips, guard them well and if you do choose to bluff, choose the better players that know enough to be bluffed out of a pot.

On the other hand, the reason bluffing is essential to tournament poker is because it is the language of power in poker. The geniuses of the game are the Doyle Brunsons and Gus Hansens of the world who aren't playing their cards at all, but are playing you when they bluff at you. That is the magic that you can only experience and learn by coming out and playing the game with the best in the world—in order to see how you stack up on the green felt. But be aware that to win a major poker tournament today, you will absolutely have to steal blinds and antes from time to time and bluff at some pots with a mediocre hand or no hand at all. And that is what makes the game so damn great.

The Final Table

Once you make it to the final table, nothing really changes—but everything changes. You want to continue trapping players and playing your chips, as well as theirs. But now an important element is added. Every player that goes out means a significant jump in the piece of the prize money for those that remain. The big players say that they are always shooting for first place, but as prize pools rocket into the stratosphere, it clearly affects how people play. The thing to remember is that in order to win, you only have to knock one player out of a tournament—the guy who gets second. On the other hand, if players are being tight, it provides an amazing opportunity for you to mix up your game, pick up chips, and become a poker superstar.

AN INVITATION

Tournament poker is just about as fun as anything I have ever witnessed. World Poker Tour events have all the trappings and all the thrills of major league sporting events with the unique twist that you can come and play. And while your risk is limited to the buy-in, the multi-million dollar upside has changed the lives of participants. The WPT millionaires club is adding new members every month of our season. With a little preparation and the right focus, you have a legitimate shot at becoming the next member of that exclusive club. We encourage you to get your feet wet and begin exploring the tournament side of your game. The cameras are rolling. We look forward to seeing you at the WPT final table.

GLOSSARY

ACTIVE PLAYER
A player still involved in the pot.

ADVERTISE
To bluff with the intention of being caught by the other players in order to get them to call a future bet that's not a bluff.

ALL-IN (OR "GO ALL IN")
To bet all the money you have on the table.

AUTOMATIC BLUFF
A bluff, usually attempted in lowball, that a player makes because of a particular situation. Depending on the circumstances this kind of bluff will almost always be made regardless of a player's hand value.

BABY
A small card, especially in razz and high-low split, that has a value of eight or less, or sometimes, five or less.

BACKDOOR
When a player makes a hand he wasn't originally drawing at.

BAD BEAT
When a big hand is beaten by a longshot draw.

BEAT THE BOARD
Having a hand that can beat any other hand in sight.

BELLY-BUSTER STRAIGHT
Used interchangeably with *inside straight*.

BET INTO
To take the initiative in the betting action with the knowledge that your opponent has a potentially strong hand.

BETTING THE POT
To bet the total amount of money currently in the pot in a pot-limit or no-limit game.

BICYCLE
The lowest and best possible hand in lowball. In ace-to-five, A-2-3-4-5; in deuce-to-seven, a 2-3-4-5-7. Also known as a wheel.

BIG BLIND
The largest blind bet in a game that has multiple blinds. See also *Blind*.

BIG DOG
A big underdog to win the pot. See also *Dog*.

BIG FULL
The highest possible full house in hold'em and Omaha.

GLOSSARY

BIG HAND

1. A hand with a relatively high value such as a full house. 2. A hand with a big draw, meaning that it has excellent possibilities of winning the pot. For example, flopping a straight-flush draw in hold'em.

BLANK

A card that is not of any value to a player's hand.

BLIND

A forced bet that a player puts in before he receives his cards.

BOARD

The cards that are face-up in a poker game.

BREAK

To draw a card instead of staying pat. Often used in lowball when, for example, a player with a nine pat, throws away the 9 and draws one card to improve his hand. He is breaking the nine.

BRING-IT-IN-FOR

To make the first optional bet in any poker game.

BUST OUT

1. Miss your hand completely. 2. Lose all your money.

BUTTON

When there is a house dealer, a button is put in front of a player to show that he is playing the dealer's position. The button is passed to each player in clockwise order.

BUY-IN

The minimum amount of money necessary to secure a seat in a particular game.

CALL

To put money in the pot that's exactly equal to the previous bet or raise.

CALLING STATION

A player who's next-to-impossible to bluff and who'll call almost any bet made.

CASE CARD

The last card of a particular rank. For example, if you catch an ace after the other three aces are in the discards, then you have caught the case ace.

CATCH PERFECT

A situation in which only one or two cards will win the pot.

CATCH-UP

To improve a hand so that it will be approximately equal to an opponent's.

CHANGE GEARS

Adjusting play from loose to tight or vice versa.

CHASE
Trying to beat a hand that is superior in value.

CHECK-BLIND (OR CHECK-DARK)
To check a hand without looking at it.

CHECK-RAISE
To check and then raise in the same round when the action returns.

CHIP (OR CHECK)
A plastic token used in place of cash money.

COLD CALL (OR CALL COLD)
When a player who has no money invested in the pot besides the ante calls a raise and a reraise.

COLD DECK
A term often used to describe the deck by players who feel they're not getting enough playable or winning hands.

COMPLETE BLUFF
A bluff made with a completely worthless hand.

CONCEALED PAIR
A pair where both cards are face down.

COURTESY BET
A bet, usually a bluff, made when it is fairly certain that an opponent will call or raise.

COWBOY (K-BOY)
A king.

CRIPPLED DECK
A deck with almost nothing left that can help a hand. For example, if a player held a pair of aces and two others were in play, the deck would be crippled.

CRYING CALL
To call with an inferior hand.

CUT
1. To separate the deck into portions (usually in half) after it has been shuffled. 2. See also *Rake*.

DEAD CARD
A card no longer in play or with no other like cards that are live.

DEAD HAND
A misdealt hand that is not valid.

DEAD IN THE POT
When there is no way for you to win, you're said to be dead in the pot.

DEUCE
A two.

DEUCE-TO-SEVEN LOWBALL

A form of lowball in which the best hand is a 2-3-4-5-7, the ace is a high card, and straights and flushes count against the player. Also called Kansas City Lowball.

DOG

Abbreviation for underdog—the opposite of favorite.

DOORCARD

The first upcard in a stud game.

DOUBLE BELLY-BUSTER

A two-way inside straight.

DOUBLE-POP

When you immediately raise a raiser you've double-popped it. That is, re-raising so the next player to act must call two bets.

DOUBLE-THROUGH

To double the amount of one's chips by being all-in and winning an amount equal to what was bet.

DOWNCARD

A card dealt facedown.

DOYLESROOM.COM

Internet poker-playing site, www.doylesroom.com, endorsed by Doyle Brunson.

DRAWING DEAD

Drawing to a hand that it would be impossible to win with, regardless of the card or cards drawn. Also known as dead in the pot.

DRAW OUT

To improve and beat an opponent who had a better hand prior to the draw-out.

DRIVER'S SEAT

The advantage a particular player has because it appears as though he has the best hand at the time. That player is said to be in the driver's seat.

DUPLICATE

In lowball games, two cards of the same rank. For example, the two fours are duplicates with 8-7-4-4-2. Also called counterfeit.

EARLY, MIDDLE, AND LATE POSITION

The early positions in an eight-handed game are the first three players to act on their hand, the middle positions are the next three and the late positions are the last two.

EXPOSED PAIR

A pair on the board.

FAVORITE

The player with the highest probability of winning the hand or the contest, as opposed to dog.

FIFTH STREET

1. In stud poker, the fifth card dealt to each player. 2. In hold'em and Omaha, the last community card that is dealt.

FILL

To draw a card that completes a hand, for example, to fill a straight or a flush or to improve two pair to a full house.

FLAT CALL

To call a bet without raising.

FLOP

A hold'em and Omaha term describing the first three community cards that are turned simultaneously.

FLOPPING A SET

In hold'em and Omaha, when a player forms a three-of-a-kind hand with one or two of the flop cards.

FLUSH

A hand with five cards of the same suit.

FOLD

To discontinue play and forfeit the pot.

FOUR-FLUSH

To have four cards of the same suit.

FOUR OF A KIND

Four cards of the same rank with a side card, such as four jacks and a seven.

FOURTH STREET

1. In stud poker, the fourth card dealt to each player. 2. In hold'em or Omaha, the fourth community card dealt—the card after the flop.

FREE CARD

A card that's received without any money having been put into the pot because all active players check on that round of play.

FREE RIDE

See *Free Card*.

FREEROLL

1. In high-low split where one player has one half of the pot won and is competing for the other half. 2. In hold'em and Omaha, where two players have identical hands except for one who has a possible flush. The suited hand would have a freeroll.

FREEZE-OUT

A game that's played down to one winner and where no player can add more money to his original buy-in.

FULL HOUSE

Three cards of the same rank and one pair, such as 5-5-5-7-7.

GLOSSARY

GETTING A HAND CRACKED

When a big hand is beaten by an opponent who started with an inferior hand.

GETTING AN EXTRA BET

In limit poker only, the art of extracting more money from an opponent by check-raising him.

GIVE A CARD

To let an opponent get another card by checking to him.

GUT-SHOT

An inside straight draw.

HEADS-UP

A poker hand or game involving only two players.

HELP

To improve a hand.

HIGH ROLLER

A gambler who plays for large sums of money.

HOLD'EM

A high poker game featuring two starting downcards, a flop of three community cards, a fourth community card, and then a fifth for a total of five cards and four betting rounds. Any combination of the best five-card hand wins the pot. Also called Texas hold'em.

IGNORANT END OF A STRAIGHT

The lowest possible straight. For example, with a flop of 8-9-10, a player holding a 7-6 would have flopped the ignorant (low end) of the straight.

IN THE LEAD

The player who's aggressive and does the first betting on each round is said to be in the lead.

IN THE MIDDLE

A player caught between the original bettor on his right and a potential raiser on his left.

INSURANCE

A side bet made on the possible occurrence of cards being drawn or hands being made.

INTERNET POKER

See *Online Poker*.

JAM

A pot in which several players are raising and reraising.

KICKER

Side card to a pair or better, such as A-J-J (a pair of jacks and an ace kicker).

KICKER TROUBLE

When two opponents have the same pair, the player with the smaller side card is said to have kicker trouble.

LEAK

When something is wrong with someone's playing technique or strategy.

LIMP IN

To call a bet.

LITTLE BLIND

The first and smallest blind bet in a game that has multiple blinds.

LIVE CARD

A card that has not been dealt (or seen), that is, a card that's still in play.

LIVE ONE

A rich sucker.

LOCK

See *Nuts*.

LOOSE PLAYER

A player who tends to play most hands, weak or strong, and gets involved in many pots.

LOWBALL OR LOW POKER

A form of poker where the lowest hand wins the pot—as opposed to high poker.

MAKE A PLAY

See *Put a Play On*.

MISS THE FLOP

When a player's starting cards are not improved by the three community cards of the flop.

MIXED GAMES

Poker played with multiple games that are alternated on an agreed-upon schedule.

MONEY MANAGEMENT

The intelligent use of a player's bankroll.

MORTAL NUTS

Given the cards on the board, the best possible hand at the moment.

MOVE-IN

In a no-limit game, to bet all one's chips on a single play.

NO PAIR

A hand with five totally unrelated cards.

NUMBER TWO MAN (SECOND DEALER)

A card cheat capable of dealing seconds. See also *Seconds*.

NUTS

1. The best possible hand at that point in the pot. 2. An absolute winning hand.

OFFSUIT

Cards that are not of the same suit—as opposed to suited, cards of the same suit.

OMAHA

A poker game featuring four starting down cards, a flop of three community cards, a fourth community card and then a fifth for a total of four betting rounds. Any combination of the best five-card hand—formed by using exactly two cards from the player's hand and three from the board—wins the pot. Can be played as high or high-low. See also *Omaha High-Low*.

OMAHA HIGH-LOW EIGHT-OR-BETTER

A version of Omaha where the best high hand splits the pot with the best low hand. However, to qualify for low, a player has to have five unpaired cards of 8 or less or the best high hand will win the entire pot.

ON THE COME

To bet on a hand with potential as opposed to betting on a hand that is complete.

ON TILT

When a player plays poorly after losing one or more big pots.

ONE PAIR

Two cards of the same rank with three side cards such as 10-10-A-5-3.

ONLINE POKER

Poker played on the Internet on sites such as www.doylesroom.com.

OPEN-END STRAIGHT

A four-card hand where a straight is possible on either end, such as a 4-5-6-7.

OUTS

The number of cards that will improve an inferior hand to a possible winner.

OVER-BET

To make a bet that is out of proportion with (much bigger than) the size of a pot in a no-limit game.

OVER-CALL

To call a bet (usually a big one) after another player or players have already called.

OVERCARD

A downcard in a player's hand that's higher than any card showing. For example, a player holding an ace in hold'em has an overcard to a flop of K-Q-3.

OVERPAIR

A pair in the pocket in hold'em that's higher than any card on the board.

PAINT

A facecard—a jack, queen or king.

PAT HAND

A hand that's complete or one that a player does not draw to.

PEDDLE THE NUTS

To bet a winning hand hoping that an opponent will call. Also called *selling the nuts*.

PICKED OFF

To get called when bluffing.

PICK UP

Win a relatively small pot without a contest.

PLAY

1. To sit in on a poker game. 2. To get involved in a particular pot. 3. To do something dramatic or creative during a particular hand, as in *to make a play*.

PLAY-BACK

To reraise.

POCKET CARDS

Downcards held by a player in hold'em and Omaha.

POSITION

Where a player sits relative to other active players in a particular pot.

POST OAK BLUFF

A small bet in a large pot in the hopes that opponents will give up the pot.

POT

1. The total amount of money bet on a hand. 2. An area near the center of the table where the bets of the players are placed.

POT ODDS

The odds of a bet compared to the amount of money already in the pot.

PREMIUM HANDS

The top starting hands in a game.

PROTECTION

Having a hand in high-low split that prevents a player from being scooped.

PUT A PLAY ON

To attempt to outmaneuver an opponent by unconventional betting.

GLOSSARY

RAG

A low-valued card that appears to help no one. Also called a *blank*.

RAIL

A barrier that separates spectators from players.

RAILBIRD

A spectator.

RAISE

To bet more chips than a previous bettor within a round of play.

RAKE

The percentage extracted from the pot by a house dealer.

RAPPING PAT

This term is used in draw poker when a player draws no additional cards.

RAT-HOLE

To put chips (or money) in your pocket during a game.

RAZZ

Seven-card stud played for low only.

READ

To make an educated guess on what an opponent holds in his hand.

RELEASING A SET

To throw away trips when it is thought they are beat.

REPRESENT

To make it appear that you have a hand that you don't.

RIGHT PRICE

To get good pot odds on a bet or raise.

RING GAME

A game with a player in every seat, that is, a full game—as opposed to a shorthanded game.

RIVER CARD

The last card dealt in a stud or flop (Omaha or hold'em) game.

ROCK

A player who plays only good hands and thus bets infrequently.

ROLLED-UP

In seven-card stud when the first three cards are of the same rank. For example, 7-7-7.

ROUGH

A term used to describe a lowball hand with relatively weak supporting cards, for example, an 8-7-6-5-3 or 8-7-3-2-A would be a *rough eight*—as opposed to smooth.

ROYAL FLUSH

10-J-Q-K-A of the same suit, the highest hand in poker without wild cards.

RUSH

A rapid succession of winning hands. Also known as a winning streak.

SANDBAG

Checking the probable best hand with the intention of raising.

SANDWICH

Two players having another opponent stuck in the middle of their betting.

SCOOP

To win both the high and low ends of a pot in high-low games.

SEAT POSITION

The actual seat a player has—not to be confused with his position in the pot.

SECOND (OR THIRD) NUTS

The second—or third—best possible hand.

SECOND PAIR (OR SECOND BUTTON)

A pair made with the second-highest card on the board in hold'em or Omaha.

SELLING A HAND

1. Getting opponents to call a bet. 2. The art of making a bet of the perfect amount to extract the maximum value out of a hand.

SEMI-BLUFFING

Bluffing with a hand that has possibilities of improving.

SET

A three of a kind hand.

SET HIM ALL-IN (OR MOVE HIM ALL-IN)

In a no-limit game, making a bet so big that it would force another player to commit all his chips to the pot.

SEVEN-CARD STUD EIGHT-OR-BETTER

A high-low version of seven-card stud featuring three starting cards—two down and one up—then three successive rounds of upcards with a final seventh card dealt face down for a total of seven cards and five betting rounds. To qualify for low, a player has to have five unpaired cards of 8 or less to win half the pot (the high hand wins the other half) or the best high hand will win the entire pot.

SHORT CALL

To call a bet with an insufficient amount of money in a game when the amount of the call is all the money that the player has left on the table.

SHORTHANDED GAME

A poker game that is not full—one that has many seats open. The opposite of ring game.

GLOSSARY

SHUT OUT

In a no-limit game, to force an opponent out with a bet bigger than he is willing to call.

SIDECARD

See *Kicker*.

SIXTH STREET

The sixth card dealt to each active player in seven-card stud poker.

SLOW-PLAY

To play a strong hand weakly, that is, to check or only call and let opponents take the lead in the betting.

SMOOTH

A term used to describe a lowball hand with relatively strong supporting cards, for example, an 8-4-3-2-A would be a *smooth eight*—as opposed to rough.

SMOOTH CALL

1. When someone slow-plays a hand or makes a difficult call. 2. When a player calls, anticipating a raise by a player behind him.

SNAPPED OFF

To get called when bluffing.

SNOW HAND

In draw games when a player stands pat on worthless hands and bets at the pot hoping his bet, rather than his hand, will win the pot.

SPEEDING AROUND

A player who plays real loose with no definable pattern is said to be speeding around.

SPLIT PAIR

A pair in seven-card stud poker in which one of the cards is face-up and one is face-down.

STEAL (OR STEAL A POT)

To win a pot on a bluff.

STEAM

See *On Tilt*.

STRAGGLERS

Players who limp in from early positions.

STRAIGHT

Five cards of mixed suits in sequence, such as a 7-8-9-10-J.

STRAIGHT-FLUSH

Five cards in sequence and in the same suit such as 5♠ 6♠ 7♠ 8♠ 9♠.

STUCK

When a player's losing, he's said to be stuck.

SUCKER

A player who thinks he knows how to play, but really has little chance of winning consistently because of his ineptitude.

SUITED

Cards of the same suit.

SWING HAND

A hand in high-low split that has a chance to win both the high and low ends of the pot.

TELL

A mannerism of a player that gives opponents an indication of the strength of his hand or whether or not he's bluffing.

TEXAS HOLD'EM

See *Hold'em*.

THIRD STREET

In stud poker, the third card dealt to each player.

THREE-OF-A-KIND

Three cards of the same rank and two side cards, such as K-K-K-6-9.

TIGHT PLAYER

A player who tends to play only strong hands and gets involved in few pots.

TIP YOUR DUKE

To reveal the quality of your hand.

TOKE

A gratuity. Commonly used in gambling circles instead of the word "tip."

TOP KICKER

The highest (or higher) side card when two or more players have identical hands and that card is used to determine the winner of the pot.

TOP PAIR

Pairing a hole card with the highest card on the board in Omaha and hold'em.

TRAP

See *Check-Raise* and *Sandbagging*.

TREY

A three.

TRIPLE DRAW

Form of draw poker played as low with the distinguishing feature being three separate draws where players may exchange unwanted cards for fresh cards for a total of four betting rounds. Typically played as deuce-to-seven with the deuce being the lowest card, aces counting high, and straights and flushes counting against the low hands.

GLOSSARY

TRIPS

Three of a kind.

TURN

1. The fourth card placed on the board in Omaha and hold'em. 2. A word previously used by players from the South and southwestern part of the United States instead of the word flop.

TWO PAIR

Two two-card sets of identically-ranked cards, plus a side card, such as K-K-5-5-7.

UNDERDOG

See *Dog*.

UNDERFULL

A full house less than the highest possible full house—given the board cards—in Omaha and hold'em.

UNDER THE GUN

The first player to act in a round.

UNGLUED

See *On Tilt*.

UPCARDS

The exposed cards in a poker game.

VIGORISH

A percentage extracted by the house to enable it to make a profit on the game.

WALK

Letting the blind win unchallenged.

WHEEL

See *Bicycle*.

WHEN ALL THE CARDS ARE OUT

The point when there are no more cards to be dealt.

WHIPSAW

The caller between two players who are both raising.

WIRED PAIR

A pair on the first two cards in any poker game.

WORLD POKER TOUR (WPT)

Innovative mass-audience reality television poker tour that has popularized poker.

THE CHAMPIONSHIP SERIES
POWERFUL BOOKS YOU MUST HAVE

CHAMPIONSHIP OMAHA (Omaha High-Low, Pot-limit Omaha, Limit High Omaha) by Tom McEvoy & T.J. Cloutier. Clearly-written strategies and powerful advice from Cloutier and McEvoy who have won four World Series of Poker titles in Omaha tournaments. Powerful advice shows you how to win at low-limit and high-stakes games, how to play against loose and tight opponents, and the differing strategies for rebuy and freezeout tournaments. Learn the best starting hands, when slowplaying a big hand is dangerous, what danglers are and why winners don't play them, why pot-limit Omaha is the only poker game where you sometimes fold the nuts on the flop and are correct in doing so and overall, and how you can win a lot of money at Omaha! 230 pages, photos, illustrations, $39.95. Now only $29.95!

CHAMPIONSHIP HOLD'EM by Tom McEvoy & T.J. Cloutier. New Cardoza Edition! Hard-hitting hold'em the way it's played today in both limit cash games and tournaments. Get killer advice on how to win more money in rammin'-jammin' games, kill-pot, jackpot, shorthanded, and other types of cash games. You'll learn the thinking process before the flop, on the flop, on the turn, and at the river with specific suggestions for what to do when good or bad things happen plus 20 illustrated hands with play-by-play analyses. Specific advice for rocks in tight games, weaklings in loose games, experts in solid games, how hand values change in jackpot games, when you should fold, check, raise, reraise, check-raise, slowplay, bluff, and tournament strategies for small buy-in, big buy-in, rebuy, incremental add-on, satellite and big-field major tournaments. Wow! Easy-to-read and conversational, if you want to become a lifelong winner at limit hold'em, you need this book! 388 Pages, Illustrated, Photos. $39.95. Now only $29.95!

CHAMPIONSHIP NO-LIMIT & POT-LIMIT HOLD'EM by T.J. Cloutier & Tom McEvoy. New Cardoza Edition! The definitive guide to winning at two of the world's most exciting poker games! Written by eight time World Champion players T.J. Cloutier (1998 and 2002 Player of the Year) and Tom McEvoy (the foremost author on tournament strategy) who have won millions of dollars each playing no-limit and pot-limit hold'em in cash games and major tournaments around the world. You'll get all the answers here—no holds barred—to your most important questions: How do you get inside your opponents' heads and learn how to beat them at their own game? How can you tell how much to bet, raise, and reraise in no-limit hold'em? When can you bluff? How do you set up your opponents in pot-limit hold'em so you can win a monster pot? What are the best strategies for winning no-limit and pot-limit tournaments, satellites, and supersatellites? You get rock-solid and inspired advice from two of the most recognizable figures in poker—advice that you can bank on. If you want to become a winning player, and a champion, you must have this book. 304 pages, paperback, illustrations, photos. $29.95

CHAMPIONSHIP TOURNAMENT POKER by Tom McEvoy. New Cardoza Edition! Rated by pros as best book on tournaments ever written and enthusiastically endorsed by more than five world champions, this is the definitive guide to winning tournaments and a must for every player's library. McEvoy lets you in on the secrets he has used to win millions of dollars in tournaments and the insights he has learned competing against the best players in the world. Packed solid with winning strategies for all 11 games in the World Series of Poker, with extensive discussions of 7-card stud, limit hold'em, pot and no-limit hold'em, Omaha high-low, re-buy, half-half tournaments, satellites, and strategies for each stage of tournaments. Tons of essential concepts and specific strategies jam-pack the book. Phil Hellmuth, 1989 WSOP champion says, "[this] is the world's most definitive guide to winning poker tournaments." 416 pages, paperback, $29.95.

VIDEOS AND STRATEGIES BY MIKE CARO
THE MAD GENIUS OF POKER

CARO'S PRO POKER TELLS
$59.95 Two-Video VHS Set • $49.95 DVD
This video is a powerful scientific course on how to use your opponents' gestures, words and body language to read their hands and win all their money. These carefully guarded poker secrets, filmed with 63 poker notables, will bring your game to the next level. It reveals when opponents are bluffing, when they aren't, and why. Knowing what your opponent's gestures mean, and protecting them from knowing yours, gives you a huge winning edge. Says two-time World Champion Doyle Brunson: "Mike Caro's research will revolutionize poker!" Prepare to be astonished!

CARO'S POWER POKER SEMINAR
$39.95 VHS 62 Minutes
This powerful video shows you how to win big money using the little-known concepts of world champion players. This advice will be worth thousands of dollars to you every year, and even more if you're a big money player! After 15 years of refusing to allow his seminars to be filmed, Caro presents entertaining but serious coverage of his long-guarded secrets. The most profitable poker advice ever put on video.

CARO'S MAJOR POKER SEMINAR
$24.95 VHS 60 Minutes
Caro's poker advice in VHS format. Based on the inaugural class at Mike Caro University of Poker, Gaming and Life strategy. The material given on this tape is based on many fundamentals introduced in Caro's works and is prepared in such a way that reinforces concepts old and new. Caro's style is easy-going but intense with key concepts stressed and repeated. This tape will improve your play.

CARO'S PROFESSIONAL POKER REPORTS
Mike Caro, the foremost authority on poker strategy, psychology, and statistics, has put together three powerful insider poker reports. Each report is centered around a daily mission, with you, the reader, concentrating on adding one weapon per day to your arsenal.

These highly focused reports are designed to take you to a new level at the tables. Theoretical concepts and practical situations are mixed together for fast in-depth learning in these concise courses. *Caro's Professional Reports* are very popular among good players.

11 Days to 7-Stud Success. Bluffing, playing and defending pairs, different strategies for the different streets, analyzing situations—lots of information within. One advantage is gained each day. A quick and powerful method to 7-stud winnings. Essential. Signed, numbered. $19.95. **12 Days to Hold'Em Success.** Positional thinking, playing and defending against mistakes, small pairs, flop situations, playing the river, are just some sample lessons. Guaranteed to make you a better player. Very popular. Signed, numbered. $19.95. **Professional 7-Stud Report.** When to call, pass, and raise, playing starting hands, aggressive play, 4th and 5th street concepts, lots more. Tells how to read an opponent's starting hand, plus sophisticated advanced strategies. Important revision for serious players. Signed, numbered. $19.95.

POWERFUL POKER SIMULATIONS
A MUST FOR SERIOUS PLAYERS WITH A COMPUTER!
IBM compatibles CD ROM Win 95, 98, 2000, NT, ME, XP - Full Color Graphics

These **incredible** full color poker simulation programs are the absolute **best** method to improve your game. Computer opponents play like real players. All games let you set the limits and rake, have fully programmable players, adjustable lineup, stat tracking, and Hand Analyzer for starting hands. MIke Caro, the world's foremost poker theoretician says, "Amazing...a steal for under $500...get it, it's great." Includes free telephone support. "Smart Advisor" gives expert advice for every play in every game!

NEW! Windows Versions More Features!

1. TURBO TEXAS HOLD'EM FOR WINDOWS - $89.95 - Choose which players, how many, 2-10, you want to play, create loose/tight game, control check-raising, bluffing, position, sensitivity to pot odds, more! Also, instant replay, pop-up odds, Professional Advisor, keeps track of play statistics. Free bonus: Hold'em Hand Analyzer analyzes all 169 pocket hands in detail, their win rates under any conditions you set. Caro says this "hold'em software is the most powerful ever created." Great product!

2. TURBO SEVEN-CARD STUD FOR WINDOWS - $89.95 - Create any conditions of play; choose number of players (2-8), bet amounts, fixed or spread limit, bring-in method, tight/loose conditions, position, reaction to board, number of dead cards, stack deck to create special conditions, instant replay. Terrific stat reporting includes analysis of starting cards, 3-D bar charts, graphs. Play interactively, run high speed simulation to test strategies. Hand Analyzer analyzes starting hands in detail. Wow!

3. TURBO OMAHA HIGH-LOW SPLIT FOR WINDOWS - $89.95 -Specify any playing conditions; betting limits, number of raises, blind structures, button position, aggressiveness/passiveness of opponents, number of players (2-10), types of hands dealt, blinds, position, board reaction, specify flop, turn, river cards! Choose opponents, use provided point count or create your own. Statistical reporting, instant replay, pop-up odds, high speed simulation to test strategies, amazing Hand Analyzer, much more!

4. TURBO OMAHA HIGH FOR WINDOWS - $89.95 - Same features as above, but tailored for Omaha High-only. Caro says program is "an electrifying research tool...it can clearly be worth thousands of dollars to any serious player. A must for Omaha High players.

5. TURBO 7 STUD 8 OR BETTER - $89.95 - Brand new with all the features you expect from the Wilson Turbo products: the latest artificial intelligence, instant advice and exact odds, play versus 2-7 opponents, enhanced data charts that can be exported or printed, the ability to fold out of turn and immediately go to the next hand, ability to peek at opponents hand, optional warning mode that warns you if a play disagrees with the advisor, and automatic testing mode that can run up to 50 tests unattended. Challenge tough computer players who vary their styles for a truly great poker game.

6. TOURNAMENT TEXAS HOLD'EM - $59.95
Set-up for tournament practice and play, this realistic simulation pits you against celebrity look-alikes. Tons of options let you control tournament size with 10 to 300 entrants, select limits, ante, rake, blind structures, freezeouts, number of rebuys and competition level of opponents - average, tough, or toughest. Pop-up status report shows how you're doing vs. the competition. Save tournaments in progress to play again later. Additional feature allows you to quickly finish a folded hand and go on to the next.

Order Toll-Free 1-800-577-WINS or go to www.cardozapub.com